GOVERNING GAZA

ILANA FELDMAN

GOVERNING

GAZA

Bureaucracy, Authority, and the Work of Rule, 1917–1967

DUKE UNIVERSITY PRESS   DURHAM AND LONDON   2008

© 2008 Duke University Press

All rights reserved

Printed in the United States of America

on acid-free paper ∞

Designed by Heather Hensley

Typeset in Adobe Jenson Pro by

Keystone Typesetting, Inc.

Library of Congress Cataloging-in-

Publication Data appear on the last

printed page of this book.

IN MEMORY
of my mother, Marcia Feldman,
and my grandmother, Sylvia Smith

CONTENTS

ACKNOWLEDGMENTS

My thanks go first to the people I knew in Gaza. This book could not have been written without the many retired civil servants and other Gazans who welcomed me into their offices, homes, and lives—who let me tape record our conversations and shared their memories and insights with me. Though my commitment to honor their privacy means I cannot name them here, I am forever grateful to them. Of those people I knew in Gaza whom I can name, special thanks must go to my research assistants, Emad Karam and Mushir Amer, who with amazing dedication and resourcefulness helped me transcribe the tapes of my interviews and work through some of my documentary materials. I am also grateful for their good humor and the pleasure of their company. Others in Gaza who helped me with my research include Dr. Assam Sesalem, Wedad Sourani, Majda Taleb, Ahmed Saleem, Wedad Nasser, Yusuf El-Hindi, Abdul Latif Abu Hashim, and Rajab Sarraj. I thank them all for their efforts, and also thank Wedad for the many excellent meals. I wish them and everyone in Gaza and in Palestine more generally better days ahead.

I conducted archival research for this project in a number of places. I am grateful to the archivists and librarians at *Dar al-Watha'iq* and *Dar al-Kutub* in Cairo; the Israel State Archives and the Jewish National Library in Jerusalem; the Library of Congress; the New York Public Library (particularly the Middle East and Jewish Divisions); the National Archives/PRO in London; the American Friends Service Committee Archives in Philadelphia; and the United Nations Archives in New York. Staff in the Gaza City offices of the Palestinian Housing Ministry, *Awqaf* Ministry, Comptroller General's Office, Pensions and Social Security Administration, 'Omari Mosque library, as well as the Gaza City Municipality, aided my research into Gaza's local documentary history immensely. The New York Public Library deserves an additional word of thanks for providing not only resources for my research, but wonderful spaces in which to write. I wrote the dissertation that was the first incarnation of this project in the Wertheim Study and wrote much of this book in the Allen Room. I cannot imagine better conditions in which to work. Some of the ideas explored in this book were first published in my "Everyday Government in Extraordinary Times: Persistence and Authority in Gaza's Civil Service (1917–1967)," *Comparative Studies in Society and History* 47, 4 (2005): 863–91.

I was extremely fortunate to receive generous financial support at all stages of this process, support that gave me the opportunity to dedicate myself not only to research but to writing. Dissertation research was funded by the Near and Middle East Program of the Social Science Research Council (through two grants), the Council of American Overseas Research Centers, and the Wenner-Gren Foundation. The writing of the dissertation was made possible by support from the Horace Rackham Graduate School at the University of Michigan and the Charlotte W. Newcombe Foundation. I conducted follow-up research in Palestine with a grant from the Palestinian American Research Center. The writing of this book was supported by a Richard Carley Hunt Fellowship from the Wenner-Gren Foundation. I thank all these institutions for their support.

My research experience was made eminently more pleasurable by the many wonderful people I knew in Gaza and Ramallah. I treasure my friendships with Khalil and Ana Ansara, Christo Bursheh, Marwan Hamad, Lubna Ghaneim, Amelia Peltz, and Nisreen Shyoukhi. Abu 'Ali Harara and Jamal Harazin helped me in my everyday life in Gaza in innumerable ways, keeping a careful, but never oppressive, eye on my well-being. Bassam Nasser helped me get settled when I first arrived. A special word of thanks goes to Samah Zaroub and her family. I can't imagine a warmer welcome than I received from this large, wonderful family. I was delighted to share the joys of their life and honored to be included also in their sorrows.

My intellectual interest in the Middle East, and my first inkling that I wanted to be an academic, began when I was an undergraduate at Wesleyan University. I especially thank Hope Weissman, my senior thesis advisor, for reading everything and always challenging me to do more. It is certain friends from college—most especially Jen Douglas, Erin Kelly, and Elizabeth Meister—whom I most count on to keep me true to myself. I began my graduate work in the Near Eastern Studies program at New York University. Courses I took there with Lila Abu-Lughod, Samira Haj, and Timothy Mitchell influenced my thinking in important ways. While at NYU, I also began my study of Arabic with Ahmed Ferhadi, who provided an excellent foundation. Anyone who works on the Middle East will find the rest of my path of Arabic language learning (Middlebury, CASA) familiar. I am grateful to my teachers in these institutions and also for the many friendships forged in the struggle of learning Arabic. My CASA cohort was especially close, and I appreciate the continued friendships of Christina Civantos, Ken Garden, Parastou Hassouri, Kate Kolstad, Nancy Reynolds, Karen Rignall, Jessica Winegar, and the other *shilla* members Lee Keath and Karim Mostafa.

I cannot think of a better intellectual training ground than the University of Michigan's doctoral program in anthropology and history. Certainly it provided me with exactly what I needed to be able to imagine and embark on this project. I especially thank the members of my doctoral committee—Brinkley Messick, Ann Stoler, Juan Cole, and Val Daniel—both for their intellectual examples and for their encouragement throughout. The influence of what they taught me is evident throughout these pages. Fellow students at Michigan—including Lee Belhman, Carla Daughtry, Karen Rignall, and Laura Stevens—enriched all aspects of my life. I was especially fortunate that an extraordinary group of colleagues and friends also came to New York for dissertation writing. I cannot imagine a better writing group than we had—its strength perhaps evident in that it has continued in various forms even beyond the dissertation. For their insightful comments, helpful nudges, careful readings, and the pleasure of their company, I thank Pamila Gupta, Rachel Heiman, Mani Limbert, Brian Mooney, and Karen Strassler.

I began the process of reimagining my dissertation while a fellow at the Society of Fellows in the Humanities at Columbia University. While teaching contemporary civilization occupied a great deal of my time, what I learned from the experience has influenced this text in unanticipated ways.

I am glad for the presence around the Heyman Center of Bashir Abu-Manneh, Sandrine Berteaux, Rashmi Sadana, Mark Swislocki, and Miriam Ticktin, all of whom stimulated my thinking enormously. I consider it especially fortuitous that Miriam and I landed at Columbia at the same time. Our conversations and ongoing collaborations have been important to so many aspects of my work. I am thankful to my colleagues at the Kevorkian Center at New York University for providing a congenial place to work and to write. I am most especially grateful to Zachary Lockman for making it possible for me to have the time to do so. My gratitude to the people who took the time (out of always busy schedules) to read parts or all of the manuscript is enormous. I thank Robert Blecher, Elliott Colla, Rachel Heiman, Mandana Limbert, Zachary Lockman, Shira Robinson, and Rashmi Sadana. The book is immeasurably improved by their thoughtful suggestions. I am grateful to Hamdi Attia for his work on the maps and to Tracy Maher for her help with transliterations. I also thank two anonymous readers for Duke University Press for their comments and Ken Wissoker, Courtney Berger, and Mark Mastromarino for their enthusiasm for the project and their expert guidance in bringing it to completion.

I am grateful to my husband, Hani Alam, for his love and care and for the pleasure of life beyond work. I am thankful to my family for their unfailing support for me and my work—even when they have found it troubling. My grandmother died shortly before I completed this book; my mother, ten years earlier. Both were tremendously strong women: loving, smart, and stubborn. The qualities I inherited and learned from them have been crucial not only in my work, but in my life. It is to them I dedicate this book.

NOTE ON TRANSLITERATION

I have used a modified version of the IJMES transliteration system, excluding diacritical marks. When quoting from spoken Arabic or referring to terms used in spoken Arabic, I have transliterated them according to local pronunciation.

PALESTINE
Administrative Boundaries

1 5 10 20 30 Km

DISTRICT ———————
SUB-DISTRICT ─ ─ ─ ─ ─

Note:
Maps published after 1940 show the
sub-districts of Jericho, Bethlehem and
Jerusalem combined into the single
sub-district of Jerusalem.

Tyre
Mituella
Banyas
S Y R I A
Al Quneitira
LAKE HULA
SAFAD
Tarshiha
Safad
Acre
ACRE
Haifa
LAKE
Tiberias TIBERIAS
Nazareth
TIBERIAS
NAZARETH
HAIFA
BEISAN
Irbid
JENIN
Beisan
Hadera
NORTHERN
Jenin
Nathanaya
Tulkarm
Ajlun
TULKARM
Jarash
Qalqilya
Nablus
JAFFA
NABLUS
Tel Aviv
Jaffa
As Salt
RAMALLAH
Amman
Ramle
Ramallah
JERICHO
RAMLE
Yibna
JERUSALEM
Jericho
Isdud
Jerusalem
Qassina
Bethlehem
Madaba
Al Majdal
Al Faluja
BETHLEHEM
GAZA
Bureir
Hebron
DEAD SEA
Gaza
JERUSALEM
TRANS
SOUTHERN
HEBRON
JORDAN
Rafah
Khan Younis
Beersheba
Karak
Khalesa
Khanxira
Asluj
BEERSHEBA
EGYPT
Al'Auja

MAP 1. Map of Mandate Palestine's Administrative Boundaries. SOURCE: THE LIONEL PINCUS AND
PRINCESS FIRYAL MAP DIVISION, THE NEW YORK PUBLIC LIBRARY, ASTOR, LENOX AND TILDEN
FOUNDATIONS. REDRAWN BY HAMDI ATTIA.

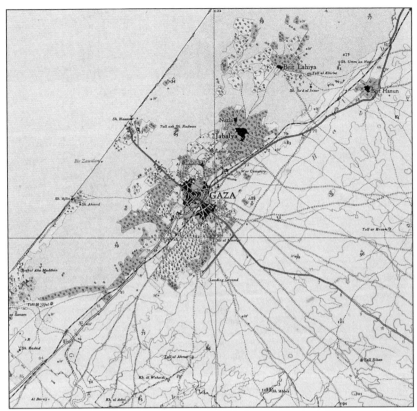

MAP 2. Detail from map of Gaza area, survey of Palestine. SOURCE: THE LIONEL PINCUS AND PRINCESS FIRYAL MAP DIVISION, THE NEW YORK PUBLIC LIBRARY, ASTOR, LENOX AND TILDEN FOUNDATIONS.

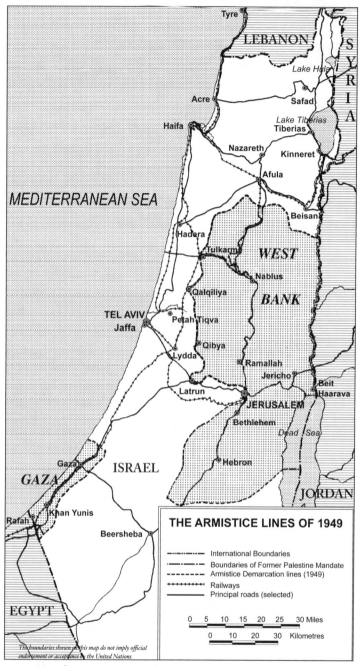

MAP 3. Map of 1949 Armistice Lines (no. 547.1). SOURCE: UNITED NATIONS. REDRAWN
BY HAMDI ATTIA.

GOVERNMENT PRACTICE
AND THE PLACE OF GAZA

G aza has had more than its share of difficult times and crisis conditions. It is often described as, and has often seemed to be, on the verge of being ungovernable. Yet it also has had, if anything, a surfeit of government. While one can easily imagine the security concerns that mobilize certain extraordinary government measures, the everyday work of government continues even (and sometimes especially) in crisis conditions. What constitutes such everyday work is to a considerable degree shaped by the situation itself. Under certain conditions—such as those pertaining in Gaza after 1948—providing daily rations to refugees becomes part of everyday government work. Similarly, in other settings—such as the Gaza of the 1920s—public utilities such as electricity are not part of this field. The terrain explored in this book—a historical ethnography of the civil service in Gaza during the British Mandate (1917–48)[1] and Egyptian Administration (1948–67)—is persistent conflict and ongoing tension as well as ordinary bureaucratic procedures and unremarkable office work. Consideration of this slice of Gazan history highlights the tremendous significance of such quotidian bureaucratic practices even in unstable places.

Even with all of the changes in Gaza over the course of the fifty years under consideration here (as well as before and after) and the crises that produced and accompanied them, there have been important continuities in its government. This persistence of government attests to the fundamental correctness of Max Weber's insights into the role of bureaucracy in producing stability when state regimes change. At the same time, even as bureau-cratic practice can continue across regimes, it is also dramatically reshaped by changing conditions and circumstances of rule. Cognizant of this complexity, I give attention to both continuity and rupture, both stability and crisis, in bureaucratic practice. In this exploration it becomes possible to see not just how government in Gaza worked, but how its workings shed light on more general (even more "ordinary") conditions of modern rule.

In focusing on the daily work of government, this book calls attention to distinct rhythms of history, charting processes of transformation that do not always match the ruptures of Palestinian political history.[2] My primary interest here is not the significant dates, battles, and political maneuvers in Gaza's history, but life and government in the in-between: the time and space between such dramatic events, the tenuous domain of the everyday that was never entirely lost. This attention not only sheds light on quotidian forma-tions of place and people, but can also produce a new sense of events them-selves. To understand what may be *the* defining date in Palestinian history—the *nakba* (catastrophe) of 1948—and the utter transformation of life in Gaza produced by it, for instance, we need to know more than the political facts of dispossession. We need to comprehend the multiple mechanisms through which such loss was managed—whether it be the transformation of an ethics of care, the reconfiguration of service bureaucracies, or the development of new forms of documentation. Each of these areas (and many more) is most clearly illuminated in the workings of everyday government. In focusing on bureaucratic practice, this study explores the effects of government on those caught up in its dynamic.

This book is an exploration of government in Gaza, yet what Gaza is and was has changed significantly over time. In terms of administrative classifica-tion, Gaza has been variously a region, a district, a subdistrict, and, after 1948, a strip—a unique entity. Gaza City, the administrative and commercial center of the area, is also known simply as Gaza. During the British Man-date, the Gaza district was an inseparable part of the larger entity of Pal-estine. During the Egyptian Administration, the Gaza Strip was decisively and painfully cut off from the rest of this territory. In the course of this book, I refer to all of these different senses of Gaza. I also explore how transforma-tions in the shape of the place have influenced what it has meant to be Gazan, and what impact such identification was likely to have on people's lives. These transformations were at once a result of shifts in government and something to which government had to respond.

I consider a variety of service sites and practices, attending to both the specificity of particular services and the general conditions of civil service bureaucracy. The first part of the book (chapters 2, 3, and 4) examines general practices and procedures of rule, exploring the production of authority that is crucial for governing. Under conditions where government was tenuous and lacked a stable ground, it was the repetitions of filing procedures, the accumulation of documents, and the habits of civil servants that produced the conditions of possibility for authority. The second part of the book (chapters 5, 6, and 7), which looks at a variety of government services (shelter, utilities, and education among them), examines the practice of what I call tactical government—a means of governing that shifts in response to crisis, that often works without long-term planning, and that presumes little stability in governing conditions. It was through tactical government that the crises and difficulties which were endemic in Gaza during this period were managed by government. And it was this practice that contributed to the tenacity of government, despite its instabilities.

To do the research for this exploration of fifty years in Gazan government, I spent two years in Gaza (1998 and 1999) during another distinct moment in its troubled history. I conducted both ethnographic and archival research, the latter taking me also to Cairo and Jerusalem. I subsequently undertook further research in London and in the United States and also returned to Palestine in the summers of 2003, 2004, and 2005. The bulk of my ethnographic work was conducted with retired civil servants, with whom I spent time in government offices, in retirees' associations, and in their homes with their families. Archival and ethnographic research sometimes came together, as it was my reading of government documents that afforded me the opportunity to spend extended time in government offices—the Pensions Administration, Gaza City Municipality, *Awqaf* (pious endowments) Administration, and Housing Ministry among them. While I lived in Gaza City, my research took me throughout the Gaza Strip—to Rafah and Khan Yunis (the other main towns) and to refugee camps such as Nusseirat and Jabalya.

The amount of movement necessary to carry out my research—not only within Gaza, but between Gaza and the West Bank—serves as a reminder that I was extremely lucky in the timing of my fieldwork. I conducted the bulk of the research for this book during what turned out to be the latter part of the Oslo period.[3] What at the time seemed to be part of a new stage in Palestinian history appears now to have been only a lull in the violence of conflict between Israelis and Palestinians. While the luster of the Oslo Accords—which had been heralded as bringing an end to conflict between Israelis and Palestinians and leading to the establishment of a Palestinian state—had worn off by 1998, replaced by growing frustration with Israeli intransigence and Palestinian National Authority (PNA) corruption, the easiness of everyday life (for someone like me, at least) had not yet been disrupted. Aided by my American passport and the Michigan license plates on my car (which I had shipped from the United States), I was able to travel freely and easily. The fact that the only way to get from here to there in Palestine was with an American car—and that with an American car there was almost no difficulty—speaks volumes about the peculiar and difficult conditions of the post-Oslo world. Cars with Palestinian license plates were not generally allowed out of Gaza, and cars with Israeli plates were not allowed in. More important, Palestinians were not allowed to travel between the West Bank and Gaza without difficult-to-obtain permits, so the two parts of the Palestinian territories were almost entirely cut off from each other. The overt violence of occupation had, for the moment, been replaced by a system of bureaucratic stricture and degradation.

In the wake of the establishment of the PNA in 1994, American, Japanese, and European aid money had flowed into the West Bank and Gaza, generating numerous improvement projects. The "de-development"[4] of the Israeli occupation was replaced with a drive for both economic and political development (the latter a favorite of the U.S. Agency for International Development). As I talked with people about the governing work of the Mandate and Administration, projects of infrastructure development were all around. Roads were paved, water networks improved, hospitals built, parks created, and traffic lights installed. The permanent nighttime curfew imposed in Gaza by Israel was replaced by vibrant street activity after dark. At the same time, even as life was easier in these ways, the economy of Gaza suffered terribly from the Israeli closure policy, which dramatically reduced the numbers of people permitted to work inside Israel. Seizures of Palestinian land continued, and the natural resources of the area remained disproportionately available to the eight thousand Jewish settlers in Gaza.[5] Compounding people's frustrations with Israeli actions was the deep disillusionment with the PNA—as, for example, "returnees" and political cronies got jobs over better qualified "local" candidates.[6] As frustrated as people were, though, this was a moment when people expected something from government.

Even as troubles were in the air and people spoke frequently about the possibility of another *intifada*, the newly possible ordinariness of life had yet to be disrupted. The civil servants who worked in government offices where I conducted so much of my research were able to focus on the everyday work of government. These places did not form a space apart from the politics of Palestinian experience—political talk was ubiquitous in offices and everywhere else—but they did allow for "getting stuff done," that is, for keeping electricity flowing, streets clean, police patrolling, and schools operating. Not long after I completed my fieldwork, the second intifada broke out, and in the years since everyday life in Gaza has been disrupted to an almost unimaginable extent. Not only has the level of violence been extremely high, but the daily work of government has been upended, both by the demands placed on it by the increasingly difficult conditions in which people live and, more recently, by the cutting off of financial support (including the money needed to pay civil service salaries) in the wake of the Hamas victory in Palestinian elections.[7]

Ruling Histories

While conditions during the intifada have been extreme, it is obviously not the first time Gaza has experienced trouble and disruption. Throughout its long history, Gaza has often been a battleground between empires, located at the crossroads of major incidents and historical transformations, though its inhabitants have rarely directed those events.[8] The twentieth century was no exception. The histories in which Gaza was engulfed during the British Mandate and Egyptian Administration were also dramatic. The dramas of colonialism, anticolonial nationalism, and nation-state building have all had an impact on Gaza, though none can entirely define its government.

During the Mandate, Gaza was a district within the larger territory of

Palestine. Palestine was part of the larger British colonial empire, though mandates, authorized by the international community in the form of the League of Nations and designed to end (even if in practice bringing them to an end required forms of resistance typical of other colonies), were a quite distinct form of colonialism.[9] The mandate system was developed in the aftermath of World War I to manage German colonial holdings and the territories of the Ottoman Empire. Emerging out of negotiations over the future these areas should properly have, this system proceeded from the claim that "the well-being and development of such peoples form a sacred trust of civilization."[10]

Mandates were commissioned by the League of Nations, which, formally at least, retained authority over them.[11] The countries which were granted mandates were supposed to shepherd the native population to independence, providing "administrative advice until they can exist unaided."[12] Where sovereignty actually lay, however, was never a fully settled question.[13] In practice the mandatory powers exercised the powers normally associated with sovereignty, though they purported to be doing so on behalf of the governed territory and its "latent sovereignty."[14]

This was, then, a colonial form that was intimately connected to the nation-state, albeit a nation-state that was more envisaged than actual.[15] As Antony Anghie argues about the mandate system, "It did not seek merely to qualify the rights of the sovereign, but rather to create the sovereign."[16] The language of legitimacy deployed by the mandatories (when it was deployed) was that not of a general "civilizing mission," but of "trusteeship" specifically connected to the idea of a future independent state.[17] In the case of class A mandates, places such as Palestine which were in a "high stage of development,"[18] that future was supposed to be near.[19] While the mandatory powers did not entirely share visions of imminent independence, the idea of a future nation-state was important to their operations. And although to the populations subject to it the mandate system may have felt very similar to other forms of colonialism, its distinct form did make a difference.

Within the mandate system, Palestine was unique, in part because of the multiple and conflicting responsibilities the British had assumed there.[20] In addition to its obligations to the native population of the country, Great Britain had taken on the task of promoting a Jewish national home.[21] A great deal of British policy and practice over the course of the Mandate was comprised of efforts to manage, however imperfectly, its "dual obligation."[22] Over time, it became increasingly difficult to conceive how the Mandate could succeed in the face of these conflicts.[23] At the same time, the increasing conflict on the ground made it difficult to envision an end to the Mandate. As one of the many commissions sent to Palestine to investigate the causes of strife noted, "The Mandate cannot be fully and honourably implemented unless by some means or other the national antagonism between Arab and Jews can be composed. But it is the Mandate that created that antagonism and keeps it alive. . . . Real 'self-governing institutions' cannot be developed, nor can the Mandate ever terminate, without violating its obligations, general or specific."[24] One effect of these circumstances was that despite the international authorization of the Mandate the language of legitimacy in fact provided a very poor foundation for government. Distraction and deferral, on the other hand, proved to be crucial to Mandate government.

As particular as British rule in Palestine was, the Egyptian Administration of the Gaza Strip was even more so. The 1948 war over Palestine was a life-shattering experience for Palestinians, and Gazan government and society were utterly transformed.[25] When Great Britain gave up on the Mandate and turned the problem over to the United Nations, the UN agreed on a plan to divide Palestine into two states—one Jewish and one Arab. The Palestinians and surrounding Arab countries rejected the legitimacy of this dispensation, and fighting over the territory began well before the British departed in May 1948. The war concluded disastrously for the Palestinians, with massive displacement and dispossession of most of their land. The armistice agreement between Israel and Egypt which ended the fighting around Gaza defined the "provisional" boundaries of what was now the Gaza Strip—an area twenty-eight miles long and six miles across at its widest point. The prewar population of eighty thousand was joined by around a quarter million refugees.[26] The Egyptian government, which had entered the war to prevent the partition of Palestine, found itself instead the custodian over this small sliver of Palestinian territory.[27]

The terms of Egyptian rule over this territory were profoundly unclear. The armistice agreement stated that the boundary line "not be considered a political or territorial border and that it does not prejudice the rights and demands that derive from settling the Palestine question."[28] In the immediate aftermath of the war there were negotiations over a U.S.-supported suggestion that Israel take over the area (in exchange for the repatriation of some refugees),[29] British discussions about taking over Gaza as a base for its troops then stationed in the Suez Canal zone,[30] and even suggestions by some Palestinians that Egypt annex the territory.[31] While none of these outcomes may have been terribly likely, that they were discussed at all indicates how uncertain Gaza's status was. British officials, after some question about how to understand the territory, identified it as "res nullius, i.e. nobody's property, since Egypt which is in control does not claim sovereignty."[32] The British position did, though, recognize Egypt as the controlling authority in the territory.[33]

The status of the "Egyptian controlled areas of Palestine" thus remained undefined and contested. Yet, even as the Egyptian Administration had a less certain legal status than the Mandate, it had greater, though still limited, capacity to reference authenticity and legitimacy in its rule. Without ever claiming sovereignty and at least formally supporting the All-Palestine Government, which did claim such authority, Egypt administered the territory until 1967 (except for a four-month Israeli occupation of Gaza in 1956–57).[34] While Jordan annexed the West Bank, the other portion of Mandate Palestine still in Arab hands, Egypt presented itself as the sole remaining defender of Palestine and insisted that Gaza be governed as a separate Palestinian space.[35] It was not insignificant to Gazans that Egypt ruled as a result of a war on behalf of Palestine. It was also not insignificant that Egyptians, while foreign, were also Arabs. Egypt defined its role in Gaza as that of a caretaker, preserving the space of Gaza to take its future place in the Palestinian nation-state. In part because of its concern not to lay claim to Gaza, the Egyptian Administration was reluctant to undertake major policy initiatives, although, like Mandate officials before them, Egyptian government officials, in the work of governing Gaza, ultimately produced many significant transformations in legal, economic, and political structures.

The Administration took a more proactive stance in the second period of its rule in Gaza. As Gamal Abdul Nasser's government was pursuing a broad governmental agenda in Egypt, many similar policies and procedures were enacted in Gaza. The tremendous expansion in educational opportunities, the concomitant expansion of civil service, the provision of housing to civil servants, the ubiquity of security services, all these policies had counterparts in Egypt. The similarities of practice may have derived in part from Egyptian reluctance to intervene too deeply in Gaza and therefore to develop distinct initiatives for this territory. Aspects of this similarity were connected as well to general Egyptian security concerns, which mandated strict control over political expression. At the same time, these practices inevitably had specific effects on and in this space. There was, as well, a distinction of scale between the initiatives in Gaza and major public works projects enacted in Egypt. This disparity was immediately connected to the difference between governing the nation-state and governing the uncertain territory of Gaza.[36]

Political activity in Gaza was severely curtailed throughout the Administration, as it was in Egypt itself. After the outlawing of political parties as breeders of factionalism, the only sanctioned means of organized expression were the Legislative Council and the government-sponsored Arab National Union. The council, established in 1957, gave Gazans a greater voice in government, though the governor-general retained final authority. The National Union, the only party allowed in Gaza, was established in 1959. It was created, as the governor-general put it, "with the goal of actualizing the message of Arab nationalism and building a democratic socialist society and to engender cooperation among all Palestinians to liberate the rest of their homeland."[37] This was Gaza's version of the National Union established in Egypt during the same period and, like that union, should be seen less as an opportunity for independent political action than as a mechanism for involving Gazans in the Nasserist project.[38] In 1964, when the Palestine Liberation Organization (PLO) was established, Nasser formally, though not practically, declared it to have authority in Gaza.[39] Under the auspices of this new organization, which was by no means independent of Egypt and the other Arab states, the Palestine Liberation Army (PLA) was created, and in 1965 military conscription was instituted.[40]

A distinguishing feature of the governmental terrain in Gaza was that, from 1950 on, Egypt shared administrative responsibility with the United Nations Relief and Works Agency (UNRWA). UNRWA, which provided aid to Palestinian refugees wherever they lived, was itself a unique UN agency.[41] Whereas all other refugees are "serviced" by the United Nations High Commission for Refugees (UNHCR), Palestinian refugees have an agency devoted specifically to them.[42] This distinctive attention recognized the long-standing involvement of the international community in, and its responsibility for, the fate of Palestine.[43] This agency has also had a more expansive jurisdiction than the UNHCR, being responsible, as its name suggests, not only for relief, but for works (rehabilitation).[44] That refugees formed a large majority of the Gazan population gave UNRWA an especially prominent role in this locale and meant that it, as much as Egypt, governed Gaza.

As the presence of these two governing bodies indicates, government had considerable reach during the Egyptian Administration. The Mandate witnessed a significant expansion of government, but during this earlier period there were people who had little direct relation with its offices and officials (often relying on intermediaries such as *mukhtars* [village leaders] to manage whatever contact was necessary) and who therefore may not have felt government as a daily presence in their lives. The number of such people diminished steadily over the course of the Mandate, especially in the later years, when government employment opportunities increased. After 1948, owing in large part to their tremendous need, almost no one would have been able to avoid involvement with the governing apparatuses—whether through the receipt of rations, participation in the expanded educational opportunities, or employment by either the Administration or UNRWA. Despite the absence of a stable state structure, then, Gaza provides an example of a remarkable degree of government. While defying classification according to any state model, therefore, rule and life in Gaza can be comprehended through an analytics of government.[45]

Analytics of Government

An analytics of government requires attention to the form, context, and details of the exercise of rule. In Gaza's case, the rich body of work on colonial processes of control is a helpful starting point for such an exploration. In the literature on colonialism, there is considerable debate about how to classify colonial relations with subject populations. Do legitimacy, hegemony, and governmentality apply in colonial conditions? Or does the importance of force and coercion to the persistence of colonial rule render such instruments irrelevant?[46] Does continued resistance to colonial rule mean there is no consent? Or does the tenacity of colonialism indicate that it could not have been sustained through force alone?[47] Ultimately, it seems that understanding the character of colonial rule entails not choosing consent or coercion as *the* significant factor, but rather recognizing the dynamic relation between them. As John Comaroff suggests, studies of colonial governance must seek to understand its "essential paradox": "its capacity to be ordered yet incoherent, rational yet absurd, violent yet impotent; to elicit compliance and contestation, discipline and defiance, subjection and insurrection. Sometimes all at once."[48]

Students of colonialism also remind us that such explorations must trace the specificities of different colonial conditions—in the case at hand the specificities of the mandate system and of that system as applied in Palestine.[49] One of these distinguishing features, as I noted, was that mandate governments were not as fully "states without nations"[50] as were other colonial forms. The idea, if not the actuality, of the nation-state was crucial to their operations. In the Egyptian Administration, the deferred nation-state occupied an even more central place in the dynamics of rule. The Egyptian Administration should not be easily subsumed under the category of colonialism, if for no other reason than that Gazans do not consider it to have been colonial. Unlike mandatory powers, which claimed the colonial prerogative both to develop the capacity for self-rule and to judge that capacity, the Administration claimed merely to be a placeholder for the nation-state, safeguarding the territory from annexation or occupation by those who might wish to dissolve Palestinian national ambitions. While this future-oriented stance, under conditions in which the future was murky at best, helped promote the persistence of Administration rule, it also ensured that such rule operated without a stable basis for legitimacy in the present. Such lack of stability and clarity characterized government during both the Mandate and the Administration.

What analytic approach is, then, the most helpful in understanding government in Gaza during this difficult period, when government was both colonial and not and was concerned with the nation-state though not defined by it? Clearly one must give attention to the significance of mandates and their relation to broader colonial conditions; one has to attend as well to the peculiar form of Egyptian authority in Gaza. Yet there is clear evidence of a governing dynamic not entirely defined by the political periods of Palestinian history, by the nationality of its rulers, or by the legal status of the territory itself. An understanding of government across this period must do more than define its state.[51] To this end, this book explores three main sets of questions. How is governing authority produced and reproduced? How does government persist, particularly under conditions that seem untenable? And what does government do? How, that is, does it shape (and how is it shaped by) the people and places that are its objects and agents?

In this exploration, a careful balance is required between identifying Gazan distinctiveness and capturing its general characteristics. Neither Palestinian exceptionalism[52] nor an undifferentiated understanding of governmentality[53] can provide sufficient analytic purchase. Government in Gaza persisted within a field in which the familiar catalogue of ruling techniques associated with governmentality—expertise, statistical exactness, administrative certitude, resource concentration—was present, but not dominant. This difference suggests that the analytic of governmentality which has been so fruitful for thinking about the work of modern rule needs to be given further nuance. If governmentality is meant to describe "governmental rationalities," as Michel Foucault suggested, then such rationalities and their associated practices must be explored in their historical specificity.[54]

In addition to its clear connections with the large anthropological and historical literature on state and government, this book builds on the insights of scholars concerned with the history and practice of everyday life.[55] Such work, diverse in its interests, highlights the "micro-physics" of power that are enacted in the most apparently ordinary of interactions.[56] Training attention on putatively marginal people and seemingly insignificant moments, explorations of the everyday show the import of the mundane.[57] Rather than focusing on ordinary experiences in the home, the marketplace, or the neighborhood, though, I highlight the domain of the office and the circuits of quotidian practices of bureaucracy.[58] This space of ordinary bureaucratic operation provides a helpful entry point for understanding Gaza's government.

The combination of archival and ethnographic perspectives on bureaucracy makes it easier to approach it not as a bounded institution, but as a regime of practices. Bureaucratic practices "are not just governed by institutions, prescribed by ideologies, guided by pragmatic circumstances . . . but possess up to a point their own specific regularities, logic, strategy, self-evidence, and 'reason.' "[59] With bureaucratic practice at the center of analysis, it becomes possible to see how contradiction and connection, rupture and continuity, regularity and exceptionality participated in a governing dynamic that was both tenuous and effective. Archival research in government documents illuminates how compilations of minutiae both follow and produce a governing logic that exceeds the scope of their immediate interests. Ethnographic work with civil servants makes clear that governing dynamics persistently overstep the boundaries that formal structures try to set up. It is in ordinary encounters and daily practice that the workings of government become clear.

Spending time with retired civil servants as they lived their postwork lives and with working civil servants as they managed the daily struggles of the office helped me better understand both the constraints of government in Gaza and the dynamics of governance more broadly. I saw how the uncertain status of the post-Oslo Palestinian Authority found expression in the ways that civil servants debated proper procedure among themselves. I saw as well how the imperative to appear authoritative meant that they rarely voiced such uncertainties in interactions with the public. At the same time, I witnessed many occasions in which members of the public explicitly challenged civil servants' authority—sometimes by refusing to accept their directives or to acknowledge that they had the authority to make such decisions, sometimes by comparing Palestinian civil service unfavorably to other regimes that had ruled Gaza, the most pointed criticism being to say they were acting worse than Israeli occupying forces. The ways that past and future governing arrangements remained present in people's understandings of their daily bureaucratic experiences further underscored the importance of understanding these regimes.

Within the methodological attention to the ordinary (under conditions that were almost always extraordinary) emerges the closely connected theoretical insight that the authority and tenacity of government in Gaza derived not so much from legitimacy, authenticity, or even "good policy," but from the form, shape, and habits of its daily practice. The unstable governing conditions that almost always existed in Gaza, conditions which provided so little grounding for ruling authority, illuminate the significance that bureaucratic *practice* has for government. Rather than measuring practice against policy—whether to judge the degree of perfection in its enactment or to highlight the failures of ideal types in capturing bureaucratic complexity—the Gazan case suggests that we need to consider this practice as itself productive of governing form, intent, and direction. The intersections and occasional collisions of the habits of civil servants and the paths of papers that were part of everyday work helped define the terrain of government. This was not a terrain marked by coherence and unity, but rather was a domain in which seemingly, and often actually, contradictory practices coexisted. Government regularities—expressed, for example, in the codification of bureaucratic forms and office procedures—existed alongside extraordinary and sometimes even erratic governing work, such as "crisis services," which were meant to be temporary, were not intended to generate further governmental obligation, and often shifted rapidly.

During both the Mandate and the Administration, such contradictions were not simply managed by government but were made productive for it. While there were moments of political crisis that threatened their persistence, these governments utilized both the regularity of repetitive bureaucracy and the mobility of tactical practice to manage the unstable conditions in Gaza. Under very difficult conditions, they were able to persist by turning those difficulties to their advantage, for instance, by deflecting the questions of legitimacy that neither administration could answer. The advantage of such practices was that governments were able to survive challenges that seem as though they should have brought the entire edifice crashing down. Their disadvantage was that, being tactical more than strategic, it was nearly impossible to predict what outcomes might result from their enactment or what shape the persisting government might take. Both the British Mandate and the Egyptian Administration survived by, in effect, relinquishing control over their future.

Reiterative Authority

For any government bureaucracy, the question of authority is a crucial one. However highly developed its mechanisms, however organized its networks, it cannot long function unless both its practitioners and the public recognize its demands as being authoritative. Considered through the lens of its daily practice, this authority is best understood not as an objective achievement, but rather as an ongoing process. Richard Sennett describes it as a "process of interpreting power."[60] Authority is enacted through practice, not established once and for all. All bureaucracies depend on such repetition; Gaza's experiences shed much light on this dynamic. As this book highlights, relations of authority within the civil service are never so "rationalized" as an ideal-type definition of bureaucratic organization might imagine. Authority does not rely simply on clearly stated regulations or minutely plotted jurisdiction. Its formations are much more diffuse, traversing boundaries that from a purely administrative perspective might appear inviolate.

While, following Weber, they recognize bureaucracy as the quintessential form of modern government (and of management more generally), explorations of governing authority in modern states often highlight formations of authority that lie elsewhere. For instance, the nation-state, the still-dominant global state form, seems to deploy the authority of affective ties, moral claims, and authentic arrangements.[61] Michael Herzfeld emphasizes the importance of this last term in engendering not only authority, but the related capacity for domination in bureaucracies that claim foundation in the nation. He argues that "it is the claim to authenticity that allows the bureaucrat to justify a stance of intransigence."[62] In Gaza, and in colonial conditions generally, this claim to national authenticity could not provide a basis for authority. In the absence of a felt organic connection between government and population, the formation of governmental authority demands other mechanisms.

In the elaboration of authority in Gaza during the Mandate and the Administration, when conditions on the ground offered little stability, the capacity of bureaucracy to produce its own authority was crucial.[63] This auto-authorization was a distinctly circular process, and the extent to which it was successful was owing precisely to its circularity. While external sources of authority were occasionally called upon—whether the promise of future independence, the benefits of reform, or the connection to cultural identity— none could provide a stable ground for authority. Promises, improvements, and connections were too often undermined by betrayals, regressions, and dislocations. Most reliable, in fact, were the general characteristics of bureaucracy itself—the reiterative networks of filing (see chapter 2) and the repetitive habits of civil servants, habits which, as I explore, were expressed in both belief and practice (see chapters 3 and 4). By demanding that attention be paid to these routines of governmental operation, Gaza thus shows clearly how bureaucracy works more generally.

Bureaucracy is certainly not the only space in which reiteration is important to authority. Jacques Derrida and Judith Butler indicate the importance of reiteration to discursive authority, though there are differences with the form I am describing. They argue that discursive authority relies both on citational practice and on the obscuring of this practice.[64] As Butler puts it, it may be that a subject "appear[s] as the author of its discursive effects to the extent that the citational practice by which he/she is conditioned and mobilized remains unmarked."[65] Subjects appear agentive by not seeming to be merely repetitive. If this is so, then dissimulation marks a divergence between discursive and bureaucratic authority. In bureaucracy, not only is repetition not obscured, it is highlighted. Files must not only *be* like other files, but also *appear* like them. Every personnel file needs to look alike; every government form needs to fit the mold. Civil servants are anything but surreptitious as they accumulate and repeat habits of service; they trumpet their mastery of these habits as signs of their competence.

Citational practice also worked distinctively in Gaza. Michel de Certeau identifies citation as "the ultimate weapon for making people believe . . . replacing doctrines that have become unbelievable, citation allows the technocratic mechanisms to make themselves credible for each individual *in the name of the others*."[66] Citation, he suggests, makes people believe without "providing any believable object." In the case of Gaza's bureaucracy, reiteration did not stand in for an original belief that had lost its power. To the extent that belief was invoked, people were asked not so much to believe that bureaucracy stood for something else as to believe in it for itself. Perhaps even more vital than such belief, though, they were asked to participate in its workings. It was, again, authority (of bureaucracy itself) rather than legitimacy (of the regime) that bureaucratic repetition promoted.

The self-referential characteristics which produced authority in Gaza are the same features that often lead to bureaucracies being criticized as obscurantist, opaque, and antidemocratic.[67] A common complaint about bureaucracies is that they privilege rule over reason, following their own internal procedures even to ridiculous and unjust ends.[68] Weber certainly identified the all-encompassing character of bureaucratic organization as potentially deadening, and not only for the broader society. As he notes, bureaucratic authority subjects not only the population, but also its civil servants. He describes these employees as "small cog[s] in a ceaselessly moving mechanism which prescribes to [them] an essentially fixed route of march"[69] and argues that "the individual bureaucrat cannot squirm out of the apparatus in which he is harnessed."[70] At the same time, this expansive and referential governing domain did not work simply to control people, but also defined a space of maneuver within which challenges, demands, and contestations were enacted. The reliance of Gaza's government on the self-referential, reiterative aspects of bureaucracy offers an opportunity to explore more precisely how they work.

Even with Gaza's peculiarities then, readers who are familiar with regions and states that have more "normal" governing structures will find much that is familiar in the processes described here.[71] For this reason, exploring how they worked to produce governing authority in Gaza can help explain the more general condition of modern rule. The Gazan instance suggests the importance of considering how seemingly exceptional bureaucratic features may also be part of more regular governing conditions. Their importance may be masked precisely by this regularity. The claims of the nation-state, for instance, to provide stable authority for rule may in fact obscure the ways in which reiterative authority, which does not rely on the claim to authenticity, is also crucial in those conditions.

Tactical Government and the Abeyance of Legitimacy

Bureaucratic authority made possible people's continued participation in government, whether working in it as a civil servant or approaching it as a private citizen. Yet such continued participation should not be taken as evidence of legitimacy. While authority and legitimacy are generally thought to be essentially the same—in Weber's formulation authority is legitimated domination[72]—in the Gazan instance, at least, they need to be distinguished.[73] Bureaucratic authority is, and was, different from the legitimacy of a specific government.[74] In the Gaza of the Mandate and the Administration, any sustained claim to legitimacy was almost certain to fail, a circumstance which demanded even more reliance on bureaucratic authority. There were, to be sure, instances in which each government made gestures toward legitimacy (as well as moments when Gazans confronted this question), but they were localized, often aborted, and never dominant modes of governing.

This is not to say that an absence of legitimacy cannot undermine bureaucratic authority, for it often does. The two do not simply exist apart but rather need to be held apart by government work. Lisa Wedeen's analysis of Hafiz al-Asad's rule in Syria identifies ways in which governments sustain themselves neither by relying on legitimacy nor by using force in every instance.[75] I draw insight from her work in this exploration of a variant sort of avoidance of legitimacy. While the Syrian government relied upon public, often spectacular displays of support for Asad, in Gaza no such declaration was demanded. If anything, the less attention paid to the regime, the better. Rule in Gaza worked not so much through the absence of belief—an absence which Wedeen argues added to the power of the Asad regime—as through a lack of attention. That is, if rule in Asad's Syria was characterized by a politics of "as if," in which people performed a consent they may not have felt, in Gaza, rule operated through a dynamic of abeyance, in which questions of consent and coercion remained suspended.[76]

To understand how this worked, one must turn to the details of government services, details which also accentuate the distinctions between the Mandate and the Administration. Questions of what services to offer and how to provide them were answered somewhat differently by each administration. Even in this domain of distinction, however, the service practice of each evidenced a shared governing style. Responding to the difficult conditions in Gaza and to the uncertain status and future of rule itself, government there was tactical, that is, focused more on coping with current conditions than with long-range planning, took actions based on partial understandings rather than comprehensive analysis, and could count only on limited resources and often tenuous authority as it did so. All governments are tactical to some—even a considerable—degree. Some governments, though, whether by legitimacy or by a degree of force that could render legitimacy irrelevant, achieve a degree of stability that allows them to be strategic also. In Gaza such stability was largely absent.[77]

In developing the term *tactical government*, I draw from de Certeau's work in *The Practice of Everyday Life*, but I am expanding his insights about persons' responses to a disciplinary environment to include the domain of governmental practice. In de Certeau's view, the tactical is eminently the realm of the everyperson, the consumer, the ordinary subject.[78] Tactics are, he suggests, the preserve of the weak. To call government tactical, though, is not to say that it does not exercise power over persons, but rather to note its distinctive style of operation. This difference is not about degrees of purposefulness, aggressiveness, or meaningfulness in government practice. Foucault calls attention to the "coherence of a tactic."[79] The distinction, rather, has to do with scale of action, scope of imagination, range of planning, and stability of resources.

The remarkable extent and depth of the difficulties facing officials were one of the distinctive features shaping Gaza's governmental practice. Neither British nor Egyptian administrators had time, space, or money to settle down in Gaza. Not only were government budgets severely constrained, but government policies were often exceedingly uncertain.[80] As noted earlier, the British Mandate was charged both with overseeing the development of Palestine (an internally contradictory proposition that entailed both shepherding it to independence and establishing a Jewish National Home) and with maintaining order in the country (a goal which privileged the status quo). Egyptian administrators, who came into Gaza as a consequence of the failed attempt to defend Palestine in 1948, were concerned both with maintaining Gaza as Palestinian space (which mandated preserving existing legal structures) and with protecting Egyptian interests in the region (which required strong control over the space of Gaza). How to both stand for Palestine and not provoke either retaliatory action by Israel or interference by the international community was a source of tension throughout.

Even as they tried to mitigate the contradictions of administration, each regime was confronted by a persistent temporal uncertainty. Both the Mandate and the Administration were governments that were supposed to end, but neither had a clear path to that end. At the same time, each feared the end might be not so much produced, as forced. Temporal insecurity meant that even when government attempted to plan, to develop policy, it was never possible to imagine with any degree of accuracy what future it might be planning for. When Mandate officials averred that after a successful effort to promote greater adherence to building regulations in Gaza, town planners could begin "concentrating on the future,"[81] they turned out to be wrong, not so much about the success, as about the future (see chapter 5). When Egyptian authorities insisted to UNRWA that educational policies should prepare refugee students not to settle where they were living, but to be "good citizens [*muwatinin salahin*] when they return to their country,"[82] this insistence reflected more an imagined future than an evident possibility (see chapter 7). Similarly, when refugees refused a service expansion proposed by UNRWA in order not to be settled in their exile, they could not have anticipated that their unsettled conditions might persist for another forty years (see chapter 6).

Tactical government offered a means for the Mandate and the Administration to cope with these conditions. Furthermore, it provided a mechanism through which questions of legitimacy that could never be resolved or entirely occluded could be held in abeyance. In this dynamic, the very instability of government was mobilized to promote its persistence. If it was unclear what the future would bring, how long any particular government would be in place, what ruling arrangements might come next, then (this practice seemed to argue) it might not be necessary to direct too much attention to the question of the legitimacy of that government. Abeyance suggested that these questions need not be resolved; tactical government provided a mechanism through which such resolution could be diverted.

With its preference for the temporary, the piecemeal, the makeshift, tactical government permitted deferral and distraction to occupy the space of resolution. Deferral meant putting aside questions of legitimacy to a vaguely imagined future time when there would be Palestinian self-determination in Gaza. Distraction meant that the attention of government, of civil service, of the population was averted from the challenges of consent and coercion and focused on the mundane, the day to day, the getting by. In this way the stakes, and the possible outcomes, of practices and policies were often not discerned, by either practitioners or the public. The dynamics of abeyance permitted the persistence of rule, under always fraught and uncertain conditions, in Gaza.

Governing Practices and the Shaping of Gaza

As I explore authorization and persistence, in each part of the book I am also concerned with what government does and with how it shapes and is shaped by Gaza and Gazans. Having discussed the historical trajectory of its ruling forms, here I briefly outline shifts in its local formations. Before 1948, Gaza City was a moderately prosperous town, as noted, the administrative and commercial center of a provincial district. It had a long history that its residents termed illustrious; it could not compare to Jerusalem or Jaffa perhaps, but was not without its charms. While the city housed government offices, courts, a port, and major markets, most of the inhabitants of the Gaza district would have gone there only occasionally. The vast majority of Gaza's population, like that of most of Palestine, were peasants (*fellahin*), who worked either their own or other people's land. The years of the Mandate were a time of crisis for the Palestinian peasantry, a crisis connected in part to the increase in Zionist settlement in the country. It became increasingly necessary for people to seek work outside their villages, and the needs of the British army during World War II created large numbers of jobs.

Gaza City had a municipal council, established by the Ottomans in 1893, as did Khan Yunis, the next largest town in the district. As in other facets of Mandate governance, British officials argued that their version of these councils was much improved over that of their Ottoman antecedents,[83] though Palestinians often disagreed.[84] The formal regulatory framework for municipal organization remained Ottoman until the promulgation in 1934 of a new Municipal Corporations Ordinance. This ordinance confirmed a system of centralized authority in which government oversaw and had to approve almost all municipal decisions.[85] In general, there were elections for council members, but the mayor and deputy mayor were appointed by the government from among those elected.[86]

The membership of the council over the years of the Mandate and beyond illustrates the dynamics of local power, which was admittedly quite circumscribed. Like other regions of Palestine, Gaza was dominated by a number of powerful families, including the Shawwa, Husseini, and Sourani, families whose prominence was as much economic as political. As one Gazan recalled about this time, "The people who had land, which gave them an income . . . They were relaxed—compared to the exhausted worker, say, the peasant who worked all year long to pay his taxes. . . . Family unity was political, economic, social unity . . . the family situation was what determined one's social position."[87]

Gaza was identified by British and Palestinians alike as an area that was a bit behind the rest of the country. When the Mandate was first being staffed, a British officer was assigned to the Southern District, which encompassed what was later called the Gaza district, with the comment, "The somewhat backward district over which it is proposed to place him will, I confidently believe, make considerable progress under his guidance."[88] Toward the end of the Mandate a Palestinian official echoed this comment, saying that the area had "always been backward and almost neglected."[89] Its economy was almost entirely dependent on agriculture and lacked significant industry. The town of Majdal was known for its weaving and Gaza City produced soap and pottery, but these crafts had not been industrialized.[90]

Not only was Gaza perceived as backward, it was also provincial, far from the center of political action and government decision making in Jerusalem. This characteristic of Gaza has proved helpful to my investigation. Looking at the history of government from the provinces makes it easier to focus on practice, not policy, on how government is enacted rather than imagined, on its effects instead of the intentions of its decision makers. At the same time, it becomes possible to see how the conditions of the place also exerted an effect on government, how it was never a simple process of application.[91]

Whatever hardships the Palestinian population might have endured during the Mandate, they were nothing compared to the aftermath of 1948. The massive dispossession and displacement of the population and the division of what had been Palestine into three separate areas, West Bank, Gaza Strip, and the new state of Israel, produced unprecedented impoverishment and social disruption. In Gaza, the crisis was felt in the tensions and cooperations that quickly developed among the new categories of the population—refugee and native. The entire population shared the experience of dispossession, as the land of many native Gazans lay beyond the armistice line, but refugees embodied the meaning of displacement. Coping with these conditions, managing this new population, was a primary task of government, whether enacted by the Administration or by UNRWA.

Driven in part by a desperate need for food, in part by attachment to their homes, in the first years after 1948 many Palestinian refugees crossed the armistice line to retrieve belongings and foodstuffs left behind.[92] These journeys were dangerous, and many people were shot by Israeli soldiers. The crossings into what was now Israel also contributed to Egyptian suspicions about the population. Gazans told me that people caught crossing the border were treated as spies. Although people also told me that these relations changed as Egyptians came to know the population better, the period before 1956 was marked by considerable tension over Palestinian demands for arms and the opportunity to defend themselves against repeated Israeli attacks on Gaza. It was not until 1955, following a raid which killed a number of Egyptian soldiers and which provoked large demonstrations in Gaza, that the Administration acquiesced to these demands and established *fida'iyyin* (guerilla) units.[93] This change in policy indicated both a transformation in Egyptian attitudes about confrontation with Israel and an effort to contain a potential crisis in Egyptian rule.

It was the mechanisms which were developed to respond to crisis, as much as the crisis itself, that shaped the new Gazan landscape. As educational opportunities were dramatically expanded in the latter part of the Administration, for instance, families who had never before been able to send their children to school produced university graduates, many of whom took jobs in the also dramatically expanded civil service or went abroad to teach and work in other Arab countries. These new conditions meant that family was no longer entirely destiny. There were new opportunities for social mobility, opportunities that, many people told me, refugees were quick to take advantage of. As one native Gazan told me, "The refugees exceeded us in education, and civilization. . . . In my house I had water and electricity, but he was living in a shack, so he says to himself, 'Why don't I go to Saudi Arabia and earn money?' Of course he studied and worked. . . . The refugee says 'I want to have a better social status.' . . . That is why they are more educated than we are."[94] In addition to the expansion of the public sector, Egyptian policies also created new economic opportunities within the Gaza Strip. Gaza was designated a free-trade zone, and it became a tourist destination for Egyptians seeking cheaper goods. Hotels went up along the beach, and economic opportunity improved.[95]

These policies did much to improve life in Gaza from the low point of the years immediately following 1948, but their impact should not be overstated. Conditions in Gaza remained very difficult for large portions of the population. Unemployment and impoverishment remained a problem throughout the Administration. The large numbers of Gazans who went abroad to work reflected the continued paucity of opportunity in Gaza. An Egyptian report from 1959 calculated unemployment at 87 percent.[96] Even the end of the "era of unemployment," as the Executive Committee of Arab UNRWA Employees put it, did not mean an end to economic hardship. As the committee complained, the greater economic activity in the strip had led to an increase in prices, an increase that was especially burdensome for civil servants on fixed salaries.[97] These difficult economic conditions, caused in no small part by the continued lack of a political resolution to the Palestine problem that would have permitted refugees to return home, created tension throughout the Egyptian Administration. The place that Gaza became in the years after 1948 was shaped by multiple pressures of population and security, regional political considerations and local demands.

That governmental practices can be fundamental in forming a place is perhaps self-evident at this point.[98] In Gaza, government practices were shaped by the reluctance of the Mandate and the Administration to claim too much connection with the place. The uneasy relationship between government and place that ensued was perhaps a more extreme expression of an unease that characterizes modern government more generally.[99] I highlight here the complexity and multidirectionality of these processes in Gaza. The relation was never simply that of government imposing itself upon a place and transforming its character, whether by reorganizing local power relations through the development of new ruling institutions or the transformation of everyday life through the development of new infrastructure. Rather, this place imposed just as much upon government—demanding deployments of resources beyond what policy dictated and forcing interventions into areas outside its apparent jurisdiction.

In the making of place and people, services play a crucial role. They both bind and produce places, people, and government. The existence or absence of paved roads between towns shaped senses of place. Significant transformations in the means through which water was procured for households shaped social relations. Changing details in an ethic of care through which food needs were met transformed people's relationships not only with government but with each other. It matters very much where one looks for help when one is in need—to one's neighbors, to the local mukhtar, or to a government official. An expansion in government services necessarily increases the sites where the public and government officials might meet. Even as services expanded quite dramatically over the period under consideration here, however, the civil servants whom the public most often encountered were members of that public themselves. The limits of services—processes by which some people were excluded, some spaces not incorporated, or certain services simply not offered—were equally important in shaping encounters among people and personnel and in constituting places.

The Shape of the Book

I have relied on a multiplicity of sources to explore the trajectories of service and the formations of government, place, and people in Gaza. As noted above, my research was both archival and ethnographic. Here I want to say a bit more about this research and the ensuing shape of the book. As I discovered in the course of my research, the materials available for this investigation were both considerable and incomplete. Despite its difficult history and sometimes marginal location, a considerable array of documentary materials from and on Gaza is available.[100] Despite the passage of time and the existence of other pressing concerns, I found former civil servants to be tremendously generous with their insights and recollections. Still, both the archival and ethnographic record are filled with half-finished stories, sometimes because a change in regime truncated a governmental practice or a file (or set of files) was lost, sometimes because memory failed or the subject was changed.

I have sought to make analytic use of this expansive incompleteness, considering a diversity of practices and moments as a means to understand a regulative and regulated history, a style of government, a way of being. The exploration of bureaucratic practice calls attention, as noted above, to distinct rhythms of history. These rhythms find expression on a small-scale—in the form of a document, the layout of an office, the pattern of daily life—but their import is broad. This is not to say, though, that bureaucracy constitutes an autonomous domain, unconnected to the major political transformations of the time; it is in fact entirely entangled in such transformations.

The historical record of bureaucracy displays these same complexities. In the course of conducting research in the Israel State Archives, to give just one example, I came across a file that seemed, literally, to be trash. It looked as if the documents in the folder had been scooped out of the garbage and transferred to the archives. The papers, which came from both the Mandate and the Administration, were ripped and crumpled, some mere fragments, none in any meaningful order. To the extent that their subject matter could be discerned, they were an eclectic assortment of notices regarding landownership laws, letters from the agriculture department, town planning materials, assorted blank forms. In contrast, most of the files I looked at in my research offered relatively orderly collections of documents, often with clear references to other files (see chapter 2). This assortment, then, was not a government file in the usual sense. And yet there it was, in a box with other files referring to Gaza (most from the Administration) and with a reference number like any other file.[101] That governmental trash ended up preserved in an archive speaks volumes about both the evident power of bureaucracy and the history of Gaza. The fact that the material was acquired from the Egyptian Administration and housed in Israeli archives helps explain the fate of this office detritus.[102] Whoever took hold of these fragmented papers and whoever placed them in the file must have recognized them as government documents and seen their potential value. Whatever the specific trajectory of decisions, in some sense Gaza's history produced this file.

This difficult history—and the ways in which successive and rapid regime change has helped shape the place, its people, and its government—is evident almost anywhere one turns in Gaza.[103] A lot of my time was spent with retired civil servants, who tend to have a lot of time on their hands for conversation. Such conversations often shifted rapidly among complaints about corruption in the Palestinian Authority, to recollections of Israeli occupation policy, to debates about the impact of the British Mandate. People rendered distinct political evaluations of these regimes and also were highly cognizant of the ways in which governing work did not always follow these same divides. As they recalled their careers, they described a persistent tension between the goal of regularity in their work and the often exceptional conditions under which that work was conducted.

The time I spent in government offices, observing and to a limited degree participating in the work of bureaucracy, enabled me to see some of these complexities firsthand. I was not, of course, put to work filing but was sometimes called on to be a participant in bureaucratic conversation, for example, in debating specific practices, or in bureaucratic ritual, such as accompanying civil servants to offer holiday wishes to the director of the bureau. Present-day bureaucratic conditions are neither identical to the conditions of the Mandate and the Administration, nor entirely disconnected from them. What I experienced in these offices, and everywhere in Gaza, helped me make sense of the archival materials I gathered and interviews I conducted. Given that my object of study was not only bureaucratic events, that is, the specific contests, deployments, and services enacted in the Mandate and the Administration, but also bureaucratic ethos, habits, and styles that were not contained within the boundaries of regimes and that extend beyond the temporal limits of my project, participant-observation in a time that was not the time of my study proved to be immensely useful. While I do not often make explicit reference to my experiences with Gaza's bureaucracy, what I learned from them does inform my analysis of the civil service condition.

The form of the book grew directly out of my experiences in researching it. Part 1, with chapters on files and archives, civil service habits, and bureaucratic competence, is focused most directly on the formations of bureaucracy and government itself. I examine the regulation of filing and the development of civil service personas. Given my interest in explicating a work of rule that is more evident in practice than in policy, more apparent in everyday workings of government than in comprehensive reflections on it, it should not be surprising that my focus is on middle- and low-level civil servants. I also focus on Gazan employees, rather than on their British and Egyptian colleagues and superiors. These practitioners (rather than planners) of government, who were also participants in the life and society of the place of rule, offer an especially good avenue through which to explore the work of government.[104] The intersection of the civil service domain with the place and public of Gaza is noted in these first chapters and is traced in more detail in part 2.

It was through consideration of the experiences of ordinary employees, apprehended through conversation, observation, and archival research, that the distinctive rhythms of Gaza's history became more clear to me. The daily struggles of doing a job, of procuring a service, serve as a reminder that Gaza is more than a stage for conflict and violence. It is as real—if also surreal—a place as any in which we live, and people there continue to be concerned with and to strive to better their mundane quotidian lives. Gazans are not simply martyrs and victims (or terrorists and fanatics, depending on your perspective), but also ordinary people with common concerns. While bureaucratic practices were never simply regular in Gaza, their clear regularities highlight Gaza's location within a broader field of modern government. By opening with them, I intend not only to describe the broad contours of the civil service domain, but also to highlight the more ordinary face of Gaza.

Gaza's distinctions are important as well, not only for understanding its history, but for a broader consideration of governing practices. These specificities figure most prominently in part 2, where I turn to the details of service work. This work and the challenges it produced illuminate the complexity of relations among the various participants in government: civil servants, members of the public, foreign officials. These chapters also foreground the tremendous significance of crisis and crisis management in Gaza's government. Gaza's government has always entailed both mundane and extraordinary aspects, both regular and exceptional practices. In the organization of the book I seek to permit consideration of each.

Gaza's government, furthermore, in telling us about the shaping of this place and these people, sheds light on broader dynamics. As distinctive as Gaza's governing techniques were, they were not entirely unique to this place. The self-referential authorization so clearly evident in Gaza's bureaucracy also seems to be at work in governments that *do* claim authenticity. The distraction and deferral that kept legitimacy in abeyance may be tactically mobilized by states that *do* depend on an acceptance of legitimacy. The centrality of these practices in Gaza's government and the relative absence of other structures that might appear to authorize and stabilize this government make it easier to see how they work. What we can learn from looking at government in Gaza is helpful, then, in understanding Gaza, and Palestine, as well as government generally. Thus this often extraordinary place no longer appears so radically exceptional—and this in and of itself is a crucial lesson.

PART ONE

Producing Bureaucratic Authority

2

RULING FILES

The management of the modern office is based upon written documents ("the files"), which are preserved in their original or draft form.
. . . the body of officials actively engaged in a "public" office, along with
the respective apparatus of material implements and the files, make
up a "bureau."

MAX WEBER, *ECONOMY AND SOCIETY*

Filing, as Max Weber reminds us, is among the most quintessential features of modern government. Almost every-
one is familiar with the need to gather and compile a huge amount of paper in
order to "succeed" in seemingly minor encounters with governing authorities.
Rule in Gaza has been no exception to this general condition. The British, of
course, are notorious documenters, and it is no surprise that Mandate rule
was file heavy. Building upon the scaffolding of Ottoman documentary production, the Mandate developed an expansive system of paperwork.[1] The
Egyptian administrators who took over in Gaza after the departure of the
British were trained in government paper by years of British colonial rule, and
in addition they had their own histories and concerns which led to a proliferation of documentation. Bureaucratic authority in each of these governments
depended in significant part on the work of filing—work that was mundane,
repetitive, and (to the extent possible) unexceptional.

The conventions of filing, its methods for information presentation and
retention, are not particular to a given government or to any office within

that government.[2] The generality of this technology of documentation, which can be found in both colonial and national governments, in offices both private and public, with a multiplicity of intentions and effects, has had specific importance in Gaza. Because it is so general in form, the governing authority produced in filing does not immediately (or necessarily) connect to the specificity of a regime. Files can be authoritative and can impart authority to the government that does the filing without conferring legitimacy on that government. Even as files *are* embedded in the particular conditions and governments where they work, and even as they also are shaped by those conditions, the mechanisms through which their authority is produced tend to obscure this specificity.

The practices of filing in Gaza evidence the condensed presence of multiple forces and administrative arrangements—the formation of Ottoman modernity, the practice of British colonialism, the struggles of nationalism, and the shifting of regional and international authority. Even as I focus on British and Egyptian practices, the very important Ottoman beginnings of this form of documentary authority must be acknowledged. Carter Findley has traced the emergence of what Foucault calls "disciplinary writing"[3] in nineteenth-century Ottoman filing practices. His descriptions of the new centrality of uniformity and rationality in filing, as well as the increasing attention paid to the individual as the subject of files,[4] illuminate Foucault's argument that by lowering the threshold of knowledge, disciplinary writing was able to make of description "a means of control and a method of domination."[5]

One of the ways filing contributes to governing authority is by defining a space and style of interaction among people, whether civil servants or members of the public.[6] Filing delimits both the terrain of possibility and modes of objection. As it occupied an ever-larger place within the governmental field of the Mandate and then the Administration, filing became the ground on which confrontations and challenges to policy, behavior, and political arrangements took place as well as the medium through which programs were implemented and refined. To a certain extent, then, this was an authority of expansiveness, one that worked by occluding other alternatives.

Expansiveness alone cannot ensure the potency of paper, though. This potency relies just as much on the mechanisms of filing, on the system within which a file circulates. The authority of government files was self-consciously connected to the uniformity and regularity of documents. Uniformity produced both familiarity—each document was recognizable—and grounds for judging authoritativeness—resemblance to other documents. Regularity helped manage the placement of documents within the broader network of filing, which was crucial to the stability of that network. As Foucault underscores, one of the features of disciplinary writing was the development of mechanisms to "integrate individual data into cumulative systems in such a way that they were not lost."[7] Each of these aspects of filing authority is largely self-referential, depending more on other files rather than external forces to define and enhance this authority.

If the power of files is dependent to a great degree on the system of filing, it is perhaps not surprising that one can most often study this authority only when files have been re-placed into another system, that of the archive.[8] Archives themselves play an important role in the production and shaping of governmental authority, but this role is not identical to that of files. Both files and archives, though, are deeply concerned with temporal relations: collecting information in the present which will be available to the future as a record of the past.[9] This chapter opens with a consideration of the relations among and distinctions between files and archives, highlighting their respective roles in the production of bureaucratic authority. Discussion then turns to the moments of filing itself, exploring the writing, compilation, and storage of files. In so doing, I draw on different types and circumstances of filing, in both the British Mandate and the Egyptian Administration.[10] Tracing the filing process in its multiplicity illuminates the effectiveness and authority of files as well as the confrontations and conflicts that are an inherent part of the process.

Archives and Files: Disruption, Loss, and Accumulation

Because of their history of dispossession, Palestinians are acutely aware of the importance of having evidence of their past and proof of their claims about history. To this end, they have generally been scrupulous in their preservation of evidence of their lives and property before 1948. Many Palestinian families have the deed to their homes and lands, the keys to their house, their land registry documents, or some combination of the above. Discussion of *ayyam al-balad* (lit.: village days; fig.: pre-1948 period) often includes an offer to produce these documents. At the same time, the conditions of Palestinian existence have also made archival accumulation difficult. Whether at the national level—evidenced in the Israeli seizure of documents from the Palestine Research Center in Beirut—or at the local level—as when the Gazan Civil Servants' Association destroyed its own records in 1967 to avoid their being captured by Israel and used in its efforts to suppress Palestinian resistance to occupation[11]—the archives of Palestinian history have been directly affected by the violence in Palestinian life.

Even under conditions far less fraught than those in Palestine, the production of archives always involves procedures of exclusion. Archives have conventions that allow entry to certain materials only; they deploy techniques that can render lived experiences almost unrecognizable; they demand conformities of form that can reshape documents. Archives themselves, that is (and not just the historians who use them), work "extractively" on the files of rule.[12] Whatever else they do, they necessarily displace and disempower the documents that constitute them. The various processes of archiving files, whether through state-issued regulations concerning deposit of official papers, seizure in war, or individual extraction, remove them from their systems of practice. In the transformation from file to primary source, these documents are stripped of their authorizing location and operations, a process which lessens and sometimes destroys their original authority. For files to work for government, they need to resist extraction from the immediacy of their practice.

Before going too far into this consideration of how files work and how that work may be disrupted, it may be helpful to step back and define a file itself. In the most basic terms, a file is a compilation of documents that is part of a larger network of such compilations which relate both vertically and horizontally. Horizontal relations include the keeping of similar files (with the same subjects and numbers) in successive years and the keeping of the same type of file about multiple subjects (as, for example, in personnel files). Vertical relations include both differential scope of files (such as municipal files as compared to central government files) and hierarchical distinctions among producers of files (such as reports from low-level employees to their direct superiors as compared to correspondence among high-level appointees). In archives, all types of files are preserved, though these relations may not be.[13]

Whatever their power, as a technology of textual rule, files are notably mundane. Their concerns may be either trivial or weighty, but they are generally quotidian in their form. They are lowly texts, not often gracefully written or especially well formed. While those who write the documents of files take opportunities to reflect upon and critique the policies they pursue and the frame of government within which they operate, filing as a process does not encourage a bird's-eye view of government. This kind of total reflection is left more to the archival stage, where files become part of history. Archives not only permit but encourage or demand the production of meaningful narratives of their producing states.[14]

Unlike other kinds of documents, which may acquire authority through the status of their author, the elegance of their form, or the significance of their content, files are authoritative by virtue of their compilation. Files do not have clear lines of descent the way canonical texts might; the idea of the authoritative original does not play the same role.[15] The accumulation and reiteration of mundane detail in files help produce facticity and potency. Furthermore, the mechanisms of filing, that is, their internal structure and their means of dispersal in a system that regulates people, places, and things, are crucial to the process of authorization. When files are archived, the bonds of this network are loosened, but the files do not become free floating. Rather, they are re-placed in the system of the archive, a system with its own conventions and demands that are effective in shaping their use.

The particular files that constitute the materials for this study have had distinct archival experiences.[16] This book explores and relies upon many types of files, including administrative correspondence and official reports, personnel files, and records of police, *waqf* (pious endowment) administration, municipal councils, and civic associations, all of which have distinctive conditions of production and retention.[17] Not surprisingly, given the history of Gaza, assembling the archive of this project required engagement with several states and their institutions (including, Egypt, Israel, Great Britain, and the Palestinian Authority). Not being part of a nation-state, Gaza has no national archives. Because of the frequent wars and conflict, documents "belonging" to one state are often in the hands of another; Israel, for example, seized and holds both British and Egyptian records. Because Gaza had different administrative status from one period to the next, there is little continuity in its documentary record (as one district among many during the British Mandate, Gaza was the subject of less specific attention than during the Egyptian Administration, when it was a distinct entity).

Many materials *of* Gaza are not *in* Gaza. The history of Mandate-era documents of Gaza, housed largely in the Israel State Archives, highlights the complications involved in archival collection. On the one hand, these documents are among the most regular archival materials available about Gaza. British mandatory officials both created a considerable amount of paper and formulated precise, comprehensive systems for archiving this paper. In these papers one finds classic archival conventions such as series A–Z and files numbered sequentially and with clear referents and markers. Still, the unfortunate history of Palestine has had its impact on this archive as well. It was not supposed to be left behind when the British left Palestine. Apparently, the documents of the Palestine government were prepared for shipping back to Britain, but in the chaos that accompanied the departure something went wrong, and they never made it there. Most of the materials were lost, and those that were found were preserved in the archives of the new Israeli state.[18] As complicated as the history of these archival materials appears, this is the simplest collection in the documents of Gaza.

Consider Egyptian records housed in the Israel State Archives. These papers from a variety of bureaus within the administration were seized by the invading Israeli army in 1956 and 1967. These were active papers of government, and no doubt many of them would have been destroyed over time in the normal course of government business. And certainly those files saved would have been categorized according to Egyptian methods and guidelines about availability. Once in Israeli hands, this potential documentary trajectory was halted. The documents appear to have been kept in their entirety by the Israelis, though they have not been catalogued, organized, or, as it turned out, classified.[19]

Normal archival processes have not been applied to these materials, a condition which worked both to my advantage and disadvantage. Because the files were not closed, I was able to do research in these materials. However, the files had never been formally declassified, and concern was raised when another researcher requested permission to investigate "sensitive matters" in the Jordanian equivalent of the Egyptian papers. A decision was then made to shut the files until such time as someone could examine each document and make a decision about whether to declassify it. Fortunately, I was able to photocopy large portions of the files before this happened. These records now lie in an in-between space, neither within the filing system that gave them authority nor re-sorted according to archival conventions. Investigating the authority of these, and all the files under consideration here, requires working back through the layers of their postwork histories to understand their systems of operation.

Producing Files

The moment of writing—the drafting of documents, the production of paper—lies at the core of the filing process. The conditions of document production were not identical during the British Mandate and the Egyptian Administration in Gaza, but during each both the content and the style of file writing were heavily regulated.[20] Administrative writing during the Mandate often included translation (both cultural and linguistic) as a fundamental component. There were three official languages in Palestine during the Mandate, English, Arabic, and Hebrew, and document producers had different languages as their native tongue as well as differing levels of proficiency in the others. During the Egyptian Administration, the local population and the foreign administrators had a common language and cultural background. They shared as well the experience of British rule and thus were familiar with certain documentary forms.

The potential audience for files also varied between these periods. In addition to the possible public perusal of certain files, documents produced in Mandate Palestine had to consider three distinct governmental readers: local administrators, officials in Britain (in the Colonial or Foreign Office, say), and members of the League of Nations (under whose auspices Britain governed Palestine and to whom it had to report). The Egyptian Administration, on the other hand, did not proceed as a subsidiary of a larger body. The United Nations, the successor to the League of Nations, was a party to rule in Gaza, but as a partner (through UNRWA), not a supervisor. As these disparities remind us, even where files appear to be self-contained, to have only each other in mind, they are clearly also embedded in broader contexts and produced for a multiplicity of audiences.

The extent to which files were shaped by the conditions in which filing took place is highlighted in both the history and content of the filing regulations of the Chief Secretariat, the central executive office of the Mandate government. The extant records of these regulations are reiterations of the code of procedure destroyed in the bombing on July 22, 1946, of the Secretariat offices in the King David Hotel in Jerusalem by Jewish militants. In the aftermath of the bombing, which took the lives of more than ninety people and was part of a process that led eventually to Britain's departure from Palestine, a series of office orders were issued restating the most important of these regulations.[21] As unfortunate as was the need for this restatement of office procedure, it did provide the opportunity to remind personnel of existing procedures they may have been lax in observing.[22] The orders also reflect the general character of filing practice.

As with filing more generally, the significance of these regulations did not lie in their grandeur. On the contrary, the office orders provide instructions for the most minute aspects of document drafting. One such regulation governed the form of dating in correspondence: "No mention should be made when quoting the previous correspondence to the current year. When reference is made to a Secretariat letter it is not necessary to quote the file number, e.g., a reference to Secretariat letter dated the 21st June 1947, if made in the year 1947, should simply be 'my letter dated 21st June' and *not* 'my letter No. SF/—of the 21st June 1947.'"[23] The reasons for such ordered uniformity are not specified, though the regulation ensured that each letter, each document, produced by government would resemble every other structurally similar document. By providing grounds for determining documentary equivalency, the enforcement of uniformity in written style contributes to the consolidation of a largely self-referential authoritative field. That is, a document could be judged accurate and authoritative by virtue of its equivalence to other documents. This equivalence is not the resemblance of a copy to its original—in the case of these files there is no original—but a resemblance of each to each.[24] At the same time, the specific form of a document marked it as belonging to a singular bureaucratic realm: personnel files, for example, were all like each other and distinct from police files or committee reports.

The extent to which the regulation of style was also a regulation of content is made clear in another order stipulated in the above notice. This order decreed that letters from government officials to private individuals should not include a distribution list, but "if it is specifically desirable to bring the fact of such distribution to the notice of the addressee an appropriate addition should be made to the text."[25] Like the date format regulation discussed above, this order is concerned with producing uniformity, but it does something else as well. By dictating style, the regulation also served to control content. It seems directly concerned with minimizing the quixotic effects of civil servants on the content of government papers. It would not be possible to categorically forbid notice of distribution, as such notice was occasionally desired. At the same time, to permit the use of distribution lists would increase the likelihood that a careless clerk might provide accidental, potentially embarrassing information. Through this precise, somewhat picky regulation, an effort appears to have been made to forestall human error.

This regulation and others like it were immediately concerned with the boundary between government and the public and attentive to the unintended effects that documents might produce in their readers.[26] Other aspects of style management were focused more specifically on the internal life of the civil service, a life that, to be sure, always had permeable boundaries. The files of Palestine government correspondence, for instance, were organized to permit conversation among civil servants. They generally share the same basic format: letters, drafts, and legislation form the body, or folios, of the file, which opens with the minutes, a running commentary by various interested officials on the papers in the file.[27] The folios of a file represent the formal discussion of policy, and expressions of disagreement tend to be polite. The minutes, on the other hand, were much more casual and frequently appear off the cuff and most decidedly off the (public) record. Here officials allowed cynicism, prejudice, and frustration to show through. In the minutes one finds comments such as, "I regard the whole thing [a draft bill] as so bad that I think they ought to start all over again. The drafting is Mr. Bentwich in his worst style, and resembles a sort of incoherent chattering" and further, "Clause 3 occupies nearly two pages of drivel, in order to provide

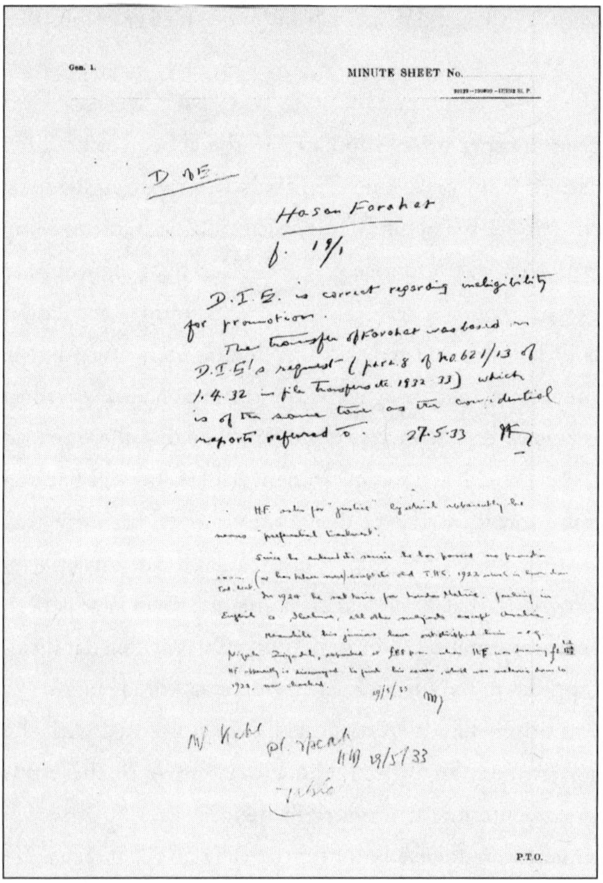

FIGURE 1. Minutes from personnel file, Mandate Department of Education. SOURCE: ISRAEL STATE ARCHIVES.

what could be provided in a few lines."[28] The minutes appear to be a sanctioned arena for such expression.[29]

The form of administrative files offers insight into both relations among administrators and private individuals and the governmental milieu within which civil servants worked. The audiences for any comment or letter were generally multiple and were likely to exceed the named addressees. The distinction between the two styles of administrative conversation discussed above has a great deal to do with the presumed level of privacy of the correspondence. Minutes were designed to be internal commentary, whereas formal letters might reach the public's attention. By providing a private space for written communication among government officials, minutes appear to have contributed to forming a civil service culture. Here, in the margins of files, civil servants were afforded opportunities to address each other and each other's work in spontaneous and natural ways—a more informal style permitted in these nonpublic parts of files. Infighting and jockeying for position, while present in folios as well, are particularly evident in the minutes.[30] Even in the presence of an apparently clear line of distinction between the spaces of a file, conversation was carried on across that divide.

The various registers provided by this filing form did not simply offer civil servants a comfortable space for communication, though this in itself is significant. Rather, the form of administrative conversation was of considerable importance in shaping government policy and practice. The regulation of style served to police the boundaries of bureaucratic discourse—there is a "content of the form"[31]—as only ideas that could be rendered as policy and articulated within the framework of debate could be entertained.[32] The following of proper procedure was as important as independent judgment in guiding government action. As I trace the details of bureaucratic operations, the ways in which administrative style was intricately bound up with administrative practice will become ever more clear.

EGYPTIAN STYLE: ADVICE FOR ADMINISTRATIVE WRITING

Preoccupation with the mechanics of administrative writing was no less important during the Egyptian Administration than in the Mandate. In this case the concerns were linked both to bureaucratic imperatives and to broader transformations in styles of Arabic prose.[33] This interest was evident in the journal of the Egyptian Civil Service Commission, *Majallat al-Muwazzafin*.[34] An article titled "The Literature of Memos" (*Adab al-Mudhakkirat*), published in the magazine in 1956, described the best style of document writing, teaching civil servants how to write the most effective memos. "Above all," the article argued, a memo was a "sign of the understanding of the author of its subject matter. Secondly, it is a way of evaluating you and indicating your competence."[35] Memos thus have a double address. If done correctly, they give clear expression of their subject matter. And, whether well or poorly executed, they express the professional capabilities of the civil servants who write them.

The advice given in the article stresses the demands made by the Arabic language on memo writers. One need not become an Arabic expert, the article assures its readers, but one must "be able to express what you want with a 'clear' expression and with formulations that have 'limited, precise meanings.'" One should be careful not to choose words that have more than one meaning, as these can obscure one's ideas. Arabic, the article stresses, can be a simple language, and in writing memos one should not affect a literary pose. Rather, one should focus on using correct syntax and grammar, mistakes in which can alter the meaning dramatically. The author of the article compares grammar to cooking: "Cooking is vital to the flavor of that which requires cooking. Can you eat *qulqas* [taro] without cooking it? . . . I don't want to mention what Sibawiya [a medieval Arab grammarian] said . . . I want you to always remember what your teacher explained to you about nominal sentences and verbal sentences, and the arrangement of each of them. . . . This is the grammar that is needed in order to cook the meaning of your memo until it is ready." The need for such instruction points to the difficulties of writing in Arabic, even for native speakers. It also suggests that nearly a century after the widespread use of print technology had provoked "the decline of a preference for rhyme in favor of straightforward prose, and the rise of a taste for simplicity and avoidance of little-known words"[36] further education in style uniformity was required. The article ends by averring that good memo writing can be a means of advancement for civil servants and suggests that each should "strive to make your memos a means of achieving a good evaluation."[37]

While the suggestions in this article do not delineate as precisely as British regulations the form of the document, they do express an interest in standardization. If administrative writers followed its advice and steered clear of "perverse and infrequent words" and complicated constructions, the result would certainly be a minimization of stylistic diversity in official writing. By emphasizing the effect on civil servants' careers of the form of their documents, this article seeks to invest them in the project of standardization. At the same time, this process enabled superiors and citizens to observe and document the practices of the civil servants. The uniformity of documentary style not only supported the authority of those documents, but also offered a means for comparing and judging civil servants. Not coincidentally, it also constituted a mechanism for shaping civil service personas (see chapter 3).

PERSONAL FORM: CIVIL SERVANTS WRITE ABOUT THEMSELVES

That a civil service culture did develop among government personnel and that these civil servants (*muwazzafin*) did feel invested in the projects of regularity and standardization that defined civil service quality is evident in the ways they talk about their careers and positions. Their writings reflect their participation in these projects. When petitioning their superiors on their own behalf, as in asking for promotion, complaining about work conditions, evaluating their coworkers, they made use of a shared rhetorical style which largely followed prescribed contours. The personnel files of retired muwazzafin are filled with such missives and afford an excellent venue for considering the regularities of civil service style.

Administration-era requests for promotion, to take one example, display a high degree of continuity of style and content.[38] In these letters, civil servants both express deference to their superiors and engage in self-promotion. The employee generally lauds the Administration as the defender of justice and refers to correct procedure as the best mechanism for fulfilling this objective. The petitioner details his work history, calling attention to the dedication with which he has served government and explaining the error or violation that has resulted in his failure to be promoted and therefore in a denial of justice.[39] The letters usually close with a plea to the addressee to turn his attention to this case and to fulfill his obligation and desire to see that right prevails.

In one such letter, Musbah Ahmed,[40] a tax collector, compares his circumstances to those of his colleagues:

> Sir, I have worked as a government tax collector in the Finance Department since 1943—meaning 18 years—and I am in Grade 3. The breadth of my work and my qualifications are present in the government file. I have been in service for a long time but have not yet received a promotion. All of my colleagues who were appointed at the same date were promoted to Grade 2 three years ago, and I am still in my old grade. My work carries a lot of responsibility, and my region is a central and large one. . . . In light of all I have presented to you, I ask that you respond to my request for promotion to Grade 2. You, who still strives for justice and social equality.[41]

According to this letter, the principle that has been violated here is that of equality. The procedural mechanism that has been infracted is that of promotion of employees with the same seniority to the same grades. According to Musbah's argument, the length of his service is sufficient to warrant promotion, but he is careful to also highlight its importance and note that these details are documented in his file, thereby suggesting that the violation of procedure is markedly unjust in his case.

Another employee, 'Ali Taleb, in a letter that begins almost identically (he began work in the Agricultural Administration in 1937), cites the end of the British Mandate as the precipitating cause for his failure to be promoted:

> Sir, I was nominated to be transferred to Grade 3 under the previous Mandate government, as the opportunity for promotion and transfer was in the terms of the position. A number of my colleagues from this time were graded and reached Grade 2. However, before my turn arrived the Mandate ended and the Arab Administration came to the Strip. Naturally, I should not be deprived of my rights for transfer and promotion because of a lack of meaningful understanding of the position I am doing currently. Therefore, I petition you, Sir, to look into my transfer to permanent Grade 3 after my long service.[42]

In this petition, 'Ali Taleb chastises the Egyptian Administration for not fulfilling its obligations to its employees and implicitly compares it unfavorably to the British Mandate in this regard. Like Musbah in the previous letter, 'Ali situates his service in the context of that of his colleagues, noting that they have been duly promoted, and emphasizes the length of his employment. The criticism of the Administration, while muted, is sharper than in Musbah's letter. 'Ali's mode of critique is common in civil servants' letters. The Administration is never called unjust, but rather is simply called to account for instances of failure to achieve its own principles and goals.

This rhetorical style was chosen for its perceived effectiveness. Certainly not all requests for promotion were granted (in the case of the two letters cited above Musbah was promoted and 'Ali was not), but appropriate address seems to have been important for getting a hearing. Although 'Ali did not get his transfer, he did win the support of his direct superior in his efforts. Even if not every letter was effective in achieving its aims, as a body they were effective in contributing to a broader uniformity of civil service style. The resemblance imperative was clearly at play, as civil service correspondence echoed other such correspondence. Through the mechanism of accumulation, a style that was highly self-conscious and no doubt sometimes artificial could become also a real expression of civil servants.

Style management offered an important means of regulating file content, but it was not the only such mechanism. Content was also governed by the demands of bureaucratic procedure. Files were not simply repositories of bureaucratic memory, but also actors in the bureaucratic field. Their content was effective in shaping administrative action, and vice versa. As Egyptian-era personnel files show, the particular document compilations that made up a file were connected to the concrete requirements of administration. Much of the content of the personnel files was dedicated to tracking the personal status of their subjects. All employees had to update their information annually, indicating their marital status and the number of their children (and in the case of men the number of their wives). Additionally, if an employee's status changed in the middle of the year through marriage, birth, death, or children reaching the age of majority, he was required to report the new information immediately to his superior for inclusion in his file. There was nothing abstract about this requirement; the monthly allowances that complemented base salaries were calculated according to family size.[43]

As much as bureaucratic imperatives mandated the inclusion of content, they also, sometimes as an almost accidental effect, produced exclusions. Because personal information was reported for the purpose of determining allowances, those family members whose existence did not affect the allowances were absent from the files. Thus, when children reached their majority and were no longer considered dependents for allowance purposes, they simply disappeared from the files.[44] Despite the wealth of information about family life contained in personnel files, therefore, they do not offer a straightforward opportunity for data collection. Like all files, archives, and documents, personnel files have interests which govern their content and their form.

Different sorts of files, of course, have different interests. Unlike personnel files, police files appear to consider no information irrelevant, a principle of content management that says include everything.[45] The imperative to collect all this information was rooted in the security concerns that shaped Egyptian rule in Gaza: the threat of Gazan action provoking an Israeli attack on Egypt, of political parties challenging government policy, of despair and

FIGURE 2. Police report on public opinion. Egyptian Administration. SOURCE: ISRAEL STATE ARCHIVES.

disillusionment driving Gazans, natives and refugees alike, toward destabilizing protest. In tracking the contours of public behavior and attitudes, the Egyptian-era files of *Idarat al-Mabahith al-'Amma* (General Investigations or Criminal Investigations Department, part of the Interior and Public Security Administration) seem to collect as much information as possible about individuals. The tremendous breadth of scope of these files does not indicate a lack of purpose. While much of the information collected could not have been of immediate practical value, it did function as a database that could assist the administration in controlling the behavior and attitudes that the files tracked.

These files include incident reports about specific events, daily and weekly reports by police officers to department inspectors, and monthly reports by regional governors and inspectors to the head of the Interior and Public

Security Administration. The reports focus on public matters like political activity, public opinion, and organizational formations but treat private life as well. All public meetings were attended by an officer of the *mabahith*, and private gatherings were noted and observed. Conflicts between and within families were detailed, and their mediation by mukhtars (village leaders) discussed. Individual behavior, especially if unusual or potentially political, was included in the files. Mabahith reports were concerned as much with talk as with action and thus reported on public opinion and on prevailing rumors. For the most part, these files do not analyze or (in terms of rumors) distinguish between fact and fiction. The work of making meaning out of these files takes place elsewhere; the files themselves focus on the work of compilation.

Accumulation works to give weight and significance to seemingly insignificant moments. The mabahith files are filled with events of no apparent import and people of no obvious significance.[46] These kinds of reports were effective in their compilation, not in their individuality. Not one of them contains complete information about an incident, but rather serves as data in the building of a profile or picture of a situation or person. Many reports give, in considerable detail, accountings of incidents that seem entirely trivial. For example, according to one such report, several people drove cars to Khan Yunis and stopped at a school for several hours before leaving the town.[47] The cars and their passengers are described in detail. The times of their movements are carefully noted. This is the sum of the report's information, except for a note that the teachers at the school were familiar with the people involved and believed they were there to have a meeting, subject unspecified.

The import of such a report is necessarily relational. If any of the participants already had files, then their personal profiles could lend an interpretation to the event. Similarly, if something threatening were to happen in the future, this report could be included in a dossier. Or if a previous report indicated that something was likely to happen, this report could serve to confirm it. Police reports created an archive of information which could be drawn upon if need be. Their role was to police the possible, to inform about what could happen as much as about what had happened. Such an orientation no doubt contributed to the authority of the files, raising the level of fear among people as to what they might contain. The files operated through accumulation: no moment was too mundane for inclusion in them, and thus no moment was guaranteed to be free from surveillance.[48]

This compilation imperative is important not only for security files. Compilation and accumulation are crucial to the production of filing authority. In filing, compilation both gestures toward the future and expands the reach of files horizontally across the social and political field. It is part of the way in which documents are made into files and through which files are located within a network populated by other files. This process of accretion makes files effective as records of the past and indicators of the future. This feature further makes filing effective in the formation of ruling subjectivities and spaces, as the threshold of knowledge is lowered and individual lives are accounted for in files.[49] Filing is not a practice that simply captures individuals. Rather, it forms an arena for regulated self-expression, as in complaints, petitions, and analyses, and self-fashioning.

In addition to the incidental accumulation of almost undifferentiated information evident in mabahith files, compilation in filing also worked to distinguish and define categories of people and place. Gaza, not surprisingly, does not have pride of place within the British Mandate filing network. A provisional district and town, Gaza did not warrant the same kind of attention as, say, Jerusalem. In files that cover Palestine as a whole, Gaza occupies the periphery, often no more than a sentence or two, sentences frequently devoted to comment on the backwardness of the region.[50] The Municipality and Local Government files offer more extended examples of compilations about and from Gaza.[51] The Gaza files included budget estimates, election regulations, citizen complaints, and municipal ordinances. They contributed to the consolidation of Gaza as an administrative category in at least two ways. First, through the compilation of municipal policy and procedure for central government approval, Gaza was located within a hierarchy of rule. Second, by providing an arena within the files of central government for the enactment of local conflict (particularly clear in complaints and petitions addressed to government), the accumulation of Gaza files within the group Municipalities and Local Government participated in distinguishing Gaza as a locale. Files, then, not only document, but also help make a place.

Palestine's government during the British Mandate was highly centralized, and almost all local decisions required approval from the central government. Gaza's municipal ordinances, such as those which determined the

FIGURE 3. Petition to British Mandate government from Gazans complaining about proposed water meters. SOURCE: ISRAEL STATE ARCHIVES.

rates of market fees (vendors to be charged a 5 percent tax on all fruits and vegetables sold and purchasers $2^1/2$ percent) or prohibited pollution of the public water supply (no bathing allowed), had to be forwarded to the chief secretary for approval and confirmation.[52] Municipal budgets required similar approval. Thus, when several towns of the Gaza district wished to pool their resources and hire a municipal engineer, the chief secretary's permission was required. The Gaza district commissioner wrote on the municipalities' behalf (the towns in question were Gaza, Majdal, Khan Yunis, Beersheba, and Faluja) and noted that "this appointment would supply a longfelt want, and I wish to recommend it. I should be glad if advance sanction would be given for the provision of his salary in the estimates of the Municipalities concerned so as to enable him to start work as soon as possible."[53] These kinds of requests and passings up for approval of local decisions are repeated throughout the local government files, thus marking the subordinate position of municipalities (Gaza's and others) in the structure of Palestine's government.

Even as Gaza was like other municipalities in its formal relations to government, the local government files also mark its distinctive character. If the first major subject in the files was the seeking of government approval for local administration, the second was local complaint about local administration. In the files, central government came to provide a venue for, as well as serve as an arbiter of, local conflict. These files also display another aspect of Gaza's hierarchies, as it was for the most part the elite who could make use of this filing opportunity. For example, in 1930, a number of Gazan notables, most of whom were members of the municipal council, wrote to the high commissioner complaining about the town's mayor, Fahmi Husseini. These notables were particularly incensed that the mayor had been granted permission to maintain his private law practice while serving as mayor. According to the complaint, "The Mayor of Gaza is kept occupied with his own private business to an extent as to neglect the interests of the town which is more needy of organisation and attention probably than any other town in this country."[54]

Because the mayor's business kept him away from town so much, the complaint argued that conditions in Gaza, rather than progressing under his leadership, had in fact deteriorated. The complaint notes, among other problems, that "winter is well in season, the roads are in a deplorable state, while the walls of many houses are falling to bits. The mud in the streets actually makes it impossible to walk, while due to the hopeless lighting system it is an actual danger to be outdoors at night." The notables call government's attention to the strength of public opinion against the mayor and close by reminding the high commissioner that "the public demands that only he who possesses the best conduct and enjoys a good reputation and who has the faith of all the people should be eligible for this position. This is a point which we believe Great Britain respects more than any other nation, and we feel sure that you have intimate knowledge of all the people in Palestine, including our most undesirable and unpopular Mayor."

In this complaint and in the many similar ones which can be found in these files, the category of the local—and particularly of the Gazan locale—was invoked to frame and forward the petitioners' arguments. The peti-

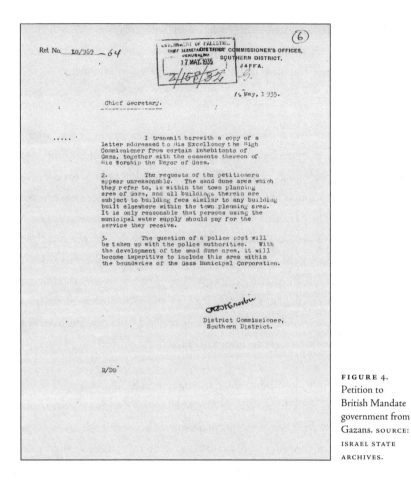

tioners even used the centralization of Palestine's government to make an argument for the importance of the local: "The fact that the Government still grants some right of authority to the Palestinians in the form of Municipal Council is a recognition by the Government of the necessity of the existence of Municipalities. That high Government Officials are engaged in formulating municipal laws re-enforces this argument." Good local administrators were, that is, vital to Gaza's progress. The specificities of Gaza were highlighted in the conflict between particular parties for power in this local arena, in this case between the mayor and opposing notables. In the accumulation of charges and countercharges found in these complaint files, the category of the Gaza locality is continually consolidated. Even as Gazans ask for help from government, the files further consolidate this conflict as local, one in which government *could* intervene if it so chose, but vis-à-vis which it was always an outside party. The varieties of accumulation found in files work not only to articulate relations between and among different participants in government, but also to shape and manage those relations.

Access and Control

As concerned as bureaucracies are about the stylistics of writing, equal attention is paid to the pragmatics of managing file circulation and accessibility. This attention includes regulations governing availability of files, procedures guiding the circulation of files, and layouts organizing offices to control exposure of files. The practices of the Mandate and the Administration were no exception to this general condition. Weber stresses the secrecy principle of bureaucracy, arguing that it "always tends to exclude the public, to hide its knowledge and action from criticism as well as it can."[55] It seems, though, that this formulation does not entirely capture the relationship of bureaucracy to information, a relationship which is marked by a tension between the principles of public access to information and the protection of government secrecy.

While Weber may well be correct to suggest that "the concept of the 'official secret' is the specific invention of bureaucracy,"[56] without a principle of publicity, there would be no requirement for such a regulation of secrecy. That is, if no government files were available to the public, there would be no need to define some of them as secret. Certainly, concern with both containment of and access to information was evident in filing in Palestine. In these practices of filing management, as in the writing process, regularization and repetition formed crucial means of effecting information management. Furthermore, as in the writing process, the regulation of circulation was concerned with producing and safeguarding the authority of files.

REGULATIONS OF SECRECY

Mandate Secretariat regulations recognize three types of files: top secret, secret, and open. Top secret files were not allowed to be sent out of the Secretariat;[57] were "to be seen and handled by British officers only"; could only be transferred by hand, not sent in dispatch boxes; and could be typed in the top secret registries only. This regulation is reflective both of the broad colonial character of Mandate rule, which limited access and opportunity for natives, and of the specificity of the Palestine Mandate, where conditions of so-called national conflict demanded that Jewish and Arab civil servants be kept away from certain materials. Access to secret files, as compared to that of top secret files, was circumscribed not by nationality but by rank. The regulations delineate which officers were permitted to handle such files and specify that "in no circumstances may a secret file be handled by a messenger."[58] To guard against accidental exposure, regulations stipulated that "top-secret and secret files when not in actual use must be kept in a locked steel box or steel cupboard. It is permissive, however, if an officer leaves his room *for a short while* to go to another room in the Secretariat, to leave a top secret or secret file on his table provided he takes such steps, by locking doors and windows, as will ensure that no person can enter the room in his absence." The regulations further state that "the fact that an officer is authorised to handle top-secret and secret files concerned with certain subjects does not entitle him to see top-secret or secret papers dealt with on other schedules." These regulations are interesting for a number of reasons. First, they further elucidate British interest in limiting the quixotic effects of individual action upon files. Like those regulations which sought to minimize individualizing style in the writing of documents, these orders anticipate and attempt to forestall accidental exposure of confidential information by imposing a uniform management style. Second, the regulations highlight dynamics of the relation between publicity and secrecy.

A central aspect of this problematic is the question of access by the public to government information, but this is only part of the matter. The secret files regulations mark distinctions internal to the civil service as well and serve as a reminder that the category civil service is by no means monolithic. Distinctions were drawn by nationalities and ranks as well as by job description. Lurking around the edges of these regulations—not articulated but present nonetheless—was a degree of uncertainty about government's own civil servants. The possibility had to be considered that, faced with issues of nationalist significance, civil servants might have loyalties to something other than government.

In Egyptian-era filing practices, the management of access to files was no less central, though the worries underpinning such management were distinct. Orders governing file disclosure can be found throughout the record of the Administration. In one such order, the director of administrative affairs reminded officials of the laws and commands governing the protection of secret documents:[59] "1) No employee is permitted to receive any visitors during official work hours or to show them any papers. 2) Each violation of the above clause will expose the responsible employee and his direct superior to severe and deterring action. 3) It is the responsibility of the heads of departments and directors of administrations to see that this order is implemented with precision."[60] Like British regulations, this order both marks a line between members of the public and government employees and internally distinguishes the civil service. By making an employee's direct superior responsible for his misdeeds, this order solidifies the hierarchies of the organizational structure of the civil service. The order seems designed to result in extremely close supervision of employees by their bosses, an effect that should ripple up the chain of command. This order does not distinguish among types of files but rather serves as a blanket prohibition of exposure. Some government files *were* allowed to be seen by members of the public. However, by categorically forbidding disclosure to visitors to government offices, the order mandates a regularity of procedure and minimizes the possibility of error on the part of individual civil servants.[61]

CIRCULATING FILES

As the regulations discussed above indicate, even the most secret of files circulate, albeit under tight restrictions. The guidelines which governed the circulation practices of files during the British Mandate and Egyptian Administration indicate that the movement of open, nonsensitive files was also carefully regulated. The circulation of files encompasses the multiple kinds of movement that files undergo, as parts of files (documents) move from one to another, as whole files circulate among government offices and as information in files is selectively disclosed to private citizens.

The Mandate Secretariat regulation of correspondence determined that "where copies of papers on one file are placed on another, the file should always show clearly which is the copy and should indicate the number of the file on which the original is to be found."[62] This order, which seeks to mark all documents, seems to work to ensure that documents remain embedded in the networks that generate their authority. A copy that is marked as such would not risk losing the meaning derived from its place in a network of signification, but rather could accrue further meaning by becoming part of yet another chain of relations. In this manner, a document could operate in multiple locations and do so in an orderly, systematized fashion. This order demands that documents not make accidental or unmarked appearances in other files. Rather, when they come to rest, documents should signal their multiplicity and call attention to their paths of movement. This material attention (within the file itself) to the trajectory of the document and its network of relations could operate to make a compilation of a single paper.

The circulation of whole files among government offices in the Mandate appears to have been perceived as an unavoidable, but at the same time undesirable, facet of administration. Each time a file was removed from its home department, there was a risk of disorder and mismanagement. Probably for this reason, the unnecessary circulation of files was discouraged: "Far too many files are being referred to Departments and it would be appreciated if, except in certain unavoidable circumstances, letters could be written instead of the file being sent out. The principle to be observed is that files should only be sent out when the amount of typing necessary for a letter (especially enclosures) is so great that this extra work far exceeds the inconvenience of absence of the file from this office."[63] Administrative preference was to keep the file within the office where possible, and where not possible to carefully manage the conditions of its movement: "Officers minuting such files are requested to indicate clearly on the margin a specific date by which they wish the file to be returned to this office."[64] Once again, relations among differently located civil servants were important for the proper functioning of the circulation system. Another order in this series reminded officers of the importance of properly instructing messengers in circulation practices, noting that they should "explain to their messengers the systems of the distribution number card and when necessary, notify them, at the time of the collection of the files, of the names of the officers to whom they are to be taken and the location of their rooms. In default of such explanation the files are likely to be misdirected and to reach their intended destination only after some delay."[65] These practices of file movement operate to maintain and regularize the general system of information management.

Increasing standardization of movement was a concern during the Egyptian Administration as well. In one instance, a bureau was established precisely for the purpose of systematizing the flow of information from one office to another. In 1960, the Gaza Executive Council mandated the formation of the Personal Investigation Bureau, as an office of the Interior and Public Security Administration, to respond to requests for individual criminal records. By serving as a central storehouse for information, the bureau could regularize the transfer of information, both in and out of the office. At one end of the process, police and court officers provided information to the bureau. The courts, for example, were ordered to forward to the bureau "1) judgments issued in capital cases, 2) judgments issued for imprisonment of six months or more"[66] as well as judgments for a specified list of other crimes. After the papers arrived at the bureau, following detailed instructions, files of individual criminal records were to be prepared. The first steps of the procedure required that "when a charge sheet for the accused is sent from the police, the sheet is registered in the appropriate registry, and numbered in sequence. After sheets have been registered and have been so marked, they are sent to the head of the alphabetical filing department who will undertake a search for criminal records of the accused in the alphabetical files."[67] In this process of file transfer, new files were created, as court and police records were used to constitute individual criminal files. The attention to detail at each step in the process indicates the felt importance of regularizing this file circulation.

This concern was also evident in procedures for making information available to members of the public. Content from the Personal Investigation Bureau files were intended to be made available "upon request of the convicted person or request by public authority [*sulta 'amma*]"[68] for certificates of conduct. The regulations also specified what information was to be included in the certificates. They would not list "1) judgments that were overturned on appeal; 2) judgments where the punishment did not exceed six months in jail . . . and no other crimes were listed in the file in the Personal Investigation Bureau."[69] These regulations appear concerned both with protecting individual privacy and with increasing the efficacy of the criminal justice system. The centralization of criminal records ensured that they could be more easily accessed when needed. The precise delineation of the information to be kept in these records, as well as the conditions for their release or expurgation, minimized the risk of accidental exposure or erasure.

Since these files were *of* people, rather than, say, government policy, privacy concerns played a central role in the regulation of their disclosure. The exposure of other types of files was governed by concerns specific to those files, but general to all files was an interest in having control over when and how the public (whether as a whole or particular individuals) had access to the files.

File Storage

The government emphasis on file accumulation was bound to raise pressing problems of storage.[70] By opening with a discussion of archives, in some ways this chapter began with the end of the process. The destiny of files, after all, is either the archives or the garbage (now perhaps the shredder).[71] Practices of record retention were internal to the filing process. Sometimes these systems of retention were immediately connected to the constitution of historical archives—the British especially were careful about building archiving into their filing system—but office archives were not always intended for inclusion in a national archive. Choices about what documents to keep (and how) and which to discard (and how) impact the regulation of information as well as the practice of compilation in filing.

The Mandate chief secretary's office provided guidelines to its employees for determining the fate of files. These regulations indicate the multiple levels of file retention. Active files were stored in the filing cabinets of the central registry of the Secretariat, according to an internal indexing system. In order to relieve overcrowding in the storage cabinets, it was necessary, on occasion, to destroy or archive unused files. It is noteworthy, considering the general attention to detail in these regulations, that the regulations provided almost no specificity in terms of what kinds of files should be kept.[72] Rather, such decisions were left to the discretion of the employees, though they did have to be approved by a number of officers:

> Clerks in charge of sections of the central registry will go through old files year by year, starting with the earlier years, to ascertain which in their opinion (a) can be safely destroyed and (b) should be placed in archives. They should bear in mind the possibility of such files being required for ready reference in the future. . . . lists should then be submitted to the Assistant Secretary or Administrative Assistant in charge of the schedule

for examination. Each file on these lists should be examined both by the section clerk and by the senior officer concerned before submission in final form to a Principal Assistant Secretary for approval of the action proposed.

The objective behind this process of file storage and destruction was to both simplify the daily practices of office filing (by minimizing the number of files that would have to be sorted through in the process) and to make easier any future move of the Secretariat to a new office (by decreasing the amount of paper that would have to be transferred).

In this process of the culling of files, the destroyed or archived files did not entirely vanish from the active filing system, but rather left two distinct traces. First, material components of the files were to be saved for reuse in other files. The order specified that prior to destruction of files, "serviceable material, e.g. file covers, tags, unused minute sheets, pins and clips, will first be salvaged." Second, "the lists of files destroyed and sent to archives will be passed to the indexing section for recording on the appropriate card the date [of action]. The lists will then be returned to the registry for filing." That the office-file storage practice continued to account for those files that were absented from its workings ensured that the integrity of the system—which included its mechanisms for referencing file location—would not be under-mined by the removal of physical files. Even files that no longer had an internal life (that is, their content was no longer important) continued to be part of the scaffolding of filing.

When the British began to prepare for their departure from Palestine, the question of file storage took on a new dimension. Questions arose as to whether files should remain in Palestine, and if so, which ones, to become part of the administrative apparatus of a possible successor government or should be removed to Great Britain to enter the historical record of British overseas rule. While there are obvious political and ideological interests underpinning such questions, they were addressed almost entirely in practi-cal terms. What were the administrative requirements for such files, and how would they be most efficaciously utilized?

For example, as the Mandate wound down and the need to prepare for pension payment became increasingly urgent, the Civil Service Commission issued a set of orders for how to manage personnel files. It was decided to set up an Accounts Clearance Office of the Palestine Government in Cyprus to handle any ongoing financial obligations of the government.[73] To this office were to be dispatched "all the personal files and history cards of all the non-expatriate officers belonging to . . . departments" as well as "all personal files and history cards of non-British expatriate officers held by the Civil Service Commission."[74] Not going to Cyprus were records of British expatriate officers—those held by the commission were to go directly to London and those in the departments were to be either destroyed or given to the officers themselves—and the files of nonexpatriate officers held by the Civil Service Commission, which were to remain in Palestine to be handed over to the UN Palestine Commission.[75]

In its final weeks and days, Mandate administration largely fell apart. As Henry Gurney, the last chief secretary, described the situation at the end of April 1948, "The Courts have stopped, and so has the Post Office, except for urgent and official telegrams; nearly all our prisoners have escaped, and the prisons are not functioning either."[76] The chaos which accompanied the end of the Mandate meant that the orderly plans for the files were not executed (indeed the UN commission did not assume any authority), but they do highlight the sorting out of the Mandate whole into its parts that accompanied the end of the Palestine government. Differences between British officers and local-hire civil servants were evident throughout the Mandate, in both regulation and practice, but the process of ending that Mandate also ended any semblance of equivalence among these people. Thus, the final moments of mandatory archiving, even where they did not succeed in creating an archive, did form a record of civil service differentiation and stratification.

Unlike the British Mandate, the Egyptian Administration of Gaza did not come to a planned end. It ended, of course, with the war of June 1967 and the occupation of Gaza by Israel. There were, therefore, no preparations for final storage, compilation, or culling. Of the many documents that survived the Administration, it is nearly impossible to determine which might have been intended to be saved, which would have been discarded entirely, and which might have been subsumed into other files, leaving a trace of their original production. Within the various offices of the Administration, there is some information about how files were stored. The head of the Personal Investigation Bureau, for example, supplied a list of the guidelines for file retention in his bureau. The guidelines indicate that during the Administration file retention continued to apply principles similar to those that were prevalent during the Mandate. These principles accorded primacy to the file system as an operational unity, making the mechanisms for filing sometimes more important than the files themselves.

According to the bureau's regulations, registers of charge sheets and fingerprints were to be kept permanently, whereas the registers of requests for certificates of conduct as well as the registers of the certificates themselves (which were the files produced from the above registers) were to be kept for only two years.[77] The lines along which distinctions were made seems relatively straightforward and logical. The primary data files, which served to create other files, were kept permanently. There was no need for the second-order files to be permanently saved, as they could be re-created if necessary out of the first set of files. These specific practices of retention and regular culling of files highlight the mobile processes of signification which are always integral to filing.

Filing as a practice exceeds the significance of any individual file. Maintaining the capacity to keep filing is more important than any particular content. Limitations in the space available for storing files was a real and pressing issue, and thus file culling was essential for continued filing. At the same time, the regular replacement of certain files within the filing system kept awareness of future filing at the center of this practice. Each file that was discarded created space for another, structurally similar file. The process of file replacement has an additional significance. In limiting the importance of any particular file, and emphasizing practice over product, the significance of the loss of particular files (something which happened a lot in Gaza) was minimized. Filing envisions future filing and in its self-referential structure renders the systemic location of files as crucial as their content. Practices of file storage illuminate how filing operates as both a compilation of the past and an anticipation of the future.

Conclusion

Filing, while a fundamental part of government, is also in some ways an odd sort of practice. It is executed primarily by civil servants and forms a record of information about both civil servants and private citizens. At the same time, many of the defining features of this regime of practices operate to minimize the apparent agency of these persons. Filing is a fully "peopled" regime of practices, but one in which those people cannot appear as *primary* (or prior) actors. Files cannot work without civil servants, but they exercise an authority that often seems to refer only to other files. Filing is a domain that often appears autonomous. Files seem to have their own principles, unconnected to any single administration or regime. To a great degree this is true—and this chapter has highlighted this general character—but files are also embedded in the particular bureaucracies they make work and are formed by those demands. They are both shaped by and shape people and places. Files are part of a broader governing dynamic that relies equally on the practices of civil servants. No single bureaucratic instrument can be fully effective on its own. It was the interactions among these instruments that consolidated ruling authority, even as such authority may never have acquired legitimacy.

3

ON BEING A CIVIL SERVANT

The English, of course, know their duties. . . . I learned from them how to treat people, how to treat someone who wants something. I say to him that I am not his master. The government placed me to serve you. I don't want to say that I am his servant, but that I serve his interests. If this person was good and polite, I had to help him regardless of his being a Muslim, a Jew, or a Christian. I lived on this basis.

SALIM RASHID, RETIRED CIVIL SERVANT, GAZA CITY, 11 MARCH 1999

Since I am a member of society, I have to demand of myself what I demand of people. . . . I was appointed to serve the people. I was not there to give orders "you come here" or "go there." This is shameful, because there is dignity. I should respect him, for he is a citizen as much as I am. I'm there to help and serve him, not more, so good treatment is required.

JAMAL YUSEF, RETIRED CIVIL SERVANT, GAZA CITY, 3 MAY 1999

Civil servants, as much as the files they write and organize, are at the center of the bureaucratic process. Their effective operations are essential to both the work and authority of government. At the same time, these personnel, especially the rank-and-file ones who have pride of place in this discussion, often occupy an uncomfortable position. On the one hand, they are functionaries and representatives of a government or administration. On the other, they are also members of the community which is being governed. They are served as much as they serve. They are both the face of government to a disgruntled public and members of that public who may be as dissatisfied as their clients. While such tensions can be found in bureaucracies of all types, they were accentuated by the circumstances in Gaza, where the relationship between government and the public was so uncertain and where the parties were so often at odds. As local hires employed by a foreign regime, and operating on a precarious fault line between public servant and private citizen, the personas and practices of Gazan civil servants were vital to the authorization and persistence of government.

The authority of personnel was articulated first and foremost at a small, even intimate, scale—in terms of character and reputation, of comparison with other civil servants, of relationships with the people being served. It was not only *who* these civil servants were that was important, but *how* they were—lest this personnel authority be mistaken for simply personal authority. Gaza's civil servants also explicitly distinguished their work and their authority from the government in which they were employed. This separation made possible their own positive sense of their work and also kept this authority distinct from legitimacy. Civil service authority partly entailed carving out a space that distinguished its practice from other sorts of practice—personnel from personal, government from regime, authority from legitimacy.

To explore this civil service experience, it is necessary to understand who counted as a civil servant. This definition was, as we will see, a matter of some contention during both the British Mandate and the Egyptian Administration. To be a civil servant in Gaza did not always mean conforming to a classic image of a clerk sitting at a desk, surrounded by papers, receiving members of the public.[1] Further, and increasingly over the time period considered here, it did not indicate with surety a person's class or social status. When I told people in Gaza I wanted to meet retired civil servants, in addition to administrative employees, I was introduced to teachers, policemen, clerics, electricians, and nurses—a diverse array that highlights the breadth of the category.[2] Being a civil servant in Gaza was primarily defined, it seems, not by the type of one's job, but rather by the ethic, style, and benefits of one's work. The difference that being a civil servant made for people was not limited to their work, but extended into all aspects of their lives.

Civil servants (*muwazzafin*) worked for government (and also for UNRWA: see below) and provided services to the public. They were institutionally distinguished from other workers (*'ummal*) employed by government by their conditions of employment, namely, monthly pay, pension upon retirement, membership in a civil servants' association. As one retiree put it to me, "The civil servant received his salary at the end of the month—meaning, for example, that he could buy on credit from stores and pay his bill when he was paid. Someone who wasn't a civil servant couldn't borrow money from others—if he worked he could buy food and eat. The life of the civil servant was different."[3] Civil servants were self-defined as being especially concerned with matters of respectability and duty.

During the Mandate, when the civil service was relatively small, it was largely the province of the upper-middle class. Palestinian society was highly stratified, and civil service status was part of the larger social condition. Civil servants were educated, wealthy, and cultured, and the job was a high-status position. According to 'Arif al-'Arif, a Gaza district officer during the Mandate and local historian, in 1943 the entire civil service in Gaza consisted of 2,775 people (the bulk policemen), of whom 162 were English and the rest Arabs.[4] These numbers reflected a dramatic growth in the civil service during World War II. Over the course of the Egyptian Administration, as both educational opportunities and the ranks of the civil service expanded, its salaries diminished, as did the value attached to such employment. Civil servants were necessarily confronted with a certain amount of tension about how much they could, or should, be distinguished from the broader Gazan population. At the same time, differences of class, of training, and of salary distinguished the civil service not only from the public, but within itself. The diversity of civil service ensured that there was also considerable tension inside its ranks. All these tensions were part of the definition of civil service.

This chapter explores reflections upon and debates about this definition. The question of what a civil servant should be was a subject of considerable concern, both among muwazzafin themselves and in the broader public. These processes, which I term reflective habit, were themselves part of the formation and consolidation of bureaucratic authority. In the absence of a secure foundation for such authority, the habitual character of civil service played a particularly important role.[5] It is a feature of bureaucracy that those parts of its work which appear the least creative, the least individual, and the least exemplary are the aspects that lend it the most authority. In this instance it was also the focus on the work itself, rather than the regime that required it, that provided a means through which government could be disassociated from the nationality of the rulers.

Weber highlights the significance of habit in permitting bureaucracies to persist in the face of major disruptions, such as a change in regime, and even to survive the loss of the files. "However great the practical importance of administration on the basis of the filed documents may be," he suggests that one cannot overlook "the settled orientation of *man* for keeping to the habitual rule and regulations that continue to exist independently of the documents."[6] These habits and routines were not static or undifferentiated. Different locations, jobs, and times made a difference to people's habits, to how they understood the proper character of a civil servant.[7] Furthermore, as important as habit seems to be for bureaucracy in general, and as it has proven to be in the specific case of Gaza, it is not an indestructible force. Weber describes bureaucracy as "practically unshatterable,"[8] but it is not entirely so. The ways in which doubt, the counterpart of habit, can enter into the workings of civil service illuminates the possibility, if not the probability, of noncompliance on the part of civil servants and civilians.[9]

Habit, as C. S. Peirce understands it, can be "either a habit of action or a habit of thought."[10] Belief is a habit, one that both shapes and provokes actions.[11] For civil servants in Gaza, belief in their work, commitment to their understandings of their personas, was certainly a habit of thought. This chapter focuses precisely on habits of belief, on ideas about good and bad work. The next chapter turns more directly to habits in / of action, looking at the ways in which habits are inculcated through the practice of civil service work. As we will see, civil service habits, being at least partially inculcated even before one was hired and lasting long beyond retirement, exceeded the moments of a career. Civil servants' discussions about the nature of this work are also part of the process of producing and reinforcing these habits.

Reflective Habits and Memory Processes

With its emphasis on experience and practice, this chapter draws heavily on conversations I had with retired civil servants. In addition to innumerable casual conversations, I tape-recorded interviews with people who worked in, or had experiences with, both the British Mandate and the Egyptian Administration. These conversations are not easily classifiable. They straddle the divide—to the extent that there is one—between the historical and the ethnographic. They are part oral history, recollections of people's lives and work in earlier moments,[12] and part evaluative reflections on what government should be and how people understood themselves. These conversations, then, both provide evidence about habit and are part of habit formation itself.

This is what I mean when I refer to habits of belief as reflective habit. Contrary to common conceptions of habit as a space of nonreflection (as in fact relying on an absence of active thought), the civil service habits I trace here are deeply embedded in contemplations on the nature of service and its practice. The bodily practices of bureaucratic work—the act of filing, the scripted interactions with the public—and its reflective practices—the development of a sense of oneself as a public servant, the elaboration of notions like good work, respectability, and duty—are profoundly interconnected.[13] Understanding the meaning and power of civil service requires attending to this relation.

In style and in content, my conversations with retired civil servants were clearly part of the practice of reflective habit. Respectfulness, pride, and duty, important features of civil service experience and habit, loomed large in the ways former civil servants interacted with me. In this twofold expression, the continuities between thought and action were manifest, as were the connections between my probings and their own concerns. Before I started conducting interviews, I was not certain how my queries would be received by people. I did not expect hostility, but I thought that perhaps the intensity of the national problem in people's experience would make my project, which did not focus on this struggle, seem irrelevant. What I found, to my pleasure, was that even as people *were* interested in what a book on Gaza might do for their cause, they were also deeply engaged (entirely apart from me) in their own processes of reflecting on the workings of government, the significance of its mundane routines, and the effects of its demands on people.

I talked with people in a variety of settings, including homes, offices, and the outdoors. Interviews conducted in people's homes were most likely to involve other participants, as family members gathered around to hear what they had to say. I had ongoing relationships with many of the people with whom I had tape-recorded conversations; other people I met only for the interview. Judging from those people whom I knew well, the concerns and evaluations expressed in formal interviews extended into ordinary life.[14] I also learned something about civil service experience from the locations of my interviews. I spoke with one former UNRWA teacher sitting between rows of peas growing in the small plot of land he had purchased with the money he received at retirement. I interviewed many people in the offices of the Retired Civil Servants' Association and the Retired Arab UNRWA Employees' Association, places where retirees, now that they no longer had offices to go to, spent their days drinking coffee, playing backgammon, and arguing about politics. For a conversation with Khalil Rishad, a retired director of *Diwan al-Muwazzafin* (Civil Service Commission), he and I were given the use of the office of the Pension Administration's director, a courtesy that reflected Khalil's status as a former high-ranking official. Each of these settings—and the variety of homes where I met people, in refugee camps, in cities, and in towns—afforded its own insight into the working histories of these former civil servants.

The narrative expressions, evaluations, and recollections articulated in conversations I had with people in Gaza constitute an interpretative moment within the memory process.[15] Conceiving of memory as a process reminds us that there is no inherent object that is falsified over time, or by politics (which is not to say that there cannot be false memories).[16] In the case of Gaza, the intense politics of the place and the multiple ruling authorities who have influenced the civil service complicate civil service memories. When former civil servants spoke about their work during the Mandate or the Administration, they frequently made explicit comparisons with the Israeli occupation or the Palestinian Authority, and sometimes with Ottoman practice. The various administrations were judged in relation to and in terms of each other. The practice of narrative imbrication necessarily complicates, but does not invalidate, the use of these interviews in an analytical project that focuses on the first two administrations. That people have something to say about the present does not mean they don't have anything to say about the past.

At the same time, just because people are silent about something does not mean it is unimportant.[17] With the tape recorder rolling, for instance, people were often reluctant to criticize the Palestinian Authority. Even though my research was not about the Authority, people wanted to make sure that I would not use their names (I am not) and that I was not a journalist who was going to put their words in the newspaper the next day. This concern, while pervasive, did not engender a complete narrative absence, but rather a narrative thinness. In casual conversation criticism never ceased, and it did sometimes make its way into interviews. There is no doubt, however, that concern about the Authority's security forces influenced people's talk.

Other narrative absences reflected more complicated social phenomena. For example, when I raised the question of relations between native Gazans and refugees, people tended to gloss over problems and discrimination. It seemed clear to me that this reluctance stemmed from a concern that I not think there was disunity or internal discord among Palestinians, who were supposed to be united in struggle after all. Of course, it was only because enough people told me about the complexity of the relations between *Ghaz-zazwa* (native Gazans) and refugees that I was able to interpret this narrative thinness in this way.[18] My own understandings of Gazans' reflections on civil service experience rely both on an accumulation of conversations and on the multiplicity of perspectives on these reflections that I acquired throughout my research (in archives, in newspapers, in local histories, and so forth). That is, my account of the memories and evaluations of civil servants is also part of the interpretive process.

The Sense of Service: Reflections on Practice and Character

In my conversations with civil servants, we talked a lot about what it meant to be a good muwazzaf, and conversely what might constitute bad work. In implicitly or explicitly comparing their work to that of other civil servants or to civil service in other times, the retirees I knew in Gaza not only defined themselves, but also offered clear arguments about what government *should* be. At times, people suggested that the work they did in the Mandate was an improvement over conditions during the preceding Ottoman regime. At other times, they drew contrasts between Egyptian service and the humiliations of Israeli occupation or the corruption of the Palestinian Authority. Retired civil servants' evaluations of rule also sometimes felt to me like suggestions for the future—how a Palestinian state might best be able to serve its people. Gaza's muwazzafin did not create their ideas about service sui generis. They were schooled in Ottoman, British, and colonial traditions of service that shaped the contours of their definitions. These broad notions both helped people cope with the difficult conditions in Gaza and were themselves inflected with Gaza's particularities. Being respectable and respected, doing one's duty, working with efficiency and sympathy, distinguishing oneself within the community, these were all features of the complicated and sometimes contradictory definition of good civil service work.

IN SERVICE TO DUTY: DOING GOOD FOR
NATION, FAMILY, AND SELF

The widespread agreement among muwazzafin that service was a duty lent their work importance, even if the details of their job seemed trivial. Sense of duty was also connected to civil servants' production of themselves as authoritative subjects. It permeated civil servants' idea of themselves, of their work, and of their lives. At the same time, ideas about duty were remarkably concrete and often instrumental. Some people linked this work with their obligations to the community, but just as many highlighted their responsibility to their families and their need to earn a living. This instrumentality distinguishes duty from the much more general ideas about respectability that were also crucial to civil service self-perception. One might choose to take the job for a specific, even narrow purpose. But once a civil servant, one had to embody that persona. Varying reasons for taking the job did not seem to produce diverse senses of what civil service should mean.

Those who defined their duty entirely as service to community and nation tended to be wealthy, people whose families did not depend on their monthly salary. Most women who worked in service during the Mandate were from this class, people for whom a job as a teacher (the most common option for women) was a means of doing good, rather than a way of earning a living.[19] A former teacher who now runs a charitable society for women described the purpose of her work: "I never thought of money. I thought of how to serve my people . . . to serve my people and to serve my women."[20] Another teacher, Hanan, said almost the same thing: "I was concerned for the people, I loved the people and I still love them now. . . . I liked my job, and it was a hobby more than an employment."[21] For these civil servants, duty to serve the people was perceived as a form of charity, an obligation on the part of the well-to-do to those less fortunate than themselves. To this extent, duty was implicated in the distinctions that civil service produced in the community.

Given the extreme impoverishment most Gazans faced after 1948, it is not surprising that most people who began their civil service careers during the Egyptian Administration accorded as much importance to their duty to their families as to their duty to community. Ahmed Ismail, who worked first as a laborer and then as a clerk for UNRWA, explained that even though he was educated, he was willing to take any job to support his family: "I was the only person who could take care of the family. What to do? I thought that the best thing was to find a job, but from where?"[22] He submitted more than sixty applications to UNRWA before finally receiving a summons from the director, who told him that the only available position was a job as a laborer in a rations distribution center, a position far below his qualifications: "He said, 'Do you know what I mean by laborer?' I told him, 'Yes, I know, I see the laborers when I go to the distribution center [to get my monthly rations]. I told him, 'I want to work.'" Convinced that Ahmed was willing, the director gave him the job. Then, he recounted, "I worked as a laborer, but I determined that I accept for now and would be a hard worker and obey my bosses, and I could also help them in clerical work." Ahmed's hard work paid off, and he was appointed to a clerical position within a short time. He received steady promotions throughout his career and retired as a field distribution officer. He stressed that his duty to his family was the impetus behind his success: "My family situation required me to work hard and strive to bring my family into safety and security."

Working in the civil service afforded people a salary with which to feed their families, but it seemed also to transform their experience of loss. By enabling muwazzafin to be active in improving people's living conditions, rather than being passive recipients of relief, civil service mitigated the humiliation they might have felt about their desperate conditions. There is no doubt that, especially after 1948, public services were vital to many people's survival. Da'ud Ahmed certainly understood his work as a clerk in the Egyptian Administration in these terms. He described his feelings of humiliation in 1948 and explained that while he needed work to help his family—

"my family thought of me as a savior"—once employed he focused on his ability to effect change for other people: "We saw how people were living, and we tried hard to ease these bad conditions. It was a responsibility to serve my community through my job and to work honestly in this regard."[23] Reflecting a different attitude from those who saw civil service as charity, Da'ud emphasized the equality of the service relation: "I was put in this job to serve the people, not to control or humiliate them." Whatever the disparities in their attitudes toward the people, civil servants were in agreement that they and their work deserved respect. Evidence suggests that this conception was widely shared, that civil servants' self-constitution as authoritative subjects contributed to their authority. Respectability was one of the terms through which civil service authority was translated into everyday interactions.

RESPECTABILITY AND CIVIL SERVICE ETIQUETTE

Everybody in Gaza told me that civil servants had to be respectable—respectful in their dealings with people, worthy of receiving their respect, and well mannered in their life. This was a habit that defined civil servants and provided a grounds for judging them. Respectability both indexed and produced their authority. To be deemed respectable, the smallest details of one's interactions mattered. Ibrahim Mahmoud, who retired as a school principal, explained his view of this etiquette. A civil servant, he said, "should have taste and good morals. I come to you, for example, you should offer me a cup of coffee. You can't greet me without a kind word. So, I drink something better than this cup of coffee [this small gesture goes a long way]."[24] Treating people right, easing their encounter with government, was perceived as an essential part of civil service respectability. Reflecting on his own experience in civil service, Salim Rashid gave prominence to his style of dealing with people: "I learned from them [the British] how to treat people. . . . I don't want to say that I am his servant, but I serve his interests. If this person was good and polite, I have to help him, regardless of his being a Muslim, a Jew, or a Christian."[25]

While Salim did not suggest that only civil servants were respectable—and civilian respectfulness was clearly important to him—he did intimate that respectability was intrinsic to civil service in a way that was not true for the general population. He did not imagine that all civil servants lived up to these standards, but he viewed such failures as having serious consequences: "If you behaved in your work in a good manner, straight, the people will respect you. . . . It is up to you. You have to prove yourself in society as a civil servant. There are civil servants who retired without anyone mentioning them and there are others in high-ranking positions, but nobody says good morning to them."[26] Being perceived as respectable could bring concrete benefits to civil servants. That is, it was an effective habit, one that could engender habits of respect in other people.[27]

At the same time, a lack of respectability could affect not only one's position in society, but also one's ability to advance at work. Muhammad Ghazi, a clerk in the Egyptian-era health department, attributed his success to his distinction from other, less respectable employees: "Some employees had bad habits. Some drank coffee at their desks, some talked, some smoked cigarettes, this was not me. I progressed a lot, even compared to the employees who had seniority over me."[28] Respectable behavior also made the work itself go more smoothly. In his accounts of events at work, Salim stressed that he accomplished his goals "through sweet speech and logic and not through shouting or fighting. . . . When the employee shouts and raises his voice, he gets a headache. . . . Through understanding everything works out—it depends on the mentality of the muwazzaf."[29] Salim noted the effects of behavior—the instrumental aspect of respectability—yet he also believed respectability to be its own reward. As a civil servant, one should be respectable, not just because it will help achieve some immediate end, but because that is what it means to be a civil servant. Respectability participated in the consolidation of the authority of civil service personnel, creating grounds for public respect and suggesting the contours of interactions.

DISTINCTION: BENEFITS OF AND TENSIONS IN SERVICE

The distinctions that went along with civil service reflect some of its internal contradictions. Along with respectability came high social status, a distinct benefit of government work and evidence of the successful inculcation of its habits. The status accorded civil servants in Palestine was an accumulation of attitude over time. The Ottoman origins of the Palestinian civil service created new forms of education and training that distinguished civil servants within the broader society.[30] When British officials considered employment in their version of this service, they looked to hire people with service histories in their families, thereby ensuring that a sense of civil service status would extend beyond the confines of any one job. The expansion of civil service during the Administration, which made these positions much less rarified, risked undermining, though not eliminating, this special status.

Even as civil servants appreciated this benefit, these social distinctions created a certain amount of tension within and around civil service, in part because, in contrast to conditions of patronage, occupation, or corruption, civil service interactions were supposed to take place among equals.[31] Many former civil servants stressed precisely this equality in describing their relations with the public. As Bahat Hassan put it, "We had values, principles, obligation, respect, and compliments. The employee was not a tyrant. Civil servants are ordinary people who respect all people. His salary doesn't make him a high-class person."[32] In this view, service should be neither servitude nor domination.

Many civil servants, though, enjoyed a sense of superiority. This superiority was linked to class differences and was most often expressed by the same people who viewed their work as a form of charity. Reflecting on her work during the Mandate, the teacher Hanan commented that "the Southern District—the Gaza Strip and the south—was less civilized. . . . Education in the rest of Palestine was more advanced." Despite the fact that she herself is from Gaza, Hanan, being the daughter of a powerful, well-known man and highly educated, most definitely did not include herself in this evaluation. Her sense of distinction from the people around her was even stronger when she discussed the refugees who came to Gaza in 1948: "The refugees who came to the Strip were from the most backward class in Palestine. . . . The villages—and I am an urban person [madaniyya]—there was a big difference between a village in the north and a village in the south." In addition to a north-south distinction, Hanan highlighted the difference between urban and rural life—and firmly identified the former as superior.[33] Hanan insisted that her superiority did not undermine her service work, but those on the receiving end might have disagreed.

Distinction did sometimes create tensions with the broader public. Rachelle Taqqu notes, in a dissertation about Arab workers during the Mandate, that when local civil servants "adopted British manners, they sometimes set themselves apart from the rest of the population."[34] Even as people respected and accorded status to civil servants, there was some resentment about "the 'professional' pose assumed by many government employees."[35] There was also resentment within the ranks of the civil service about internal class distinctions. As one retiree, Abu Jamal, complained to me, "Junior employees had low salaries, and the senior employees had high salaries and were indifferent to the plight of junior employees and unconcerned about increasing their salaries."[36] These sorts of tensions never developed into out-and-out conflict, but they were a persistent feature of civil service experience.

Still, even civil servants who were not from the upper class benefited from service distinctions, and many remember their high social status fondly. People recall that in the British Mandate, "We were the top."[37] A former teacher described how association with teachers was enough to raise the status of others: "Someone who wanted to be notable, during Ramadan he invited the teachers to show that he has a connection. So, the people say, 'Oh! Oh, the teachers are coming to the home of *fulan* [so-and-so].' "[38] During the Egyptian Administration, one retiree (Abu Jamal) commented to me, "the civil servant felt comfortable and everybody wanted his daughter or sister to marry a civil servant because he earned a good and steady salary. When a civil servant wanted to become engaged to somebody, her family immediately agreed; they said that this employee will get a *dunam* [plot of land] in the future and his salary is good." In large part because of a devaluation in civil service salaries, such high status is a thing of the past, and Abu Jamal went on to lament that today "people hesitate when an employee wants to marry their daughter, even if he has good morals and conduct, but when an uneducated day-worker wants to marry, they agree immediately."[39]

Distinction both created and was a characteristic of tension in civil service. Bureaucratic authority seemed to depend on the presence of both "equality" and "social differentiation" in civil service practice. There were, that is, multiple sources of authority which were both interrelated and mutually dependent. That civil servants made claims about approaching their clients as equals afforded the civil service a certain amount of moral authority. That they sometimes approached these clients from a position of higher status gave them social authority. This was in addition, of course, to the legal authority that their office gave them. The relations among these sorts of authority were complex, and they did not necessarily form a coherent whole. Bureaucratic authority appeared to depend on keeping this variety of relations in constant play.

Bad Habits: The Other Side of Civil Service

One of the factors that had to be accounted for in this variety was the possibility of poor work—"bad habits"—among civil servants. Even as civil servants articulated their expectations of themselves and others in their position, and even as they asserted that these expectations were not simply ideals but rather the practiced habits of civil service, they were cognizant of failures. People more often talked about the bad habits of other people, other departments, or other regimes than about their own. That civil servants were vehement in their objections to perceived misbehavior by colleagues could serve to further underscore the importance of civil service virtues as well as the commitment of most civil servants to maintaining them. These reflections on the boundaries of good behavior also served as a reminder that habit was not stasis: it required work, reflection, and active participation.

While my conversations with retirees about failures to behave up to standard took place long after the fact, archival records indicate that working civil servants did make formal complaints about their colleagues when they disapproved of their practices (and perhaps when they saw personal advantage in slowing someone else's career trajectory). In 1947, Mustafa Bseiso, the *sharia* advocate of Gaza wrote to the attorney general, complaining about the work habits of a colleague in the Gaza court. The attorney general forwarded the complaint to the chief secretary, who asked the Supreme Muslim Council to investigate.[40] The petition both presumed and described a whole order of work, which Bseiso thought was being undermined by the irresponsibility of one civil servant: "[He] inquires whether the regulations governing hours of attendance in Government offices do not apply to officers of the Supreme Muslim Council and the Sharia Courts who arrive late in the morning and absent themselves whenever they like, while the public wait to pay their fees. For instance, Sheikh Adel Shareef, Chief Clerk at the Sharia Court, Gaza, often arrives late unheedful of the hours of attendance. On Saturday the 12th July, 1947, he arrived after 11 A.M., while he often has a haircut and invites guests to eat and drink with him during office hours in the office behind closed doors, while people are waiting outside to finish their business."[41] Bseiso identified timeliness, regularity, and equality of treatment as crucial to office order. Petitions such as this one, even as they complained about poor civil service performance, reinforced the importance of good habits. Making its way from one government office to another, the petition became a circulating sign of the pervasiveness of a civil service ethos, even as it addressed a failure of this practice.[42]

Bseiso's complaint was about a habit of negligence, a disorderly practice. Other bad habits appeared more proactive—sins of commission, as it were. Abu Jamal, who worked in the Gaza Municipality water department, contrasted the work of his department with that of other civil service sites in terms of *routine*.[43] Adapted into Arabic, *routine* indicates inefficiency, bureaucratic red tape, and a use of procedural mechanisms to obstruct the citizen's efforts to receive services, rather than suggesting something like an organized work schedule or a regular following of procedure: "We as employees offered services to the citizens and were efficient in our dealings with them so they would feel comfortable and not annoyed by *routine*. There were departments which operated by *routine*—for example, they said to the citizen to come tomorrow or after tomorrow, but we were serious in our job, and we respected the public and the public was satisfied."[44] In Abu Jamal's view, relying on routine showed one to be neither serious nor respectful. While he distinguished the work of his department from that of departments who did not effectively serve the public, there was an evident risk to the entire apparatus of authority if the latter were perceived as representing the civil service milieu.[45] This risk, which could also undermine the status of civil servants, was one reason that identifying and denouncing bad work was so important.

Bad habits are no less complicated than good ones, and there were many possible reasons that a civil servant might not appear serious in his work. In one of the few conversations in which a civil servant reflected on his own practices with the same critical eye generally directed at colleagues, Bahat Hassan described some of the difficulties involved in being a good civil servant. Bahat, who worked during the Administration as a market inspector charged with ensuring that merchants were pricing items according to government regulations described the negative effects of *wasta* (connections) on his work habits. He highlighted the ways in which it interfered with his capacity to do his job fairly and effectively. Bahat's comments also indicate another side of social differentiation vis-à-vis civil service: those circumstances in which the civil servant approached a private citizen from a position of lower, rather than higher, status. Wasta, in this context, operated as the negative side of social authority, differentiating among civil servants on the basis of family origins or personal connections.[46] Personnel authority did not, and does not, always trump personal authority, a reminder of the complex field within which authority is articulated.

In response to my question about what he did when he discovered someone was not in compliance with the official prices, Bahat responded, "I will answer you frankly. What I did is what happens now. I am from a weak family. If I found that he was from a weaker family than mine and he couldn't hurt me, I would punish him. If I found that he was from Hillis, Shawwa [powerful families] . . . I couldn't do anything to him, I could only notice. Because, my back wasn't covered. . . . I wanted to eat, to continue to eat."[47] The amount of attention accorded to pricing violations in police records from the Administration suggests that this sort of civil service failure was very likely to have been noticed by the general public.[48] A report from 1962, for example, indicates that merchants were raising prices on basic commodities and states that "people are asking the government to intervene and stop merchants from exploiting them."[49] People I knew in Gaza remembered the prevalence of corruption: "The needs of the people were achieved by wasta. There began to be a style that we hadn't seen before—bribes—a merchant who wanted to import had to pay something. . . . Someone who wanted to resolve a problem—even if he wasn't in the right—could get a good outcome."[50]

Bahat's failure to do his job was, as he certainly felt, a serious matter. He was both frustrated by and resigned to this bad habit of Gazan life. His comments describe more than his personal failures and frustrations though. They reveal how the different obligations and duties of service could come into conflict. In his work as a market inspector, Bahat had to choose between fulfilling his duty to himself and his family and pursuing his duty to the community as a whole. That he was confident in his inability to actually fulfill this latter duty when faced with a well-connected malefactor seems to have made his choice easy, though no less troubling to him. Whatever the public might see in Bahat's work, he saw himself as trapped in a circumstance ruled by privilege and distinction.

Public Perspectives on Civil Service: Habits of Complaint and Comment

As the public outcry about overpricing confirms, muwazzafin were not alone in viewing civil service as a duty. Public attitudes toward the civil service shed light not just on how its practices played among the broader population, but also on people's ways of interacting with government and its servants. That Palestinians were quick with their commentaries about civil service practice suggests a view of government as potentially responsive to public needs. The content of the commentaries implies that belief in the importance of respectability was widely shared, as it was in these terms that complaints were often forwarded. The terms and tone of complaints did not necessarily pose a challenge to the authority of civil service or its habits. Like civil servants' own accounts of corruption and inefficiency, by calling attention to particular failures as the problem, public complaints may sometimes have further consolidated bureaucratic authority. Some complaints, though, did point to the possibility of systemic problems, suggesting that failure might not be only individual.

During both the Mandate and the Administration the Palestinian press evaluated civil service performance, critiquing muwazzafin's professionalism, efficiency, and effectiveness. In the newspapers of each period one can find examples of both praise and complaint.[51] In May 1935, for example, al-Difa',[52] a paper published in Jaffa that was widely read in Gaza, complained about the behavior of employees of the customs department: "It has come to our attention that these employees come late for their shifts, which is causing negligence and delays in their dealings with people."[53] In this case, the complaint was not about merchants, but on their behalf. It was frequent practice in the press to report and champion public complaints about government practice. The choice of which complaints to highlight no doubt reflected the paper's readership, a readership limited by class and literacy. This particular complaint illuminated the network of relations—between employees, their superiors, and the public—which constituted the civil service. Reflecting on the negligent behavior, the article asked, "Could this be true? And, if it is true, who is responsible for these actions, we wonder?" The piece ended with this question, further underscoring the importance of a well-functioning bureaucratic apparatus for the inculcation of proper civil service values in individual employees.

Similar techniques were employed in press articles which praised civil servants, sometimes defending them in the face of mistreatment by their superiors or misunderstanding by the public. The press, after all, did not simply reflect public views of the civil service, but participated in creating those views. In the early days of the Egyptian Administration, a new Gazan newspaper, *Sawt al-ʿUruba*, published a panegyric to the Gazan civil servant. The commentary praised Gaza's employees for doing their job well and for defying expectations. The article recounted a story told by a Quaker volunteer (the Quakers provided relief in Gaza before the establishment of UNRWA), "who expected Palestine to be like unknown Africa." Comparing Gaza's civil servants to those in Jordan, the man explained that it had taken him a long time in Jordan to complete his paperwork, but in Gaza "they asked me to sit in a chair and they offered me cigarettes and coffee. And, in five minutes—without connections—they completed what had taken four days in Jordan. God bless all the civil servants of this region because they brighten the image of their country."[54] In doing their job well—being respectable and efficient, doing their duty, and showing sympathy—these civil servants were not only mediators between government and the public, they were the face of their country to a skeptical foreigner. In praising this work, the press contributed to the consolidation of their authority.

Petitions submitted to government by individuals further underscore how widely shared ideas about civil service quality were. A complaint sent in 1945 to the director of the land registry about two of its employees in Gaza mobilized general ideas about civil service character to respond to a particular circumstance of misbehavior. The petition alleged that the employees were letting down both the public and the government, noting that "it is the duty of a Government officer to serve the public interests and to be faithful to Government."[55] Pulling out all its rhetorical stops, the complaint commented on the reputation of the civil servants in question among Gazans: "Last evening I was sitting in the 'Al-Nuzha' Café in Gaza where I over-heard some of the people discussing the ill reputation of the Registrar of Lands Gaza and that of the Chief Clerk Habib El-Sayegh and how those officers are actually committing shameful acts in over-loading the poorer classes of the public by imposing on them exorbitant fees because they do not give them bribes and how, in return of bribes they receive, they subject Government to heavy losses in fees."[56] Positioning himself as an unconnected bystander who merely happened to overhear this talk and was concerned for the sake of good government, the complainant urged that the director come to Gaza at once to investigate.[57] I can't comment on the veracity of this complaint (the registry did not believe it to be accurate), but it discloses the widespread currency of the categories through which civil servants defined themselves. Character and practice, reputation among and relations with the public, duty to government and citizenry—all of these terms according to which the land registry employees were criticized, were those through which civil servants recognized themselves.

The same criteria were invoked in Administration-era complaints about civil servants.[58] When, in 1958, a group of students complained to the director of the Interior and Public Security about their teachers, they relied on shared conceptions of appropriate civil practice in their claim that the teachers' behavior was outside its boundaries. In their letter, the students said, "We would like to inform you that some of our teachers evidence bad morals and set bad examples. They break the fast of holy Ramadan by smoking and eating in front of the students—in addition to other disgraceful acts."[59] A police investigation determined that the charges were true—the evident explanation for such behavior being that the teachers in question were Communists. Such an ostentatious display of political affiliation was definitely at odds with the prevailing understanding of appropriate civil service behavior (not to mention the general security climate in Gaza). Accordingly, the security forces ordered the education director to take disciplinary action against the teachers.

Regulating Civil Service: Politics and the Repose of Habit

The complaint about civil service practice involving Communist misbehavior raises the curtain on politics, the arena that posed the most significant potential challenges to civil service habit. The severe restrictions that the governments of both the Mandate and the Administration placed on political activity by civil servants indicate their awareness of the risks posed by such expression. Consequently, civil servants were prohibited from fully participating in the public life of their communities. For these employees, at least as far as politics was concerned, there was no available realm of private conduct. The restrictions, as much as political participation itself, created tension in service habits.

This challenge was not to the idea of service, but to its enactment, threatening to destabilize the ability of civil servants to be comfortably "reposed" in habit.[60] The political realm had the potential to create doubt, discomfort, uncertainty, which could undermine the stability of civil service. Such doubt could also be threatening to civil servants' sense of self. As William Connolly notes, "To become severely disaffected from that which one is called upon to do in work, family, and consumption is also to become disaffected from the self one has become. When the distance between what one is and what one does is great, one is likely to hold oneself in contempt."[61] Given the expansiveness of the civil service persona, which was deeply connected to how civil servants understand their persons, this threat was very real in Gaza.

It was in the political domain that questions of legitimacy might be raised—despite a general practice that held them in abeyance—that in turn might undermine authority. Habit is tenacious, though. The recollections of civil servants about how they maneuvered through these challenges indicate that the abeyance of legitimacy was not a policy simply imposed from above (in fact it very often may have been at odds with policy initiatives), but a practice that made things work, however tenuously, for all those who participated in the governing process. The second part of this book, which explores the details of bureaucratic service, further illuminates this practice. There were clear moments of rupture in civil service habit over the fifty years under consideration here, instances in which abeyance seemed to fail. The first Israeli occupation of Gaza in 1956 was one such instance—and many civil servants seemed to have stayed at home for those four months.[62] More often, though, politics produced a shudder of doubt which was then reabsorbed into the habits of bureaucratic practice.

CHOOSING WORK AND PROHIBITING POLITICS IN THE MANDATE

During the British Mandate, civil servants were categorically forbidden from engaging in political activity of any kind. As unsurprising as this restriction was, given the importance of controlling the national conflict in Palestine, it shows some of the inherent difficulties involved in the Palestinian experience of working for the Mandate government. Constantly negotiating the restrictions of one's employment and the sentiments of one's nation created tremendous tensions for civil servants. Retirees described their work as having been for the benefit of their people, and yet they felt frustrated by their inability to publicly express their support for this cause. Qasim Jamal, a former teacher, described the position of civil servants. Each one, he told me, knew he had made a choice: "He had two options, either to do the work he had accepted or, if he got involved in politics, they said, 'Bye-bye. You chose politics.' Then, maybe he wouldn't find any other work. Job opportunities were limited, and most of them were government positions."[63] The two kinds of duty—to nation and to family—through which muwazzafin invested their work with import appeared to be in conflict.

How were civil servants able to cope with this conflict? How was doubt put to rest? Civil servants appear to have utilized two primary mechanisms to maneuver among their conflicting demands: subterfuge and disassociation. Through subterfuge—and by taking some risks—some civil servants *were* able to find ways to participate in political life.[64] Hanan, who could afford to take greater risks than those dependent on the income their jobs provided, managed to write secretly for the nationalist cause even as she worked as a teacher: "I wrote and signed my articles in my sister's name . . . Istiqlal [Independence]—our names inspired what was inside us. Inside school I didn't do anything. . . . I obeyed them at work. They allowed me to broadcast on the school public address system, but to speak only about cultural things, not politics. . . . So, I falsely signed my writings."[65] Hanan seems to have created two distinct realms in her life, and she was able to feel positive about both, indeed, to believe in her work in both.

Even civil servants who could not afford to risk such subterfuge were able to take some comfort in the disassociation such divisions allowed. Civil servants distinguished between their work *in* government and government itself, drawing a line between British policy and Mandate service delivery. Yasmin, a retired teacher, expressed this sentiment: "We never felt we were working for the government."[66] When she said this, I thought she meant that work in education was different. When I asked, she insisted, "[No,] work in the government does not mean that all civil servants are spies for the government or collaborating with the government." Qasim Jamal echoed these sentiments and explained when and how civil servants might be thought of as collaborators. A civil servant, he said, "felt that he provided services for the citizens, whether he was an employee in health, education, or public security. Except for public security—if he had to enter into matters which were considered against the nation. Then it would be said, 'This man is political, he's from the *mabahith* [CID].' And people talked against him. But, this didn't happen a lot." Thus, even as civil servants chafed against the restrictions imposed by the British on their political activity, they were largely able to keep this frustration separate from their valuation of their work and service.

The kind of separation described by Yasmin and Qasim was enabled by the very habits that political restrictions disturbed. These habits, which were not grounded in a particular government or policy agenda, were identified as more fundamental to the work of civil service than that agenda. It was when one's work was directly implicated in the pursuit of objectionable policies that it became difficult to disassociate. Such disassociation did not entail creating a division between practice and belief or between official and hidden transcripts.[67] Even as all sorts of divisions were demanded of civil servants, both by the conditions of their employment and by their efforts to take part in the life of their communities despite those conditions, such divisions do not comprise a map of the "truth" or "falsity" of people's positions.[68] In the process of making themselves feel better about their work and defusing the challenge politics posed to their own comfort, civil servants contributed to the consolidation of governmental authority.

NATIONAL SENTIMENTS AND POLITICAL CONVICTIONS:
EGYPT, UNRWA, AND CIVIL SERVICE PRACTICE

During the Egyptian Administration, control of civil service political activity was affected by Egyptian concerns about politics "at home" and regionally and by the sometimes uncomfortable relationship between the Administration and UNRWA. The control of political activity in Gaza, which went through several distinct stages in the course of the Administration, mirrored what was happening in Egypt itself. The most important parties on the local scene were the Muslim Brotherhood and the Communist Party. The Muslim Brotherhood was especially popular since Egyptian members of the organization had fought for Palestine during the 1948 war. After the war, however, the party was banned by the Egyptian government.[69]

In 1952, after the Free Officers' revolt, which overthrew King Farouq and ultimately gave Gamal Abdul Nasser the presidency, the Muslim Brotherhood was legalized again. For the next two years it was extremely active and drew much of its membership from the ranks of the civil service. Rema Hammami notes that "the head of the movement until 1954 was the head of the Gaza Municipality and also a shari'a court judge. Other leaders were also employees in the Gaza Municipality or school teachers."[70] The attempt on Nasser's life by a Muslim Brother in 1954 transformed the government's relationship with the group from one of cooperation to one of repression. This second banning of the movement, and the departure of much of its leadership, reduced the organization's strength considerably.[71]

If 1954 marked the low point for the Muslim Brotherhood, 1958–59 proved to be that moment for the Communist Party. While Communist support for the partition of Palestine had antagonized the Egyptian government, during the mid-1950s there was a "thaw in communist-regime relations"[72] such that, in Egypt proper at least, jailed party members were released and greater activity was possible. The Iraqi revolution of July 14, 1958, and the increasing rivalry between Nasser's Egypt and the communist-supported regime of 'Abd al-Karim Qasim ultimately led to a crackdown on communists in Egypt, Syria (at the time part of the United Arab Republic), and Gaza.[73]

The Gazan membership of both the Muslim Brotherhood and the Communist Party had included many civil servants, though after the crackdowns most were afraid to be involved in politics. Still, according to Hassan Rashad, some continued to be active: "The civil servant was afraid. . . . Other than teachers, most civil servants did not participate in political activities, but teachers did. They were active with either the Communist Party or Muslim Brotherhood."[74] Police reports from throughout the Administration support Hassan's contention, indicating that the Communist Party had quite strong support.[75] There was also continued mention of Muslim Brotherhood support among teachers as well as support for the Ba'th party.[76] All political activity was closely monitored, and the threat not only of dismissal but of prison hung over any civil servant who remained active.

Ibrahim Mahmoud was imprisoned in 1959. He explained that the government arrested anyone who expressed a political opinion: "We had made a group who defended the homeland and the land. We pressured the Egyptian government to bring arms and recruit. . . . they accused us of being Communists even though none of us were. When we disturbed them, they accused us of being Communists and put us in the military prison. . . . We remained isolated in the prison without trial. I stayed there for twenty-one months. [The group was made up of] teachers and others, but the majority were teachers."[77] Despite this experience, Ibrahim continued to speak positively about aspects of Egyptian rule, insisting that "not all the Egyptians were bad." Even more striking than Mandate civil servants who evaluated their own work as being good while disparaging the Mandate, Ibrahim disassociated the service work of the Administration from its political repression: "In the education field, we respected all the Egyptian teachers because prominent scholars and professors were among them, so why should we express our antagonism against them. They [the teachers] did not interfere in politics but only in education—they gave us lectures in literature and morals. The educational apparatus was good. In the health field, there were good Egyptian physicians. . . . Politics was something else." In fact, despite the repressive aspects of Administration rule, most Gazans described this time as the golden age for Gaza.[78] The uniformity of this judgment hints that disassociation was an effective tool for mitigating frustration with political repression.

The Administration did recognize the necessity of affording Gazans an outlet for political and nationalist expression, however controlled. The legislative council and the Arab National Union were intended to provide such an outlet, but also to build further support for the Administration and the Nasserist project. Even if the union did not really represent a space of political freedom, it was still too political in the eyes of UNRWA, and the organization prohibited its employees from joining. This stance created a conflict with the Administration, which sought to encourage widespread participation. It also produced an alliance between the Administration and Gazans who, despite its limitations, were eager for opportunities to organize.

In September 1959, the agency issued a staff circular that highlighted the importance of political neutrality among its employees:

In accordance with the established principles and practices of the United Nations, staff members are required to maintain at all times—in both their official and their private conduct—the independence and impartiality which is implicit in their status as Agency staff. . . . Although staff members are not expected to give up their national sentiments or their political or religious convictions and are naturally free to exercise their rights to vote in elections, they shall not make public speeches, or write articles or speeches for publication or broadcasting, or otherwise actively support a particular political party or group of candidates.[79]

According to UNRWA, to be a civil servant, or at least to be an international civil servant, was to be independent and impartial. Such a view was somewhat at odds with the definition of service as duty—duty to family *and* to community—that was so important to Gazans. Egyptian administrators couched their objection to the restrictions in precisely such terms. They expressed concern that literal interpretation of the impartiality clause "would require dealing with Israel as a normal country, not an enemy one. The price of working for UNRWA . . . is not that one has to forget one's nation or one's consideration that Israel is an unlawful country."[80] Despite the Administration's efforts and employee petitions to UNRWA, the agency seems not to have been swayed.[81] UNRWA employees appear to have managed this conflict in their work in a manner similar to that of Mandate employees, namely, by expressing frustration with and criticism of the agency and its policies even as they saw their own work as in the service of their people.[82]

CIVIL SERVICE ASSOCIATIONS AND
THE DEFENSE OF EMPLOYEE RIGHTS

While restrictions on political activity posed at least potential problems for civil servants' comfort with their work, the efforts of these employees to organize collectively to confront government about work-related problems had the perhaps ironic effect of shoring up the stability of such repose. Civil service associations provided a mechanism for muwazzafin to distinguish themselves from government while remaining inside it. Despite the apprehension with which both Mandate and Administration officials viewed these associations, which seemed perilously close to unions, they ultimately reinforced, rather than undermined, muwazzafin's connection with government.

They offered a means of expressing discontent without threatening the bases of civil servants' perceptions of their work or their selves.[83]

Civil service associations were moderate in their politics and conservative in their methods. Even as they appealed for better working conditions and made complaints about government practice, they consolidated a shared sense of civil service identity based precisely on their relationship with government. As Mary McGuire comments about civil service organizing in the United States and Germany, "At every step of the way the vast majority of organized postal civil servants organized within a perception of themselves *as civil servants*—with all that meant in terms of their duty, responsibility, obligation, honor and loyalty as servants of the state."[84] In Gaza, civil service organizing ultimately confirmed the habits of service.

When civil servants during the Mandate sought to organize, they first had to convince Mandate officials that their organizing was qualitatively different from trade union activity, activity which the government "had found it necessary to oppose."[85] Provisional officers of the new association assured the chief secretary that "the Association will have little or nothing in common with a Trade Union, either in its aims or its methods. It is the chief aim to place before Government the reasoned views of its members and to act only on recognized constitutional lines. It is anticipated that it will render material assistance to Government inasmuch as it will deal mainly with wide questions of the general policy applicable to the Service."[86] With such reassurance, and despite its misgivings, government eventually acquiesced, and an association representing members of the senior civil service was formed, followed by a second one representing members of the junior service.[87] There was some continued tension over the political outlook of these associations—the 1944 annual report of the First Division Association complained that they were still sometimes described by the government as "the Association of Bolshies"[88] —but, for the most part, worries that organized activity by civil servants would lead to a disruption of service work proved unfounded. The one notable exception was a strike in 1946 by the Second Division Civil Service Association, an action which produced substantial government concessions.[89]

In raising questions about the character of the civil service and the nature of its relationship with government, widely held notions about the propriety and respectability of civil servants were confirmed. In response to a First

Division Association request, J. W. Shaw, the chief secretary, commented, "I agree . . . that it is desirable to foster a spirit of greater cordiality and co-operation between 'Government' (what are all these civil servants if they are not 'government'?) and the Civil Service (1st Division) Association and for my part I am prepared to do my part to achieve this."[90] Shaw further confirmed that civil servants had a "'special' relationship to the state"[91] when, in response to another association request, he stated, "I was in favour of complying with the request coming as it did from a responsible body of Government's own servants which was a different thing from dealing with the General Public."[92] Civil servants themselves certainly concurred with the idea that they were *different* from the general public. To cite one instance of an explicit statement of this difference, the First Division Association president reported in 1945 on his efforts to get better car insurance rates for members. He suggested that special consideration was likely to be forthcoming because "civil servants as a body are generally quiet and careful people and not likely to go rushing all over the roads to the injury of innocent passersby."[93] Even as civil servants confronted government, they reinforced their distinction from the general population and their identification as government employees.

The civil service associations during the Administration—here divided not by level (first and second division), but by employer (government and UNRWA)—continued to be an outlet for personnel frustration that served to buttress the repose of civil service habit. The two associations were not identical in style, though. The UNRWA employees' association deployed a somewhat more confrontational tone in addressing its employer, calling personnel policies it disagreed with unfair and unjust and at times even raising the threat of political activity. In a letter to the agency director complaining about the cost of living in Gaza, the association's executive committee warned of trouble if salaries were not increased: "You may consider that this Committee shall not certainly be happy to see that this untolerable [*sic*] state of affairs should thrust staff members into such attempts aiming at expressing their unrest as it is felt that they can no longer endure any further patience in this respect."[94] The threat of unrest was not entirely idle, as on several occasions UNRWA offices had been the object of the local population's wrath, but the association seems not to have ever resorted to such measures.

The government association did not employ such threats, even for rhetorical effect. The extent to which civil servants internalized the restrictions on political activity and fit them into their sense of their own identities is evident in the ways people remember their work in the association. Abu Sami, a onetime head of the government civil service association insisted that they "had nothing to do with politics, only civil rights."[95] As he put it, the association "did not interfere with the basic laws, but only in personal rights." He described the association as responsive, not proactive, in its activities, saying, "The association did not get involved in anything just for the sake of proving its existence. It was just a means of defending the rights of the employees when needed: demanding promotion, raises, etc." The association, he seemed to suggest, was always respectful in it interactions with government and focused on doing its duty to its members. To be gentle, not aggressive, was also to be respectable and a good civil servant.

Conclusion

That civil service habits were both flexible and reflective contributed to their tenacity. Throughout their careers, and indeed throughout their lives, civil servants made different senses of their work as conditions changed. Even within a given moment, different positions could produce distinct understandings of civil service work and habit. These internal distinctions, tensions, and differentiations worked—by making such habits adaptive—to promote the general significance of civil service habits. Habits illuminate how bureaucratic authority could be engendered and also how it might fall apart. It is a strength of bureaucracy that it can produce its own authority. It is also a weakness that doubt among its personnel can also produce doubt among the population—that it can undermine its own authority when repose in its habits is disturbed. Doubt does not, though, flow automatically from strain or inconsistency or even dissonance. Such contradictions and tensions could be a source of strength for service habits. Doubt arises, rather, when the logic itself seems faulty, when tensions become crises, when contradictions become conflicts. Under acute conditions, doubt can become resistance or rejection. For the most part, habit was an effective instrument for sustaining the civil service apparatus and, with it, the broader authority of rule.

4

CIVIL SERVICE COMPETENCE AND
THE COURSE OF A CAREER

The government of any country depends principally upon organised thought and organised thought depends upon exact record and assemblage of all the material which is necessary before the thought can be translated into effective action. We suggest that the clerical service of a government is concerned principally in the mechanism of maintaining and assembling the record upon which governmental action depends.

REPORT ON REORGANIZATION OF CLERICAL SERVICE, 31 JULY 1926

A clerk has more information than any other person in a directorate because he sees everything that comes into the directorate, and everything that goes out—and he should be trustworthy.... [The directors] maybe didn't have all the information about the subjects that came in. I had a simple position, but I saw everything.

MUHAMMAD GHAZI, ON WORK IN THE ADMINISTRATION, GAZA CITY,
24 APRIL 1999

Governing authority must be repeatedly produced, and it does not have a single form. The authority of files and of personnel each contributes to a field of bureaucratic authority, but in distinct and sometimes disparate ways. Furthermore, bureaucratic authority is itself embedded in a broader social and political field, within which it must be both general and specific, expansive across the social domain and distinguished from other possible forms of authority. The power of official documents is distinct from that of other forms of writing, but not entirely separated from them. Civil service affords status and privileges—distinguished from other socially powerful positions, but not unconnected to them. The terrain of civil service, that is, has to be clearly marked, even as it claims that government values are general social values. In any government, people and papers work together in the production of bureaucratic authority. In Gaza's government, where the foundations of this authority were exceedingly tenuous, these relations were of particular importance in sustaining rule. The processes through which civil servants were acclimated to their work, through which they developed their personas, were central to sustaining the sometimes awkward balance among the various parts of this authority.

Having considered the general features of repetitive filing and the articulations of bureaucratic habit, this chapter turns to the course of the civil service career in order to examine how such habits were instilled and how such repetitions were ensured. From hiring to retirement (or firing), these moments shed light on working conditions, relations among colleagues and with the public, and the active promotion of a civil service style. Habit was operationalized as competence—a way of being was articulated as a way of doing. As civil servants sought personal advantage throughout their careers and strove to be competent in their work, they became ever more acclimated to the service milieu. The moments of a career worked to define civil service both by schooling personnel in its contours and characteristics and by identifying its borders. The processes of including and excluding certain sorts of people on the basis of things like character, gender, and class and certain sorts of jobs from the civil service apparatus helped shaped the character of service competence. Such competence not only helped shape the personas of civil servants, but also participated in shaping the population as well. I will explore these intersections in greater detail later. This chapter focuses on how civil service was inculcated in civil servants, how the general idea of good work was concretized in specific notions of competence, making the significance of reiterative authority for Gaza's government even more clear.

Ethics, Techniques, and Local Knowledge:
Defining Bureaucratic Competence

The development of competence highlights the "repertoires of authority"[1] available to civil servants. These repertoires were often articulated as forms of bureaucratic competence. In developing and declaring specific kinds of competence, civil servants also declared themselves to be authoritative figures. In judging such civil servants to indeed be competent, the public accepted this claim to authority, though it was not an unconditional acceptance. The ways in which competence was defined in Gaza further signal the contours of its government. The distinction between authority and legitimacy, and the emphasis on the former in Gaza's government, is crucial for understanding how bureaucratic competence was conceptualized and articulated. Lacking a framework to confer legitimacy, bureaucratic authority depended especially closely on the authoritative personas of its personnel. Further, conditions in Gaza helped define bureaucratic competence in this context, producing notions of competence that both are recognizable as part of a broader practice of modern government and reflect local distinctions.

Gaza's civil service required a technical competence that was not exactly expertise, a social competence whose goal was not disinterested interactions but differentiated service, and an ethical competence that did not guarantee (or even necessarily promote) a moral outcome.[2] These forms of competence were instruments in intertwined, yet distinct, repertoires of civil service authority. The reliance on not entirely expert technical knowledge was directly connected to the practice of tactical government. The articulation of this kind of work as competent bureaucratic work lent authority to the broader governing dynamic. The linking of competence with local knowledge that enabled civil servants to appropriately distinguish among the population further reveals the ways in which civil servants' authority sometimes blurred the distinction between personal and personnel authority. The centrality of ethical considerations in judgments of competence calls attention to the relation between the authority of individual civil servants and the broader authority accrued to government through their work. Each of these aspects of bureaucratic competence offered an opportunity to claim authority and also proved to be a mechanism through which such authority could be challenged.

While most governmental histories describe a tension between the roles of "generalists" and "experts" in civil service,[3] it is widely agreed that the advent of the expert—"a protean image of authority and rational knowledge"[4] —marks the emergence of modern government. Expertise might not define all governmental practice, but it seems to occupy an increasingly crucial place as governments become more modern.[5] Looking at government from Gaza, however, necessitates a reconsideration of this picture. Gaza's government during the British Mandate and Egyptian Administration was indisputably modern—it was concerned with the welfare of the population, it developed techniques of knowledge accumulation and population management that enhanced its efficiency, and it was focused on progress and increased rationality—even as expertise was not a centerpiece of its practice.[6]

Making government work, even with the limited money, infrastructure, and planning that were available in Gaza, required a technical competence that emphasized not mastery of elaborated models but coping skills. The colonial roots of Gaza's civil service explain in part its emphasis on generalists, as this kind of organization was typical of colonial civil service, which required personnel who could be transferred among the different colonial administrations and be qualified for each.[7] As Robert Heussler notes about the colonial civil servant, "An unusual combination of qualities was needed— courage with adaptability; firmness with sympathy; enterprise with reliability; obedience with authority. In lonely stations, far from the restraints of European public opinion and supported by lavish remuneration, the officer must remain dignified and incorruptible."[8]

Conditions in Gaza offer further insight into the form of its technical competence. The possibilities of government itself, the kinds of interventions that were feasible, the sorts of undertakings in which civil servants engaged were so severely constrained in Gaza (by both circumstance and policy) that expertise was rarely brought to bear. Timothy Mitchell, exploring the work of rule in twentieth-century Egypt, describes the importance of the "reorganization and concentration" of knowledge in marking the threshold of a particular sort of expertise.[9] As the interests and reach of government shifted and its projects became more immense, the variety of localized knowledges and capabilities (which constituted their own form of expertise) that made agriculture, say, work in Egypt had to be replaced with a broader and more controlled capacity to manage such production. In Gaza, such large-scale government was neither possible nor often sought. Rather, government coped, made do, was tactical rather than strategic in its interventions. In this practice it was the skills of the *bricoleur*, not the expert, that were required.

Technical competence was only one part of the skill set required to be a good civil servant. The execution of technical skills defined by Gaza's conditions required a social competence based in local knowledge. It was through understanding the people with whom one interacted (colleagues, superiors, and clients) that it was possible to produce satisfaction from an encounter with government, even if that encounter did not produce the desired results. As Muhammad Ghazi, a retired health department employee, put it, "As a civil servant, you have to meet the people in a good way. At the least you have to make him feel content when he comes to you. We have a proverb that says, Take him to the sea and leave him thirsty. That is, if you serve him a cup of tea, he will be content, even if he came to complain. A good meeting of the people helps." This emphasis on attitude rather than outcome was itself connected to the self-referential quality of bureaucratic authority, where what might define an encounter as good might have less to do with achieving a specific end than with feeling that the process was right.

According to common conceptions of civil service, the encounter between bureaucrat and client should be disinterested, but in Gaza's civil service this was decidedly not the case. Rather, *muwazzafin* described their ability to make distinctions among the population, that is, to know how to treat people appropriately according to their social position, as crucial to their work. One had to be sensitive to how someone coming to a government office might feel, know how to put her at ease, and, as well, how to create a balance between the person and the result she achieved. Social competence was expressed as a matter of style, of etiquette, as much as anything else. Salim Rashid highlighted this point:

> Someone comes to me to make an application [for a travel permit]. I tell him "good morning, what is the problem?" I know this man, he is not a merchant—he stands on the sidewalk, laying out a blanket with some goods and things on it. However, if someone comes to me and wants to import TVs from England with a cost of one million dollars, I do not treat him in the same manner as I treat the previous one. I give the importer a

travel permit for one month and to the other a week. Some people tell the latter, 'Go and make a problem and shout at him in order to give you more than a week.' He comes to me to complain about the permit. I ask him if he drank coffee with his wife. I ask the messenger to bring coffee to him. . . . After he drinks the coffee he apologizes and tells me to give him the time I want.

Given the awkward place of civil servants as mediators between the often clashing demands of government and of the diverse parts of the public, it took considerable skill to create satisfaction in the bureaucratic encounter. Simply being a local did not guarantee that a muwazzaf would have the social competence to manage these interactions. Neither was it only a matter of accumulating knowledge; one had to be deft in the management of information. The respectability that was so important to muwazzafin was connected to the development of a competent persona—a civil service presence that suggested authority.

This civil service persona also required, as Thomas Osborne has shown in the case of India, attention to the cultivation of ethical practice among employees.[10] Ethics and bureaucracy often appear to be opposed domains, and Gaza's bureaucracies do not seem especially likely to have been driven by ethical considerations.[11] A bureaucratic practice that distinguished people by class and context, that often sought to deflect people from the attainment of their goals, that could not promise a better future does not on the face of it seem defined by ethics. How can this circumstance be squared with what we have already seen were civil servants' concerns with duty and respectability, with good work and honorable practice? This contradiction can be addressed not by opposing ethical claims to immoral outcomes, but rather by exploring the ways in which ethical self-cultivation, in the sense described by Foucault, shaped bureaucratic sensibilities.[12]

That colonialism frequently sought to justify itself in moral terms has been much written about.[13] What Osborne traces in India and what I am interested in for the case of Gaza is something slightly different. Here I consider not only how rule was justified to others, but how civil servants came to feel themselves competent to occupy their positions. Osborne suggests that bureaucratic ethics were first and foremost expressed in the cultivation of an ethical persona among civil servants—that the care of self made possible concern for others.[14] This seems to have been the case in Gaza as well. Saba Mahmood notes that Foucault considered this cultivation to involve technical practices, "corporeal and body techniques, spiritual exercises, and ways of conducting oneself—all of which are positive in the sense that they are manifest in, and immanent to, everyday life. Notably, the importance of these practices does not reside in the meanings they signify to their practitioners, but in the *work they do* in constituting the individual."[15]

In Gaza's government, this practice also involved perceptions of bureaucratic action, though the claims that were made about ethical practice had a high degree of circularity. Civil service was defined in terms of good work, which then became tautologically defined as the work of government. Such self-referential ethics, not unexpected in conditions in which authority was also to such a large degree self-referential, can appear to be ungrounded in anything other than its own conceptions. This sort of circularity produces a potentially "dangerous ethics," in which almost anything can appear justified in its self-reflective terms. Yet even in the absence of a clear ground for ethical practice, it was not in fact entirely self-contained. Bureaucratic ethics were a domain of contestation, as members of the public, civil servants, and high government officials sought to shape the field. Even as, in the absence of a governing framework that could solidly ground a bureaucratic ethics, it was only through developing and preserving their own capacities that civil servants could lay claim to ethical competence, self-cultivation was embedded in these contestations.

This self-cultivation was clear in the conversations cited in the last chapter, in which civil servants repeated to me, and to themselves, their sense of themselves as honorable and respectable, of their work as good and as providing a service. Self-cultivation was also evident in the moments of a career as civil servants sought jobs and promotions, as they went about their days and planned for their retirement. How they interacted with their colleagues and with the public shaped their sense of themselves as ethical subjects and therefore as "authoritative subjects with the authorization to subject others to authority."[16] Self-cultivation took place throughout the civil service career and even beyond. Such attention to the self was both a service to oneself, as it made possible a more successful career, and crucial to one's development as an authoritative persona, thus making possible a more successful bureaucracy. Just as files were formed in part through repetition, civil service personas also required repeated articulation and reinforcement. The development of competence throughout one's career was a mechanism for such articulations. The moments in a civil service career divulge the production, deployment, and contestation of repertoires of authority

Acclimated Applicants and Civil Service Hiring

Muwazzafin acquired bureaucratic competence over the course of their career, as they became habituated to civil service. If one sought a job in the civil service, though, it helped to be already possessed of at least some of the habits of service, to be already somewhat competent in its execution. The hiring policies of the Mandate government explicitly sought out those people, mostly men, who were likely to have such competence. Recruitment policy sought out "sons or relatives of old government servants, who have traditions or experience behind them."[17] It was not only technical competence that was sought in this preference; government hoped as well to harness the social authority of these families for the authority of government. That some of this prestige had been acquired precisely in government service is a reminder of the multidirectional flows of authority. Even when government looked beyond this narrow group for its employees, it worked to develop competence and habits through schooling. As in the Ottoman Empire, education during the Mandate was often intended to produce civil servants for government.[18] When applicants emerged from the Palestinian educational system, they had been trained, if not for service specifically, than at least with British values in mind.

The potential problems in hiring the wrong people were made evident even before the formal start of the Mandate. In a letter of June 1921 to Secretary of State Winston Churchill, Herbert Samuel, the first high commissioner for Palestine, acknowledged that he had created some difficulties for himself: "When the Civil Administration was started in July last year and I was selecting officials for the various posts, I found that in order to retain the services of the officers of the Administration it was necessary to offer them some security of tenure. . . . After one year's experience in Palestine, I find that some of the officials selected, whose services were retained by me, in the above circumstances are not suitable for the posts they occupy. . . . I shall be grateful, therefore, if you will inform me whether, although a particular official has been offered permanent engagement, I can now inform him that his services are no longer required."[19] The minutes of this file indicate a considerable degree of frustration among British officials that such premature offers were made at all. It seemed clear that, at the very least, this decision would have negative financial implications for government. As Churchill noted in his reply, "In some cases it may be possible to state definitely that the officer in question is not fit to occupy the post which he at present holds, but to dispense with an officer's services on grounds of inefficiency is a strong step which can only be taken in clear cases, and these are no doubt rare. In the remaining cases it is clear that the Government cannot treat as non-existent the very definite and precise offers of permanent employment which have been made and some compensation will certainly have to be granted for loss of employment."[20] These mistakes at the outset further underscored the importance of hiring the right sort of person, but what constituted the right sort of person was a matter for further consideration. Different circumstances could produce different understanding of good civil service material.

Reflecting on a group of employees who now seemed unsuitable for promotion, a British official noted a few years later that "most of these officers were engaged during the Military Administration to act as Advisors and Translators to Military Governors who had little knowledge of Arabic, and that in most cases they were selected for their linguistic attainments rather than for any special administrative aptitude."[21] With governing needs turning more to the daily work of administration and technical competence becoming increasingly important, these personnel no longer seemed well suited for government service, prompting the suggestion that "it would appear desirable, before offers of pensionable employment are made, that careful reports be made on all Palestinian Officers, with a view to terminating the services of those who are unsuitable and making room for better qualified candidates, capable of being trained for eventual promotion to higher posts in the service."[22]

Over the course of the Mandate, personal character came to occupy a central place in hiring decisions, a centrality shown in an effort in 1946 to fill a vacancy in Gaza's district administration. Commenting upon the quality of the applicants, the district commissioner rejected one applicant partly on the grounds that "he is very pleased with himself and his manners are deplorable."[23] Recommending others for further consideration, the district commissioner praised one candidate's "character and drive, which, with proper training, might enable him to develop into a useful public servant" and commented on another that he was "genuinely interested in works of social amelioration and is intelligent enough to see the great needs of his own people at the present time." Of one candidate who was over the age limit for the position and did not possess the requisite university education, the district commissioner argued he should nonetheless be considered because "he is sensible and presentable and well acquainted with Government routine." Wherever an applicant acquired his sense of style and form, it was awareness of and comfort with service habits rather than any specific skills or expert knowledge that appeared a prerequisite for getting and doing the job. The difficult political conditions in Palestine, combined with the broader colonial concern for "quality people," shaped the character of the Mandate civil service.

In the switch from the Mandate to the Egyptian Administration, appointment procedures became even more fraught, a change directly related to the tremendously difficult conditions facing the population after the *nakba*. Dislocated and dispossessed, people were in desperate need of employment. In the first years of the Administration, when government jobs were scarce and other jobs practically nonexistent, applicants stressed civil service continuity and previous government employment. In the immediate aftermath of the 1948 war, the best way to secure a job in the new administration in Gaza was to have been employed as a civil servant during the British Mandate.[24] To the extent that financial restrictions made possible, the Administration tried to rehire these former civil servants. In later years, as financial and political conditions improved somewhat, applications contained a new appeal to the sympathy of the Administration and figured civil service jobs as a form of welfare. In both forms of appeal, applicants highlighted their familiarity with the contours of service work, presenting themselves as already competent in the ways of being which defined civil servants.

In August 1949, a group of civil servants originally from Beersheba complained that they, unlike the bulk of their fellow employees, had not been given positions in the new administration. Their complaint suggested it was an ethical imperative that they be given the jobs they deserved: "We went to work for the Egyptian forces in Hebron and Bethlehem by order of the Governor General. After the Egyptian forces left Hebron and Bethlehem, we came to Gaza on May 1, 1949, following the Egyptian army. We wanted to continue our work as in Beersheba, Hebron, and Bethlehem. . . . We are in desperate need. . . . 90% of the employees of Beersheba are working now as they did in the past and receive their salaries; to keep 10% of the Beersheba employees in such difficult circumstances is not just. We consider the Egyptian government good and just. Please help us."[25] The ethical claims implicit in this petition rest on the importance of technical competence, of doing the job. These former Mandate civil servants "went to work" as per the "order" of the new Egyptian governor. Having done their job, they wanted simply to "continue our work." The Administration, though, rejected the position of these muwazzafin. The deputy governor-general explained, "When we left Hebron and Bethlehem to the Jordanians, we asked the employees to stay there, because the administration in Gaza could not handle any new employees being added to the employees already working in it—after the withdrawal from Beersheba, Majdal, Faluja, and their surrounding villages, and the inclusion of the employees and teachers from these areas in the administration. Despite this, a large number of these employees came to Gaza with the Egyptian Army on their own responsibility, and all of them have asked for work. They were refused because they came without request or need, and there is no money in the budget to pay for additional salaries."[26] The Administration response to the petition stressed the importance of acting *like* a civil servant if one hoped to continue to be one. In flatly disobeying orders, these employees had shown themselves to be outside boundaries of service. Having chosen to leave their posts in Hebron and Bethlehem, the Administration implied, they were no longer civil servants and therefore not beneficiaries of the principle of continuity. Their employment was now "their own responsibility," not government's.[27] In addition to consolidating the contours of civil service, this argument had the added benefit of removing a potential financial obligation on a government ill-placed to take it on.

In the second half of the Administration (after the Israeli occupation in 1956) the financial circumstances of both the Administration and the Gaza Strip in general were much improved. Government became more willing and able to view the general problem of unemployment as a governmental responsibility. In this period, the number of positions increased dramatically, part of the emergence of civil service as a form of welfare. This transformation impacted both the style of application—as applicants began to add personal suffering to their list of qualifications—and working habits—as an overabundance of employees diminished the work required in any individual position. Thus, what one had to know to get a job and what one had to know to do a job shifted in this period.

When Hussam Abdullah, a refugee from Nazareth, sought to get a position that opened up in 1958 at the main Khan Yunis mosque, he did not simply apply for the job. In keeping with the new welfare discourse, he sent letters to the Khan Yunis *qadi* [judge], the head of the Islamic appeals court, and the administrative governor of the Khan Yunis district. In each letter he detailed his qualifications and his suffering in the years following the *nakba*. He put himself at the mercy of the addressee and left it up to him to determine the right course of action. Hussam appears to have been a skilled strategist, crafting his application to appeal to its various recipients, but not relying on any one party to get him the job he was after. In his letter to the Khan Yunis governor, for example, after explaining that he had graduated from al-Azhar, Hussam stated, "I am separated from my family because they have not sought refuge in any Arab country, but have stayed in our village until now. . . . I did not find any refuge except in this beloved Strip. I petition you to find me work, whether as a [Qur'an] reciter at government parties or any work that you think is appropriate that will give me an honorable life."[28] The governor forwarded this letter to the *awqaf* director for his consideration, as did the other recipients of the appeal. With support for Hussam coming from all directions, the awqaf director soon replied to the administrative governor, informing him that the appointment had been approved by the Supreme Muslim Council.[29] This process revealed Hussam to be adept at managing the new application climate, to be, as it were, habituated to the new demands of civil service hiring. Not everyone could have managed this dynamic so effectively.

The emergence of civil service as a welfare provider in Gaza paralleled a similar trend in Egypt itself. In both places this transformation meant that many more people were employed as civil servants than were actually needed to execute the work.[30] As one former department head told me, "They brought me twenty persons, what could I do for them, I had a complete staff? I gave every three or four a desk to sit at, gave them newspapers to read, and I sat with them to pass time."[31] Further, because Egypt promoted and funded widespread education, the number of university graduates needing jobs exploded. One former principal recalled, "The school that needed twenty teachers, they gave it forty teachers. . . . There were many graduates and they [the Egyptians] wanted to employ them. I, for example, needed twenty teachers and I made the timetable for twenty teachers. Then, another group would come because there was pressure on the government, so they hired four or five more teachers. So, I would change the timetable. Each time there was pressure on them they sent teachers."[32] The practice of overfilling the ranks of the civil service had contradictory effects. As the boundaries of civil service broadened, the domain became a presence in an ever-greater number of people's lives, perhaps making it easier to claim authority. Indeed, many people told me how, over the course of the fifty years considered here, the public had increasing occasion to deal with government and were ever more likely to do so directly rather than through the intermediary of such persons as *mukhtars*. That ever-greater numbers of people were likely to have a civil servant in the family certainly contributed to this transformation. At the same time, this expansion of the service also worked to devalue the jobs themselves, as the work became more makeshift, thereby undermining some of the dignity and respectability associated with government employment.[33]

Improving Civil Service Character: Education and Training

Whatever the working conditions, considerable effort was directed toward training civil servants in the habits of government service. Civil servants certainly identified such education as important. As a report from 1946 by the Second Division Civil Service Association put it, "Training should be carried out systematically and so planned as to provide the new entrant with practical instruction in actual duties, accompanied by individual supervision and proper guidance in general routine, coupled with study by the trainee of the text book, ordinances, regulations etc. relating to the branch of work in which he is engaged."[34] Debates about how and whether to deliver such training reveal uncertainty about the extent to which competence could in fact be taught and the extent to which it was an inherent quality.

One Mandate official stood squarely on the side of nature against nurture when he criticized a proposed training course for clerical officers designed to treat "the absence of powers of supervision [which] is a common and serious defect experienced generally with regard to senior clerks throughout the departments of Government."[35] Rejecting the idea that further training could help, the education director argued,

> It is of course obvious that "absence of powers of supervision," being a trait of character, is probably congenital and irremediable. If, however, the phrase is intended to mean "imperfect acquaintance with office organisa-tion," a judicious admixture of theory and practice might improve the present low standard of clerical work in this Government. I incline how-ever to the belief that the root of the evil is the recruitment of persons with inferior natural and educational endowments, the lack of incentive or compulsion to improve acquirements, inadequate salaries on first ap-pointment and poor prospects of advancement.[36]

This argument for a focus on better hiring rather than on more training implies a conviction that the boundaries of civil service were best policed at the outset of a possible career. Personal authority, in this view, could be converted into personnel authority, but the latter could not be produced from nothing. In practice, though, training was both necessary, as there was a limited pool of competent persons, and effective, at least in inculcating peo-ple in the demands of the service.

In the Mandate, such training was intended not simply to promote general civil service character and practice, but to develop sensibilities suited to a particular place within the civil service. For example, a course for messengers "which will fit them to improve their status," was explicitly limited in its aims: "Training should *not* aim primarily at creating aspirants to the Clerical Ser-vice. . . . Nevertheless, exceptionally intelligent and reliable messenger boys are always eligible from promotion to clerical or other classified posts."[37] A balance was sought between essential capacities, such as those exhibited by "exceptionally intelligent" boys, and those which could be taught. In addition to the vocational curriculum, which included bookkeeping, arithmetic, and English, the organization of the course was intended to teach service habits like duty and respectability. Training offered practical exposure not just to the work of service, but to the character it required.

That the Egyptian Administration also offered on-the-job training to its civil servants is evident in the personnel files of those employees, which include frequent references to training furloughs.[38] The available archives do not offer many details about such training, but the recollections of civil servants suggest that continued learning throughout one's career was vital. Muhammad Ghazi, for instance, told me that he advanced in his career by keeping the importance of training (including self-training) at the forefront of his awareness: "Someone who knows how to read the alphabet and is open-minded *can* be a writer; someone who can count from one to ten *can* be an accountant. Then he will acquire experience and open his mind for the job—he can know everything. . . . I worked in many positions. It was *like* I was born in all jobs, to the extent that I was a dictionary for everything. No one ever came and asked me about a certain subject that I didn't know about it—I had information about everything. I joined the health school and got a high school diploma through my experience [emphasis added]."[39] Like the Mandate education director, Muhammad assigned character a prominent place in the building of civil service competence. Unlike the director, however, he believed that such character could be developed. As a general rule, engagement, not expertise, marked the competent employee. Anyone who had a few basic skills and a willingness to work could be a civil servant in the service environment of the Administration.

Getting to Work: Spaces of Service

The space of service was as important as training and education, rules and regulations in the habituation of civil servants.[40] Whereas a training course came to an end, one went to one's office everyday. One walked the streets, guarded the classrooms, managed the clinics throughout one's career. The space of service both expressed ideas of service—articulating notions about how service should be rendered and what the nature of the relationship among the providers and the public should be—and acclimated civil servants and the public to the practices of such service, thereby mandating certain behaviors and styles. Furthermore, the ability of civil servants to display competence was connected not only to an individual employee's abilities, but to the setting as well. If the space of service complicated interactions with the public, it was that much more difficult for a civil servant to appear competent.

Office architecture had an obvious effect on the character and quality of service. In discussions about office layout, a tension emerged between the needs of one party, the civil service, for control of its space and productivity in its work and the needs of the other party, the public, for access to information and for efficiency in obtaining responses to its requests. These practices and regulations served in part to define these two categories, both in themselves and in relation to each other. The practices of office management contributed to creating a circumstance such that, when people in Gaza confronted one another, they did so through their locations as members (and in some ways representatives) of a group. The basic concerns about organizing space for good service seem to have been consistent from the British Mandate to the Egyptian Administration, but the stylistics differed. If in a Mandate office, service was best expressed through efficiency, in an Administration office it appears to have been expressed through personability, for example, in the cup of coffee, the kind word, the space of sociality.

The Mandate records of inspection of the Gaza land registry office highlight the attention paid to the details of office organization. They also disclose something about the robustness of the real estate market in Gaza and indicate that it was not only locals who were doing the buying. In 1934, for example, the inspecting officer recommended that the registry office be supplied with an iron safe to "enable the clerk in charge of cash to comply with article 58 sub para 3 of the Financial Regulations which authorise him to keep in his safe amounts not exceeding LP 50." Such a safe would not only bring the office into compliance with the law, but also improve the efficiency of the office, as the recommendation went on to note: "This is needed because with the increase of land-purchases in the Gaza Sub-District some people come with the train from the North which reaches Gaza between 12.30 and 1 P.M., and by the time they reach the Land Registry Office they find that the cash is closed and they get into difficulty about payment of fees."[41] The immediate interest behind this suggestion was to improve the level of service offered by the registry to members of the public. In addition, it would create another setting for interaction between clerk and private citizen, providing a reminder that office space helped habituate the public as much as civil servants. Rather than confronting a closed door and an abstracted notion of inefficient bureaucracy, people who came to the Gaza land office after it had a safe would deal with a clerk both authorized and able to provide services.

While the safe is an example of an easily solved problem, management of documents and files created greater difficulty. Here, where privacy was a central worry, the ability to protect papers from accidental exposure to the public came into direct conflict with the needs of people to have access to the office and its services. Soon after the land registry moved into Gaza's new government building in 1941, the director expressed his concern about problems with the office layout: "Room No. 2, the archives rooms, is completely filled, as will be seen from the plan, and cupboards containing valuable and irreplaceable documents, the property of private individuals, are scattered all over the office. An additional archives room is essential, as in any case it is impossible to place any more cupboards in the general office. . . . It is equally unsatisfactory to perpetuate the practice of placing such archives in the corridor and in the hall in which the public collect. . . . In addition the surveyors' stores have to be placed in a passage and are thus open to interference by members of the public."[42] As the director's comments make clear, the comportment of civil servants and the public was in part dependent on the proper arrangement of office space and of papers. These arrangements helped make it possible to distinguish appropriately between members of the public, in this case to give people access to only their own papers, and to manage the boundaries between civil service and that public. The placing of personnel papers in a public space created a concrete risk of interference; it also divulged the broader challenges of inculcating appropriate attitudes in all the participants in government.

The milling about of the public that so troubled government officials during the Mandate appears to have been par for the course during the Egyptian Administration. Less information is available about Egyptian-era office organization, but by comparing descriptions of office life in Egypt at this time with current practice in Gaza, it is possible to imagine what they might have been like. What I saw in offices in Gaza in the late 1990s nearly replicates a description of an Egyptian office written by an American sociologist in 1957: "As a visitor enters, indeed, he usually finds many others there before him, most of them whispering to each other quietly, yet not in a conspiratorial air; this is simply the way things are done, for in Egyptian government offices the really private audience is almost unknown. The official simultaneously handles three or four items of business and converses with three or four visitors or colleagues who stand or sit around his desk.

The number of such persons milling around an office gets to be considerable."[43] Today, private conversation is certainly not an attribute of people's interactions with government officials. When I was reading files in one civil servant's office, he would frequently turn to me in the middle of dealing with someone's case and tell me their whole story. This made me very uncomfortable, but it did not appear to bother anyone else involved. Service in Gaza, at least in the 1990s, did not require privacy.

This difference in organization reflects as well a difference in the display of competence. In the Mandate office, a civil servant's competence could be judged in part by his ability to guard information from public view. In the Administration it appears that competence was displayed through a public performance of knowledge. The openness of Administration offices likely had other practical effects as well. Perhaps the presence of other civilians in the offices of civil servants offered allies in dealings with government. To use my experience in Gaza's government offices as guide once again, not only did civil servants tell me people's stories, but people themselves often involved me in their interactions with officials, looking for agreement on the merits of their case or sympathy for the difficulty of their situation. As is clear from both Mandate and Administration attentions to the organization of space for service, the obligation to provide service was about more than the outcome of an encounter between a civil servant and a civilian. It was, in addition, about the quality of that encounter.

This encounter, though, sometimes required that a civil servant take an adversarial position vis-à-vis a member of the public; it also sometimes took personnel out of the confines of their offices. Civil servants had to know when to be forceful, and they relied on the authority engendered by their position and their person to make such confrontations effective. At the same time, such actions also worked to further solidify their authority. A seemingly minor story told to me by a former head of the Gaza municipality electricity department, Khaled 'Emad, manifests the import of this practice. Going into the field to respond to complaints or to inspect the quality of work was a regular part of his job, Khaled told me, and if he found problems, his force would be directed against the negligent employee. One day he was sent to investigate a complaint made by a citizen about garbage collection at his house. When Khaled and the complainant left the municipality offices, however, the citizen seemed to lose interest in the investigation: "The man invited me to smoke *argile* [waterpipe] with him at a café, and not to go to his house. I returned to the mayor and told him that the guy wanted me to smoke *argile* with him at the café instead of checking the worker's work. The mayor told me to leave the garbage at the man's house for a week as a fine."[44]

Whether the complaint was fabricated or the man simply thought his long-term service prospects would be better with Khaled as an ally is not clear. What is clear is that this infraction demanded a response. Further, and equally important to Khaled, the punishment had to be appropriate. As he told me, "I had contacts with the people and through my contacts I knew everyone—the good and the bad, the educated and the uneducated—and understood that you have to cope with them all. It is illogical to beat someone who asked you to smoke "*argile* with him at a café." So, being a good civil servant and treating the public with respect meant not only producing a pleasant encounter with government, but also exercising a carefully calibrated forcefulness meant to contribute to engendering respect among the population.

Career Advancement: Resemblance and Recognition, Opportunism and Equality

Having gotten a job, a civil servant's thoughts quickly turned to compensation and promotion.[45] Personnel files were filled with civil servants' complaints about their inadequate salaries, descriptions of their arduous duties, and self-reviews of their excellent performances. In their writing, civil servants participated in and produced a regulated civil service style that emphasized equivalence among civil servants even as it (sometimes contradictorily) sought to make a place for individual recognition. Equivalence suggested that competence was a general civil service attribute, while individual recognition identified the skills of particular civil servants. Just as the distinctions that civil service produced between and among the population created tensions, so too did the emphasis on resemblance among muwazzafin. The promotion process, fraught as it often was for personnel seeking raises, was a crucial mechanism in their continuing inculcation in the service milieu. The terms in which they pressed their cases and the grounds on which their appeals were accepted or denied were part of the terrain of habituation.

The British formed numerous commissions, issued multiple reports, and produced considerable regulation on the problem of managing promotions. In 1926, noting that the existing promotion system in the clerical service had "been formed under a system of opportunism" and that "inequalities and injustices are inherent in its constitution," an official committee proposed a new system of cadres, grades, and grounds for promotion.[46] The report recognized that many clerical officers might never want the added burden of administrative responsibility, preferring "the routine of their function because it involves them in little anxiety." Therefore, the proposed system was to include regular promotions within the clerical service that would "afford opportunity for a normal, if undistinguished, career." The cases of those exceptional civil servants who sought advancement to the highest grades would be considered by a promotion committee which "should have before it the complete history of each officer recommended by the Chief Secretary for consideration and the recommendation should be by way of vote of the majority. We can think of no more impartial way in which to decide the public values of individual officers."[47] Even in recognizing exceptional individual qualities, the system was supposed to operate according to a principle of equivalence.

The stated aim of the reorganization was to produce a fair system, one that created genuine equivalences among members of the service, offered guarantees for the future, and allowed distinguished individuals to be identified and rewarded. In order for these goals to be achieved it was necessary to produce sufficient knowledge about both individual civil servants and the general needs of the service and the public. Thus, this reorganization not only mandated a habitual resemblance among civil servants but promoted the proliferation of instruments of knowledge production, including more complete personnel files, assessment of public needs, etc. Information had to accumulate. For civil servants, it helped shape both the contours of and the conditions for acquiring a proper persona. The values of resemblance and recognition also defined the quality employee, one who was like other employees but who stood out as exemplary in his/her achievement of these common values.

The dynamics of equivalency and recognition remained similar during the Egyptian Administration.[48] Given the enormous financial constraints facing the Administration, though, opportunities for promotion were more limited than during the Mandate. Perhaps for this reason, Khalil Rishad, former director of *Diwan al-Muwazzafin*, described complaints about promotion as the most persistent difficulty in his job: "Most people's protests were about employees' promotions. Promotions created confusion, in that each employee felt that he had right to be promoted, which is natural. In order to make the employee accept that someone else deserved it more than him, I had to sit with him and make him understand. The problem is that the employee thinks that you are the one who is standing against his promotion."[49] As head of the department charged with employee affairs, Khalil had a personal investment in viewing the promotions process as fair and effective, yet he recognized that no system could be perfect ("Let me tell you something, there is no 100 percent justice"). In case of injustice, however, each employee had the right to have their complaints investigated. Khalil stressed, "If someone was wrongly or unfairly treated, we could know it, why?, because we were limited in number and we knew each other." His comments point to his interest in achieving a balance between correct procedure and situational flexibility.

While Khalil clearly had an investment in remembering the system as being largely fair, other retired employees had mixed memories. One retired police officer recalled that "the government was poor during the Egyptian period. It was selling the promotion process for money. The government had no money."[50] Memories of corruption were by no means limited to the Egyptian period; one person described *wasta* as part of every government: "Everything depends on relations and knowledge of people. If I know you, my issue is solved in no time. If I don't know anyone, I have to wait for a long time. And so on. This is the way it was in the days of the Egyptians, the Jews, whenever. . . . Today [under the PNA] if you want a job, you pay a thousand dollars to be hired."[51] And yet, a former railroad employee insisted that "when someone was going to be promoted we used to examine his file—and sometimes we did find some negative issues. Still, it was very rare to find someone who was taking bribes, who looked at women, who did not do his job as required. . . . If [the employee's record] was inadequate, then we stopped promoting him."[52] The promotions process no doubt included a bit of each. Civil servants needed to be able not only to handle members of the public, but also to maneuver among the complex relations of class and connection which could hinder or guarantee their own advancement.

Punishment

My focus thus far has been on civil servants' claims to competence and on the administrative techniques for producing and judging such qualities. Of course, not all civil servants *were* competent—or judged so by their superiors. Punishment for incompetence or willful disobedience was in part about weeding out bad civil servants, those who had been neither excluded during the hiring process nor corrected through training. Additionally, by identifying the boundaries of appropriate civil service behavior, punishment further taught good employees how to be better. The ways the civil service apparatus responded to mistakes, misbehavior, and insubordination by civil servants, as well as the ways these employees reacted to punishment, helped define the bureaucratic field.

Punishment again raised the question of whether competence was rooted in practice or in character. In cases where the harshest punishments, such as dismissal, were meted out, failures of both tended to be identified: "I have observed this man at his duties on numerous occasions and found that in addition to being grossly incapable and inefficient, he possesses an inflated ego which will always prevent him from stooping to absorb knowledge."[53] Displays of incompetence of both character and practice were highlighted to support arguments that rehabilitation or improvement was impossible. These sorts of charges refer directly to the ethos of office, to the ethical dispositions which were supposed to be part of civil service personas. In judging the character of these employees, their superiors, colleagues, and even the public called them ethically deficient. Not surprisingly, fired civil servants often rejected these charges.

In one such case, a former station clerk at the Gaza railway station (Khalil Hammanieh) wrote to the chief secretary complaining about his dismissal.[54] He recounted the events leading up to his punishment, starting with his arrest for rape, including his suspension from duty, ultimate acquittal, and finally dismissal after the resolution of the case. In his complaint, Hammanieh noted that he was fired before his acquittal and that the acquittal removed any grounds for firing him: "The gross misconduct which, as the

G.M. says, was the immediate cause of my being dispensed with, is non-existent, otherwise I would not have been acquitted by the Court of Justice. . . . without the false charge against me there would not have been any cause for my discharge and in view of my clear acquittal my being dispensed with is rendered illegal."

The administrative response to this complaint indicated that while Hammanieh had legal justification for claiming that a dismissal in response to the rape charge would have been improper, his acquittal was not entirely "clear" nor was the charge used as the "immediate cause" (though it seems pretty obvious it was the underlying cause).[55] The general manager noted that Hammanieh was acquitted despite the fact that the girl in question had accused him of assaulting her and that medical examination had indicated that she had been raped: "The fact that he married the girl before the case was heard, thereby rendering her evidence inadmissible, had, I believe, a bearing on the finding."[56] The general manager stated that he was fired not because of the rape charge but because of other charges associated with the event—that he had aided her in traveling without a ticket and that he had taken her into the railway rest room in Gaza—as well as his past conduct, which included two fines, two warnings, and eighteen cautions in his service file.

The general manager closed his letter by stating, "It being apparent that Hammanieh was not *of a type* who should be retained in Railway service, his services were terminated with effect from the date of his interdiction. . . . His discharge from the service was decided upon independently from the charge of rape preferred against him by the Police [emphasis added]." Despite the distinction made between the rape charge and the dismissal (necessary for legal purposes no doubt) it seems obvious that this charge was instrumental in making it "apparent" that Hammanieh was not of an appropriate "type" to be a civil servant. He was fired for failures of both practice and character. The ethical violations at issue here were not limited to an ethics of office, but charges of this sort were central to the case against him. Having so thoroughly failed to acquire good civil service habits and to develop a proper persona, Hammanieh proved himself to be irretrievably outside the limits of the service domain.

As during the Mandate, punishment during the Egyptian Administration expressed an interest in both practice and character, that is, doing the job well and being the right kind of person to do it. During the Administration, however, there seems to have been a bit more reluctance to conclude that someone was not civil servant material. Perhaps in part because of the importance of civil service work as social welfare, administrators might have been hesitant to deny someone the opportunity to receive a salary. In the nearly one hundred Egyptian-era personnel files I read, I found no cases of employees being dismissed (though there were instances of employees of the Egyptian Administration being fired during the Israeli occupation).[57]

Dismissal was always the extreme end of a range of possible responses to civil service misbehavior. Most such misbehavior was relatively minor, and the punishments were accordingly limited. The personnel files of Gaza's civil servants are filled with instances of people being warned about their behavior, fined a few days' salary, or given similar sanction. Even in these lesser punishments what was at issue was more than the infractions of certain regulations. What made punishment an imperative was what the infractions evidenced in the way of failures of service habituation: not being respectful, not doing one's duty, dishonoring the service. The ethos of office that stabilized civil service practice could be disrupted by such misbehavior by individual civil servants. In these cases, it was precisely the disposition of a civil servant qua civil servant that was at issue. Given the importance of authoritative personnel to the broader authority of government, its protection demanded attention even to apparently minor threats to its stability.

Mariam Samira, a nurse at Nasser Hospital in Khan Yunis, was sanctioned four times over the not quite four years of her employment in the Administration (she was hired in November 1963).[58] The causes for the sanctions were inventory deficits, in which cases she was fined the cost of the missing object, and fighting with her colleagues. In the most serious of these instances, the director of the Health Administration recommended that she be fined two weeks' salary. Such a large fine required the approval of the governor-general,[59] who decided to dock Mariam's pay only one week—still a substantial penalty. The cause of this severe penalty was that Mariam had hit another nurse at the hospital, as the health director explained to the civil affairs director, who oversaw the civil service commission: "I am sending you a copy of the investigation papers that were sent to me by the director of Nasser Hospital . . . in the matter of nurse [Mariam Samira] hitting the nurse [Rana Zeinab] inside the hospital on June 14, 1964. The above-mentioned nurse hit her colleague and cursed her in front of the patients. This behavior does not conform to the honor of the nursing profession, is considered to be a violation of her colleague's rights, and harms the reputation of the hospital. Therefore, I have decided to deduct two weeks (fourteen days) from her salary and to give her a final warning that she will be fired if she does something like this again."[60] The infraction was viewed as especially serious, touching as it did on the honor of both the nursing profession in general and the reputation of the hospital in particular. Not only was this action in and of itself dishonorable, but it took place in front of patients, thereby impacting the public perception of the civil service.

Concern not only about a particular infraction, but its possible ramifications is evident in many punishments levied against civil servants. In one case, a department director requested that an employee be transferred out because of his "lack of cooperation and laziness in his work [and] his recalcitrance in implementing the directives and commands that come to him from us." The director argued that "if an employee like this were to remain in the directorate it would spread the spirit of recalcitrance and slowness among the other employees."[61] Whereas in the case of Mariam's sanction, the concern was about the possible effect of such misbehavior on the public, here the concern was about effects on other civil servants.

In a dispute between an employee and his direct superior, the principal issue was that of respect. The employee, Da'ud Khaled, was four hours late to work one day and refused to answer his superior's questions about his absence. In response to this infraction, the director of civil affairs informed the governor-general that he intended to dock his pay two days (double the sanction his boss had recommended) because "this action is a severe disrespect."[62] In Da'ud's statement about his behavior, he claimed he refused to answer questions because his boss had insulted him in front of other employees, saying, "You are always late. You are a *himar* [donkey], and you don't fulfill your responsibilities."[63] His boss denied this accusation, a denial that was supported by other witnesses. It doesn't matter very much who actually said what; what is interesting for my purposes is the general agreement about the nature of the problem. To treat someone with disrespect, to cause him to lose face in front of his colleagues, was a serious violation of workplace standards. Such disrespect not only reflected on the character of the offender, but could impact the entire workplace and therefore the whole civil service domain.

Retirement Benefits and Struggles Over Civil Service

The promise of a pension on retirement was one of the clearest personal benefits of a civil service career, a benefit which, like the monthly salary of a working civil servant, distinguished these employees from the larger population, which had no such social security. The British are praised by Gazans for continuing to pay pensions to Mandate civil servants long after the government for which they worked had ceased to exist.[64] Conflicts that arose during both the Mandate and the Administration over who was eligible for pensions suggest that the definition of a career in service was often determined in the character of its closure. Not surprisingly, it was in relation to potential government expenditures that it became crucial to define with precision who was a civil servant. Whether one received a pension and what sort of pension one might get determined the conditions of life in the aftermath of a career and also cast light back on how the career itself was evaluated, by both employers and personnel.

During the Mandate, two major pension conflicts formed around categories of gender and religion. Specifically, should married women civil servants (whose husbands were presumed to support them) be allowed to receive pensions? And should personnel of the *shari'a* courts be considered civil servants like any others and therefore eligible for pension benefits? The issues were somewhat different in each case, but they both exhibit the stakes of service definition. There was a long tradition of treating female civil servants differently from their male counterparts by paying them lower salaries and restricting the positions open to them. The problem posed by allowing these women to receive pensions was "the possibility of husband and wife, both civil servants, drawing two full pensions at the same time."[65] This problem was ultimately resolved by forcing women who married to resign their positions and therefore remove themselves from the pensionable ranks but permitting them to be rehired on a "temporary" basis, thus meeting government needs for their work.[66]

This resolution addressed the financial concerns posed by married women's presence in the civil service, but it did not solve some of the other associated problems, such as "the embarrassment caused to other members of the staff and to members of the public by their presence in a certain condition."[67] That pregnant women were thought to pose a disruption to the proper functioning of the office is a further reminder that the contours of civil service required not simply the positive development of civil service habits, but the exclusion of discomforting presences.[68] We saw in the last chapter how gender differences impacted civil servants' self-conceptions; we see here how much anxiety those differences could produce in civil service space. Concern about issues of propriety continued, leading to a recommendation, in 1936, that married women no longer be rehired in the clerical service since "it is now possible to obtain competent shorthand typists without difficulty and in my opinion the only grounds for the retention of married women officers is the impossibility of replacing them within a reasonable period of time by competent shorthand typists."[69] The problem of pensions brought to the fore a much broader set of concerns about women's employment and its stakes for the civil service.[70]

In the matter of the shari'a court employees, the principal problem was their working conditions, particularly that they operated under the authority of the Supreme Muslim Council, not the high commissioner.[71] This difference of authority was enough, according to the colonial secretary, to render them ineligible for civil service pensions. It was, he said "clearly undesirable that there should be created in Palestine a special class of pensionable officers who could not be retired for inefficiency or compulsorily retired on grounds of age; and, indeed, whom the High Commissioner would have no power to dismiss in the case of misconduct or misbehavior even when of a criminal nature."[72] The concern here was clearly about authority, both the articulation of regulated authority within the civil service and the potential challenge that other forms of authority might pose for the former. The Palestinian Civil Service Association tried to minimize those concerns, highlighting how firmly inside civil service shari'a judges were. In its petition to government on their behalf, the association stressed that this position was the oldest government post (going back thirteen hundred years) and that it had always been pensionable before. Furthermore, the association noted, "Members of the Shari'a Courts are subject to Government Regulations. Their whole time is at the disposal of Government. Their salaries are paid wholly from Government funds."[73] In the crucial areas, the association argued, these employees were like other civil servants.[74]

In the letters that went back and forth for several years among government officials, the civil servants' association,[75] the Supreme Muslim Council, and shari'a court officers, these points continued to be debated, with each party indicating another reason these officials either should or should not be considered civil servants.[76] Not long after this exchange, for reasons and under circumstances that are not clear from the archival record, government decided to grant the pensions, but under a special ordinance. In this way, the immediate problem was solved, but the underlying question about the definition of civil service was not entirely resolved.[77] In the case of "religious affairs" employees, the resolution was always uncertain—these employees ultimately *were* civil servants in the Mandate, and this categorization was also always a problem.

In the Administration, religious services did not pose the same problems that they did during the Mandate. These employees continued to operate under somewhat different conditions than other civil servants—their personnel files were (and are) kept in the awqaf administration, which had direct authority other them—but they received pensions without apparent problem.[78] Even where there was no debate about whether employees were civil servants, what kind of civil servant they were could make a tremendous difference for their retirement. I refer here to the difference between the government and UNRWA as civil service employers. In regards to pensions, the difference is this: government provides a monthly pension from retirement until death, whereas UNRWA pays a lump sum to its retiring employees, with which they can do what they like. Many people I spoke with told me they had not realized the importance of this difference until they retired. One person said that through the course of his career with UNRWA he had never considered working for government because the UNRWA salary was much better, but that "now that I am retired I regret not working for the government because UNRWA is not fair with employees in terms of retirement. . . . The government gives the employee a life pension, which guarantees that he would not have to ask people for money. Now I am facing this problem. I have spent the money I received on the education of my son.

Thank God, my son is employed now, but what if he wasn't?"[79] Remembering that the persona of the civil servant, and even the inculcation of that persona, continued throughout people's lives, these pension disparities could also make a difference in people's dispositions. Both benefits offered an opportunity for financial security, but one continued the same sort of security as the career, that is, a guaranteed, although relatively low, monthly salary. The second afforded the opportunity to begin a new venture—in the last chapter I mentioned a retired UNRWA employee who had purchased and cultivated land with his retirement money—but also entailed a risk of outliving the benefit.

It might seem that retired civil servants would no longer be concerned about the authoritativeness of their personas, about how well they embodied the various sorts of bureaucratic competence. Yet, as they worried about their futures in retirement, they also revealed a desire that they continue to be perceived in this same light. As one retiree explained his pleasure at having worked for the government rather than UNRWA, "When you retire from UNRWA, it gives you your money. Maybe the retiree is less powerful in the house, maybe his sons asked him to build a house, or they wanted to marry, so the money goes easily. But I go and receive my salary at the first of the month. I don't need my son or my daughter to give me money. So I keep my dignity until the last day of my life."[80] Retirees' authority might no longer directly matter to government, but it clearly continued to matter to them.

Conclusion

Across the breadth of their careers, civil servants both acquired and exhibited competence and authority. The different aspects of competence, the distinct repertoires of authority, highlight both the expansiveness of bureaucratic authority and the persistent challenges it faced. Debates about who could be a civil servant—what sort of job, what kind of person—and then what made a competent civil servant—what kinds of practice, comportment, attitudes— were often the ground for working out formations of authority. While civil servants were often as worried, or even more so, about their own positions as the stability of government, to the extent that they developed authoritative personas in the quest for personal advancement, they also helped produce governmental authority. To the extent that government sought to harness social and personal authority for its own purposes, it contributed to the strength of such forms. Each deployment of authority, furthermore, provided an opportunity for challenges. The processes of defining, elaborating, and challenging bureaucratic competence and authority were always inflected by the particular governing conditions in Gaza—its demands and its limitations.

PART TWO

Tactical Practice and Government Work

5

SERVICE IN CRISIS

> In the Turkish period [during World War I], there was starvation.
> People were quarreling over an orange. . . . We were starving during
> the period of the Turks and blessed during the period of the British.
> . . . Though they were occupying us, we led a life of ease and comfort.
>
> ABU SAID, REFUGEE FROM HAMMAMA, GAZA CITY, 23 FEBRUARY 1999

> When we first left our villages [in 1948] there was starvation and
> hunger. . . . We remained about four or five months with no food or
> supplies or anything. . . . After four months, an agency came—the
> Quakers—and started to distribute flour, supplies, blankets and
> things like this. . . . They opened supply centers . . . and the people
> went to these centers every fifteen days or every month and received
> flour, sugar, and supplies.
>
> ABU NADIM, REFUGEE FROM YIBNA, GAZA CITY, 22 FEBRUARY 1999

If the domains of filing and personnel illuminate formations of authority that relied on repetition, reiteration, and regularity, the particular services these instruments worked to provide highlight practices of tactical government that often appeared singular, limited, and even irregular. The work of service provision in Gaza further elucidates distinctions between authority and legitimacy and clarifies the ways in which Mandate and Administration government produced the former without the latter. Services occupied a curious position in Gaza's governing dynamic. In many ways, they lay at the heart of government's relation with the population. At the same time, both governments evinced considerable anxiety about getting too involved in service provision (though what counted as being "too involved" changed over time). Services were, then, both the center and the periphery of a governing relationship. They were both the most ubiquitous site of encounter between civil servants and the public and an obligation to be avoided when possible. In a dynamic of tactical government, the apparent paradoxes of this condition were, while not resolved, productive for the work of rule.

This chapter focuses on what I call crisis services, those services—such as food and shelter—which were understood to be temporary, brought on by extraordinary need, and destined to be removed from the service domain at some future time (even if that time has never yet come). Crisis services highlight the process of defining both *need* and *service*, as well as movements between these categories. Everyone needs to eat, but what counts as adequate and appropriate food requires elaboration. When needs come to be thought of as services, it is a result of a further process whereby responsibility for their fulfillment shifts, from personal to public, from family to society, from community to government. In the case of crisis services, this movement was not conceived as permanent. Precisely because these services were defined as exceptional, as beyond the "proper" service domain, they produced acute anxieties in governments that were always anxious about extending the domains of their obligation.

They produced anxiety for other reasons as well; the very crises that made these services necessary indicated that the population was unsettled, in a dangerous condition, constituting a possible threat. During both periods, there was a great deal of discussion about such threat, and not only on the part of government officials. It was security concerns as much as governing compassions that made the Mandate and the Administration venture into the realm of providing food and shelter to the Gazan population. To a certain extent, then, one source of anxiety trumped another, as security considerations kept governments involved in a broadening array of services. If crisis services were marked by both security and compassion, they were also distinguished by their location on the cusp of formal government. These practices consistently traversed the boundary—and called into question the extent to which such a boundary was clear—between the state and society.[1] They were connected to community relations as much as to government procedures and regulations.

These crisis-driven interventions into the service domain must also be understood in relation to the dynamic of abeyance. With their tactical focus on averting threat, the claims of these services were limited. In part because of the apparently exceptional quality of this service provision, even as it produced anxieties, its stakes were not always clear. In conditions where service recipients felt at risk, their attention was often (though importantly not always) focused on the immediate fulfillment of basic needs and less on the significance of their participation in a broader governing regime. The ways distraction and deferral entered into the details of service provision are made clear in these crisis services.

Crisis servicing also highlights the practice of an ethic of care that governed relations among people and between people and government. The phrase "ethic of care" was famously used by Carol Gilligan to describe an image of a network of relations, a "nonhierarchical vision of human connection," as opposed to a hierarchically imagined one, "an order of inequality" in which relationships "appear inherently unstable and morally problematic."[2] I mean it here, however, more in the sense of what Foucault describes as the Greek problematic of "the care of the self." Such care was, Foucault argues, "ethical in itself; but it implies complex relationships with others insofar as this *ethos* of freedom is also a way of caring for others. . . . it is also the art of governing."[3] As such, this ethic was "a way of being and of behavior. It was a mode of being for the subject, along with a certain way of acting, a way visible to others."[4] And, importantly, this practice of care *was* hierarchical.

Gaza, of course, was not ancient Greece, and the demands which underpinned its similar ethic of care were not identical. In Gaza, this ethic was linked to shifting definitions of obligation and relation in the transformation of services. In the deployment of, and transformations in, practices of care, we can see how tactics shaped the practice of both persons and government. The practice of care, whether delivered as a service or imagined as a social practice, was of considerable importance in subject formation. When governments responded to crises through service provision they, like the population, benefited from increased stability, from strengthened bonds, and from an enhanced (though still limited) capacity to affect the social, political, and economic environment. The transformations in the practice of care that were part of the trajectory of crisis services in the Mandate and the Administration did not make this practice less hierarchical. On the contrary, as the pathways of service became more clearly marked, more bureaucratically codified, certain networks of hierarchical relations became even more elaborate, revealing just one of the ways in which crisis services always did more than respond to immediate need.

The Contours of Crisis

Probably the single most wrenching event in Palestinian history was the *nakba*, but this was by no means Palestine's only upheaval. When British rule in Palestine began in 1917, much of the country—and certainly Gaza—was in very poor shape. It took three major battles for British forces to defeat the Turks in Gaza, in the course of which the city was decimated and "many [Gazans] were forced to leave by the Turks, who feared the population would get in the way of the troops."[5] The Gaza Municipality records this expulsion as "the Gaza Emigration," saying "this disastrous event has been engraved in the minds and souls of the Gazans."[6]

The years of the Mandate were marked by one crisis after another—political, economic, security—often brought on by the intensifying conflict between Zionist settlers and Palestinian Arabs. There were riots in 1921, 1929, and 1933 and full-scale revolt in 1936–39 (by Arabs) and 1946 (by Jews). The 1929 riots, sparked by rumors that Jews were planning to take over the *Haram al-Sharif* in Jerusalem, provoked a serious reconsideration of British policy in Palestine, as did the 1936 revolt. Each time political unrest erupted into violence, British administrators sent commissions to the country to probe the underlying causes, whether peasant poverty and landlessness, displacement by Zionist settlement, frustration over British support for the Zionist project.[7] The discussions surrounding these commissions show that Mandate officials were acutely aware that poor living conditions could produce unrest and could lead to security threats. The solution most often imagined for such problems, though, was the prospect of development, conceived as a private, market process, not a government project.

Palestine's crises did provoke occasional, and exceptional, relief efforts;

during the 1936–39 rebellion, for instance, assistance "was given at first to families where the breadwinner was detained under Emergency Regulations and was later extended to families which suffered indirectly from the prevailing conditions—the unemployed and the chronic poor."[8] In the later years of the Mandate, concern for such chronic conditions and a broader empirewide interest in development and welfare led to a consideration of government-sponsored development. As the report of a committee convened to study the question stated, though, the crisis conditions of the country severely constrained the possibilities for such a government project.

The report noted that any major development program would require an expansion of existing government departments, "the normal departmental organization forming the nucleus from which such expansion would take place."[9] In Palestine, however, there were many departments that lacked such a stable nucleus: "Owing to the disturbances and on financial grounds, the departments in question have been reduced in strength to such an extent that, far from being in a position to expand, they are unable to discharge, with that degree of efficiency which might reasonably be expected of them, even those day to day duties which now fall to their lot." Before the question of development could be really tackled in Palestine, that is, the crises which made ordinary government so difficult needed to be resolved. As the report put it, "The service rendered by the various departments of Government fall short of the reasonable requirements of the country." The authors of the report were convinced that not only could Palestine not afford what it called "luxury services," but under existing circumstances "a far longer list of activities, of practically equal importance and in many cases vital to the development of the country, must be abandoned as beyond the power of Government to undertake." While in the first part of the Mandate the government hoped to be able to control and conclude crises in the country, by its end this hope seemed vain. Indeed, the British government relinquished the Mandate not because it had successfully completed its tasks but out of frustration.

Under the Egyptian Administration, exceptional conditions were the norm throughout, and crisis services had to expand accordingly. In this post-1948 service expansion, defining and categorizing the population posed an acute set of problems, as Gaza's native population was dwarfed by the influx of refugees. On the one hand, distinctions between the two groups were obvious and codified by the United Nations. The UNRWA definition of a Palestinian refugee, finalized in 1952, was a person "whose normal residence was Palestine for a minimum of two years preceding the outbreak of the conflict in 1948 and who, as a result of this conflict, has lost both his home and means of livelihood."[10] On the other hand, this categorical distinction between people who had lost their homes and those who had not was not an accurate accounting of need. Much of the native Gazan population, many of whom had lost not home, but land and their means of livelihood, was as destitute as the refugees. But, lacking the label refugee, they were not eligible for most UNRWA services.[11]

The crisis facing the Gazan population was immediately seen as being about more than basic needs. It was also about a potential decay in morals and possible emerging security threats. In the first years of the Administration, Egyptians and international observers alike offered sobering evaluations of the decline in values and social capacity among Gaza's population. The Egyptian newspaper *al-Ahram* described the refugees as "living in a society with no religion, no morals, and no community life."[12] Such an evaluation may seem extreme and indeed does not entirely correspond to other reports about refugee sociality.[13] This kind of response to the presence of large numbers of "people out of place"[14]—displacement provoking not only compassion, but fear and even revulsion—is in fact a common response to refugee crises.[15] In Gaza this concern was neither abstract nor only social. Egyptians worried that, wittingly or not, an uncontrolled population might put the Egyptian government at risk. Border crossings to retrieve food and possessions might provoke an Israeli attack. Political and or military organizing to reverse the dispossession of 1948 could be even more threatening. Having suffered a bad defeat, the Egyptian government had no interest in a confrontation with Israel; Palestinians did not necessarily share that reluctance.

Whatever its political and security concerns, the Egyptian Administration described its interest as humanitarian. The Department of Refugee Supervision, Government Assistance, and Social Affairs (henceforth Refugee Affairs) explained its work as follows: "Our mission for these people is humanitarian in the first degree. . . . We need to be close to the attitudinal currents that are moving among the people. And we have to expend great effort in spreading reassurance and hope among them in order to stop the decline into depravity or the rot of Satan or the fall into destruction which has already afflicted some of them because of the [difficult conditions] in which they live."[16] UNRWA, in its annual reports, also expressed concern about "the psychologically debilitating effect of giving relief over time" and about the "development of a professional refugee mentality." It reported some of the (mis)behaviors that accompanied the refugee condition: "To increase or prevent decreases in their ration issue, they eagerly report births, sometimes by passing a new-born baby from family to family, and reluctantly report deaths, resorting often to surreptitious burial to avoid giving up a ration card."[17]

UNRWA worried further about the long-term negative effects of unemployment and poverty: "A refugee who has lost, or has never acquired, the habit of self-reliance and self-supporting work will be a useless burden on the community, whether he is later to be repatriated or resettled."[18] By the later years of the Administration, the immediate threat of starvation or exposure was much diminished, but the threat of idleness remained: "One of the tragic aspects of the life of a refugee is that he often has nothing to do. This is . . . particularly true in the Gaza strip, where 300,000 people are concentrated in a small area of largely unproductive desert land. . . . Although a man may not be aware of it, the debilitating effects of ten years without regular work is considerable."[19] Gazans themselves, especially natives, expressed similar concerns about the corrosive effects of relief. As Salim Rashid said to me, "From my point of view, and I say it to everybody, it was better if there was no agency [wikala]. Prophet Mohammed said 'the high hand is better than the low hand.' What does this mean? It means that the one who gives is better than the one who takes."[20] Another person contrasted the dignity of Palestinians before 1948 with their conditions after receiving UNRWA aid: "After UNRWA started to distribute rations, the Palestinian started to take. He started begging—and morals were destroyed."[21]

While UNRWA and Administration descriptions of the deleterious psychological and moral impact of poverty were constrained by their measured bureaucratic language, judgments by native Gazans were sometimes much harsher. This harshness reveals deep-seated tensions within this population. While few people spoke in great detail about problems between native Gazans and refugees, one elderly woman I talked with, Hanan, did not hesitate to express her opinions. Hanan saw clear connections between "bad habits" and impoverished living conditions:

The refugees were really in a catastrophic condition. When they first came to Gaza, they occupied schools and took refuge everywhere. Nothing was prepared for them. Then camps were made for them; the camps, of course, offered very humiliating conditions. . . . In addition, there was the matter of begging—for provisions. Can you imagine, a mother, father, and son going to ask for food? The child carried the basket and begged. This, of course, was reflected in the psychology of the child, how they taught him to beg. It was a terrible thing. . . . There was an unimaginable decline in values. . . . This in fact had a very negative impact. I always say that our country has gone, but we can regain it in a fierce battle—but the morals of the people cannot be restored in one, two, or three days as the structure was corrupted. . . . Actually we are in bad need of awareness and I always call for going to houses and educating women there.[22]

Hanan also described the "class rancor" (haqd al-tabaqi) between refugee and native Gazans. She suggested that the effects of this rancor remain very much alive today: "Even when the boys of the camps were throwing stones, they said that the boys of the city [that is, nonrefugees] cover the stone with tissue before they throw it at the Israelis. This is strange. Really we dealt with them as human beings regardless of anything else and they were in bad need of care. They, however, remain wretched."[23] Given Hanan's disparaging comments about refugees, her surprise at expressions of hostility toward native Gazans seems, if not disingenuous, then at least naive. Even if Hanan's comments were more harsh than most—and they were—they reflected widespread sentiments among native Gazans about the impoverished character as well as the material conditions of refugees. Such comments also reflected the anxiety on the part of the natives about their new position in a population defined by poverty. That the nakba had produced a social crisis was not only an evaluation by outsiders, but was a concern among the population as well.

Providing for Oneself and Caring for Neighbors: Getting Food in the British Mandate

The British Mandate began and ended in crisis, but at least so far as food was concerned its middle was relatively stable. The beginning of the Mandate followed the devastation of World War I, which decimated Gaza City. In the final years of Ottoman rule, Gaza had been a peaceful, relatively prosperous town, though such serenity defined only one moment amid a history marked by conflicts. The life of this "modest stone-and-mud-built town"[24] was shattered by the war, in which Gaza became a frontline zone in the struggle for control of the Middle East. Caught in the war and in a broader regional famine, the population faced starvation.[25] Musa, an elderly man who was a child during the war, described these hardships: "The Turks used to take our fathers to the army. My mother remained alone. She had three hens that laid eggs. She used to sell the eggs in the market for 1 piaster, or 2$^1/_2$ piasters, and with the money buy turmus, *jummaiz* [dried sycamore], and five handfuls of flour. We would mix it all in a bowl with a pitcher of water and devour it. We were very hungry, thirsty, and imprisoned. There was no work."[26] Saying that he would not wish this suffering on his worst enemy, Musa commented further, "An orange rind lying on the ground covered in sand, I would pick it up and wipe it off on my clothes and eat it, I was so hungry. Hunger is cruel and life was terrible." Under conditions of acute hunger, orange rinds and flour mixed with dried sycamore become substitutes for the "figs, *sabr* [prickly pear], grapes, and everything"[27] that Gazans remember as their normal diet during the Mandate.

How exactly the transition from the cruelty of hunger to a life of relative stability was managed is not well documented. Certainly there was some limited food servicing when the British entered Palestine. This government intervention was trumpeted in British propaganda efforts. *Jaridat Filastin*, the official paper of British military forces, commented in 1918 on British efforts to aid the needy in Palestine: "[The military administration] has spent a lot of money to assist the unfortunate and the industrial sector, giving out seeds and food to those in need, and establishing camps to aid the poor and unfortunate in all parts of the country."[28] Despite this early activism, Mandate officials appear to have relied primarily on market forces, which normalized after the war, and the promise of development to resolve the crisis.[29] That land in the Gaza area was, as a British official noted, "highly fertile,"[30] made this a more realistic proposition.[31]

Gazan refugees from villages in the surrounding area often remember life during *ayyam al-balad* (village days) as being "like gold." They emphasize communal assistance and self-sufficiency—the ethic of care, for oneself and for others—as the primary mechanisms for ensuring that people had enough food. These memories are certainly at least partly nostalgic longings, colored by the dislocation and loss of home which occurred in 1948, and they cannot be assumed to be entirely accurate depictions of life in a Palestinian village prior to the nakba.[32] On the contrary, as I have noted, the problems of peasant poverty, indebtedness, and growing landlessness were concerns throughout the Mandate and repeatedly noted in government-commissioned reports. While some peasants lived well, such as a farmer described in American Friends Service Committee (AFSC) records who "owned a bit of fruit trees too and on his earnings they lived in relative comfort in the little village before fright scattered them and their neighbors,"[33] others experienced conditions of, as the Hope-Simpson report put it, "extreme poverty."[34]

Life for much of the Palestinian peasantry during the Mandate was patently difficult. For the most part, however, it was better than the famine that had come before or the total dislocation and the attendant threat of starvation that came after. People's memories cannot be dismissed as mere fantasies, and they reflect dramatic changes in self-sufficiency, abundance, and the practice of care.[35] They also reflect changing definitions of need and luxury, as people's ordinary diets were transformed over time. The ethic of care as social practice worked during the Mandate in part because of what Gazans described as their "simple life." As Abu Hassan, a retired UNRWA teacher from a village near Majdal, explained, "One lived a simple, blessed life. Today when I go to buy things for the house I buy big sacks of sugar, flour, and rice, etc. In *ayyam al-balad* I only used to buy one or two kilos total, a pound of rice or sugar, half sack of flour. I didn't have to buy tea or coffee, which I buy in kilos now, because it was only drunk and offered to guests at the mukhtar's place. Guests were offered fruit when they came at home."[36] This comment underscores the social aspect of the definition of needs. What counts as abundance or as a minimum requirement changes over time and varies according to perspective.[37] While today one is invariably served both coffee and tea when visiting a Palestinian home—and both are certainly felt to be basic necessities—during the Mandate they were luxury items.

Within the Palestinian population, there were material disparities in people's abilities to be self-sufficient. While there were many small peasant holdings in the Gaza area, as in the rest of Palestine, large landowners provided employment to many peasants who either had no land or who could no longer live off its income and produce. Amal, who was from such a wealthy family, compared life in the Mandate to current dependency: "Nowadays if you have money you eat. If you don't have money you can't eat. . . . We had all the lands in the world. Everyone had land—not only a *dunam* [approximately one-quarter of an acre] but a lot of land. . . . We lived in well-being, eating from the produce of the land, working the land, planting, reaping and eating. . . . We worked in our lands . . . and we had also workers who harvested the land with us. We hired peasants for harvesting because we had a lot of land."[38] Even as Amal offered this as a picture of universal prosperity, her description divulges a key feature of the ethic of care—its hierarchies. In marked distinction to Gilligan's claim that care is about interconnection rather than inequality, the practice of care in Gaza was both interconnected *and* unequal. Even as Amal's family may have had "all the lands in the world," not "everyone had land." Some people were workers who harvested other people's land. The conditions of hierarchy and inequality, far from undermining the ethic of care, were integral to it.

As part of a broader milieu in which *zakat* (charity) was valued, those who had land shared its bounty with those who did not. Abu Hassan described how the landless took what they needed from their neighbors' crops: "I remember when we were living in our village and had land that we used to plant. All the neighbors used to take vegetables for free. They used to take it themselves and we were happy; because we considered it as *zakat*. People were close to each other as one family."[39] Of course, as Abu Hassan's description reminds us, relations of inequality do not imply a simple distribution of power. The landless that he mentioned were not given this food; they "used to take it themselves." Abu Hassan and his kind might have been "happy" about it, but they seem not to have been entirely in charge of it. Still, the ethic of care in the Mandate appeared largely successful in managing the provision of food to the people of Gaza.

While the government tried to stay away from food services, there were times when involvement was necessary. Sometimes local events demanded a degree of intervention, for example, the aid provided during the 1936–39 revolt noted above and the distribution of water during a 1947 drought.[40] The crisis which most forcefully brought food into the domain of government service during the Mandate was, however, not a local crisis of hunger, but rather the much larger extraordinary circumstances created by World

War II. During the war British officials regulated food production and supply in Palestine and all over the Middle East.[41] Even with this increased intervention, British rationing policy mandated maintaining "normal channels of trade" to the extent permitted by the requirements of control.[42] In the efforts to maintain this balance, some of the tensions inherent in the tactical government of the Mandate came into play. To the extent that government did involve itself in food distribution and in the practice of care, it did so as a "singular" intervention, one motivated by crisis and intended to end as soon as possible. As it happens, this intervention facilitated the much larger project of food aid undertaken by the AFSC in the immediate aftermath of 1948. The Quakers relied on the village population records developed to manage this wartime rationing to help determine the number of refugees.

Government, market, and municipality all had a role to play in the Mandate food distribution network, and these roles were sometimes at odds. Some municipalities appealed to government to be allowed to assume greater control over the sale of goods within their jurisdictions. In Majdal, for example, the municipality was granted permission to monopolize the sale of flour, an enterprise funded by local merchants.[43] It then sought to expand the range of commodities under its control. The Gaza district commissioner supported this request and forwarded it for approval to the chief secretary, but the latter was wary about the effects on private business of such municipal expansion.[44] The district commissioner's arguments in favor of permitting municipal control of sales illuminate a transition that was under way in the practice of the ethic of care, wherein this practice was, at least momentarily, transferred to the site of government. In the case of Majdal, the district commissioner argued that the "public benefit" of municipal control far outweighed the potential "private" harm caused therein. Further, he suggested that those most likely to object to the proposal were "profiteers" and therefore not worthy of consideration. He clinched his argument by reminding the chief secretary that the benefits of municipal control would accrue to the entire town: "The profits are spent on improving the streets and schools for which revenue is urgently needed. There may be complaints from one or two who will be unable to profiteer but the majority of shopkeepers are quite content as they sell other articles."[45]

Such an argument both suggests and reinforces a tactical hierarchy of capability in which private persons were necessarily compromised in the practice of care precisely because of their private interests. According to this argument, in this context it was government (here in the body of the municipality) that was most capable of providing justly for the needs of all.[46] While this case represents a wholesale removal of private responsibility, food servicing more commonly traversed domains, and the ethic of care appeared both private and public, both communal and governmental. When the practice of care was transferred to government during the Mandate it was self-consciously perceived as temporary, a requirement of wartime management. The exceptional nature of Mandate interventions contributed to the broader dynamic of abeyance. With the focus on emergency, little attention was paid by either government officials or the population which was the recipient of these policies to the potential stakes and significance of such interventions.

Coping with Catastrophe: Food Services after 1948

The period of the Egyptian Administration witnessed a larger and longer-lasting transformation in the ethic of care and the character of crisis services. Under such conditions it was less distraction and more disassociation that promoted abeyance. Both the community's practice of care and government's capacity to provide were strained by the massive dispossession of Palestinians in 1948. The sheer numbers of people who required assistance in getting adequate food overwhelmed the available coping mechanisms. The nakba tripled the population of Gaza and threw almost everyone, native Gazans and refugees alike, into poverty. The practice of care was both strained and reinforced by this crisis. The normal ways of distributing food were no longer available—most of the land from which people got their food was now beyond their grasp. The ordinary hierarchies in care were also disrupted in that people who had been giving landowners during the Mandate were now forced to scrounge for food wherever they could find it. Ultimately, this crisis resulted in the enormous expansion of government food services—a nearly wholesale transformation of need to service—and a reconfiguration of people's sense of obligation to themselves and each other.

To explore how this transfer occurred, I turn first to the conditions of dispossession which mandated it. People's departures from their homes were chaotic and hurried; they often took little with them because they planned to return when the fighting was over. As Basma Haifa described, "The planes were firing on Majdal, and people were afraid because of the air raids, so they left their homes and furniture."[47] Sami Ibrahim remembered watching people heading toward Gaza: "We were young, and we were going to watch them along the shore. Women, men, one carrying her baby, some carrying things on their heads, some pulling an old man slowly, everybody was walking along the shore."[48] Once refugees arrived in Gaza, conditions were extremely difficult. Im 'Amir, a refugee from Yibna, described the early days: "We had no bread or food to cook. Our living was difficult. . . . We were fighting over the distribution of supplies and every day two people were injured. . . . The [Egyptian] army was throwing onions and soap while it passed by. . . . We had neither food nor drink. We ate dried dates and guavas, but it was not enough."[49]

As the experiences of everyone I knew in Gaza made clear, the confusion and trauma of the *hijra* (exile) threw basic needs into conflict. Shelter and health, safety and sustenance, personal survival and family and social well-being, all these important life needs were in conflict with each other during this period. While the first months of dispossession were the most difficult—with people uprooted from their lives and not yet having formed new patterns of living—the trauma caused by this experience has yet to be resolved. The immediate crisis of dispossession and starvation severely constrained peoples' abilities to care for themselves and for others. Im 'Amir's comments were echoed by other refugees, who described similar scenes of ruthlessness in the struggle over food: "One could not feed his children. People were stealing bread from those who went to the baker. People were starving."[50] The crisis of the nakba and the widespread hunger which accompanied it overrode, at least in the short term, the ethic of mutual care which motivated communal food provisioning.

In the immediate aftermath of 1948 it was not clear how a communally sited practice of care could fulfill people's needs for food. The knowledges and capabilities that had been developed to this end were, in the new Gaza Strip, no longer applicable. People were forced to develop new ways of coping, ways that relied neither on their neighbors' "happiness" to give them food, nor on the products of their own land. Im 'Amir's description of her early efforts to feed herself and her family appears as a distorted version of prior practices:

Where could we go and how could we find food? I started going to the forest and bringing wood to sell to bakers for a [small sum]. We sold wood in order to eat. Then I told him [her husband] that I was fed up with selling wood, and so we started selling radish, onions, carrots, and vegetables. I was going to [Gazans'] fields and uprooting carrots, washing, cleaning, and selling carrots for one or two pennies and buying a loaf of bread with the money. The Gazans started to put sand in the loaves of bread and selling the bread to us for one or two pennies.

This description of refugees taking (essentially stealing) whatever they could find in an effort to survive and of Gazans putting filler in the bread to be able to make more money highlights the extent to which care of the self and care for others, both integral parts of the practice of care, often appeared incompatible during this difficult period.

Both natives and refugees were in need, many natives having lost much or all of their income and land. Lacking any means to change the situation or even, in the first days and months of the crisis, to find food, people often resorted to taking from each other.[51] Even during these most trying days people tried to offer assistance when they could, but that they sometimes harmed rather than helped each other must also be recognized. These tactical practices on the part of both Gazans and refugees certainly reflect a making-do that "seize[s] on the wing the possibilities that offer themselves in any given moment,"[52] though they were tactics directed not at power but at others like themselves. In this context, personal tactics did not always express themselves as resistance, but often as force. When organized efforts to provide relief began, first by the Quakers and later by UNRWA, with cooperation from the Administration, these service providers were cognizant of the possibility that this force could also be turned against them.

If the crisis of the nakba undermined people's abilities to care for each other, it also threatened their sense of personal dignity and continuity. People who were used to caring for themselves found themselves dependent on charity, an experience that was destabilizing and degrading. Da'ud Ahmed, a retired civil servant who was a boy at the time of the nakba, recalled to me the consternation he felt when he first received food aid: "Someone put a piece of cheese in my pocket and sweets in the other pocket. . . . At that time, I felt myself as a strange beggar. I was twelve years old and I was crying. . . . The people there brought food to us like beggars."[53] Even when international aid groups began to organize the delivery of food aid and the relationship of distribution was transformed from a personal to a procedural one, the experience was still humiliating.[54] As Da'ud said, "Can you imagine how a man who lived in a great city such as Yaffa and then came to live in a tent and had nothing would feel? . . . It was humiliation and misery of the most horrible kind. . . . We lost everything, and we had never imagined we would experience such conditions."

Ultimately, this sense of humiliation was managed, and the practice of care reconfigured, through a discourse and practice of international obligation. Obligation had always been part of the ethic of care. Having abandoned the Palestinians, as Gazans saw it, the international community now bore responsibility for caring for them. They saw the work of, first, the AFSC and then UNRWA as a recognition of this obligation. Providing this aid did not, as Gazans saw it, absolve the international community of its political obligations to the Palestinian people—most particularly their obligation to enforce their right to return to their homes. Furthermore, acceptance of food aid should not be construed as a recognition of the legitimacy of either the organizations which supplied it or the conditions which made it necessary. This disjuncture left many Gazans bitter about UNRWA's role. As Abu Ayub, a refugee living in Shati camp, told me,

> In the days of the Quakers and the UN the Palestinian people had only food and drink. I mean, it is like someone who stops someone else and keeps beating and beating him and at last he brings him food. The world countries were doing the same with us. They brought us food, blankets, cheese, dry dates and everything. There was more food than you can imagine. But what is the benefit?[55]

This comment reflects a commitment to the idea that such services were limited and inadequate responses to the Palestinian problem. From this perspective, food services could always only be tactical—no matter how rationalized they became in their delivery—because a strategic response demanded a reversal of dispossession.

Even as the Egyptian Administration was not painted with exactly the same brush as UNRWA, the discourse of obligation came also to shape its

FIGURE 5. Milk distribution at Khan Yunis. CREDIT: CAMPBELL HAYES/AFSC ARCHIVES.

food service practice. Although UNRWA's jurisdiction was limited to refugees, Egypt had an obligation to the entire population of Gaza. One of the early mechanisms the Administration employed to distribute food and other supplies to Gazans was the organization of what it called mercy trains (*qitarat al-rahma*), which traveled between Cairo and Gaza to deliver goods donated by Egyptians for the Palestinians. This new practice of food provisioning was part of a humanitarian style of governing that characterized the Administration in its early years—and thus was coded as relief rather than service. This humanitarian style was connected to the initial ambivalence and discomfort in Egyptian rule. By projecting its service in Gaza as a humanitarian effort, rather than as part of a rationalized bureaucratic structure, the Administration was able to proceed without fully inhabiting the role of government. It was not, though, possible to maintain this stance for very long.[56]

While the mercy trains played an important public relations and psychological role, the provisioning of food to so many hungry people required a more regimented and ultimately bureaucratic system. As the practice of relief began to be codified as head counts were taken and eligibility determined, local village leaders [*mukhtars*] acquired a new responsibility and therefore new power. These people were called upon to identify members of their villages and were sometimes given responsibility for distributing donated goods to refugees.[57] These new powers created opportunities for corruption, and the AFSC for one was very frustrated by the extent of such malfeasance among mukhtars.[58] The continued, reconfigured importance of mukhtars further reveals ways in which transformations in the service of care could work to further elaborate social hierarchies.

There was never enough money to provide as much food as was required,[59] the capacity to perfectly regulate the rolls, or the mandate to aid everyone who needed help.[60] These problems contributed to the development of a focus on rationalization, management, and continuity in food delivery as a tactical means to maximize limited resources. At the same time, this shift indicated a change in the Administration's style of rule in Gaza from humanitarian to bureaucratic. In this regard, the first and second parts of the Administration (before and after the four-month Israeli occupation in 1956) were quite distinct. Even as the pressures of work moved government in this direction early on, the second half of Egyptian rule was marked by a much more expansive understanding of its role in the Strip. While never fully at ease with this rule and certainly never settled, the Administration gradually acquired a more de jure acceptance of its obligations toward Gaza and Gazans and thereby was increasingly bound to the population and place of governance. Conditions in Gaza meant that this move toward regularity of servicing could never be entirely stable—nor could the future of the ruling body be assured.

The emphasis on rationalization was evident in a report by the Refugee Affairs Department on the operations of the flour distribution bureau. The staff of the bureau included ten civil servants and fourteen workers. The report praised the employees and noted that

> because of the experience of the officers and civil servants . . . they have been able to implement a new distribution system whereby each recipient knows exactly which week, which day, and which time he receives his rations. Previously all of this was unknown to them, which caused a lot of

FIGURE 6. Rations distribution. SOURCE: AFSC ARCHIVES.

exhaustion among both the recipients and the civil servants who did the distributing. The new system allows the number of work hours to be cut with an increase in production. It used to take until 3pm to get through 400 ration cards, now we get through 600 before 12pm, without causing the civil servants and workers any difficulties.[61]

Developing a more rational system of distribution made the jobs of civil servants easier and, no doubt, eased the population's anxieties. If one knew exactly when, where, and how one could get food, it might be possible to not be fearful at every moment that one might go hungry.

This increased rationalization in and improvement of food service provision was threatened by ongoing instabilities in government. The procedures of flour distribution were undermined by an unpredictable supply of flour from Egypt, caused in part by financial constraints. The report stressed the importance of keeping the distribution regular, saying, "We have to continue to distribute to the poor at their regular appointments in order to protect the governmental machinery."[62] Embedded within this statement is clear anxiety about possible tactical action on the part of the population. The tactical force that people turned against each other earlier could just as easily be turned against government.[63] Just as providing some security of distribution could ease personal anxiety and therefore, presumably, make people less likely to act out against government, disruptions in that security might provoke anxious disorder among the population.

The imbrication of social concern and governmental practice highlights both the transformation in the ethic of care as it was reconfigured as service and the ongoing tension between continuity and singularity, between rationalization and exception, that characterized tactical government. The centrality of obligation in people's understandings of food servicing could potentially bring them perilously close to a consideration of legitimacy. Such an outcome was in part averted by the dynamic of disassociation that enabled people both to claim UN relief as a right, as AFSC workers noted they did,[64] and to argue that the purpose behind UNRWA was to make "the Palestinian forget his homeland since he takes the flour sack,"[65] as one Gazan put it to me. Just as civil servants distinguished their work in government from their evaluation of it, so too Gazans sometimes separated their acceptance of services from their judgment of the government or agency providing that service.[66]

Service Anxieties, Living Conditions: Planning Towns and Houses in the Mandate

To an even greater extent than food servicing, the field of housing offers an instance of governmental anxiety and of tactical government utilized as an instrument of response. It also sheds light on important differences between the Mandate and the Administration. The meeting of anxiety and service highlights the paradox at the heart of tactical government. Both governments wanted, on the one hand, not to be overinvolved with the place or the people—not to extend or expend too much—because of fears of overcommitting and of overspending. At the same time, each government *needed* to be involved because of fears of the population getting out of control, of moral disintegration, and of political challenge. Tactical government is the means through which these contradictory impulses were managed in Gaza.

In addressing housing problems, each government had first to decide whether housing should be considered a service at all, and, whether yes or no, either answer had troubling implications. Although shelter is an immediate and apparently straightforward need, fulfillment of it creates a broad array of social, legal, and political entanglements. Building houses raises questions of town planning, construction regulations, landownership, and social dynamics. These issues made Mandate officials, especially, reluctant to define housing as a service. Still, these same concerns also indicate ways in which such a service *could* be productive for government. When government was forced to fully take on housing as a service—as was the Egyptian Administration, due to the extreme crisis caused by the nakba—that service was also able to participate in social policy.

World War I wrought enormous devastation in Gaza, including the physical destruction of much of Gaza City. As Herbert Samuel, the first high commissioner of Palestine, described it,

> The town of Gaza suffered probably more from Military action during the war than any other town in this theatre of operations. Almost all its buildings have been destroyed, and its present appearance is comparable only to that of the devastated areas in France and Belgium. . . . Gaza was, before the war, in respect of population (40,000), the third largest town in Palestine. . . . It was of considerable commercial importance, being the natural emporium of the rich grain districts lying south and east of it. The original population has now dwindled to something like one third of its number, and in the present ruinous condition of the town there is little to attract the remainder of its inhabitants to return or a fresh population to settle there.[67]

Samuel made a plea for government intervention, arguing that aid would serve a humanitarian purpose and could also be of strategic benefit to the newly established British Administration in Palestine: "Not only would the population of Gaza be deeply grateful, but the political effect throughout Palestine would contribute greatly to the popularity of British rule."[68] There is more than a glimmer of interest in legitimacy in this plea—an important reminder that its relative absence from the governing dynamic was not because the governments of the Mandate, or later the Administration, did not care about legitimacy, but because it did not work for government. The immediate demands of governing crises deflected attention from strategies to develop legitimacy toward tactics to manage problems. This was certainly the case in this instance, in which, despite Samuel's efforts, no significant funds were put toward the rebuilding of Gaza.

British officials worried about the financial drain on already limited government resources, about setting a precedent that would impose future obligations on government which it might wish to avoid, and about the possibility that the relationship between municipalities and the central government would be disrupted by government intervention in what was felt to be a municipal (or possibly private) arena.[69] One Mandate official commented that he didn't understand why landlords had not made the repairs themselves: "There is no lack of credit in the country for building provided that it is an economic proposition. If it is not an economic proposition at Gaza, public funds should not be invested in it any more than private funds."[70] The tactical response to these concerns resulted in a limited government project of home building and a much more significant transformation of the regulatory landscape within which housing stock could be built. Thus, one could say that the Mandate solved the problem posed by regulatory entanglement vis-à-vis housing by making an answer out of the problem itself.

To get to this tactical solution, housing policy in Gaza went through numerous twists and turns over the course of the Mandate. This confusing array of decisions made it difficult for people on the ground, whether Gazans or government officials, to discern their effects. The Gaza Development Scheme, as the response to Gaza's housing problems was called, was a complex, not entirely workable, amalgam of poor relief, town planning, and municipal development. It did not award direct grants to those whose homes had been destroyed. Rather, it proposed to cede government land to the municipality, which in turn would sell this land and use the proceeds to fund a Gaza Building Society to make loans to homeowners whose houses were destroyed during the war.[71] By making the municipality the putative owner of the land and thus the direct service provider, and by raising money from among wealthy Gazans rather than from state coffers, government hoped to avoid the problem of overservicing Gaza. Even this limited scheme raised suspicions. Officials doubted the capacity of the municipality to fulfill the role proposed for it, and they especially worried about getting reimbursed for the value of the land. In addition, skepticism was expressed about the Gazan population's ability to live up to its commitments, that is, to pay off the loans and to actually do any building.[72] In the end, these judgments proved too harsh.

Actual implementation of the scheme was delayed by numerous complications, which meant that, despite government approval of the scheme in principle as early as 1924, a final draft of the purchase agreement was not approved until August 1933.[73] Even then, the condition of the land slowed both sales and building. Since this was a "new" area, there were no government services, such as water provision, near the land, making it a less than appealing site on which to build a home. The commissioner of the Southern District reported to the chief secretary in 1932 that out of an anticipated two thousand available plots, only seventy-seven had been sold, and of these, only four people had begun actual construction. He commented,

> I am informed that one reason why the inhabitants of Gaza have failed to take advantage of the scheme is the lack of water in the area in question. This naturally increases the difficulty and the cost of building a house, and the knowledge that the house, even when built will be without a water supply is a further deterrent.
>
> When the scheme for a new Water Supply at Gaza is put in hand it will be possible for the Municipality to provide water to the development area. This scheme is, however, temporarily in abeyance while the finances of the Municipality are being examined with a view to enabling the Council to contract a loan for the purpose.[74]

This comment about the lack of water services (see chapter 6) underscores the interconnected, mutually supporting character of government services. In the event, land sales did not begin in earnest until 1934, when 322 plots were sold.[75] This delay, as a 1941 report on the scheme by the Land Settlement Department noted, "reduced the necessity for granting loans to the would-be purchasers whose houses were destroyed or damaged during the war, which was one of the main objects of the scheme."[76] As this comment indicates, one thing this plan had never been designed to do—a feature which distinguishes it from later Egyptian housing interventions—was to remake the socioeconomic landscape in Gaza. The people who were supposed to be aided by the scheme were those who already owned property. Even in its imagined form, it did not include mechanisms for expanding the owning class in Gaza.

While much of damaged Gaza *was* eventually rebuilt, and the new Gaza neighborhood of Rimal *was* established, this happened less through government servicing than through government regulation. The plan, which had been intended as a means of providing some housing service without involving government *too* much, had evolved into a government-regulated commercial venture. There was no formal decision to abandon the service aspect of the scheme, just as there had not been only one cause for the delay in its implementation. As it was actualized, though, public funds seem to have disappeared.[77] The regulatory mechanisms which governed the implementation of the Gaza Development Scheme got the better of any original intent behind that plan. In this manner, it was folded into the general regulatory environment, which was the primary means through which the Mandate responded to the housing problem.[78]

Regulation did not bring an end to the confusion, however. In the challenging environment of the Mandate it was easier to propose a regulatory framework then to enact it. Gaza was designated a town planning area as early as 1923, but it was not until 1940 that the District Town Planning Commission began meeting.[79] Further, as late as 1945, the regional town planning scheme still did not have the force of law. As the town planning advisor commented, "In so far as the issue of permits and the collection of fees are concerned, my Office has been obliged to act as if it was in fact in force."[80] The Town Planning Commission faced additional difficulties in getting home builders in Rimal to follow these rules. In a meeting in October 1940, the commission noted that "although the Municipality had instructed owners to build in accordance with the Regulations, cases had arisen where these instructions were ignored."[81]

Faced with a public that was disregarding regulations and a municipal body that was failing to enforce compliance, government was forced, contrary to its own intentions, to increase civil service involvement in the daily life of Gaza. As a result, the commission ordered that the regional engineer be dispatched to Gaza on a monthly basis to serve as an advisor to the local planning commission.[82] The commission also regulated the activities of municipal civil servants, ordering the municipality, for example, "to ensure that one of its building inspectors visiting [sic] the site and explained to the applicant all the regulations or set backs, etc."[83] The layers of governing work involved in managing regulation meant that, even as government was increasingly involved in microlevel municipal affairs, the public still confronted the municipality as agent. So, while the Mandate government may not have been successful in minimizing housing service in Gaza, it did manage (without any plan to this end) to distract attention from the significance of such involvement.

It was not until 1947 that the Planning Commission felt prepared to claim success at enforcing regulations. According to the minutes of a meeting from June of that year, "After a slow start and a lot of uphill work . . . real progress was at last being made. . . . having cleared up a considerable number of infringements which had been allowed in the past the Committee was concentrating on the future."[84] The procedures put in place, the personnel dispatched, and the products being constructed should, the commission averred, "put an end to the state of chao[s] which had been allowed in the past." It was, therefore, not until almost the end of the Mandate that the regulatory environment had been brought under enough control to begin "concentrating on the future"—a future that, as it turned out, would not be realized.

Responsibility for ensuring that building regulations were followed had been removed from the municipality, which now served as an agent of the Planning Commission in this regard. Thus, while government had initially been reluctant to undertake housing services partly because of an unwillingness to take on municipal responsibility, in the transition from service to regulation, this is precisely what occurred. Over the course of the Mandate housing went from need to service to regulatory domain. The outcome of this process was an involvement of government at a level of detail that had not been anticipated, a general incapacity to do more than react to problems in implementation, and the emergence of a complicated field of government service that rendered the stakes of its work opaque.

Housing Service as Social Service

Most of the improvements of the Mandate years were made irrelevant by the 1948 war over Palestine and the subsequent creation of the Gaza Strip. With three times the population and much less land, housing became a crisis, not a development problem. Indeed, the severity of the situation which faced the refugees coming into Gaza did not afford the Egyptian Administration or UNRWA the luxury of debating—as did Mandate officials—whether or not it was appropriate to service housing. It was evident to all that housing was a pressing and immediate need. The very severity of the need meant that the implications of this service work for the nature of government, and for the relationship between the (transformed) local population and that government, could not be the focus of anyone's attention. This condition-produced distraction later shared space with a practice of deferral that was equally connected to conditions in Gaza.

The housing crisis highlighted an important distinction between refugees and native Gazans. Since it was precisely in terms of losing one's home that a refugee was defined, housing both was a marker of distance between the two groups and was productive of that distance. At the same time, the housing crisis in Gaza also brought these people, newly defined as two groups, into intimate relations with each other. Jamil Nizar, a refugee from Asdud who was a child in 1948, described the close quarters in the house where his family rented space from native Gazans: "In the house where we stayed, we lived in one room, and the owner's family lived in the other room. If I were my father, I would not have been able to survive."[85] Not surprisingly, these kind of conditions created tensions between Gaza's native inhabitants and the refugees. As Hassan Muhammad, a refugee from Hammama, explained, "We had no relatives, but I knew a man from Jabalya. . . . We lived with him for some days, but his house was small, and his father was always nervous, I thought maybe it was because of us, so I said goodbye. He is still my friend."[86] Sometimes refugees with no money squatted on private land, but, as Im 'Amir recalled about her family's squatting experience, "The people of Gaza did not tolerate us and kicked us out."[87]

Even as housing created tensions between natives and refugees, many refugees also recall the efforts by Gazans to help them when they first arrived.[88] Certainly, Gazans remember: "We used to go to the sea—a big ship would come carrying girls and women from Jaffa. A man would go into the sea carrying a rope, and would swim and swim until he reached the ship. Then he would tie the rope to the ship and two hundred or three hundred people would pull and pull until they dragged the ship in, carrying the women and children."[89] The refugees then took up residence wherever they found space, in fields, schools, and mosques.[90] As relief agencies, and eventually UNRWA, came to Gaza, refugee camps were established which eventually moved people out of mosques and into tents, later replaced by concrete and asbestos houses.

From the start, Egyptian administrators understood the dimensions of the housing crisis to extend beyond the need for shelter. From their perspective, the crisis was a social one as well, with improper living conditions leaving society in general at risk for a "decline into depravity."[91] Social relations and mores were normally imbedded in spatial arrangements of housing and neighborhoods that helped sustain "proper" interactions between men and women, as well as within and among different families. All of these relations were put at risk by the conditions in which refugees in Gaza had to live in the first years after 1948. Egyptian administrators saw these conditions as dangerous to the moral welfare of the society. According to a report by the Refugee Affairs department, conditions in camps were not much more satisfactory than those in mosques: "Where there was a family living in their nation in a spacious independent house, they have come to a life where they live in one narrow room, or a small tent. The family needs to tend to all of its needs in this small space—sleeping, cooking, washing, showering, meeting guests, etc. There is no doubt that this situation cannot be sustained." Even worse, the report went on to comment, "there are many circumstances of two families who have no connection having to live in one tent or room,"[92] thereby forcing unrelated men and women into the same intimate space. Calling the situation abominable, the report stressed both the importance and the difficulty of alleviating these conditions.

It was not only "nation," but potentially "society" that was lost in the disaster of 1948. While the former loss could not be quickly rectified, it was possible to do something about the latter. Hence, in the response to the first-order need for shelter, housing service during the Administration quickly developed a second-order interest in social policy. Even as it remained defined as a response to crisis, housing became a mechanism for regularizing and regulating the lives of refugees and native Gazans. It participated in reshaping the social landscape, as new towns and neighborhoods were formed and new neighbors emerged, reconfiguring the moral climate, as people lost and gained privacy, and redefining the boundaries of government,

FIGURE 7. Khan Younis refugee camp, 1954. CREDIT: M. CHAUMENY. SOURCE: UNRWA PHOTO ARCHIVE.

as UNRWA and the administration determined the contours of their shared responsibility.

UNRWA also saw the need to improve conditions in the camps and was eager to replace tents with solid houses[93] as quickly as possible, a goal that was achieved in Gaza before any other area of UNRWA operation.[94] In other places, most notably Syria and Lebanon, refugees actively resisted any projects that they thought "might mean permanent resettlement."[95] Accordingly, "experimental houses, erected by the Agency, have been torn down; and for many months, in Syria and Lebanon, there was widespread refusal to work on agency road-building and afforestation schemes."[96] UNRWA reports do not indicate why Gaza projects did not encounter such resistance, though UNRWA's firm and stated conviction that "the reintegration of refugees on the Gaza strip is impossible, since it can hardly support its previous inhabitants" may have eased refugees' possible concerns about the implications of housing improvements. When there were clear efforts to engage in resettlement projects, such as a proposal to move refugees to the Sinai, resistance was indeed strong.

With new houses in place, the UNRWA Annual Report for 1954 noted that "many refugee camps are thus increasingly taking on the appearance of villages and towns, with school buildings, small workshops and communal facilities such as bath houses and recreational centres, as well as small shops opened by enterprising refugees."[97] Of course, this almost rosy picture of emerging small-town life does not capture the overwhelmingly makeshift and destitute character of the landscape of these camps. Even after the tents were replaced with houses, these camps were temporary in design and dilapidated in execution.

Another way in which refugee camps were unlike normal towns was that none of the inhabitants owned their homes or the land on which they sat. Rather, the land, at least nominally, retained its original ownership, and the homes were owned by UNRWA itself. The public ownership of camps increased UNRWA's regulatory oversight of the use of the houses. Any construction within the camps required permission from the officer in charge of the camp, and such construction would itself become UNRWA property.[98] The camp regulations also stipulated how camp residents could make use of their dwellings. Residents were responsible for keeping their homes and yards clean, were not allowed to offer shelter to others, and were prohibited from installing water taps in their homes or using land for cultivation.[99] The land on which refugee camps sat was for the most part state land, and these regulations were developed and enforced with cooperation between Egyptian authorities and UNRWA.[100]

The joint management of refugee camps—in which UNRWA provided services and the Egyptian Administration was responsible for security—further complicated the governmental field. That their respective authorities were entangled seemed clear to the population—a complexity which was reflected in the multiple directions of complaint and critique. Petitions about UNRWA practice were sent to the Administration; protests about Administration policy were staged outside UNRWA offices. These complicated relations certainly contributed to a lack of clarity about the meaning of particular policies for judgments of government, though it did not in any way limit critique of those policies themselves. Refugees were acutely aware of both their need for housing assistance and the potentially negative implications of such assistance for the resolution of their condition. The establishment of refugee camps was a response to the incapacity of the population to care for its own housing needs (owing to the crisis of dispossession), but it also ensured that this capacity for self-sufficiency would be continually deferred and risked making a return to their homes less likely.

The housing services provided by refugee camps were limited not only in their capacity to fulfill the broader social needs the Administration saw as crucial, but also in their very capacity to house refugees—only about half of the refugee population ever lived in camps.[101] In these conditions of perpetual deferral, Egyptian administrators eventually had to develop additional, more permanent housing policies. Mirroring a practice used in Egypt, the Administration sold public land to civil servants as a perquisite of their service to government. Through a lottery system, plots of state land were made available at "symbolic" (that is, very low) prices to employees—first to those with more than ten years' experience and later to those with less.[102] These sales highlight the paradoxical place of deferral in Gaza's government. One the one hand, they were a *sign* of the continued deferral of refugees' return to their homes. On the other, they were an *instrument* through which the Egyptian Administration shored up its authority, authority based partly on the deferred promise of independence.[103]

This distribution of land, taking place as it did in the new circumstances in which Gaza was inhabited by both natives and refugees, had a significant effect on the social landscape. As civil servants, refugees had the opportunity to acquire land in Gaza. Property ownership did not diminish people's desires to return to their homes or lessen their claims to lands left behind, but it did bind them to their new place of residence. It also muted some of the differences between refugees and natives inhabitants. While clear distinctions between the groups remain even today, the fact of living in the same neighborhoods and sharing the same everyday space did blunt the edges of the differences. In the elaboration of housing services in the Administration, it is clear how even a crisis service, deployed in a practice of tactical government, could participate in effecting social policy and shaping social life. Even with all the profound limitations, both chosen and imposed, on government in Gaza, it still had a fundamental impact on transforming this place and its population.

The land sales met with an enormously positive response. Judgments by Gazans about the Egyptian Administration vary considerably, but nearly all speak with glowing praise about two aspects of Egyptian rule: the provision of free university education to vast numbers of Gazans and the low-cost sale of land to government employees.[104] That Gazans were so enthusiastic about this service further highlights the complexities of tactical government. The coexistence of the promise of independence with the delivery of services that might be contrary to such a promise was made possible by the particular scale of tactical practice. Their limited breadth of vision and scope meant that they did not easily cohere into a totality. Both promise and service were necessary for the persistence of rule. In tactical government, not only did the contradictions between them not require resolution, but they were productive for rule.

At stake in the details of Egyptian housing service, as in the details of Mandate services, was nothing less than the persistence of government. These practices, which kept people participating in a dynamic to which they could not assign legitimacy, also formed material through which both community and place were shaped. When frustration over perpetual deferral seemed likely to produce a crisis, the distraction afforded by improved services could avert it. Alternately, when political demands rendered distraction insufficient, future promise could counsel patience. The way these things worked together was not necessarily planned, but it was productive. At the same time, this mode of practice both represented and was produced out of genuine limitations of governmental capacity. When government worked in Gaza, when it participated in the shaping of place and people, as it clearly did, it did so in ways that neither policy makers nor practitioners could entirely control or even understand.

Conclusion

The location of crisis services on the edge of government—persistent but not permanent; provided by both state institutions and community practice— illuminates the contradictions at the heart of tactical government. Crisis services were motivated by concern both for people's well-being and for the potential threat they posed. Food and housing services expanded the reach of government into new domains, even as they proclaimed these domains to be beyond the proper sphere of the state. In the Mandate, the government sought to limit its service interventions, thereby developing a housing project that was quickly overtaken by market forces and by regulation, and to limit the implications of those services it did provide, defining its food rationing as an exceptional instance that was not characteristic of government responsibility. In the Administration, government explained the expansion of services by reference to a language of international obligation and humanitarian relief—such that food rations could be universal, but not precedent setting—and took advantage of being compelled to broaden services to turn crisis services to a social policy end—as housing services attempted to create better social and moral conditions among the population.

These contradictions were very real but also productive for the persistence of rule. Crisis services, with their presumed exceptionality and impermanence, reveal the ways in which the practice of tactical government, as opposed to any particular policy, served to keep questions of legitimacy in abeyance. In their efforts to contain the scope of their servicing, the Mandate and the Administration also worked to obscure its significance. The way these services were embedded in a broader social dynamic of care further worked to distract attention from their relation to the governing regime. At the same time, even as they might have averted attention from their own significance, these exceptional services had important and lasting effects on the place and people of Gaza. As ways of coping with difficulty and patterns of living shifted across domains, relations among people also shifted. However limited their scope and their vision, the impact of crisis services always exceeded their intentions.

6

SERVICING EVERYDAY LIFE

> [*Ayyam al-Balad*] was an easy life, not hard like today's. There was no electricity. Water was free. Farmers used to give people vegetables and fruits.
>
> ABU SAID, REFUGEE FROM HAMMAMA, RAFAH, 12 JUNE 1999

> We used to bring water from [wells]. We filled water in jars and put them on our heads. Every three women went together, or a woman alone. Water was different from now where you can use the tap, or light the lamp, it was different in the past.
>
> IM ʿAMIR, REFUGEE FROM YIBNA KHAN YUNIS, 15 JUNE 1999

In 1943, two histories of Gaza were published, both written by civil servants. The first was by ʿArif al-ʿArif, a Jerusalem-born Mandate official who was a district officer in a number of locales, including Gaza. *Tarikh Ghazza* (The History of Gaza), was one of his many publications. The second history, *Tarikh Ghazza: Naqd wa-Tahlil* (The History of Gaza: Critique and Analysis), was written as a rebuttal to parts of al-ʿArif's book. The author, Hilmi Abu Shaʿban, was certainly known in Gaza, but he was not a historical figure like al-ʿArif. Rather, Abu Shaʿban, who was a Gaza native and from a prominent local family, was a municipal clerk and a regular contributor to Palestine's newspapers.[1] Abu Shaʿban took issue with many parts of al-ʿArif's account, seeming to suggest that al-ʿArif's outsider perspective on Gaza hindered his ability to accurately represent it.

He prefaced his book by explaining why he felt compelled to write his critique:

> Since this book is about the city in which I was born and under whose skies I grew up, and, desirous of the commitment that its greatest citizens have shown for preserving its history, I embarked on writing my notes about this book and criticizing some of the information in it—about which the author did not succeed in obtaining the truth. His excuse for this is clear, as he could not collect everything about the history of Gaza.[2]

Indicating that al-'Arifs efforts to "collect" the truths of Gaza's history were "irreproachable," even if his conclusions were not, Abu Sha'ban offered what he hoped was a "positive and constructive" criticism.

Abu Sha'ban criticized al-'Arif for relying too much on "what he heard from people" and for letting his biases influence his history. Even as Abu Sha'ban criticized al-'Arif for producing a located and partial history, in contrast to the objective and accurate account that he sought to offer, it seems clear that the problem with al-'Arifs version was not *that* he was located, but *where* he was located. Because he was not Gazan and interacted with the Gazans only as a government official, al-'Arif misinterpreted "Gazan character," which he described as "nervous and quick to anger." Abu Sha'ban suggested that the source of this misinterpretation was al-'Arifs limited contact with the people of Gaza: "He did not mingle with all the people of Gaza, rather by reason of his position he knew a portion of them—those who had injustices to present to the authority, rights to demand, problems to solve, or needs to have met. What applies to someone in need, as it is said, does not apply to the rest of the Gazans."[3] Abu Sha'ban, a Gaza native who worked in local, not national, government, suggested throughout his commentary that he knew Gaza in a way that al-'Arif never could.

The significance Abu Sha'ban attached to the difference of locality—both of person and position—highlights the importance of perspective in the formation of governing relations. Perspective both provides an analytic hook for making claims to and about government—demanding better services, contesting restrictions—and gives rise to particular senses of place. As Donna Haraway reminds us, all knowledge is situated, coming from "somewhere in particular."[4] By attending to these locations and to the "embodied objectivities" they represent, it becomes possible to see how contestations among a multiplicity of partial visions help give shape to a shared experience of place. People's perspectives are obviously derived in part through their social, political, and economic locations, and they are made robust by the details of everyday life.

Intimate connections with people and place are forged in significant part through regular practices of living, such as the gathering of water, the traveling through the landscape, the communicating across its space. It is these practices and the services which aided them that are my interest here. My focus is on the quotidian formations of place that emerge out of the everyday practices of government services.[5] If crisis services were distinguished by their exceptionality, everyday services were marked precisely by their mundane quality. It was in the repeated enactment of these mundane services that place took shape. Services such as utilities, roads, and transportation helped shape the pathways of people's lives, influencing daily routines, determining trajectories of movement. The similar, but not identical, use of such services by many people underscores both networks of connection and recognition that are forged in part in service use and the spaces for creativity and contestation that exist in these unremarkable experiences.[6]

Jurisdiction, Locality, and Everyday Services

For government, one expression of these contests over location was the persistent debates over jurisdiction. Questions about which branch of government should provide which services are part of any government. In Gaza these questions were complicated by the difficult conditions pertaining in the place and the lack of stability that characterized governmental practice. In the British Mandate, these struggles often took place between central government, municipalities, and the local public. In the Egyptian Administration, with the presence of international aid organizations and the United Nations, the jurisdictional questions became even more complicated. While efforts to avoid responsibility were often couched in terms of economy, and efforts to claim authority over service were often described as procedural imperatives, it is clear that the stakes of jurisdiction were tremendous.

Contests over jurisdiction also further illuminate the layers of government that Gazans experienced. During both the Mandate and the Administration, government was highly centralized, and yet local bodies and personnel—municipalities, village councils, *mukhtars*—were the sites of government with which many Gazans had the most contact. In the Mandate, as an early report on British administration in Palestine put it, local councils were to "serve as the collective mouthpiece of the people towards the District Governors, and as the means for carrying out the general requirements of the Administration."[7] To balance these two roles, Mandate officials attempted to remain aloof from the details of municipal conflict, while at the same time exercising control over the output of municipal councils. The central government reserved for itself the right to oversee all decisions of local bodies as well as the prerogative not to intervene.

Gazans frequently petitioned government with complaints about municipalities, generally to no avail. For example, in 1946 several Khan Yunis families appealed to the chief secretary, asking for more representation on the local elections committee: "We have one representative out of seven on the committee and he is ill. We are at a loss as to whom we should address our grievance. Should we address ourselves to the Secretary of State or to His Majesty the King or to God alone? We pray that an enquiry may be instituted to ensure free and unbiased elections."[8] These families charged the mayor and the district officer with conspiring against them and obstructing their ability to contest elections. The government's response, in which it declined to intervene in the domain of municipal authority, was typical during the Mandate. In the files I examined, I found no instance in which government intervened on behalf of petitioning locals against a local council.[9]

During the Administration, government was, if anything, even more centralized. Local councils and their employees were fully integrated into the strip-wide governing structure. Being located more firmly within this structure, municipalities became a site for conflict, not only between government and local communities or within those communities, but also within government itself. Such conflict was evident in a 1960 complaint sent by the *qa'imaqam* (administrative officer) to the governor-general about the Deir Belah administrative governor. In this complaint, the *qa'imaqam*, Said Abu Sharkh, reminded the governor-general that "the councils are under your supervision" and that "the purpose of these administrative organizations was to have each area work according to its jurisdiction to benefit the public good in terms of

FIGURE 8. Report of Deir Belah village council meeting. SOURCE: ISRAEL STATE ARCHIVES.

quiet and order." Abu Sharkh charged the Deir Belah governor with interfering in the council's work and with forcing council members and employees to spend the town's money without going through proper procedure.[10] He detailed several specific complaints and asked that the governor-general "ensure proper behavior and appropriate jurisdiction division."[11]

If the space of municipal autonomy was somewhat decreased, though, the presence of UNRWA added another layer to the governing dynamic and offered another space for contestation over government action. So too did the legislative council that was established in the second half of Egyptian rule in Gaza. The legislative council, initially headed by the governor-general and later turned over to more fully Palestinian representation (Haidar Abdul Shafi was its chair), was empowered to debate and propose legislation, though the governor-general retained veto power.[12] UNRWA, while making no claim to govern Gaza, was as important an administrative actor as the

Administration. The apparently fixed division of jurisdiction—UNRWA responsible for services to refugees, the Administration to natives—was in fact not without challenge on the ground. The Administration often sought UNRWA funding for public projects undertaken outside of refugee camps, arguing that those projects would benefit refugees. A great deal of the correspondence between the two parties is taken up with such questions: who would pay for (or pay for what percentage of) what.[13]

This multiplicity in the faces of government as well as the conflicts over jurisdiction was part of a governing dynamic in which it was difficult to get things done and often impossible to plan ahead. Even as these uncertainties created numerous problems, they were also productive for a practice of tactical government that depended on a dynamic of abeyance. Jurisdictional tussles demanded that attention be paid, not to the issue of government's legitimacy, but to the question of which part of government should be providing which services. The way in which layered government worked in Gaza, where the central government was both reluctant to be involved in local matters and unwilling to devolve significant powers to these bodies, meant that the location of authority was not always obvious to service recipients. Even under these conditions, there were cracks in this abeyance, moments people connected problems with service provision precisely to fundamental questions about the character of government, its relation to the place and population, and its legitimacy. These moments underscore the tenuous nature of governing practices in Gaza. Even where they worked, it was never assured that they would continue to do so.

Water Services and the Boundaries of Government

In the previous chapter I described services that were taken on by government because of a crisis of need, reflecting an inability of the population to care for themselves independently. Water, on the other hand, came to be a service through the transformation of relations of people and government to place. Whereas in crisis servicing the presumption was always that if the crisis abated so would the services, everyday services were intended to be permanent, even if in practice they rarely were. There was a shift in definitions of place and its capacities such that water distribution came to be perceived as necessarily lying within government's jurisdiction. This transformation was also connected to changes in notions of government and service themselves. As rationalization and standardization became increasingly important to government, social mechanisms for collecting and distributing water appeared increasingly inadequate.

For much of the Mandate, rural areas lay beyond the reach of water and other utility services. The practices that sustained life in a nonserviced environment were both a means of coping with difficult conditions and a productive mechanism in shaping social life. Sitting in his cramped and crowded living room in the Shati refugee camp, Abu Ayub described to me what life was like in Yibna before 1948. In the absence of government services, water gathering was women's work:

> There was no street cleaning, no water pipes, no services like this in the *balad* [village]. . . . People used to go to the grove where there was a pump for water. . . . A woman would put a crock on her head bring water in it. . . . They'd go to fill it in the morning and in the afternoon they fill it again. All of the water was brought on the head in the balad. There was no water at home, except in cities. . . . The life in the balad was like this. It was different from now. Now there are people who clean the streets, there is a water tap, and the water is checked.[14]

This account of a rural life pursued mostly without government-provided services demonstrates the difference of life in the villages both from city living and from post-1948 conditions.[15] People who lived in larger towns recalled the expansion of services into these areas over the course of the Mandate.

On a visit to the Jabalya refugee camp in the north of the Gaza Strip I spoke with a woman about utilities in Majdal (now Ashkelon). She recalled, "Electricity entered the town a short time before we left al-Majdal. At first they [the municipality] put in lampposts . . . which ran with kerosene. There was a man who lit them every day at sunset. A short time before we left al-Majdal, they brought electricity to the houses." Then I asked about water services: "Were there faucets in the houses?" "In our time," she told me, "there were. At first they brought water to the municipal wells, and then I remember that the water reached the houses. They laid water pipes to the houses."[16] Service expansion in steps seems to have been typical of Gaza-area towns.

In people's recollections, this transformation to servicing does not appear as a simple account of progress. People were cognizant of the ways in which services can produce new obligations and constraints even as they can make life easier. These new relations contributed to shaping the "character" of the place of Gaza both by reconfiguring understandings about the capacity of that place (its natural resources and its population) and by transforming that population's relationship with those resources. Place and public were formed in "minor" government practices such as water provision in several ways: in part by cohering differently located people into a horizontal group of service recipients; in part by concentrating resources in governmental hands, thereby delimiting both present and future distribution; and in part by distinguishing as well as connecting national and local government, thereby linking place not only to its public, but to its local government.[17]

PROVISIONAL HISTORIES: NEED, DEMAND, AND DEVELOPMENT

The dueling local histories of Hilmi Abu Sha'ban and 'Arif al-'Arif both discuss Gaza's water services. Their sometimes seemingly minor disagreements about the facts of this service in Gaza City divulge an even more fundamental disagreement about the stakes of government-provided water. Both Abu Sha'ban and al-'Arif indicate that there had long since been a municipal well that supplied water for some of the people of the city. Further, they agreed that the Mandate was a period of considerable expansion in government water service. They concur as well that this expansion was a definitive sign of progress and service improvement. They disagree, however, about the nature of the progress and about who the primary beneficiary of this improvement was.

Al-'Arif's account begins from the perspective that water necessarily had to be provided as a government service and, therefore, that the expansion of the service network was evidence of better government. Abu Sha'ban, on the other hand, suggested that the private mechanisms of water procurement had in the past been a perfectly adequate means of fulfilling people's needs. He too saw the expansion of the service network as vital, but its importance lay in its contribution to the rationalization of government. The expansion of municipal water services, according to Abu Sha'ban, aided in the production of more efficient government, increase of municipal revenue, and greater control over health conditions in the city. Rather than highlighting the role of service expansion in increasing the capacity of place, Abu Sha'ban focused on how it enhanced the capacity of government. Water services, from this perspective, produced government as much as they fulfilled needs.

These services also transformed people's relationship with place. Al-'Arif described how "Gazans brought up water [from the municipal well] in buckets and carried it away in leather waterskins,"[18] until 1926, when the municipality put in a motor, after which point the water was drawn into a municipal reservoir. If waterskins were a symbol of the social life of water gathering, the municipal reservoir was a symbol of its bureaucratization.[19] Over the course of the Mandate, additional wells were dug. Al-'Arif suggested that even these were not enough, and he described "the strong thirst"[20] which had faced the city in recent years. Abu Sha'ban disputed this characterization, saying that in Gaza "any small child could dig a well in the sand on the beach and drink sweet water from it." Abu Sha'ban further commented, "It appears to me that the author is ignorant of the history of water in Gaza and the reasons for digging the wells which he mentions."[21]

According to his view, the expansion of water services was not primarily about meeting the "basic needs" of Gazans, but rather about increasing the capacity and efficiency of government. For this reason, Abu Sha'ban's correction of al-'Arif's account focused on the bureaucratization of water services— a bureaucratization which he saw as all to the good. Whereas at the beginning of the Mandate there was only "a basic network of water pipes" and the subscribers to the municipal water supply numbered only in the hundreds, after the "elected Municipal council" decided, in 1928, to compel participation by forcing all Gazans to pay water fees whether they used public water or not, the water network was able to expand dramatically. Abu Sha'ban said of this endeavor,

> This step was necessary to make people participate, to protect public health, and to gather the drinking water in a reservoir that is under the supervision of the council and the oversight of the department of health. The people became interested in subscribing to the water and the overwhelming majority now consume their water through municipal pipes. Waterskins and the like have disappeared. The Municipal council has fulfilled its role and has expanded the pipe network and safeguarded their presence in the city streets. Revenue from water has increased from hundreds to thousands of pounds.[22]

According to Abu Sha'ban, it was the greater participation in water services that created the need for new government wells.

In addition, new building in Gaza created new service needs. The Gaza development scheme, which created the new neighborhood of Rimal, required new wells to service the area. As noted in chapter 5, as of 1932 water was still lacking, awaiting approval of a new water supply scheme: "This scheme is, however, temporarily in abeyance while the finances of the Municipality are being examined with a view to enabling the Council to contract a loan for the purpose."[23] Given the Mandate government's concerns about taking on municipal financial obligations, the reason for such careful examination seems clear. The project was no doubt caught up in the variety of tensions and conflicts between central government and the municipality. Given also that the stability of municipal finances depended, in part, on the capacity and willingness of the population to pay its bills in a timely manner and on the capacity and willingness of the municipality to enforce regulations, government's concerns about each of these parties may have also slowed down the project. The water scheme was approved in December 1932, when Barclay's Bank—"without a Government guarantee"—agreed to make a loan to the municipality.[24] Even when government services expanded, then, private means were not entirely left behind.

Neither Abu Sha'ban nor al-'Arif addressed any of these issues. Their "debate" about the water project focused on the quality of water produced by the well dug in 1933 with money from the loan.[25] Al-'Arif described the well as "salty and not good for drinking,"[26] an assertion to which Abu Sha'ban strongly objected. He argued that, as district officer, al-'Arif had to know that the Health Department had tested the water and found it acceptable for drinking. Rather than describing the water as salty, Abu Sha'ban suggested, it should be said that it was "less sweet" than another well.[27] In fact, a government report from 1936 did describe the water as "at present adequate and good in quality, slightly saline, but containing some fine sand."[28] In these two accounts the complicated politics and economics of water expansion in Gaza seem reduced to a "technical" problem of water quality. So, ironically perhaps, even as both Abu Sha'ban and al-'Arif sought to write a complete history of Gaza, each produced a "developmentally" inflected account that obscured some of the tactical operations of Gaza's water provisioning.[29]

The expansion of municipal authority and scope through the compulsory participation in public water services was part of a more general process of binding people and government. This binding created bidirectional obligation, responsibility, and demand. Whereas in the past most people had obtained water—no doubt often for free—from their own or their neighbors' wells, they were now obligated to pay for the privilege of using municipal water. At the same time, the municipality was now obligated to supply the piping that would enable water distribution and to ensure that its wells had enough water to meet the needs of the whole Gazan population. The expansion of service and obligation created new opportunities for challenge to government and new sites of interaction between the public and the government. At the same time, the expansion of water services reduced certain kinds of social interactions, as the walk to a nearby well disappeared from daily pathways, and the water well ceased to be a gathering spot for women. These reconfigurations were not simply the inevitable result of development but were produced in the tactical operations of government.

POLITICS OF SERVICE: PROVIDING WATER AND PROTECTING THE LOCAL

The tactical conditions of Gaza's water services were brought to the surface by conflicts engendered by the 1936 general strike, which was supposed to include a cessation of local government services. This strike highlighted the mutual obligation and dependence of Gazans, the municipality, and the Mandate government, and the problems sometimes engendered therein. Although the transfer of water provision to public responsibility, a transfer which provoked both obligation and entitlement, seems to have been largely complete by this point, tension and conflict over the contours of this responsibility had not ceased, nor would they. Debates in the Gaza City Council over its participation in the strike evidence these tensions. While the municipality had provisionally halted all service provision at the start of the strike, as recorded in the Registers of Council Decisions, the council was divided about whether this was an appropriate course of action. The mayor expressed concern about both the harm to the public and the danger from government that continued participation in these strike activities might cause. He argued that ongoing municipal stoppage of "cleaning, lighting, and water provision for city residents will lead to sickness as a result." In the mayor's view, ceding governmental responsibility for these services would create numerous problems.

"There will be a danger," he suggested, "of residents leaving their cities or of the government—per its authority according to the Municipalities Law— taking over the administration of the municipalities."[30] The threat was that the central government might be provoked out of its usual oversight approach to municipal management and into an active position as surrogate local authority. For the mayor, this threat was itself sufficient reason to ease the strike.[31] His concern about government interference reflected more than an ordinary interest in local autonomy; it suggested a conviction that this government was incapable, above all during such stressful times, of properly providing for local needs, both practical and political. Municipal autonomy was always extremely limited during the Mandate, but the political conflicts between foreign policy and local demands, heightened during periods of outright rebellion as in 1936–39, made preservation of even that limited autonomy appear highly important.

At the same time, the tension between government and municipality was not the only form of national-local conflict. There was also an inherent conflict between national(ist) political demands and the local needs which the mayor articulated. In the council debates, other members argued on behalf of nationalism that the council had to promote national unity and support the cause and therefore the strike. Ultimately, the mayor's position prevailed, and the council decided that because "the people of Gaza are dying of thirst and are suffering from illnesses,"[32] the municipality was obliged to resume its provision of basic services. This instance not only showcases an instance of the disassociation that civil servants often used to make sense of their work, but also highlights the work involved in arriving at such compartmentalization. While the Gaza City Council, and civil servants generally, may indeed have felt that their work *in* governing was different from work *for* government, it took an active effort to manage the contradictory positions in which they often found themselves.

This service question was also a potential crisis for government. It was precisely at those moments when the stakes of service had to be confronted head-on that the dynamic of abeyance was most fragile. Where people were forced to consider what it would mean—for themselves, for the nation, for the future—to either participate or not in the daily work of government, they had to contend also with the legitimacy of government. In this case, the potential crisis of legitimacy was averted by a politics of location. In its own efforts to resolve its awkward position between competing national demands, the council invoked and measured the needs and demands of the local public against these competing obligations. The municipality presented itself as the bulwark between Gaza and the threat of government intervention. At the same time, even as the decision was presented as a form of resistance to government, it also had the effect of contributing to the persistence of government—by keeping services working—and of averting the potential crisis of abeyance—by separating the daily work of governing from questions about the legitimacy of the governing regime.

ORDINARY INCAPACITIES, SERVICE OBLIGATIONS

Even after the end of the rebellion and the return of water services to more ordinary terrain, struggle over the style of service provision continued to shape the relationship of government and local public. Government remained a participant in this local dynamic, but a relatively aloof one. When local conflicts did not threaten the stability of the governmental process, it proceeded as observer of these affairs. In the triadic relations among government, municipality, and Gazans, circuits of complaint and redress were central. In one instance in 1941 of Gazan complaint to government about municipal practice, a group of almost sixty residents of Rimal, the "new Gaza" neighborhood for whom, in part, the well had been dug in 1933, submitted a petition to the chief secretary objecting to a municipal plan to install water meters in their quarter of the city—a petition preserved in the "municipal government" files of the chief secretariat.[33] This conflict, relatively late in the Mandate-era transformation of water services, illuminates the significance of this transformation. Not simply compelled to participate in municipal water, as Abu Sha'ban described, the residents of Rimal were dependent upon it.

Their new homes were built with water faucets and, presumably, without private wells. If disconnected from the municipal system, there was no private network upon which people could depend. The new municipal plan entailed this very threat; the municipality had announced its intention to discontinue water service to anyone who did not agree to install a meter.[34] The installation of meters marked a significant change from the previous system for assessing water fees, one whereby people were charged flat fees depending on the type and value of their buildings. Under the meter system, people would pay for their usage, regardless of their rent or whether their building was their home or business. The petitioners complained that their quarter was being unfairly singled out for meters (the other quarters of the city did not have them) and argued that the new system was unfair to the poor, who would now be charged at the same rate as the wealthy. Given this injustice, the petitioners asked government to step in and reverse the municipal action. In keeping with the general practice of staying out of municipal governance if it did not threaten national government, central authorities declined to intervene.

This petition, and the seemingly inevitable response, open a window on the transformations in the place of Gaza over the course of the Mandate. The concentration of the mechanisms of water collection and distribution in the hands of government meant that the resources of Gaza could be accessed only through the offices of government. Water use was no longer a private affair, or an act of beneficence by the wealthy to the poor (as one woman I spoke with remembered her father's provision of water to others in the village), but rather was a public responsibility.[35] Provision of services like water binds government (local and national, institution and process) and place (both land and population) in new ways, both delimiting action and creating new spaces and styles of interaction and challenge.

Expansion of government service is not simply a means through which government gains greater control over the lives of individuals. If Abu Sha'ban was correct that water service expansion was a means of increasing governmental capacity, its effects were just as much to increase governmental obligation and responsibility, and therefore to uncover and produce new incapacities. Servicing is a complex process that increases both opportunity and obligation for all the parties—government, public, nation, locality—that are formed in its practice. Both the social and the physical landscapes of Gaza were transformed in the shift to water services, as social gathering around a well was displaced in the change to faucets and as piping and motors appeared on the scene in Gaza.

These seemingly clear transformations from one kind of place to another and from one kind of present to another were made possible by the relative stability in water servicing. Unlike the crisis services discussed in the previous chapter, water services were defined as permanent, presumably not to be withdrawn as circumstances changed. Despite this apparent stability, however, water services and the transformations they engendered could be as easily threatened as any other governmental domain by the dramas of Gaza's history.

Service Boundaries in the New Gaza Strip

The tenuous ordinariness of everyday servicing was made even more precarious by the transformations of 1948. While during the Mandate everyday servicing was punctured at intervals by the explicit demands of politics, and tactical government was made evident only occasionally, during the Administration the domains in which tactics were not dominant and in which politics were not pressing were much more circumscribed. The compression of territory and the vast influx of refugees created enormous burdens for government, for servicing, and for place. It dramatically altered the physical and social landscape of Gaza. The capacities of the land to provide were stretched by the demands of its new population. The capacities of government were, if anything, more overextended.

Servicing under Egyptian rule was always a cooperative and often conflictual affair, with responsibility shared or divided between the Administration and UNRWA. The transformation of water services that began under the Mandate continued during the Administration, but the disruptions of 1948 ensured that it was not a simply linear development. While service in municipalities proper were not disrupted, the enormous refugee population strained their capacities.[36] The pressures of service provision are particularly evident in the camps. This division by place—where the services provided to municipalities and villages were much greater than those available in camps— was distinct from other jurisdictional divisions we have seen that were made according to type (native or refugee) within the client population. Whereas in food services native Gazans suffered from their lack of refugee status, in water servicing it was refugee spaces that were more deprived.

In the camps, at least in the first years after 1948, everyday utilities were

FIGURE 9. Water pump in Shati refugee camp, 1956. CREDIT: MOSHE PRIDAN. SOURCE: ISRAELI
NATIONAL PHOTO COLLECTION.

barely existent. Not only were there no pipes and power lines connecting these supposedly temporary places to existing networks, but there was political resistance to their incorporation, which, it was felt, might signal an acceptance of permanent displacement. The 1953 Report by the Department of Refugee Supervision, Government Assistance, and Social Affairs indicated that there was one faucet for every three hundred people in the camps and that the water was turned on at intervals.[37] And camp regulations issued by the same department in 1961 included the provision that the "installation of water taps (privately for the shelters)" was strictly prohibited.[38] One retired teacher recalled the problems that sometimes arose because of the limited water distribution in the camps: "UNRWA was in charge of the water problem in coordination with the government. Sometimes disputes or quarrels occurred between women who were going to bring water. Water time was limited, not the whole day. It was one hour a day, and this caused problems among women."[39] Procuring water was still women's work, it seems, but more difficult, more divisive work than before.

The question of jurisdiction—what agencies should provide what services to whom—was particularly challenging in relation to refugee camps. While service provision during both the Mandate and the Administration was pursued without an explicit claim to sovereignty over the territories serviced, such services did indeed entrench government. When it came to servicing refugee camps, there was an added layer of concern. Not only did the Egyptian Administration not want to claim sovereignty over Gaza, it did not want to seem to suggest or accept the idea that refugees were permanently Gazan or that the Gaza Strip itself was not temporary. Providing everyday services to refugee camps posed the risk of doing exactly that.

After 1967, the politics of servicing produced a clash between Gaza City's mayor and the Israeli occupying forces, leading to the former's dismissal. According to reports at the time, "The Israelis said the order was intended to integrate Gaza refugees into the town and make them tax-paying citizens. Four other refugee camps have been annexed to other Gaza Strip towns."[40] Ann Mosely Lesch comments, "Refugees feared that integrating the camp into the town would cause them to lose their special legal status as refugees and undermine their right to return to their homes inside Israel. Thus Shawwa's (the mayor's) refusal to obey the Israeli command received popular support."[41] That the order came from an occupying army made the political importance of such a refusal evident.

The status of camp services during the Egyptian Administration is a little less clear. Some retired municipal employees I spoke with in Gaza recalled that there *were* municipal services in camps in the latter years of the Administration. Abu Jamal recalled that, in 1960, the Gaza municipality extended services to Shati camp:

> At first, the issue was political, and they did not extend the services to the refugee camps, and they [the refugees] depended on drinking water from pumps inside the camp. Then [in 1960] the municipality extended the water network to them. . . . and then [later] the services of sewage, road paving, and electricity were provided for the camps so that they could live in dignity, and to stop the spread of diseases among them.[42]

When I asked about UNRWA's connection to this refugee servicing, Abu Jamal indicated that "there was cooperation. UNRWA helped the municipality pay for the oil for the motors that pumped water in return for extending the water network to the refugees." Khaled 'Emad, who started work in the electricity department in 1960, insisted that the municipality provided services to Shati "from the very beginning"[43] of his career. He remembered the two spaces as completely tied together in servicing: "There were not water wells for the refugees and wells for the Gazans. UNRWA contributed in health and cleaning, but the municipality presented electricity and water as well as health."

The only archival document I have found on this issue seems to indicate that there were not—or at least not many—such services in the camp. This document, a police report on an open meeting (*nadwa*) held in June 1966 in Shati camp and attended by the governor-general, the mayor of Gaza, and a large number of camp residents, records refugee requests precisely for such services. At the meeting, the residents asked the Administration, among other things, to provide street lighting and drinking water for the camp, pave the camp roads, dispense rations to camp residents because UNRWA rations were not sufficient, and increase the police presence in the camps.[44] In response, the governor-general promised to meet "some of these requests," and he "explained the difficulty in fulfilling others." Which requests were met, the report does not specify. Matters are made no more clear by the mayor's comments. He told the people of Shati camp to conserve their resources because "the municipality had cut off all the assistance it had provided." He further stated that he had asked UNRWA authorities two months prior to provide drinking water and electricity to the camp, but that he had still not received a response. Since the report does not specify what assistance the municipality was no longer providing or what the politics of this cessation were, one cannot say with certainty what the camp's service status was. Whatever the actual facts of the matter, the question of service jurisdiction highlighted the limits of the Egyptian Administration's capacity to fulfill its promise to liberate Palestine, creating potential problems for the effectiveness of deferral as a mode of abeyance.

"WE WERE SERIOUS IN OUR JOB": THE WATER DEPARTMENT
AND MUNICIPAL SERVICE PRACTICE

It was the edges of service jurisdictions that created the most obvious tensions in government. Inside service, this work could acquire an ordinariness, tenuous to be sure, that was important not only for getting work done, but also for contributing to formations of place. Abu Jamal, now an activist on behalf of retired civil servants, used to work in the Gaza City water department.[45] He was very proud of both his career and his postretirement activities, and he talked to me at length about them in conversations at the offices of the Retired Civil Servants Association.[46] His first job, which he got in 1957, was as a water meter reader, though he was quickly promoted to a clerk's position. His account of municipal water services during the Administration highlights both the particular role of the municipality as a service provider and the significance of everyday services in shaping the relation between Gazans and government and between population and place. It was during the Administration, Abu Jamal told me, that "the municipality succeeded in connecting water to every house. Water was available to everyone." Water service provision—and everyday services in general—comprised a venue for an intimate connection between people and government. And water services contributed to constituting a place in very concrete ways.

Water services tied the place of Gaza together, both literally, as the network of pipes connected each home and building to each other one, and figuratively, as patterns of water usage were replicated across town. Whenever a Gazan turned on the water faucet in her home she reinforced these literal and figurative ties. At the same time, these services also connected the places in Gaza to the municipality in an equivalent fashion.[47] Each home was charged for water according to the same system; each pipe was laid with the same technique. Abu Jamal described the procedure as follows:

> People who wanted to build a house and wanted water used to come to me and submit an application. The application is transferred to the organizational department, whose employees go to measure the building and ask the people to pay the fees for building the house. After the fees are paid, the application is transferred to the engineers in the water department to determine the diameter of the tube for the house and the placement of the waterline that would be connected to the house. The owner of the house pays the fees, and we give him a water meter, and then the technicians of the water department go and connect the water to his house, and the same thing happens with the department of electricity. . . . We determined the fees according to the engineer's measurements, the greater the distance [of the house to the main waterline], the higher the fee, the shorter the line, the lower the fee.

The ordinary regularity of this procedure may appear remarkable in a place where no aspect of life was untouched by the crises of Palestinian experience, where government was always uncertain and anxious about how to proceed. That even under such conditions everyday practices can sometimes be regular is important to keep in mind. How people work with these procedures, how they interact with civil servants and with the services they provide, can be seen, as Michel de Certeau and Luce Giard suggest about ordinary practices, as a "practical science of the singular."[48]

Not only the use of services, but the work itself constituted such a practical science. Abu Jamal described his typical workday, from the 8 am start of the day to its close at 2 pm.[49] His description illuminates both regular practice and moments of tension, an ordinary flow and mechanisms that permitted a release of pressure. This is indeed a picture of a "subtle combinatory set, of types of operations and registers, that stages and activates a making-do":[50]

> We came to work at 8 in the morning and arranged the citizens' transactions according to date or turn—we put the new transactions in a category and the transactions that were scheduled we arranged according to their date. Of course, every citizen knew his turn—when water would reach his house. . . . At noon, we prayed the noon prayers in a mosque for the employees in the same department. There was also a breakfast break from 9 to 9:30. One ate a sandwich and drank a cup of tea. We spent the time working and receiving the demands of the citizens. Because water is in demand and its problems are so many, we were under pressure. There were water problems especially in summer, for example, water was cut off at someone's house or the amount of water decreased or he had salty water, etc. We conveyed the citizens' complaints to the authorities and asked them to respond. This work took all our time, unless there was a holiday for the employee, so he can let his body have some rest the same as any other employee in any state. This was basically our daily work.

The breaks in the day and the periodic breaks from work itself were crucial to managing the tensions of even an ordinary service. A petition or complaint might provide such a break for a citizen, but civil servants required the built-in getaways that their schedules allowed. The different ways of making-do that come together in any service encounter may be clashing. Abu Jamal, for instance, felt confident that water services were well provided and that complaints were dealt with efficiently; members of the public may not have agreed. What felt like a moment of relief for a civil servant may have been perceived as shirking of responsibility by a citizen. What felt like a reasonable request by a citizen may have been seen as an aggressive overreaching by a civil servant. The negotiations and conflicts that are an inevitable part of any service provision gave shape to its pluralized experience.

"UNRWA IS RESPONSIBLE FOR WATER":

FIGHTING THE WATER-PIPE PROJECT IN NUSEIRAT

As much tension as might arise within service, such tension was even sharper at its boundaries. We have seen how questions of whether and how to provide everyday services troubled the Administration; they concerned UNRWA as well. An instance of suggested service expansion in the Nuseirat refugee camp and of local opposition to this expansion sheds further light on the complications of service provision. In camps not adjacent to municipalities, such as Nuseirat and the other "mid-camps," there was no question that UNRWA, at differing levels of concert with the Administration, would remain principally in charge of water provision.[51] Thus, the conflict over the proposed expansion involved UNRWA directly, and to the extent that political concerns were raised, they centered around the politics of international service obligation. No less than municipal expansion, this proposed service change may have been perceived as a threat to refugee status and to refugees' convictions that their life in the camps was temporary. In making the place more comfortable, more like a home, such service expansion may have threatened to undermine the delicate balance between coping with reality and hoping for more that sustained refugee lives.

Embedded in a larger file of *mabahith* (CID) investigation papers, a series of documents from April 1967 report on a proposed plan to pipe water directly into refugee homes in Nuseirat camp and detail the crisis this plan engendered.[52] The immediate question under investigation was whether a local UNRWA employee named 'Ali Harb had destroyed water pumps in Block C of the camp in an effort to force people living there to accept the project, which he had designed. The mabahith director contended, on the basis of the report of a police officer stationed in the camp, that people had refused the project because they could not afford to pay the ten-pound fee

Harb was collecting; and furthermore that he had therefore destroyed the pumps, leaving "one pump for all of the residents—more than 1,000 souls—while the other three are broken."[53] Statements on Harb's actions were taken from the residents of Block c. Most people questioned professed no knowledge of Harb destroying pumps, but some did raise strong objections to the piped water project.[54] It is these objections which most interest me here.

The varied responses to this project highlight the extent to which people had, by 1967, become accustomed to their conditions in the camp as well as their continuing conviction that these conditions were unjust. Refugees, who had been uprooted from their previous communities, habits, and practices, reshaped these formations in their new conditions and through new services. Expectations of life in the camp did not include piped water, and they did not include paying for the water services that were provided, in this case public water pumps. The refugees were willing to challenge those who threatened this fragile service arrangement. This service practice both helped shape the place of the refugee camp—as the diverse population that made up the camp was bound together in similar living conditions and in a similar structural relationship vis-à-vis UNRWA and the Administration—and confirmed its status as temporary. To suggest that there was a shared experience of place and a bond among its residents is not to deny internal division and conflict. On the contrary, the water crisis in Nuseirat evidences both the existence of a community of service recipients and divisiveness within that community about the practice and future of such provision.

One of the mabahith charges against 'Ali Harb was that he tried to alter conditions on the ground and thereby force people to "adapt" to a new circumstance under which they would pay for piped water. The mabahith director viewed this project as part of an UNRWA plan to bring the "Palestine problem" to an end. The camp residents' objections were framed in more local terms. One of the principal objections to 'Ali Harb's water project was that people were going to be forced to pay for something that UNRWA was supposed to provide. As the policeman put it in his report, "He wants to sell water pipes to the people, even though this is UNRWA's responsibility."[55] The diversity of response among the camp residents suggests that some people were willing to transform their relationship with UNRWA if it meant better living conditions, but that most were reluctant to make any change. At a meeting with the governor-general, the majority of camp residents rejected the idea.

In investigating the crisis, mabahith personnel took statements from four camp residents. They were divided on the wisdom of the project, and each for different reasons: one person agreed to pay if the majority would; another refused because he thought that pumps were sufficient and that in any case his house was too far for the pipes to reach; a third had never heard of the project, but was willing to pay because water from pipes was better than pump water; and the fourth also had not heard about the project, but he rejected the idea on the grounds that UNRWA supplied water for the camp.[56] The person who was willing to pay if a majority had agreed argued that the opposition came from people's inability to pay the fees and that "everyone would agree if it was at UNRWA's expense."[57] The principle of UNRWA responsibility seemed as important to people as immediate financial concerns, as this relationship was reiterated in several of the statements. The relationship also functioned as a community bond, bringing all the camp residents together in a common service relationship. To both implement the project and have UNRWA pay for it might have been a compromise position. It would have affirmed international obligation for refugee services (and therefore their unique status) while at the same time providing greater comforts in refugee lives, thereby settling their conditions somewhat.

In the end, a compromise was ordered, but a different one. Because of the many complaints, the Deir Belah administrative governor finally instructed that piped water be brought in, but that those residents who could not pay for it should be permitted to continue to use the pumps.[58] In distinction from the Mandate, when the compelling of all municipal residents to participate in the water network played a part in the formation of community, in Nuseirat in 1967 the residents won their freedom from such obligation at the expense of their horizontal connection. The decision to exempt people from accepting piped water would no doubt divide the camp along lines of who was able to pay, thereby creating a new marker of wealth in the water faucet. This decision might also have created divisions among camp residents between those who rejected the new service as a "settlement" of their condition and those who either saw no threat in this creature comfort or who simply felt their immediate needs outweighed a possible future implication. In the event, the occupation of Gaza by Israel in June 1967 transformed the entire social and political dynamic of the Strip, limiting the effects of this crisis.

Service Connections: Getting Around and Keeping in Touch

Water services transformed daily habits of living and shaped the relations of people and government by bringing different provisioning practices into the places where people live. Transportation and communications services produced similar effects by enabling and promoting people's connections beyond their local places of residence. These services are no less "everyday services" than water provisioning, but they attend to different aspects of this everyday life. Whether public works projects like road building and paving, services like trains and buses, or communication mechanisms like mail and telephones, connection services both shape community and transform definitions of locality and place. While water services are immediately connected to the natural resources and physical layout of a place, connection services transform the relationships of places to each other.

As in almost every aspect of life, variations in profession, in class, and in gender had considerable influence on the use people made of roads and transportation services. In Gaza during the Mandate private cars were an uncommon luxury. One person told me that "there were five or six cars in all of Gaza—in comparison with the situation now, where there are one or two cars in every house. People used primitive means of transportation—carts and such."[59] For travel between towns, most people relied on the private companies that offered car or bus service. And, it should be remembered, most people did not leave their villages frequently. This was especially the case for women. As Im Tariq recalled, "I stayed in al-Majdal, and we did not go out unless there was an urgent need for doing so. Sometimes, for example, one wanted to visit a patient in a hospital in Gaza."[60] For those who did have more regular cause to travel, what they tend to remember now is the lack of boundaries between the areas in Palestine. As Hamdi Qasim, who grew up in Majdal, recalled, "We used to go to Jaffa, Haifa, Jerusalem, etc. I used to go for a change of air. If I did not like Jaffa, I could go to Haifa, Tel-Aviv, or Jerusalem. If I did not like Jerusalem, I could go to Nazareth or Safad. I used to go wherever I wanted. It was allowed."[61] The basic capacity to move—such a marked contrast with people's lives now—gave people's memories of Mandate travel a distinctly rosy glow.

At the time, however, road conditions were a subject of considerable contention. Both government files and the Palestinian press were filled with complaints about the state of Gaza-area roads. Reflecting the constituency for these services, these complaints came mostly from car companies, chambers of commerce, and local elites. These were the people who needed the roads most immediately, though a shutdown in commercial traffic would obviously have broad effects. A letter to the high commissioner from representatives of some of Gaza's wealthiest families championed the "fellah" (peasant) as the true beneficiary of the Gaza-Jaffa road (an obvious rhetorical ploy, but not wholly without merit): "The policy of Your Excellency has always been the revival of the fellah and the improvement of agriculture in the country. . . . the greatest help that you may render to the inhabitants of Gaza District, who are wholly peasants, is through the construction of this road."[62] The fact that these roads connected places to each other meant that they were never simply local. Gaza's merchants might have a local interest in having good roads into town, but the clientele for these roads was always multiple.

The fact that a variety of persons—Arabs, Jews, government, the army—made use of the roads made them subject to further tussles over jurisdiction. Who, for instance, should be responsible for repairing a road heavily trafficked by army trucks, but about which "no definite proofs could be produced to hold the Army responsible for exceptional damage to the roads?"[63] Should a road running through Majdal be considered an "arterial road," that is, one "which carries 'through traffic' *through* a municipal area as distinct from local traffic, and therefore be partially supported by the central government, as the Gaza district commissioner argued, or was it more properly considered a "feeder road" and a municipal responsibility, as the Public Works Department decided?[64] The fact that the roads were not entirely local directed people's attention to perceived inequalities in treatment, making it harder to keep people's attention from concomitantly considering the meaning of such inequalities. "Had Gaza been Jewish," wrote the newspaper *Filastin* about the bad state of its roads, "His Majesty's government would [not] dare to delay the correction of such a problem."[65] Distraction in the service of abeyance had a somewhat more difficult time in this domain.

Contestations over construction on the Gaza-Beersheba road in 1936–37 highlight the stakes of such public works projects. Large stretches of the

Gaza-Beersheba road were not asphalted, with the result that in poor weather it frequently had to be closed. Letters and telegrams to the high commissioner from Beersheba's transportation companies and notables decry the hardships caused by these closures, which

> isolate Beersheba from big towns such as Jaffa and Gaza which are very frequently visited by the inhabitants of this District. . . . Your excellency, no doubt, cares very much for the welfare and happiness of the populations and we are confident that you will order those concerned to arrange as early as possible for the road in question to be metalled so that this District would not, during your time, be deprived of the facilities accorded to other towns in the country.[66]

In their pleas for action, the transport companies described themselves as nearly bankrupt. The state of these roads aroused interest beyond the immediate locality; the Arab Chamber of Commerce in Jerusalem specifically linked the road to the government's interest in economic development, arguing.

> For centuries, Gaza has kept commercial and various other relations with Khan Yunes and Beersheba but while this part of the country is being developed by the plantation of citrus trees and while this relation is being continually increased through the transport from one place to another of cereals and other crops, we see that Government has overlooked the question of the road between these towns and failed to assist in the further development of this area. . . . It has been the practice of the Government when small Jewish settlements are established in the country to embark on the construction of roads for the purpose of connecting these settlements together and for that reason it is the duty of Government to pay special attention to such a large area which includes Gaza, Khan Yunes and Beersheba.[67]

While government's initial responses to these petitions were to regret the financial stringencies which rendered major work impossible, eventually, and owing to the difficult economic and political conditions in the country, repairs to the road were authorized as a "relief measure," a reminder that the boundary between everyday and crisis services was not always clear. Regarding this work as relief meant that it need not commit government to future expenditures. Indeed, only a year later it was once again saying that "having regard to the present financial circumstances of the Government, it appears improbable that it will be practicable to allocate in the near future a sum of this magnitude for the permanent improvement of the road."[68]

In addition to the barrage of petitions, the Palestinian press kept up a steady drumbeat of complaint about road conditions. Alongside complaints about land sales to Jews, this was one of the most frequent topics about Gaza in the press. In the pages of al-Difa' both local and national governments were criticized for insufficient provision of connection services. Local authorities were generally charged with negligence or personal corruption,[69] while government was charged with bias and duplicity. Government, the articles implicitly argued, was using an appearance of incapacity as a tactic in its efforts to support the Jewish community at the expense of the Arab. For example, in January 1935, the paper complained that the government only paved roads used by Jews. Noting that the Gaza-Jaffa road was paved only as far as the last Jewish settlement, after which point it was merely covered with stones, the article asked bitterly, "Will we only get a road when we give all our land to the Jews? This is very shameful in the history of your government, that it cooperates with the Jews to pave the roads, but we don't get anything but stones."[70]

Again and again, articles in the paper began by exclaiming, "Oh, public works department," and then proceeding to detail how the department was callously neglecting its service obligations to Arabs. An article in May 1935 reflected on the frequency of complaint:

It could be said that all the residents of Palestine have heard the complaints of the residents of Gaza, and the owners of cars and buses, about the bad road. The local newspapers have published their demands that the road, which connects a number of Arab villages with Gaza and Jaffa, be paved quickly. Does the reader know what was the result? Government responded to the people's demand, but when?

After tens of cars and trucks were ruined. . . . We thanked government for this work, even though it was late in coming. Then later, we learned that this work is going to be "only a small payment" to make people be quiet . . . [it will extend only] a small distance past the existing asphalt— which goes as far as the last Jewish settlement. As for the holes which damage cars and trucks on their way to Majdal, these will remain. Not much time was allotted to us before we had to return to complaining and asking the government to pave the road.[71]

The paper was compelled to make this complaint, the article seems to suggest, because of its role as the mouthpiece of the people of Palestine. Still, the press, produced and largely consumed by an educated class, no doubt disproportionately addressed the concerns of this class as well.[72] At the same time, the press, playing the role of muckrakers, could be the vanguard of awareness, not only reflecting, but also shaping concerns and complaints. Newspaper discussions of transport-related services are an instance as much of the *constitution* of concern about these services as *expressions* of it. If "all the residents of Palestine have heard the complaints of the residents of Gaza" this was because the press had served as a venue for the voicing of this complaint. In this manner, the press not only offered comment about services, but participated in producing habits of complaint and resistance in regard to these services.

In all the complaints about road conditions, whether in petitions or in the press, there was a clear understanding that places were defined in part through their relationship with other places. To deny connection, to isolate a place, was also to diminish it. Services too were often understood in relational terms—compared to other times, places, and classes. For Palestinians, the obvious comparison was to the services provided to Jewish settlers. Government was consistently chastised not simply for not providing these services to Palestinians, but for not providing them *equally* with the services that were provided Jewish communities. From the Palestinian perspective governmental incapacity to provide everyday services was a result of will as much as of circumstance. The tactical government which limited government intervention had, from this perspective, a strategic purpose. Incapacity was not simply a condition of Gaza, it was a tactic used to shape Gaza. This attention to the politics of government services is a reminder that the conflict in Palestine was of such significance that it could not always be dissipated through distraction.[73]

As in all other realms of service, the *nakba* forced profound changes in the area of connection services. The abrupt formation of a border between the Gaza Strip and the rest of pre-1948 Palestine bisected roads, severed telephone communications, and cut off the railroad. As an Egyptian officer noted in a July 1949 memo, "The absence of civilian telephone and telegraph lines in the Gaza-Rafah area causes considerable exhaustion among the people because all business transactions for this area . . . require travel to Egypt or El-Arish in order to send a telegram or make a telephone call. Further, going to El-Arish requires getting a permit to enter the Egyptian train and an exit permit [from Gaza]."[74] As the officer further noted, the lack of such service was a political rather than a technical problem: "The telephone and telegraph lines exist, and so do the civil servants needed to operate them."

Not only was Gaza, in 1949, still a military area, but the broader system of which Gaza's telecommunications had been a part—the Palestinian system— had been disrupted. Gaza needed to be reconstituted within an Egyptian service network in order for these connection services to operate.[75] This reconstitution took time, but it did happen, and travel and communications among Gazans and between Gaza and Egypt were restored. This section explores conflicts over this (re)connection of Gaza and Egypt, illuminating how the provision of connection services among newly defined points of service participated in shaping these places of service. In this process, Gaza as a place was both re-placed (within a new regional context that rendered Cairo more present than Jerusalem) and re-figured (as a place of crowding, difficulty, and inconvenience).

In 1959, in an effort to win support for increasing transportation between Gaza and Egypt, the governor-general sent the Egyptian defense minister a copy of an article that had appeared in *al-Tahrir*, a local Gaza newspaper. This article, by Zuheir Rayyis, described the difficult transportation conditions and asked that something be done to improve them.[76] As Rayyis noted, the only existing means of transportation between Gaza and Cairo was a train, which he dubbed "the train of troubles" (*qitar al-mata'ib*) because of its unpleasant conditions: it was hot, dusty, shaky, and extremely slow. The time had come, he argued, that bus transport should be considered "not a tourist necessity only, but a national and public service necessity."

The importance of having good transportation services to Egypt was directly linked to the transformations in Gaza's spatial relations. The cutting off of Gaza in 1948 not only required a reconstitution of connection services as a practical matter, but also generated new habits of connection with other spaces. Gaza as a local place became part of a different regional place, demanding a new set of spatial relations and new patterns of movement and connection. In these circumstances, even "the train of troubles" was an "artery of life"—as Rayyis said the train was also known—that "connects Gaza with the beating heart of Arabism and brings to us everyday our brothers and honored visitors." No longer could Jerusalem serve as a center for Gaza; now Cairo had to be the "heart of Arabism" for Gazans.

Rayyis noted that the governor-general had expended considerable efforts trying to get bus service going; *al-Tahrir* had itself reported on his numerous communications with various Egyptian ministries. To assist the governor-general, Rayyis addressed the Transportation Ministry directly, saying, "A bus line is the easiest, fastest, most comfortable means of connection, which will not cost anything other than opposing some of the deadly and boring rules of *routine*." One of the issues surrounding the establishment of such a bus line was who would get the concession. The governor-general supported granting a Gazan company the special permission that was required for a non-Egyptian company to work the route to Cairo. The Egyptian transportation minister rejected this suggestion, simply saying, "We don't see a point to establishing a new company to have permission to go inside the borders of Egypt."[77] The Gazan company that wanted the concession, not surprisingly, saw a great deal of point to this arrangement and argued that, because of the difficulties associated with the route and the limited income potential, no Egyptian company wanted the concession. It reminded the authorities that an Egyptian company *had* briefly worked on the route and had ceased operations when it found itself with a deficit of thirty thousand Egyptian pounds.[78]

This incident calls attention to the ways in which Gaza remained a place apart during the Egyptian Administration. While it was often governed in a manner similar to Egypt, with certain evident parallels in policy, it was never governed as if it was Egypt. Evidence of whether this newspaper article helped the governor-general's case is not included in the file. What is certainly clear from the exchange is that incapacity in this instance was not simply a result of conditions in Gaza, but was directly linked to political and economic considerations. Egyptian authorities were reluctant to grant foreign operators permission to work in Egypt, even if those foreigners were the Gazans they were supposed to be helping. They may also have been worried about financial repercussions if the company was not profitable, as it would have been Egypt, through the office of the Administration, that would have had to carry the burden if the company was unable to pay its fees. The train may have created troubles for Gazans, but from the Egyptian government's perspective, a bus line seemed potentially even more troublesome.

If travel to Egypt was troublesome, though, transportation problems were exacerbated within the Gaza Strip, where travel among its locales was a daily necessity. During the Mandate many people did not travel much, and "everyone was in his own balad and busy with his own work."[79] During the Administration, fewer people had the luxury of staying at home and tending to their own affairs. Without land to work, people who lived in camps and small towns needed to leave their places of residence and travel to work (if they could find it) in Gaza City. That there was deep frustration with inadequate transportation within the strip is reflected in many *mabahith* reports. A 1963 report from Jabalya camp in the northern part of the Strip stated,

> Recently there has been a transportation crisis. People who wanted to travel to Gaza were held up at the taxi-stand because the bus company didn't send enough vehicles to Jabalya camp. In the past it used to send four buses for the Gaza-Jabalya line, whereas now it only sends one or two buses. This is not enough to transport all the passengers and is creating a transportation crisis. When a bus arrives you see the people running and pushing each other, and around 100 people end up on the bus. There is not a single traffic cop at the taxi-stand to order the movement of cars— especially in the morning. People complain to government and to the company about these actions and the failure of the company to transport the passengers. Further, the company only sends the old and dirty cars for the Jabalya line, which wouldn't be used on any other line. There is no system for sending cars for the Jabalya line.[80]

Implicit within this report of transportation crisis was anxiety about the threat of disorder the crisis was provoking. Policing and servicing had to work together to ensure that public order was maintained. (See chapter 7 for a discussion of how political concerns and control entered the community service domain.) This incident also suggests the importance of regulating movement within, not merely beyond, the borders of Gaza. This crisis of government servicing was, in the first instance, a problem of private business conduct. But it seems clear that actual provision of this service by a private company did not undermine anyone's sense that transportation servicing was government's responsibility. The ability of government to fulfill this obligation was sorely strained by the new character of the Gaza Strip.

One reason it was so difficult to provide adequate transportation for people traveling between Jabalya and Gaza was that there were simply too many people. The space of Gaza had been vastly overcrowded by the nakba, and conditions only became more crowded over the years. As a refugee camp, Jabalya was incapable of supporting or sustaining its population, conditions which forced a large percentage to travel to Gaza City on a daily basis. At the same time, this inadequate transportation was not an accident. Despite its need, Jabalya appears to have been unable to make a claim on the company, which sent "the old and dirty vehicles" to this overcrowded, dirty place. The bus company seemed to make use of Jabalya's incapacities to create its own service incapacities. It is not difficult to imagine the decision making that would have led the company to reserve its better vehicles for better-off places and to be more concerned that there was enough transportation for people who were better placed to complain if it was inadequate. Still, even if their complaints did not have the same weight as those of citizens in Gaza, the refugees of Jabalya continued to press their claims. If the refugees in Nuseirat were reluctant to accept a water-service expansion in part because of concerns about becoming too settled, the Jabalya incident indicates that refugees *were* willing to challenge discomforts that appeared to be gratuitous. If the private company could not be counted on to provide clean, adequate transport, as apparently it could not, government intervention was required.

The claim of Administration responsibility was explicitly made in a petition sent to the governor-general a few years later, also coming from Jabalya. In 1966, a group of about fifty civil servants living in and around Jabalya petitioned the governor-general, asking that the local car company be replaced, since it had "failed in its mission" to transport passengers.[81] The mabahith report about this problem and the petition itself noted that "this company has not fulfilled its duties toward civil servants in the proper manner." With adequate transportation, Jabalya could be easily tied to Gaza, whereas without such services it seemed immeasurably farther away. Barring replacement of the company, the petition suggested that "a special bus, or more, be designated to transport civil servants from Jabalya camp to their places of work in Gaza—for a monthly fee." In this case, civil servants appealed to their particular needs as government employees—and to government's particular needs for them: "The scarcity of transportation is causing them [civil servants] not to fulfill their work obligations in the proper manner, because it is causing them to be late to work." The petition evoked, therefore, the possibility of a cycle of inefficiency whereby inadequate transportation would cause civil servants to fail in their duties, thereby ensuring that Gazans would be improperly serviced. This complaint linked everyday transportation services to larger service questions of duty, obligation, and responsibility and explicitly located the responsibility for fulfillment of these service demands with government.[82]

These particular service crises highlight some of the ways in which everyday servicing was distinct from the crisis services discussed in the previous chapter. In everyday services the sense of service was sufficiently expansive to incorporate even seemingly private commercial activity within its domain. The entire episode occurred *within* service—a marked distinction from the practices in relation to food or even water. Here service was transformed from an intermittent response to crisis to a general condition of being in the Gaza Strip. And if service was expansive here, it was also productive. Relations among the various parts of Gaza, and the character of these places themselves, were produced in part in the details of service delivery.

Conclusion

The singular work of everyday servicing—provision and receipt, debate and delivery, complaint and correction—was fundamental to the pluralized production of place. In the repetition of daily acts of servicing—turning on a faucet, getting on a bus—the dense network of relations that constitute a place was produced and reproduced. These everyday services, minute though their apparent focus might be, were also far-reaching. Their significance lay not only in their effect on Gazans, but also in their impact on government. The diversity of perspectives on, and locations in relation to, everyday services was crucial to this formation. As people expressed their views, staked their individual claims, articulated their own understandings, they gave shape to the networks that formed Gaza and its government.

Government services helped produce government authority, though the multiplicity of governing bodies, practices, and participants often rendered the nature of that authorization opaque. Municipalities may have seen themselves as staking a claim for local authority in the face of a potentially hostile national government, but their effective operations also promoted the stability of central administration. Individuals might have objected to specific service conditions, but the form of their objections often worked to consolidate governing practices. The tenacity of government never meant that government entirely controlled or directed these dynamic relations. Gaza may have been formed in and by government, but this form was often unexpected and frequently reconfigured. Given the loss that is at the heart of the Gazan (and Palestinian) experience of place, it is difficult to imagine how this might have been otherwise.

7

COMMUNITY SERVICES AND FORMATIONS
OF CIVIC LIFE

The average Municipality of Palestine is an authority which plans
roads, provides water and conservancy, erects slaughter-houses and
regulates markets; but it is not yet a corporate body expressing in its
services the social sense of the community. . . . There is evidently little
sense of municipal responsibility for public welfare in the sense in
which this would be understood in Europe. . . . The participation of
the local government authorities in education, as is the English practice, is one way of enlisting civic interest and civic pride in a campaign
of general cultural improvement.

PALESTINE ROYAL COMMISSION [PEEL COMMISSION] REPORT, 1937

Purpose of the club: to raise the social and cultural level among the
Arab UNRWA employees—to have games and matches, hold lectures,
show films. The club has sports activities to strengthen bodies and
spirits. The club does not enter into political matters or sectarian
matters. The club operates according to the law in Gaza.

BYLAWS OF ARAB UNRWA EMPLOYEES ASSOCIATION, 1961

While most of the governmental practice of the British
Mandate and the Egyptian Administration was char-
acterized by its constraints—limited in financial resources, tentative in relations with the territory being governed, anxious about overextending its

reach—there were domains and moments that called for a more expansive mode of governing. The need for control, for managing political threat and security concerns, sometimes produced an intensity of regulation and a close involvement with place and population. Government concerns did lead to a proliferation of security services, but they were also addressed by community services which elaborated civic ideals and defined public mores.[1] In these services, the expression of government control was forceful without (often) employing the actual use of force.

In community services such as education and religious affairs it became ever more difficult to disentangle state from society, even as these services often relied on the apparent solidity of such a distinction to do their work. The space in which these services operated was the space of the civic, a domain that was, not surprisingly, highly contested. While at the broadest level there was agreement that civic life entailed individual, community, and government participation in the promotion of an active citizenry, an engaged public, how such goals might be accomplished and what such an engaged public might look like were sources of deep disagreement. That this public did not simply exist but had to be continually formed was certainly something of which government was aware. The necessary involvement of government in such production further complicated any imagined separation of the civic from the governmental, of society from the state.

We can think of the civic, as Pierre Mayol in volume 2 of *The Practice of Everyday Life* suggests in regard to the neighborhood, as entailing both obligation and recognition. One was obligated to participate and to conform to the demands of "propriety." Propriety, as Mayol defines it, "represses what is 'not proper,' 'what one does not do'; it maintains at a distance, by filtering and exposing them, the signs of behavior that are illegible in the neighborhood, intolerable for it, destructive, for example, of the dweller's personal reputation."[2] Propriety does not function only negatively, but also articulates obligations of what *is* proper, what *are* the best ways of living and being in a community. Fulfilling these obligations could also lead one to expect acknowledgment of one's compliance, one's civic skills, through a "lexicon of 'benefits' expected from the progressive mastery" of propriety.[3]

While the neighborhood is a more intimate space than the civic appears to be, arguments about civic virtues, as the services explored here make clear, often played out at precisely this scale. Education and religious services, while broad in their mission and scope, were enacted at a small scale: in a school, a village square, indeed, a neighborhood. The mutual obligations brought forth by these services were not simply between government and the public, but within the Gazan community itself. Civic associations, which were regulated and subject to surveillance by government, offered a space for the management of the "conduct of conduct"[4] of Gazans by Gazans. The activities of such associations, the details of schooling, the work of religious scholars and service providers were all part of a process of policing propriety.

One aspect of the locality of these community services was the bounded nature of the community they served. While community services were distinguished from crisis and everyday services by having a collective client, their clientele was also in some ways more narrow than that of those individually oriented, singular services. The "community" of community servicing was never the entire population, but rather was distinguished by religion, by nationality, by refugee status. And yet, these services often sought to exercise influence beyond the seemingly clear boundaries of their jurisdiction. Education, for example, had long been divided in Palestine according to religious community (*millet*), each *millet* providing its own schools. In the Mandate, this religious community distinction was transformed into a national community division, with two school systems, one for Jews and one for Arabs, operating. During the Egyptian Administration the line of distinction was once again transformed, and refugee and native children attended separate schools. Religious services were by definition limited to members of a particular religious community, but, as in the case of missionary activity, sometimes they attempted to expand the boundaries of that community.

The focus of community servicing on civic life further illuminates the dynamic of abeyance that was so important to the maintenance of rule in Gaza and in Palestine more broadly. While the language of propriety offered a mechanism of control, it also displaced the site of that control to the seemingly distinct realm of society. The demands of propriety, that is, could appear to be social rather than governmental demands, distracting attention from the very regimes which were imposing it. Abeyance, though, as has already been made evident, was never a perfect technique, and there were many cracks in its distractions and deferrals. Efforts by community members to bring the government in as an ally in their projects for policing society highlight the impossibility of keeping these realms entirely separate and of fully distracting people from the government's involvement in controlling propriety. Political struggles over the nature of civic life in Palestine, over the future of the community, the nation, and the state, suggest limits to the effectiveness of deferral as a means of avoiding political threat. Not surprisingly, the effects of government policies often outdistanced their intentions. In the effort to exercise control over the shape of Palestinian civic life, community services opened up new venues for challenging government.

Community services were concerned not only with defining and protecting propriety for the current moment, but also with shaping the future of civic life. Crisis and everyday services were principally focused on the near-at-hand and the current moment. Community services, on the other hand, projected their vision forward, imagining a better society, a brighter future. In conditions of tactical government like those in Gaza, this future orientation posed a problem. I have already noted that tactical government has a shortened vision of action, and we have seen some of the consequences of this makeshift character for governmental practice. Because community services articulated themselves in relation to a future they could not glimpse, they operated with an additional layer of uncertainty. This uncertainty shaped the delivery of community services in both the Mandate and the Administration.

"Commanding What is Good": Religious Services as Civic Services

Religious services, which in the case of Islamic services included work in mosques, shari'a courts, religious education and scholarship, and charitable societies, were somewhat uncomfortably located within the larger bureaucratic structure.[5] The question of whether shari'a court employees should be eligible for pensions (see chapter 4) highlighted some of that discomfort, a discomfort that was not so much about *whether* religion should have a place in public life, but *what* that place should be. How autonomous could religious services be? What kind of claims could religious expression make on a society that was broader than its own community? The process of defining a religious sphere within public life began not with the British, but with the Ottomans. In the nineteenth century, Ottoman authorities distinguished religious and secular governmental functions, limiting the jurisdiction of religious courts, for example, to personal status issues and referring all other matters to a secular court system.[6] During the Mandate and the Administration, the fact of religious servicing raised sometimes uncomfortable questions about the relationship among government and population, government institutions and civic associations, and private citizens and public officials.[7]

The dominant idiom of religious servicing was that of moral improvement.[8] Moral improvement was, though, not simply the betterment of the individual or the improvement of personal character, but was also tied to the community as a whole, to its civic life. It was, therefore, also connected to the political terrain on which civic life was enacted; hence the problem with these services. Nationalism and civic duty were articulated as internal to religious practices, potentially solidifying a means of challenging government. Connecting their mission to this question of the civic, religious service providers also often tried to exert influence beyond the limits of their client population.

The first problem for the provision of religious services in the British Mandate was the form of that mandate itself. The replacement of Muslim Ottoman authority with (Christian) British authority in Palestine raised immediate questions about the organization of religious services within the framework of the state. Under the Ottoman Empire, shari'a courts, *waqf* administration, and mosque management were all part of the state infrastructure, authorized, like all government services and activities, by the sultan. When the British entered Palestine, they took over all of the administrative functions of the former Ottoman regime, including these religious services, but under, first, military and then international (through the League of Nations) authority. These authorizing sources, being secular at best and Christian at worst, were a weak foundation on which to build the provision of Muslim services.

In order to cope with this problem and to equalize the various religions within the new ecumenical authority, a governing body, the Supreme Muslim Council (SMC), was established to authorize Islamic services in Mandate Palestine.[9] The SMC, like all government offices during the Mandate, was headquartered in Jerusalem, although, again like all government offices, it had employees working in the districts as well. Gaza City was the site of an SMC-authorized waqf committee, shari'a court, and library.[10] Despite its many similarities with other government offices, the SMC was not an entirely regular governmental body. By creating this autonomous religious body, Mandate officials hoped to both contain religious expression and defuse religious politics. From the beginning of the Mandate, Herbert Samuel tried to impress on the SMC the "undesirability of using places of devotion for the purposes of political propaganda."[11] In its 1936 report to the League of Nations, the Palestine government commented, "Whilst discussing the representative character of the Supreme Moslem Council, it will be borne in mind that it is not a political body, but an administrative body dealing with Moslem religious affairs. In so far as it is representative, it is representative of the Moslems of Palestine in their religious aspect."[12]

Despite the British insistence on controlling the limits of the SMC's representativeness, neither the council nor the variety of Islamic personnel saw their services as so limited. The moral and political futures of the Palestinian community were entirely bound together in the eyes of these service providers, and their practices indicate an unwillingness to divide them. Religious services *were* civic services in Mandate Gaza, and they also formed a field of tension about the delimitation of both religious and civic life. The similarity of these services to other civil services in terms of administrative structures, styles of operation, and budgetary strictures imbued them with governmental authority. At the same time, the similarity constrained them, as it obligated them to operate according to the same standards of civility that sought to excise (or at least contain) politics from the civil service field.

In other chapters I have discussed personnel who operated under the direct authority of the SMC, including shari'a court judges, mosque staff, waqf officials, and religious teachers. Here I turn to another sort of provider and another site of such servicing: the community leader and the religious association.[13] During the Mandate, societies were established throughout Palestine with the express purpose of "spread[ing] Islamic morals and ideals" among the population.[14] Many of these societies operated under the umbrella of the SMC. Unlike some other religious services, though, these societies had no legal authority. Their ability to command was based, rather, on moral authority. Their self-defined responsibility was for the moral climate among the Muslim-Palestinian community and the promotion of virtue in its members. They, like government, acted tactically in their pursuit of a better society.

There were several Islamic societies in Gaza during the period of the Mandate, the most significant of which was the Society for *Amr bi-l -Ma'ruf wa-l -Nahy 'an al-Munkar* (lit. Society for Commanding Right and Forbidding Wrong, a name which the society rendered in English as the "Society for the Preservation of Public Morals").[15] This society, Gaza's branch of a national network of such societies, was established after a call from the first national *'ulama'* conference (convened by the SMC) for concerted work on Palestine's moral terrain. According to Abdul Latif Abu Hashim, the Gaza society was established on June 3, 1935, at a meeting held in the *awqaf* administration offices.[16]

In organizing its civic struggle in the terms of amr bi-l ma'ruf, these Palestinian societies were joining a much longer and broader Islamic tradition of exhortation to better behavior. Michael Cook, in a comprehensive study of the history of amr bi-l ma'ruf in Islamic thought and practice, identifies a wide variety of wrongs to be forbidden and of means of forbidding them.[17] The obligation of amr bi-l ma'ruf crisscrosses the terrain of state and society. Describing this practice as it occurs in Saudi Arabia, Talal Asad notes that the government has taken on the responsibility, as part of its obligation to ensure that people do not flout God's authority, of establishing "a supervisory organization whose members devote their energies 'to commanding what is good and forbidding what is evil (*al-amr bi-l -ma'ruf wa n'nahy 'an al-munkar*).'"[18] In her study of the women's mosque movement in Egypt, Saba Mahmood emphasizes its personal enactment, tying women's involvement in such exhortation to Rashid Rida's argument that it is a *fard al-'ain* (individual obligation).[19]

In Palestine, the Society for the Preservation of Public Morals lay somewhere in between. It was not governmental, though it operated under the umbrella of the SMC and sought government support for its campaigns. Its membership was somewhat circumscribed—it was open to the following: participants in the conference, *'ulama'*, or "men of religion," and "every Muslim who follows the righteous path and laudable morals [*al-akhlaq al-hamida*]"[20] —though the specific issues around which it organized demanded the personal involvement of the entire Palestinian community. The major threats to Muslim community and morality in Palestine identified by the society were the sale of land to Zionists, Christian missionary activity, and improper dress and behavior by Muslims.[21] While all of these threats were to the entire community, they could be rebuffed only by proper behavior on the part of individuals. In defining the issues which were most pressing for the Muslim community, the society also linked them to the needs of the entire Palestinian Arab society.[22]

It was on the terrain of these preoccupations that the society struggled for its vision of civic life. Thus, while the services of the society, namely, its preaching and teaching, were limited to Muslims, its lessons were meant to be general. The concerns of the society also indicate the anxiety about the future that conditions in the Mandate engendered. The political character of some of these moral issues is evident and posed a challenge to government's idea that religious expression could be contained as social. In the society's work these ideas may not for the most part have been expressed against government, but in its charting of a political terrain they created a possibility for opposition.

Uri Kupferschmidt, in his study of the SMC, comments that the Central Society "rarely showed signs of life."[23] This may have been true of the Jerusalem branch, but it was demonstrably not the case in Gaza's society. According to the records of this society, which include reports on activities and correspondence, its members were active on a number of fronts, including preaching in villages, challenging government on its biases, complaining to government about its permitting immoral behaviors, and providing charity to the poor.[24] The obligation to act morally may have been incumbent on everyone, but the inculcation of such behavior required ethically authoritative personnel. The society's sense of its authority is evident in its 1936 request to the SMC to be permitted to oversee village preachers and to "supervise them in an official manner." The society complained that there were many preachers "who are only interested in receiving their salary and who are lazy and negligent about undertaking this holy office [wazifa muqaddasa] correctly."[25] Since it was through the offices of this wazifa muqaddasa that the bulk of Muslims in Gaza could be induced to "preserve the interests of their religion and their world," their supervision by such morally qualified individuals as the members of the society was of paramount importance.[26]

The society ended its request by tying together the various forms of community and obligation. It wanted to supervise the preachers, the letter affirmed, in order to "work with them in the public interest and for the salvation of the nation [umma] from the dangers which are facing their religion, their world, and their holy nation [watan], preservation of which will

preserve their being [*kiyanahum*] and their nationality [*qawmiyatahum*]."
There are several senses of nation embedded in these words—the Muslim
community, the Palestinian nation, and the broader Arab nation—though, as
Weldon Matthews notes, the distinctions between these terms that characterized later nationalist discourse had not yet fully crystallized.[27] Even if the
meanings of these locutions overlapped, the society's use of them all suggests it
saw itself as equipped to provide ethical guidance across these domains. That
religious thought expressed itself in a nationalist idiom in Palestine is perhaps
not surprising, but it should not be seen as self-evident (nor has such expression been employed at every moment).[28] That it did so during the Mandate
points to the expansiveness and the publicness of this thought at the time.
This expansive attitude is confirmed by the range of the society's activities.

The society sent preachers to the mosques of the city and to surrounding
villages to speak about its agenda and to attempt to elicit people's agreement
to improve their behavior.[29] The mechanisms the society employed to control conduct were varied, including social pressure and government force.
One preacher, Said Muhammad Allah, described his success in transforming
conduct in the village of Simsim. He went to the village on February 10, 1936,
arriving before the afternoon prayer. He was escorted by a teacher in the
government school, implying that he was not content to rely on his own
moral authority but wished as well to "borrow" some of the social authority
of teachers. After the prayer he commenced his preaching, focusing on the
prohibition against drinking alcohol. He spoke until the evening prayer, after
which time

> I asked them to ask for pardon, to repent, and to cease practicing abom-
> inations. I took from them an agreement for that. The *mukhtars* of the
> village swore on the Qur'an that if someone practiced these things, they
> would hurry and inform on him to you [the society president] or to the
> police. This happened in front of everyone in the mosque. The school-
> teacher gathers the boys nightly in the school and works on their reading
> and writing and tries to dissuade them from all abomination, and he
> deserves thanks for this. And so I thanked him in front of them. I am
> confident that they will not return to this behavior.[30]

The publicness of both the message and its acceptance appeared to be of
central importance: "this happened in front of everyone" and "I thanked him

in front of them." Another crucial aspect was the communal and universal nature of the experience: everyone was there to hear Said preach, he stressed, and everyone agreed to accept the message. Even as people accepted the demands laid out by Said, their behavior would be henceforth policed by their local leaders, the mukhtars, who might involve the outside authority of the society or the police.[31]

Although Said invoked the authority of the police over moral conduct, it was by no means guaranteed that the police were actually interested in patrolling this domain. An effort to get legal backing for the society's campaign against alcohol, for instance, largely failed. The society petitioned government to revoke the liquor licenses of a number of bars and stores on the grounds that they violated the law by being located too close to mosques or in solely Muslim neighborhoods.[32] The government did not seem to find these claims compelling. In the matter of an objection to the renewal of Fahmi Hakura's permit to sell alcohol in his store, for instance, the high commissioner decided not to overturn the decision of the local permits committee, being convinced, among other things, that "the store is on a main street in Gaza where a lot of non-Muslims live and a number of the neighboring shops are owned and frequented by non-Muslims" and that many of the nearby mosques "were built after the store."[33] There was more at stake in this decision for the society and for government than the narrow legal issues. But regulatory questions which made it possible for the society to request governmental involvement, also made it possible for government to refuse to intervene.

Christian missionary activity, especially missionary schools, worried the society and Gazans more generally.[34] Like alcohol consumption, missionary activity threatened to undermine both the virtue and the unity of the Muslim community. The threat of the schools seems to have been less that pupils would actually convert to Christianity than that they would learn attitudes and morals that would make then bad Muslims. As in its campaign against alcohol, the society moved in several directions at once to confront the threat. A 1936 monthly report blamed the government for not providing adequate schooling and described the society's efforts to address this problem:

> In the last monthly report, we mentioned that there is a missionary school in Gaza which is teaching children to hate the Islamic religion. They learn this false ideology because there are no [public] kindergartens. We wrote

to the mayor of Gaza asking him to open a kindergarten in the municipal school, and we asked the director of education to open a children's school in the government elementary school. We have learned that the municipality opened this class. As for the government, the education director responded that he received our request and he will look into the matter and maybe the request will be fulfilled. I hope that requests like this will be made by all the associations in Palestine, and then maybe the government will respond positively.[35]

In addition to petitioning government, the society decided to address the parents of the students directly, both in the public forum of the Friday sermon and through personal visits to their homes in order to "clarify to them the harmfulness of the missionary schools . . . and ask them not to send their children to the school."[36] The society serviced the community by involving each of the parties in the governing dynamic—government, municipality, population—in the project of creating a more virtuous civic life.

In the campaign against land sales to Zionists, the society focused its attention on individual members of society, seeking to remind them of their obligations to seek the good of all. In distinction to practices of public shaming of land sellers and *simsars* (brokers) that were often employed by the press, the society's efforts were frequently private interventions. Society members did preach against the sales in general, for example, in cases in which a particular sale was threatened or a specific seller identified, but the society tended to approach the party individually. Among the records of the society, there are a number of letters written by individual members to persons they knew to be selling land as well as mentions of delegations being sent to talk to them in an attempt to dissuade them.[37] Such individual address hints at another aspect of the control the society desired to exert. Using "sweet speech and logic,"[38] the society aimed to compel individuals to recognize their obligation to community and society.

As a community service provider, the society searched out multiple mechanisms for controlling conduct and for improving the quality of civic life. The difficulties in acquiring the government support it sought further highlight the complications that religious servicing posed in the Mandate. Distinctions had been made between these and other kinds of services, partly in deference to community feeling (that it was inappropriate for a non-Muslim body to direct Muslim services), but this distinction in turn restricted the capacity of those services to lay claim to the full weight of government power. In their practice, religious service providers made use of a variety of sources of authority, including ethical and social, governmental and national, even as these domains were held to be distinct.

STATED RELIGION: THE EGYPTIAN ADMINISTRATION
AND THE PROVISION OF RELIGIOUS SERVICES

Under the Egyptian Administration, the boundaries between the various domains of service receipt, provision, and authorization were much less sharply drawn. Whereas during the Mandate the SMC was established precisely to create a distinct authorizing body for religious services, during the Administration the SMC was integrated into government, and at its head was the governor-general.[39] Ultimately this lack of distinction led to its dissolution. Since its original purpose had been lost, this "old" body was no longer suited to the needs of service provision. As Michael Dumper puts it, "The position of a higher echelon of the Supreme Muslim Council in the Gaza Strip controlling the local waqf committee [became] increasingly redundant."[40] Accordingly, in 1957 the responsibilities of the SMC were devolved to the governor-general, the Administration, the shari'a appeals court, and the local waqf administration.[41] The dispersing of religious services across government departments suggests how unproblematically within service these practices were during the Administration. At the same time, the control exerted by the Administration over the services indicates the extent to which this provision was connected to political concerns.

Before the SMC could be absorbed and then dissolved, the Administration had to reconstitute it. As we have seen in every arena of service provision, the 1948 nakba destroyed the financial and organizational basis of religious servicing. The loss of waqf land, which provided revenue for mosques and religious schools, and of the resources of the SMC in Jerusalem had an immediate deleterious effect on the provision of religious services. As a stopgap measure, in 1949, the new governor-general of Gaza asked the Egyptian Awqaf Ministry to help support Gaza's religious institutions:

> In the areas of Palestine under the purview of the Egyptian Administration, there are a number of mosques which are now without furnishings.

Not one of them is maintained by Islamic Affairs in Jerusalem, as they used to be. . . . The need now is for the Awqaf Ministry to provide new furnishings and also to provide financial assistance to these places of worship. The salaries of the preachers and *muezzins* have been stopped. The Egyptian Administration is obliged to organize these places of worship and to arrange for assistance to them. The Awqaf Ministry is responsible for religious and charitable matters, so we ask that the ministry provide whatever assistance it can in paying the salaries of these employees.[42]

The ministry agreed to send carpets to the Gaza mosques and to contribute 190 pounds to their budget.[43] The Egyptian Social Affairs Ministry also appropriated funds (upon request) to support the operations of Islamic schools in Gaza, which had previously been supported by the SMC.[44] In the long term, as I noted, the SMC was reestablished by the Administration and then absorbed into other departments. With religious services distributed across government, Administration-era files record numerous instances of municipalities and other government bodies funding these services—the Deir Belah Council contributed to the construction of a religious school; the Rafah Municipality was ordered by the Administration to pay for the reparation of a local mosque wall.[45]

While this absorption occurred in large part for administrative reasons, it reveals the government's desire to control the domain of religious services.[46] The Mandate government was similarly apprehensive about the possibility that religious bodies would act politically, but it was more constrained than the Administration in its possible responses to such worries. The Administration, as a Muslim government, was able to more directly control religious expression by its employees and the public. Rema Hammami, echoing this point, suggests that "the Egyptian State's consolidation of its control over the institutional mechanisms of religious production in Gaza was intimately connected to its suppression of the Muslim Brotherhood [*Ikhwan Al-Muslimiin*] as a counter-hegemonic political force."[47] Still, just as the Mandate was never entirely successful in controlling these politics, neither was the Administration. In concert with its centralization of control over religious expression, the Egyptian Administration was much less willing than the Mandate to give independent religious societies room to maneuver.

Police files from the Administration include numerous accounts of surveillance of religious activities and refusals of permission for the formation of religious societies. In 1953, a group of people in Khan Yunis desired to establish a Society of the Followers of Sunna in Khan Yunis, whose stated purpose was to spread knowledge of the Qur'an and Sunna through "public lectures on exalted morals and social etiquette," to develop a collection of religious books and magazines, and to "aid the poor and unfortunate to the extent the Society's finances allow."[48] Police investigation of the founding members found them all to be supporters of the Muslim Brotherhood, but also found them all to possess "good morals and clean records."[49] Despite the lack of apparent danger such a society would pose and the nonobjection of the police to its founding, the governor of Khan Yunis recommended against approval, commenting, "In my opinion there is no cause to have this society, given that its numbers are very small, and in fact do not exceed the founders themselves—also there is no cause to have a society like this given that most of these founders were previously members of the Muslim Brotherhood."[50]

Even if religious services during the Administration were not usually provided by the kinds of religious societies that were so important during the Mandate, their provision was nevertheless not limited to religious affairs *muwazzafin*. The administrative dispersal of religious services across the governing infrastructure also produced an expansion of religious servicing. One of its most important sites became the educational apparatus (see below for a lengthier discussion of education). According to Rema Hammami, "The administration invested itself with the role of elaborating religion. . . . [and] the main terrain through which the regime promoted its reading of Islam was the school system."[51]

Hammami argues further that this reading was part of the government's project of "creating modern subjects/citizens" and made clear that "Islam was to be considered a code for personal behavior and social morality as opposed to a political will that it was the responsibility of Muslims to fulfill. Islam was relevant to shaping modern life inasmuch as it provided codes of ethics and behavior in everyday life."[52] Gregory Starrett makes much the same argument for religious education in Egypt, writing that "religious study in Nasser's primary schools altered the previous emphasis on manners like humility, time management, and good behavior, focusing instead on social values necessary to a popular reconstruction of society by the masses: sincerity, fulfilling obligations, forbearance, and the rights of the nation."[53] Compared to the Mandate, the Administration made religious servicing, if anything, more public, more imbricated in the civic life of Gaza, but it was also more controlled for political expression. Islamic education under Egypt sought to promote a kind of civic morality that would not threaten government power and could participate in its project of promoting a well-ordered public life.[54]

The civic quality of religious services and the obligations entailed therein were highlighted in the crisis atmosphere that preceded the 1967 war (and, as it turned out, the end of Egyptian rule in Gaza). At the end of May 1967, just two weeks before the war in June, the awqaf commissioner issued an order to mosque staff in which he listed the topics for sermons to be delivered in the mosques during the month of Safar 1387 AH, that is, May/June 1967. In light of the brewing political crisis, the sermons were to stress the importance of cooperation and understanding among the citizenry as well as support for and cooperation with the forces working to liberate their nation. Further, the sermons were to urge people not to hoard food and supplies because it is "the government [that] is responsible for organizing, storing, and distributing the needed supplies to the people, and it is undertaking this task." People should be reminded that hoarding food "will harm the public without benefitting the hoarder, whether he be a merchant or a consumer. . . . The Prophet, *sala 'alehi wa-salem*, said: 'One who hoards the food of a nation [*qawm*] is not of them.' "[55]

In this high stakes moment of preparation for war, the practices of policing propriety and encouraging ethical comportment were especially important in the delivery of religious services. The mutual, overlapping obligations inherent in civic life continued to shape its expression. Religious and national duty were inextricably linked in this call for responsible citizenship. The government could meet its obligations to both regulate and provide only with the participation of the entire society. To choose not to participate was to choose not to be of the society. To cooperate with government and with one's fellow Gazans, on the other hand, was to express the highest ideals of Gaza's civic life. As it turned out, of course, this carefully calibrated array of obligations was disrupted by the defeat of Egyptian forces and the Israeli occupation of the Gaza Strip.

Civics and Citizenry: Educational Services in Gaza

Education in Gaza during the first half of the twentieth century, which was partly colonial, influenced by nationalism, and indebted to enlightenment traditions and Ottoman practices, was necessarily connected to the contours of civic life that were emerging and being struggled over during this period.[56] Given the intensity of the demand for control and the ongoing uncertainty about rule, the civic life promoted through education unsurprisingly was one which excluded, or at least restricted, political expression. The contours of educational servicing were also formed by uncertainty about the future shape of the polity of which students were being educated to be a part. This uncertain civic life was expressed in education through the sometimes conflicting figures of the "national" and the "citizen."

In their most common senses, nationality and citizenship appear to be integrally connected. James Holston and Arjun Appadurai, for example, describe a general modern project of "national citizenship" that relies upon an idea of "the nation as a community of shared purposes and commensurable citizens."[57] In the Gaza of the Mandate and the Administration, however, nationality and citizenship were to a degree uncoupled, and each became a site of struggle. Given the intensity of national conflict between Jews and Arabs in Palestine during the Mandate, British officials promoted a vision of citizenship that could transcend national distinction and offer a social, as opposed to a political, sense of citizen rights. Since the Administration, on the other hand, was unable to actualize the achievement of formal citizenship (in an independent Palestine) that it promised to Gazans, it promoted the nation as the dominant space of subject positioning. During both periods, Gazans, above all the teachers who were most explicitly called on to impart these visions, challenged the government's terms and its efforts to control the limits of proper behavior.

If civil servants occupy an uncomfortable space in a ruling dynamic, the work of teachers epitomizes this discomfort. Gazan teachers, who were highly politicized during both the British and the Egyptian periods, were in the position of always having to teach two conflicting curricula at once. On the one hand, they taught the government curriculum with its particular emphases and with its important skills and knowledge. On the other hand, they also articulated and taught a contesting vision of community and civic life. They suggested, in the Mandate, that the national community was paramount, even as they reproduced the official curriculum's lessons on world history and universal civics. They suggested during the Administration that the rights of citizenship, rights that included political contestation and organization, were as important as the demands of nation as defined by the Administration. Teachers continually negotiated a terrain of contradiction and conflict.

Early in the Mandate, officials identified education as a mechanism for inculcating a broad conception of Palestinian community, one which would encompass all religions and nationalities and which would be distinctly social, rather than political. Being a good citizen was uncoupled from one's obligations to country and was figured instead as a general attribute of a proper person. Such a project would be greatly simplified, officials argued, by the establishment of a uniform, national school system. Ylana Miller describes the attitude of the Colonial Office: "The avowed British aim in Palestine was 'to get Jew and Moslem to work together and develop a common Palestinian consciousness.' The more schools were left to religious communities and local authorities, the more difficult it would be 'to get the schools to play their part in the development of such a policy.'"[58] Given the depth of the conflict in Palestine and the doubts and debates that were always present under British rule, one has to wonder, as Miller does, how much British officials really imagined they might succeed in producing a common citizenry and community in Palestine. Certainly the fact that schooling *was* separated into two systems, the Jewish community operating its own schools, seemed to guarantee that the effort would fail even before it began.[59] However unrealistic the aim, schooling for Arabs in the government system was always engaged in this project of producing non-nationalist, apolitical citizens, a project that was complicated by the uncertain future of Palestine.

A further complication in educational initiatives was that, although schooling was supposed to be compulsory, there was a sizable gap between theory and practice, with large numbers of students shut out of schools every year for lack of space. Education during the Mandate may have been defined in universalizing terms, but it was nowhere near universal.[60] The limits in educational services represent another instance of services with a limited clientele whose effects were meant to pervade society. Those families which had no direct exposure to school might acquire some familiarity with its general lessons through the social personas of teachers. Civil servants generally, and teachers particularly, had high social status during the Mandate. Given the limited availability of education, it was inevitable that this service field would contribute to the reproduction and reinforcement of class distinctions among the population. The same conditions which mandated the stagnation of much of the population were those which guaranteed the educator and the educated status and respect. Education was widely recognized as a path to personal advancement. As Qasim Jamal, a former teacher, recalled people's desires to educate their children, "The desire was that they would finish school and become respectable, could find a position, get work."[61]

Teachers were both the embodiment of this educational ideal and gatekeepers for its realization. Sami Ibrahim, a teacher in Majdal, pointed out that there were very practical reasons to cultivate good relations with teachers, as they determined which of the students would take one the few seats available at the next grade level: "It wasn't like what they did during the Egyptian Administration when there was a general examination that was corrected in Egypt or was corrected by a committee. . . . No, we made the examination and the grades—and I reported the grades. There was no one to supervise me in the question of grades."[62] The delegated authority enjoyed by teachers contributed to their social status, as did their relatively high salaries and their education.

The social authority of teachers was evident in the context of religious services—as when a preacher smoothed his entrance into a village by coming with a teacher (see above). In relation to the program of civic education promoted by the Mandate, teachers' influence was much more complicated. Since, for the most part, Palestinian teachers did not support the government's policies, their social practices often worked at cross-purposes to its program. Recall the discussion in chapter 3 of one teacher's (Hanan) extracurricular political activity. Even as Hanan obeyed Mandate commands "at work," in her personal life she wrote political articles under a pseudonym.[63] Even those teachers who did not directly engage in political activity (no doubt the majority) had an influence on people's conceptions of what Palestinian community, society, and civic life could be.[64] That people still talk about the significant effects of Mandate education, even as they complain about its restrictions, suggests that classroom work had a broad social impact.

Decisions and debates about school curricula highlight the tension between social citizenship and national identification. The students who were lucky enough to be admitted to schools were taught different subjects depending on whether they were in town or village schools. The village curriculum was limited in its academic subjects and was weighted toward agricultural techniques.[65] This curriculum was intended, in the words of one educational official, to deliver "an education that will at once enlighten the peasant, make him a contented citizen, and keep him on the land."[66] The town school curriculum included history, Arabic, English, mathematics, religion (Islam or Christianity, as appropriate), hygiene, drawing, and sports. It was designed to ensure that upon graduation students would "know in a systematic way (a) the circumstances of the development of human society and present systems of government; (b) the problems that face human society at present, and (c) the duties of the citizen to his country."[67] Each of these knowledges was general, connected to universal history and values. The duties of the citizen that students were to learn through this curriculum were not, therefore, the particular duties of an Arab Palestinian living in the conditions of the Mandate, but the general duties that any citizen anywhere would have to his country.

The politics of curricular depoliticization did not go unnoticed among Palestinian nationalists. The emphasis in the curriculum on world history was understood as a direct attack on the development of Palestinian nationalist consciousness in students. A. L. Tibawi, the education inspector for the Southern district, recorded the following complaints in his history of Mandate education: "While it contained features of the geography and history of Arab countries, [nationalists] never ceased to point out, it insisted in its content and tone on the international rather than the national character of Palestine. The Arab boy or girl was taught far less about the history of his nation and the geography of the Arab countries, the argument went, than the average Iraqi or for that matter the Palestinian Jewish child studying under a national but an independent system of education."[68] Despite their political objections to this curriculum, Palestinian teachers recognized what they identified as its pedagogical importance. It was a good education, if not always the right one. Almost every former Mandate teacher with whom I spoke echoed this view. Hanan summed up her view of British education as follows: "The level of education was high, sixth or seventh class during the British period was better than the level of the general secondary students today—truly, without exaggeration. This is true, and one cannot say anything but the truth. However, we still dislike them."[69]

Visible in this attitude of educators is how the development of citizenship was complicated not only by the practices of tactical government, which ensured that no one, clear policy could ever be pursued with consistency, but also by the sometimes oppositional practices of the teachers who had to implement any policy. There is no small irony in the fact that the arena that was supposed to produce apolitical citizens was occupied by the most political of civil servants. While teachers remember their political activity during this period as being severely curtailed, as constrained as that of any other civil servant—"They didn't allow any discussion of politics, not by us or the students,"[70] one teacher told me—politics plainly did seep through the restrictions.

Government was certainly aware that students were learning nationalism, however indirectly, from those who were supposed to teach citizenship. In an attempt to deal with this problem, the Education Ordinance of 1933 provided for the firing of any teacher who was proven "to have imparted teaching of a seditious, disloyal, immoral, or otherwise harmful character" and the closing of any school "being conducted in a manner contrary to good order and morals."[71] Through its use of a general language of "order" and "morals" the education ordinance presented itself as a nonpolitical document, a representation of the social public sphere that Mandate practice sought to promote. At the same time, of course, these broad categories were designed to permit the firing of any teacher deemed to be a nationalist.

That this effort to foreclose nationalism enjoyed only limited success is evident in Palestinians' memories of this period and was recognized at the time by Mandate officials. The Peel Commission Report of 1937 summed up the state of the problem when it identified education as a key factor in the growth of Palestinian nationalism:

The whole of the Arab educational system, unlike the Jewish, is maintained by the government . . . it is at least as purely Arab in its character as the Jewish system is Jewish. . . . A school-system thus purely Arab may be better for Arab children than a "mixed" system with a British element in its staff and its field of instruction; it is the right way, it is said, to make them "good Arabs." Whether that is so or not, it certainly makes them good Arab patriots. The general tendency of schoolmasters to be politically-minded is nowhere more marked than in the Middle East: and it is not to be expected that Arab schoolmasters in Palestine, Government servants though they are, should be able to repress entirely their sympathy with the nationalist cause.[72]

The narrowness of a school system that was "purely Arab" apparently made it difficult to create Arabs who were broadly civic. Politically minded teachers, left to their own devices, produced politically minded students. Despite the fact that education was a service domain in which government endeavored to plan strategically and from which it made an explicit effort to remove politics, it was, as we have seen, one of the more political of service areas.

When political leaders called strikes in the country, students and, sometimes, teachers obeyed. In one of his memoirs, Ibrahim Skeik, a former teacher and local historian, recalled such a strike. On November 2, he remembered from his elementary school days, he and the other young boys would run into older students on their way to school who would tell them, "Today is Balfour Declaration Day—it's a strike. So we retraced our steps, and no one was scolded or punished."[73] Tibawi noted this same phenomenon in his report on education during the latter years of the Mandate:

There is hardly any place for politics in a report of this nature but a few passing remarks are needed to touch on the subject of strikes in schools. This subject was almost negligible from 1940 to 1944, but with the resumption of political activity in Palestine . . . strikes were declared. . . . Government schools like all other branches of the Government service were bound to be affected, and attendance of pupils on the days of the strike became either scarce or nil. . . . From the range of my experience as a pupil, teacher and inspector from 1920–45 I know of no effective remedy to stop completely strikes in schools when there is a political strike. . . . Penalties of suspension, expulsion or payment of fines proved of no avail in dealing with pupils. Warnings and withholding of increment of salary was likewise useless in dealing with teachers.[74]

Both the complaints made about the school curriculum and the prevalence of political activity within and around schools highlight the extent to which the stakes of this service were evident to providers and recipients. Distraction and deferral gave way to direct political challenge. Education (not always, but at times) was a case in which abeyance failed. There was almost no service area that did not on occasion witness such a failure, but, along with policing, education proved to be the most difficult to manage. As political challenges heated up after World War II, abeyance, which offered no real solution to the problems of governing Palestine but simply was a way to manage such government in the short run, was no longer a sufficient technique. Having no capacity to govern in any other way, the British ultimately gave up on their civic project and on the Mandate as a whole.

SCHOOLING AND SURVEILLANCE: EDUCATIONAL
OPPORTUNITIES IN THE EGYPTIAN ADMINISTRATION

Educational services during the Egyptian Administration did not, as they did during the Mandate, strive to exclude nationalism from the curriculum or from the minds of students and teachers. On the contrary, during this period a carefully circumscribed version of nationalism was promoted and encouraged, and the concept of the citizen assumed a more restricted place in education. The tensions that teachers felt as participants in the practice of education were similarly reconfigured. Teachers' oppositional practices during the Administration tended to inject political citizenship, including the right of opposition and the right to organize, into students' consciousness. Another distinguishing feature of this period was the addition of UNRWA as a negotiating party that shaped the contours of educational practice. If the Administration and Gazan teachers struggled most immediately over the shape of the current civic life, UNRWA and the Administration struggled over its future. In this struggle as well, the Administration privileged nationalism as the idea that would give shape to this future, while UNRWA promoted a more prosaic notion of utility in education.

As in other service areas, Egyptian security concerns had considerable impact on educational practice. Despite, or maybe because of, these concerns, education was the site of the most expansive governmental project of the Egyptian Administration. As distinguished from crisis and everyday services, in community services like education and religious servicing the Administration hoped to do more than contain security threats. It hoped to actively transform the political positions and dispositions that could produce such threats. We have seen how religious education sought to contribute to a project of producing social subjectivities, a project that extended across the curriculum. Muslim Brotherhood and Communist Party affiliations would, it was hoped, be substituted by support for Nasserism. The prevalence of independent political attitudes among teachers made this a challenging proposition in certain ways, though the evidence suggests that Nasserism was indeed broadly popular among the Gazan population.[75] To the extent that Palestinian nationalism was encouraged, and it was, this was to be a dependent nationalism—subordinate to Egyptian political demands and not to be acted upon on solely Palestinian initiative. The simultaneous expansion of education and control of politics were pursued through increased surveillance of schools and their occupants.

Egyptian authorities transformed the social landscape in Gaza by making universal primary and secondary education a reality and by providing free university education for large numbers of Gazans. This massive educational expansion mirrored the policy in Egypt, and here too university graduates were granted government employment. The importance of Egyptian educational initiatives is universally recognized and applauded by Gazans today. Gazans who refer to Egyptian rule as a "golden age for the Palestinian people" explicitly connect this evaluation to the expansion of education.[76] As a retired government clerk put it to me, "We are completely tied with the Egyptians. No one can deny that. They were here to serve us. People used to study without paying fees. . . . Education was free. That is why if you pay a visit to a [refugee] camp you will find tens of teachers, doctors, pharmacists, and engineers who were educated at Egyptian universities."[77]

The massive educational transformation took time, of course. In the immediate aftermath of 1948, there were not enough schools, teachers, or materials, nor were there the funds to provide them. Gazans recalled to me the very difficult conditions in which education was initially pursued: "Pupils had no wooden board to write on. They wrote on the asphalt. They solved algebra questions while they were walking."[78] Mahdi Ayub, a former teacher, recalled how he began his career teaching refugee children: "In the beginning

FIGURE 10. Teaching in a refugee camp. SOURCE: AFSC ARCHIVES.

of 1949, after five months, we, the youth, gathered and discussed the situation and decided to be volunteers and teach the children. We started to teach the children in streets. The Quakers and the Egyptian Administration noticed us and helped us."[79]

Eventually, Mahdi recounted, schools were built to house these students. He insisted that, even without school buildings, refugees' desire for knowledge was such that his students' grades were better than those of native Gazans studying in preexisting schools.[80] Today, the high educational levels attained by refugees are often pointed to as proof that they have "assimilated" into Gazan society—that they have overcome their initial lower-class position.[81] In fact, class and other distinctions between these groups have not entirely disappeared.[82]

Getting enough books for all the students was a problem, as was the sorts of books that were available. Coming out of the frustrations of Mandate education, Gazans initially hoped to have a more Palestinian curriculum.

FIGURE 11. Tent school in Shati refugee camp, 1950s. SOURCE: UNRWA PHOTO ARCHIVE.

When a delegation from the Arab League visited Gaza in 1952, the mayor took the opportunity to insist that students in Gaza needed to be educated in the history and geography of Palestine and that they needed textbooks that could offer this education.[83] Providing such resources proved difficult. A committee sent from Egypt in 1959 to examine the state of education in Gaza noted that some classes still lacked books altogether. Those that did have them relied almost entirely on Egyptian texts.[84] The committee agreed that this was a problem because "some of the things in Egyptian schoolbooks will be strange to Gazan students," but designing wholly local texts would have been difficult given that, as the committee also recognized, "the current situation in Gaza is a provisional one, subject to many changes." One effect of the textbook situation, and of the educational practice more generally, was that Gaza's students received a somewhat deflected education. They were schooled in the manner of Egyptian citizens, and yet they were not schooled to be such citizens. Keeping Palestinian national feeling alive and controlled was an Egyptian priority, but the mechanisms for providing this national education (*tarbiyya wataniyya wa-qawmiyya*) were not necessarily Palestinian.

The Administration and UNRWA certainly struggled over curricular issues, and their conflicts were often about short-term practical benefits versus long-term national strategies. A conflict in 1959/60 between the two bodies over responsibility and funding for an agricultural training school in Beit Hanoun illustrates this tension. Having operated the school for a number of years, UNRWA decided to terminate its support on the grounds that, because agricultural lands were very limited in Gaza and no local work was available for graduates of the school, it did not conform to the agency's policy of funding "useful" projects.[85] UNRWA's apparently prosaic focus on training refugees in useful skills was interpreted in political terms by the Administration. In responding to the decision to stop funding the school, the Administration countered that UNRWA's responsibility was to improve the educational standards of refugees to prepare them for a future not in their temporary refuges, but in their homes: "The intent in this improvement is not to settle [*tawtin*] them in the places where they are living, but the goal is that they should be good citizens [*muwatinin salahin*] when they return to their country."[86] In the Administration's view, citizenship was defined in reference to the deferred future in Palestine, and education in the present should produce Gazans who were Palestinian "nationals." Students were to be prepared for citizenship in a country which did not (yet) exist, and whose relation to their current conditions was not defined.

While the Administration championed future civic life in this conflict with UNRWA, its own position was not and could not be stable. Even as Administration officials were accusing UNRWA of attempting to settle the Palestine problem by focusing on practical education, in another setting officials were championing exactly this kind of need-focused education. The 1959 "Report on Education in Gaza" implied that UNRWA had responded too much to refugees' desires for higher education and had lost sight of the need for the creation of work opportunities. The report indicated that the school curricula of the government and UNRWA alike—contained far too little vocational training: "The result of the current education system is that many young men graduate from their theoretical studies and the Strip is not able to find room for them."[87] In the absence of any industry in Gaza, even vocational education was less than wholly practical. As the report stated, "Establishing industrial schools in the Strip before industry is set up there will transform the study to theoretical study." These considerations seem the same as those which made UNRWA hesitant to keep funding the agricultural school. Whatever the Administration's commitment to a future Palestine (a commitment that was generally more rhetorical than practical), the immediate economic demands and political threats of Gaza's difficult conditions made it impossible to banish immediate concerns from educational services.[88]

The emphasis on national education by Egyptians was both policy and practical consideration. Unable to offer Gazans immediate improvement, administrators resorted to offering them hope for the future. Teachers' descriptions of their work during this period emphasize the importance of developing this sense of nation among their students. Ibrahim Mahmoud, a native inhabitant of Gaza who was both a teacher and a principal in UNRWA schools, described his responsibilities as the head of the "cultural committee" in his first school.[89] This committee, he said, focused on "making the people aware culturally, principally concentrating on morals and values as well as the love for the people and doing good deeds."[90] He noted that one of the achievements of the committee was implanting a sense of patriotism among the students. When I asked him how this patriotism was taught, he said, "Loving homeland and morals do not come by instruction but through practices. Practices—that means you tell stories, run school tours where cooperation among people and the respect for others prevail, where the importance of not harming others and forgiving people will be clearly manifest—through practices. Also through writings, for example, in a small newspaper. . . . These things encourage the students to search in the library about the moral values, which they then wrote about and showed to their teacher." The duties of the nationalist as described in schools were not immediately political ones, but cultural and moral ones, including care for others, cooperation, and respect. Ibrahim argued that being a patriot was a moral duty and a requirement for the betterment of society as a whole: "They must love the people so that the whole society can live in happiness and well-being."[91]

The happiness of the whole society, from the Administration's perspective at least, depended not just on patriotism among its people, but also on the control of unauthorized political expression. It is in the struggle over the control of political activity in and around schools that the extent to which educational patriotism was pursued at the expense of certain aspects of citizenship is especially manifest. Ibrahim, who spoke so proudly of his achievements in inculcating patriotism in his students and who praised

Egyptian authorities for their support of education, is the same Ibrahim whom these authorities imprisoned for nearly two years (see chapter 3). Politics was a perpetual threat, and teachers, who were always more political than the general population, were the objects of continual surveillance and regulation. In the Administration police files there are numerous reports of principals being instructed to watch their teachers (and themselves) to ensure that there were no political activities in schools.[92]

A file on the Bureij Middle School for Refugees demonstrates the extent of the surveillance of education in the Administration as well as the prevalence of politics within the schools.[93] On the morning of October 12, 1959, the janitor of the Bureij school found a leaflet posted on the door of the school. As he began to remove it, some students ripped the leaflet apart, perhaps to forestall an investigation. He was able to put the pieces together, and he then turned the leaflet over to the school principal, who sent it to the Deir Belah administrative governor, who in turn sent a contingent of police officers to investigate. The officers questioned the students who had ripped down the leaflet as well as its author and some teachers. The text of the leaflet seemed to comport with the messages being promoted by the Administration—it declared "Palestine is our country" and "Long Live Gamal Abdul Nasser"—so the disturbance produced by its posting was obviously about something other than content. This independent action on the part of a student raised the possibility of a loss of control over the school and the civic environments. The sentiments might have been proper, but their expression had not been authorized.

The investigation into the posting revealed that the school was an arena of rampant factionalism and party politics. The police identified teachers affiliated with the Communist Party, the Muslim Brotherhood, and the Ba'th party, the supporters of each organization accusing the others of creating trouble and "chaos."[94] In an incident which exemplified just how difficult educators could be to control, an informant reported on a quarrel that broke out among the teachers. They were calling each other garbage, and the principal, who was a Ba'thist, threatened to "wring the neck" of a Nasserist teacher. The principal announced to the group, "I am a Ba'thist, and I am not afraid of anyone, not even Gamal Abdul Nasser."[95]

Even as the Administration sought to promote a nonpolitical national subject, teachers injected a sense of political citizenship into the discourse about civic life. It was teachers and students who were at the forefront of demonstrations in 1955 against a proposed plan to resettle refugees in the Sinai.[96] It was teachers who were most active in the political parties the administration hoped to control.[97] Even the imprisonment in 1959 of a large number of teachers for their political activity—the incident is mentioned by Mahmoud and described in detail by Mu'in Basisu, a teacher, poet, and Communist Party activist, in *Descent into the Water*—failed to entirely contain such expression.[98]

During the Administration, political threats and the perception thereof ebbed and flowed. There were moments of genuine crisis, many of which involved teachers directly, but the dynamic of Egyptian government was never completely undermined. Through one tactic or another, and sometimes by changing a governing practice, these crises were contained, though never really solved, and abeyance continued to work. Changes in the governing structure in Gaza in the latter years of the Administration do suggest that there may have been a limit to deferral's effectiveness as a governing tactic. The Palestine Liberation Organization (PLO) was created in 1964; shortly thereafter the National Union was dissolved and replaced by the PLO as Gaza's only recognized party.[99] The PLO then established the Palestine Liberation Army (PLA), with Gaza as its primary base. Yezid Sayigh indicates that Egyptian authorities initially objected to this establishment, but that Nasser ultimately was compelled to support it in order to deflect challenges to his leadership in the Arab world.[100] Sayigh further argues that the actual establishment of the PLA in Gaza was hampered by Egyptian policies. However tempered the support may have been, in March 1965 the governor-general and Legislative Council approved a law mandating compulsory conscription.[101] This move toward the creation of Palestinian institutions, however limited their authority (and it was quite limited), does allude to the impossibility of deferring Palestinian national aspirations indefinitely. Since Israel's occupation of Gaza cut the Administration short, what exactly might have been the limits of deferral and of abeyance will never be known.

Conclusion

Government control, political struggles, and the proprieties of civic life were intertwined in the provision of community services. In these services, contestations over civic life centered around government's attempts to control political expression, Gazan efforts to expand political consciousness, debates about the role of religion in public life, and challenges to the highly vexed categories of "national" and "citizen." Ideas about civic life were always expressed in multiple tenses—struggling with past loss, striving for the future, uncertain about the present. The concern for control, for propriety, was perhaps the most difficult feature of tactical government. It was compelled by anxiety and incapacity. At the same time it required a putting aside of this anxiety and a surpassing of these incapacities. Control demanded precisely the kind of over-involvement that government in Gaza generally struggled to avoid. There was also a persistent paradox in these controlling services, as it was precisely in the domains where government was expansive that the most sustained resistance emerged.

This awkward relation among the aspects of tactical government was itself, of course, tactical. Tactical government was by its nature self-contradictory, relying now on one instrument, now on another. Government coped with the difficult conditions of Gaza by deploying a tactical mobility that allowed it to respond rapidly to changing demands, just as Gazans coped with these same conditions through a multiplicity of practices that included care and contestation, scuffles and support. The confrontations among these forces sometimes produced crises in abeyance—such a crisis led the British to retreat from the Mandate and perhaps could have undermined Egyptian rule had it continued—but also often worked to sustain rule. Within this dynamic, the parties to government in Gaza each sought, even within the constrained horizons of its temporality, to imagine a future that could provide more security, greater stability, a better life.

GAZA AND AN ANTHROPOLOGY OF GOVERNMENT

This exploration of government in Gaza has illuminated a diverse and sometimes contradictory array of governing practices. The ways in which these practices worked together—even as they did not always fit together—gave shape to a mode of government, and also to the place and people of Gaza. The relationship among government, population, and place was not one simply of cause and effect, but rather operated in multiple directions, sometimes at the same time. In addition to the national, regional, and international forces that influenced the style of rule in Gaza, the demands of this particular space, as a provincial market center or overcrowded refugee destination, shaped the details of this practice. At the same time, rule was shaped not only by the constraints of place, but also by the demands of its participants (the governors and the governed). These demands for freedom, for independence, for security, for order, for stability, for nation were formed in rule and were formative of it, shifting over time and circumstance. The efforts to manage the complexities of governing Gaza demanded a multiplicity of sometimes contradictory instruments and techniques.

The two major styles of rule I have explored here—the deployment of reiterative authority and the use of tactical government—seem, and in fact are, at odds in many ways. These practices worked together in part by not claiming to cohere into any totality. If one of the problematics of liberal governmentality is how to govern "spatially and constitutionally 'at a distance' "[1] —a technique that was often developed in the colonies[2]—in Gaza this problematic was inflected as how to govern without quite identifying what that distance was, without clarifying the relation between government and place, government and people. In the absence of a precise framework in which to place and through which to interpret these different practices, the significance of such contradictions often remained opaque. With governments that did not work through sovereignty or legitimacy, there was no whole against which the parts of government were judged. This is not to say that these governments were not judged, for they often were, but they were not judged on the basis of their incoherence. Contradictions were generally not a problem for government, and indeed they were often productive for it. If one ruling style was ineffective at a particular moment, another might help hold things together. We saw, for instance, how civil servants disassociated the work of government from its politics in order to continue to feel good about their own work. Given the difficult conditions in Palestine and Gaza and the fundamental incapacity of either the British Mandate or the Egyptian Administration to actually resolve those conditions, it is hard to imagine how rule could have worked otherwise.

Reiterative authority relies on regularity and on an expansive view of the bureaucratic domain. Files and civil servants accrued and deployed authority in part through a process that seemed to offer no alternative, no other place to go. It is in this respect that Gaza's bureaucracy came closest to the picture offered by Weber of the "iron cage" that offers no way out. Bureaucratic practice can appear as a hall of mirrors, each instance of such practice being judged in relation to other such practices, and which in fact may simply be the same practice duplicated endlessly. We saw this in the absolute importance accorded to documentary similarity—with even the smallest deviations controlled for. We saw it as well in the often circular character of civil servants' claims about their work. Public service was good work because it was work for the people, it was for the people because it was public service. While this circularity did not obviate the possibility of critique—of individual civil servants, particular practices—it did make it more difficult to conceive of an alternative structure of governance.

Bureaucracy and bureaucracy's reiterative authority shaped, constrained, and helped define possibility for all its actors. The expansion of bureaucratic apparatuses bound people and government in new ways and made demands of both. People found themselves obliged to follow government regulations, to use proper procedures, to petition in appropriate language. The government, at the same time, acquired new obligations to provide services, to respond to people's complaints, to manage social relations. Responsibility, authority, and opportunity were distributed very unevenly across the bureaucratic terrain, but this multiplicity is nonetheless significant. When Gazans wrote to the Mandate high commissioner to complain about the city's mayor, they had learned particular lessons about how best to get a hearing for their complaints. When civil servants petitioned the Administration for jobs or promotions owed them, they too displayed skills acquired through bureaucratic familiarity. That in many of these cases the complainants did not get the result they desired is a further reminder that these governments had an array of techniques at their disposal to deflect, redirect, or refuse these demands. These struggles were in part defined by the terms of bureaucracy itself and by the dynamic of reiterative authority that helped stabilize it. In these conditions there appeared to be no perspective outside service, and therefore the idea of such an outside was itself less imaginable.

Tactical government, on the other hand, depended on always keeping the possibility of spaces beyond service alive. Rather than regularity, it was exceptionality that most characterized tactical practice. Uncertain of their relationship with the place of rule, anxious about the future, constrained in their finances, and concerned about security, Gaza's governments relied on practices that were both impermanent and restricted in their claims. Service, while at the center of the governing relation, was not necessarily meant to declare anything about the character of that relation. We have seen how crisis services were a priori defined as exceptional, even when their enactment was both broad and long. In contrast, everyday services, while in theory permanent, in practice almost never were. The shifts in and contestations over these ordinary services indicate the importance of necessarily located and partial perspectives in shaping a governmental experience. The most self-consciously expansive form of service, community services, was also the domain that produced the most tension in government, a reminder that tactics were by no means an instrument available only to government. In each of these sites and forms of service, the uncertainty of government, that is, its potentially short life and limited capacity, was highlighted.

The tactical approach to governing, while helping to mitigate these difficulties, was not a technique of limitless possibility. It could not and did not work always or indefinitely. That governments did not have a monopoly on tactical practice—we have seen clear evidence of its use among the Gazan population, directed sometimes at government and sometimes at others like themselves—indicates one source of constraint. During both the Mandate and the Administration there were instances of clear challenge to the governing regimes, instances in which neither distraction nor deferral was quite sufficient. That the British eventually gave up on their efforts to govern Palestine serves as a further reminder of the limits of tactical government. It can help manage the moment but leaves the future very uncertain. If reiterative authority seemed to offer no outside perspective on rule, tactical government offered no horizon.

The coming together of contradictory practices—the nontotalizing governmental field—was practice rather than policy. That intentions do not always or even often match outcome is, by this point, a truism about government. By focusing on the practice of rule, my aim is not to highlight this disjuncture, but to understand better the effects of practice itself. The picture I have traced here, while not unrecognizable to the policy makers of the Mandate and the Administration, would also not necessarily have been identical to how they articulated their visions of government in this territory. This has been very much a description of government at work, not as imagined. Gaza is a good location from which to consider this practice of government. Provincial as it was, it was never the center of government decision making. Even during the Administration, when it was a distinct administrative area, Cairo remained the power center. It was, at the risk of overstating matters, a place where government was enacted, not planned. And yet, as this exploration has made clear, such enactment was a highly creative process. The work of government was never a simple application of policy, regulation, and procedure.

Looking at government in this way makes it possible to see something new about Gaza, to better understand how the place took shape (and what shape it took) over the course of the fifty years examined here. We have seen something of the "social life" of bureaucratic authority, how it worked to help sustain government and also to shape relations among people, to structure political arrangements, and to define spaces. At the same time, government is always a process of interaction between ruling ambitions and existing conditions. It does not simply impose itself on a place, but rather places also help shape government. This general process is perhaps particularly clear in Gaza, with its crisis conditions and (especially in the Administration) overcrowded space, untenable economy, and unsustainable population.

By exploring the in many ways extraordinary operations of government in Gaza, it actually becomes possible to see Gaza as a more ordinary place. Many locales suffer from a burden of presumptions that can get in the way of actually comprehending them. Gaza's regular appearance in the news as a site of violence has certainly tended to work against more complex understandings of the place. Investigation of the daily work of rule, in contrast, has divulged a multiplicity of facets, some of which in fact appear fairly ordinary. This book has depicted transformations in social relations as civil service employment accrued and lost both status and economic importance; as people's financial conditions were upended by the dislocation of 1948; as new population categories followed from this event; and as schools sought to produce different sorts of subjects. It has emphasized the formation of place in the expansion and occasional contraction of government services as people got water from wells, pipes, or central pumps; as roads and railroads were built, destroyed, and rerouted; and as opportunities for landownership were reconfigured. It has also described changing mechanisms for civic expression: as formal structures of local and national government were reconfigured; as paths for petitioning were redrawn; and as political circumstances and movements shifted. As this array of practices has shown, for all of its truly remarkable history, Gaza is not wholly exceptional.

Indeed, because of its provincial location and uncertain state form, Gaza has afforded an opportunity to understand government in a somewhat new light. In the lack of any definite model that could be turned to in order to explain this government, it has required a focus on the details of its practice. The governing techniques I have explored here can, in fact, be identified and understood only through the lens of practice. They could not be distinctly seen simply in ideology, prescriptive discourse, or policy. An understanding of their operations has to be teased out of the daily work of governing. This investigation illuminates a much broader governing dynamic, one that is relevant far beyond Gaza.

Government beyond Gaza

Approaching government through its practice provides a different perspective on both the historicity and coherence of governing arrangements. It is widely recognized by now that considering new actors, questions, and concerns in historical research does not simply add to our understanding of historical periods, but can generate a rethinking of these periodizations themselves.[3] In this case, looking at quotidian ruling practices underlines rhythms of transformation that do not always correspond to the periodizations of political history. Sometimes there were continuities across dramatic breakpoints, such as the retaining of personnel across regimes. Sometimes significant changes occurred in otherwise unremarkable moments, such as the transfer of government land to people in Gaza. It is in apparently mundane processes, expressed, for example, in a minor change in bureaucratic procedure, in a gradual accommodation to a new regulation, in a new style of social interaction, that both government and the formation of people and place are often most clearly grasped. While Gaza has had more distinct "periods" than many places, this shift in perspective can be helpful for exploring numerous circumstances. Further, it is precisely the focus on practice that makes it possible to understand that diverse and often contradictory techniques *could* work together in government, and how important having this array of instruments available was for enabling the persistence of always tenuous governments.

While in some ways Gaza represents an extreme case of governmental uncertainty, studies conducted in numerous settings have highlighted how uncertain even apparently stable governments and seemingly strong states can be. Colonial states, for example, have been shown to be frequently insecure in both their knowledge of the colonized and their capacity to manage relations between ruler and ruled; such insecurity shaped the practice of governance in important ways.[4] Postcolonial states have proven to be dependent on "mystifying complex[es] of practices and beliefs,"[5] on productions of "illegibility,"[6] and on varieties of both amnesia and memory[7] as means of distracting attention from often fundamental instabilities. Conditions of globalization have only underscored the uncertainty of even powerful state forms such as the nation-state.

Indeed, in a world that seems increasingly unstable, the potential importance of both reiterative authority and tactical government in a variety of settings seems evident. The number of governments across the globe that can be described as tenuous is enormous, and it is not just the classic sorts of "failed states" that fit this description. The case of the U.S. occupation of Iraq, for instance, underscores how perilous it can be for governing regimes to forget the importance of ordinary bureaucracy.[8] In its initial zeal for de-Ba'thification, the purging of the new Iraqi government of anyone tainted by the old order, the Coalition Provisional Authority (CPA) outlawed the party, dissolved the army, and fired thousands of former Ba'thists from government offices. Combined with the military's failure to intervene to stop the looting and destruction of government offices, this mass purging seems to directly contradict Weber's reflections on bureaucracy: "A rationally ordered officialdom continues to function smoothly after the enemy has occupied the territory; he merely needs to change the top officials. It continues to operate because it is in the vital interest of everyone concerned, including above all the enemy."[9] The smooth functioning of Iraqi government would certainly have been in the interest of U.S. occupying forces and of the Iraqi population as well. In the event, it was not long before the problems with this approach were realized. In following years increasing numbers of former Ba'thists have been returned to government positions, but the stability of the bureaucracy had already been disrupted.

If, on the one hand, the U.S. approach to governing Iraq seemed to disregard the importance of bureaucratic continuity and reiterative authority, thereby underutilizing some crucial governing techniques, it seems to have overreached in other areas, refusing to be satisfied with the limited claims of tactical government. In the circumstances I have explored in Gaza, governments were acutely aware of the uncertainty of their relation to the place of governance and of the tenuousness of their authority. The United States displayed no such concern when it went into Iraq. Convinced that American troops would be greeted as liberators, that the United States would automatically be granted authority, officials appear to have paid little attention to how governing authority might be produced. Further, in claiming to be the savior of Iraq—promising liberation, freedom, democracy (despite a lack of planning for how to make that happen)—the United States put the legitimacy of both its occupation and the regime it helped install front and center. As a consequence, abeyance, however useful it might have been, was not entirely available as a technique. While other aspects of tactical government, such as the focus on the near-at-hand, a lack of strategic planning, and extremely limited service resources, quickly became important, it appears to be tactical government without its advantages. As this brief excursus on Iraq suggests, the analytic developed in this book provides useful tools for investigating the work of government beyond Gaza.

Israeli Occupation

I have emphasized throughout this book that the rhythms of government and bureaucracy are not identical to the rhythms of political history. We have seen how sometimes the ruptures of this latter domain—and the abrupt changes in regime that have characterized Gaza's history—have marked ruptures in governing practice, but how they have sometimes been absorbed by the continuities of bureaucracy. A question for many readers, then, may be, What relation does this form of government practice have to the Israeli occupation that came after the Egyptian Administration?[10] How many of these techniques continued (and continue) to be deployed? While there were certain, significant, continuities, the occupation marked a more fundamental break. Certain techniques of tactical government *were* employed, but ultimately, since Israel hoped to achieve greater control over this territory and possibly sovereignty over it, a different mode of operation dominated. Similarly, legitimacy could not be held in abeyance in the same manner as during the Mandate and the Administration, though certain governing practices seemed intended to encourage it.

In contrast to policies surrounding the more recent example of Iraq, Israeli policy at the outset of its occupation suggested a familiarity with Weber's insights about the importance of keeping bureaucracies intact after changes of regime. At the beginning of the occupation, Israel sought to pursue a policy which it termed "government but not administration."[11] Existing structures of local government would be maintained and administrative tasks would continue to be executed by Palestinian civil servants. The situation envisioned by this policy was that a Gazan might "be born in a hospital, receive his birth certificate, grow up and be educated, get married and raise his children and grandchildren—all without having to resort to an Israeli civil servant, or having to see one at all."[12] This kind of separation seems designed to encourage the sort of disassociation that was one of the mechanisms through which continued participation in government was made possible during the Mandate and the Administration.

Indeed, many Gazans who had been civil servants during the Egyptian Administration continued in their jobs under Israeli occupation. This decision was a pragmatic one, as one Gazan told me: "When the Jews came in 1967, they asked us to come and work for the police. The policemen asked: 'How do you want us to work in the police while you occupy us?' The Jews said to them: 'You are not going to fight for us, no, you will only work for your country.' An officer told me: 'Don't think that we will go so easily as in 1956. He who can find a job and feed his children will be the one to win.' So, I worked."[13]

Even as the policy of "government but not administration" was declared, the military government did interfere in administration in an effort to control resistance to the occupation, thereby underscoring the crucial importance of the latter to the operations of the former. In the immediate aftermath of the war, the Israeli officer in charge of Gaza City threatened to dismiss the municipal council and cut off water and electricity services to the city if the council was unable to force Palestinians to turn in their weapons.[14] While that threat was deemed excessive and was revoked by the military governor of the Strip,[15] continued Palestinian resistance (both military and otherwise) to Israeli occupation made repeated interference inevitable. Resistance took the form of both armed struggle and civil disobedience. As part of the latter "students demonstrated in the school yards and streets, adults boycotted Israeli goods, and lawyers refused to practice in the Israeli military courts."[16] Organized armed struggle against the occupation peaked between 1969 and 1971, when it was largely crushed by the Israeli military under the command of Ariel Sharon.[17]

Resistance to the occupation in Gaza from its inception suggests that the policy of occupation at a distance was not wholly effective. Yet the many years of relative quiet that followed the initial period of confrontation mean that it was not entirely without success. Israeli efforts to eliminate armed resistance in Gaza had a direct impact on service provision of the sort explored in this book. One of the most well-known instances of administrative interference around service provision was the dismissal, in 1972, of Gaza City's mayor because of his refusal to provide municipal services to the Shati refugee camp. Palestinians understood the Israeli demand for incorporation to be part of a project to dissolve refugee-specific spaces in Gaza.[18] Housing was another site of struggle. Sharon took charge of a project to create wide streets through refugee camps, whose narrow, winding pathways afforded ample ways for resisters to evade detection by the army, and in the process bulldozed large numbers of refugee dwellings. Sara Roy states that "Israel built nearly 200 miles of security roads and destroyed thousands of refugee dwellings as part of the widening process."[19]

Infrastructure projects which built roads and created new housing outside of camps for refugees were part of a reconfiguration of space that had more than military value.[20] These projects, whether early attempts to move parts of the refugee population out of Gaza altogether to nearby al-Arish in the Sinai or the later neighborhood building projects, were read by the population as strategic efforts by the Israeli government to dissolve the category of refugee and thereby to defuse the demand for return. From the perspective of the Palestinians living under its rule, that is, Israeli occupation did not seem restricted to the tactical domain.[21]

While there were some connections, then, between the period I have considered and the subsequent Israeli occupation, the modes of rule also differed in important ways. Along with a separation of government and administration, over the course of its occupation of both the West Bank and Gaza, Israel has sought to separate population from place. The "government but not administration" policy reflected the occupation's attitude toward the people of the territories. Toward the land, however, Israel enacted, even if it did not formally state, a claim to sovereignty over the territory. In the projects that have been pursued on the ground in Gaza and the West Bank over the course of the forty-year occupation the difference between this government and the tactical government that characterized the Mandate and the Administration becomes abundantly clear. The projects of settlement building, road construction, and land and water appropriation that have gone on throughout the occupation—and that have increased dramatically in recent years—exhibit none of the restricted scope, scale, and imagination that is a key part of tactical government.[22]

However little Israel may have wanted to claim Palestinians, it has certainly laid claim to Palestine. This has had important consequences for the sorts of governmental work that were undertaken in the territory and also for the government's response to resistance to that rule when it has become vociferous and organized. While for much of the first twenty years of the occupation the Israeli government claimed to be managing an "enlightened occupation,"[23] the *intifada* (1987–93) put an end to the imagined Palestinian acquiescence. It became increasingly difficult to distract the population and civil servants from the illegitimacy of occupation, and resistance became nearly impossible to contain. In recognition of the significance of participating in government, during this period many civil servants, especially police, resigned from their positions in the Civil Administration. Unlike the British Mandate, however, which gave up on governing Palestine as soon as abeyance seemed to completely fail, the fact that Israel has had much more certainty about its relationship to the place (a certainty that has been increasingly shaken) meant that resistance led not to the end of Israeli rule but to its increased brutality.

The establishment of the Palestinian National Authority (PNA) as a result of the Oslo Accords of 1993 marked an important shift in the dynamics of occupation, but it did not mean its end. In some ways this governing arrangement seemed the successful implementation of Israel's first occupation strategy, which minimized the number of Israeli soldiers and officials that Palestinians would need to encounter in the course of their daily lives. The creation of the PNA did, though, enable Palestinian civil servants and the population to feel that the government could be legitimate. The possibility of legitimacy, in part embodied in the elections for the presidency of the PNA and the Legislative Council, remained connected to the hope for an independent Palestine. The prevalence of corruption in PNA operations in the ensuing years and people's disappointment in its progress toward independence have meant that this legitimacy was always contested.

Given how unstable post-Oslo ruling forms have been, a focus on government practice is vital for understanding this recent history. Not only did the PNA not exercise sovereign authority over the small part of Palestinian territory it controlled, the bureaucratic operations of government continued to be shared in crucial ways.[24] Border crossings, identification documents, and permits of many kinds required Israeli approval, though Palestinian civilians dealt with Palestinian offices. One effect of the Oslo Accords was the further expansion of an Israeli closure policy (enacted for the first time during the Gulf War in 1991) that dramatically curtailed opportunities for people to work inside Israel. With fewer work options available, civil service employment began to return to its earlier place of prominence in Palestinian economy and society. The export of Palestinian products from the territories and between Gaza and the West Bank was controlled by Israel. When I was doing my fieldwork, Gaza's insufficient electricity supply still largely came from Israel, and there were frequent blackouts.[25] Palestinians were certainly acutely aware of the limits of the PNA as a government and, after the initial excitement over the establishment of Palestinian governing institutions died down, were extremely critical of the Oslo Accords which had created it.

The tenuous authority of this government was made starkly manifest in the Israeli response to the second intifada, which began in September 2000, and the PNA has been increasingly stripped of any semblance of substantive power. In the course of the second intifada the level of violence of both resistance and repression increased enormously. Even with their focus turned largely toward methods of counterinsurgency that seek to exterminate the leadership of militant Palestinian groups and to restrict the movement of the entire Palestinian population, Israeli forces did not entirely forget the potential of other methods of disrupting political and social life. In April 2002 Israeli forces reentered a number of Palestinian towns, the first large-scale military occupation of Palestinian population centers since the withdrawals under the Oslo Accords. While the stated purpose of this invasion was to crack down on militant activity, Israeli attention extended beyond people and buildings. Rather, the army also attacked the administrative infrastructure of both public and private institutions.

According to a report from Ramallah, in the Ministry of Education "all school test records since 1960" were taken.[26] In the Finance Ministry "all payroll data for the Palestinian Authority seemed to be gone." The Ministries of Agriculture, Health, Civil Affairs, Statistics, the Land Registry, and the Ramallah Municipality all reported similar losses. Both paper files and computer hard drives were taken. The Palestinian minister of information called it an "administrative massacre" and said it would "lead to chaos." International officials who surveyed the damage noted that the army "seemed not to have made a distinction between the political leadership and the civil service." Asked why the army would undertake such actions, one officer commented that they were searching for security information. "A lot of these places turn up unexpected things by accident," he said; "documents have a very important value." Indeed they do, although, as this book has explored, this value does not only or always lie in the specific information they contain. In this case, the seizing of the documents worked to disrupt bureaucratic operations and undermine the capacity for governmental continuity, a "value" no doubt more significant than any "sensitive" information likely to be found in thirty-year-old school records.

One result of the intifada and of Israeli efforts to quash it was thus to pose a greater challenge to the existence of anything that looked like a stable structure and to bring about a further fragmentation of authority. Hamas (the Islamic Resistance Movement), since the first intifada a serious challenger to Fatah, the long dominant PLO faction, and the PLO for popularity among Palestinians, continued its rise to prominence. People supported Hamas because of its apparent lack of corruption, its political positions, and its extensive networks of social services, services that augmented the always insufficient government (and UNRWA) resources. After the death of Yasser Arafat in November 2004, further cracks in governing authority emerged. Reports from Gaza suggest that family ties and militia groups have come to play an increasingly important role as the PNA largely collapsed.[27]

As the second intifada began to die down, a number of events transpired that had tremendous significance for Palestinians in Gaza and the West Bank, and that further highlight the continued relevance of the analytic approach developed here. In August 2005 the Israeli army, after removing its eight-thousand-person settler population, evacuated Gaza. This pullback created new opportunities for contiguity of Palestinian government and new concerns about the boundaries of a future Palestinian state. Part of the discursive and ideological work done around this removal was precisely to reconceptualize Israel's relationship with this territory. Palestinians expressed concern that this change in Gaza may come at the expense of an even greater entrenchment of Israeli attachment to portions of the West Bank.

In January 2006 Hamas won a majority of seats in elections for the Palestinian Legislative Council. The Hamas takeover of the PNA was a major blow to Fatah, and it opened a new chapter in the history of government in Gaza. While the PNA had already been weakened by Israeli incursions into Palestinian territory and the concomitant destruction of institutional apparatuses over the course of the second intifada, the international and Israeli response to the Hamas victory was to, essentially, launch an all-out bureaucratic assault on this government. International donors withheld funds, and Israel refused to transfer the tax revenues it had collected from Palestinians, in the process essentially bankrupting the government. As a result, the authority could not pay the salaries of civil servants, salaries on which large portions of the population depend for survival. The crisis produced by the failure to pay salaries further underscores how important civil service employment has once again become. In the wake of the Palestinian capture of an Israeli soldier in June 2006, this financial strangulation was augmented by a direct attack on government officials, as the Israeli military began arresting Hamas government ministers. In the wake of these events and as the PNA seemed increasingly less authoritative, some Palestinians, including Prime Minister Ismail Haniyeh, questioned whether it could or should continue to exist at all. In June 2007, after months of Palestinian struggle over authority, Hamas seized control of the Gaza Strip and Fatah then sought to consolidate its power in the West Bank. This circumstance rendered the future of Gaza and its governing condition even more uncertain.

Anthropology of Government

At the current moment, uncertainty about the future seems a global condition. While many state structures appear increasingly unstable, this circumstance further accentuates how important an anthropology of government can be. The analytics of government developed here can be useful for understanding rule in circumstances quite distinct from Gaza. For one thing, the particular techniques of reiterative authority and tactical government described here can be found in other places, but in addition an approach to analyzing government that takes as its starting point government's everyday practices has broad utility. The landscape of possibilities for governing the modern world is diverse, but not entirely disconnected. In offering a description of government at work in particular circumstances, I hope to provide further analytic tools for exploring both this diversity and these connections.

To understand this array of techniques, one needs neither a unitary theory of "modern government" nor a vision of an entirely disparate array of alternative possibilities, but rather a perspective that considers these techniques as part of a broad, interconnected terrain of modern government.[28]

Government in the era of neoliberalism—a subject of so much recent academic attention—can look different when deployed in the development of what James Ferguson calls "nongovernmental states" in Africa, in the "graduated sovereignty" that Aihwa Ong elucidates in an Asian context, in the entrepreneurial subject that Nikolas Rose identifies as crucial to the "advanced liberalism" of Europe and the United States, or even in the "unitary executive" theory currently popular among certain circles in the United States.[29] And yet, as these authors note, these forms share important connections. Neoliberalism is often discussed as a retreat of the state as part of an ideology of privatization. While some people have suggested that this restriction of services might be better described as a reconfiguration of government —one in which security functions may expand even as services decline—the question of how to rule with limited resources which was so important in governing Gaza clearly has continued relevance.[30] The Gazan case also underscores that such questions are not entirely new.

After many years of hesitancy to take on the state, anthropologists have increasingly turned their ethnographic attention in this direction, producing innovative and vital accounts of state operations, imaginaries, and effects. Michel-Rolph Trouillot has urged anthropologists interested in such "state effects" to "look for these processes and effects in sites less obvious than those of institutionalized politics and established bureaucracies" and to turn instead to "the seemingly timeless banality of everyday life." My exploration of government in Gaza suggests, though, that bureaucracy is not as "immediately transparent" in its operations as people may presume and that it is a crucial site for exploring the fundamentals of "everyday life."[31] Indeed, in key ways, bureaucratic life is everyday life. Approaching the study of government through the lens of bureaucratic practice makes it possible to see these connections.

In placing such "regimes of practice" at the center of analysis, they become both the subject and the site of research, thereby enabling a productive reframing of research questions. In this approach, practices cannot be seen simply as instruments in the hands of particular actors or tools for domination and/or resistance, though they are certainly sometimes that. Practices appear, rather, as techniques—for living, for governing, for shaping social space—that cannot be reduced to singular causes or effects. Research in this vein may be "multi-sited,"[32] following the deployments of particular practices across different locations. It certainly requires a multiplicity of perspectives, hence my reliance on both archival and ethnographic methods. To define practice as one's research site does not mean saying less about places and peoples, the focus of most anthropological inquiry. On the contrary, as I hope this study has shown, this approach can shed new light on formations of subjects and locales.

As I have suggested, the self-referential reiterative authority that characterized government in Gaza seems to be a general feature of the bureaucratic form, but one that is often masked by other claims about the sources of government authority. One of the loudest such claimants in the modern world has been the nation-state. Nation-states claim to be and to provide everything that was absent from rule in Gaza: a stable framework for government, a clear connection between rulers and ruled, a permanent relation, and, most important, legitimacy. That such stability and legitimacy are often illusory and seem to be increasingly under threat has been much discussed and has often been taken as evidence of the decline of the nation-state, a diagnosis that has itself been increasingly challenged.[33]

In considering bureaucratic operations in Gaza I have been less focused on diagnosing the state of the state in this place that is fairly demonstrably in crisis than on trying to understand the dynamics of governing authority and persistence. Nonetheless, this investigation does propose some central tenets about how we should approach investigation of such ruling forms. If ruling authority even in nation-states has depended greatly on the self-referential mechanisms of bureaucracy, then a rethinking of where the power of that form lies may be in order. Certainly, a faltering in nation-state ideologies should not be presumed to lead automatically to their demise. Saskia Sassen has written about how even with the rise of globalization and the concomitant shifts in nation-state operations, techniques and institutions developed to govern that particular arrangement have continued life, being deployed by new actors toward new ends.[34] My exploration of government in Gaza suggests, in addition, that important techniques of rule—of producing authority, of managing continuity—are not always derived from the form of its state. Even where a nation-state seems stable, therefore, an examination of government should take very seriously the practices of its bureaucracy.

As my exploration of tactical government has indicated, to put bureaucratic practice at the center of analysis does not require presuming that bureaucracy is an entirely autonomous domain. As Gaza's experience makes clear, this practice is entirely entangled in the histories, economies, and politics of the places where it operates, even as it is not always directed by them. In Gaza during the Mandate and the Administration, the interrelations between bureaucracy's general "regularities, logic, strategy, self-evidence, and 'reason'"[35] and the conditions in which this bureaucracy was enacted gave rise to tactical government as a dominant mode of rule. In other circumstances, other conditions, different styles may be foregrounded. What I offer here is not a universal (or other) model of rule but an analytics of government. An anthropology of such regimes of practice—an anthropology of government—makes it possible to understand how the general and the specific, the regular and the exceptional, work together (and at odds) to shape place, people, and rule.

1. Introduction

1. During the first four years of British rule, until the official acceptance of the Mandate in July 1922, Palestine was governed according to military rule. In anticipation of the Mandate, civil administrative structures were put in place before the formal change-over.

2. These rhythms were deeply affected by the history of nationalism and national conflict in Palestine but were not identical to it. Given the importance and often overwhelming character of the national conflict in Palestine, the focus on nationalism in much of the historiography on Palestine is neither surprising nor entirely mistaken. From the Palestinian Arab perspective, this attention has been politically ameliorative, replacing a vision of Palestinians as passive or reactive only to Zionism with a much more complex understanding of personal and communal identity. Nonetheless, more remains to be understood about Palestinian history. For examples from the literature, see Muhammad Muslih, *The Origins of Palestinian Nationalism* (New York: Columbia University Press, 1990); Rashid Khalidi, *Palestinian Identity: The Construction of Modern National Consciousness* (New York: Columbia University Press, 1997); William Quandt, Fuad Jabber, and Ann Mosely Lesch, *The Politics of Palestinian Nationalism* (Berkeley: University of California Press, 1973); Jamal Nasser and Roger Heacock, eds., *Intifada: Palestine at the Crossroads* (New York: Praeger, 1990); Zachary Lockman and Joel Beinin, eds., *Intifada: The Palestinian Uprising Against Israeli Occupation* (Boston: South End Press, 1989); Nels Johnson, *Islam and the Politics of Meaning in Palestinian Nationalism* (London: Kegan Paul International, 1982); Adnan Abu-Ghazaleh, *Arab Cultural Nationalism in Palestine* (Beirut: Institute for Palestine Studies, 1973).

3. The Oslo Accords, signed by Yasser Arafat and Yitzhak Rabin in September 1993, provided for the establishment of a Palestinian National Authority in parts of the West Bank and Gaza Strip and for a withdrawal of Israeli troops from Palestinian

population centers. While the Accords were greeted with much acclaim by many, others understood them to be deeply flawed, a reading that was vindicated in the years of their enactment, as settlement building continued at an increased pace, the Palestinian economy was extremely restricted, and corruption was rife in the authority. All of these problems contributed to the outbreak of the second *intifada* in September 2000.

4. This is Sara Roy's phrase (*The Gaza Strip: The Political Economy of De-development* [Washington, D.C.: Institute for Palestine Studies, 1995]).

5. These conditions have been documented by various human rights organizations, including al-Haq (a Palestinian organization) and B'Tselem (an Israeli one). In May 2005 Israel removed the settler population from Gaza, making that land once again available for Palestinian use.

6. The Palestinians who returned from abroad—especially PLO folk from Tunis—were known as returnees.

7. In the summer of 2006, after an Israeli soldier was captured and taken into Gaza, Israel arrested a large number of Palestinian legislators and cabinet ministers, leading Prime Minister Ismail Haniyeh to question whether the Palestinian Authority remained a viable entity (Ha'aretz, "Haniyeh questions whether PA can function without key lawmakers," 9 August 2006).

8. Situated on "the main highway between Asia and Africa"—a road that is "one of the oldest in the world" (Gerald Butt, *Life at the Crossroads: A History of Gaza* [Nicosia, Cyprus: Rimal Publications, 1995], 6)—Gaza, itself one of the oldest cities in the world, has been a concern for neighboring ruling orders in every era. It has been a site of battles for control by, among others, Egyptian pharaohs, Alexander the Great, and Napoléon Bonaparte. Its population has ebbed and flowed with the vicissitudes of the times. After its conquest in 332 BCE by Alexander, the city was emptied and repopulated by people from surrounding towns. In the fourteenth century its population was depleted by disease. For accounts of Gaza's early history, see Martin A. Meyer, *History of the City of Gaza from Earliest Times to the Present Day* (New York: Columbia University Press, 1907); Salim al-Mubayyad, *Ghazza wa-Qita'uha: Dirasa fi Khulud al-Makan wa-Hadarat-a al-Sukkan min al-'Asr al-Hajari Hatta al-Harb al-'Alamiyya al-Ula* (Cairo: al-Haya al-Misriyya al-'Amma lil-Kitab, 1987); 'Arif al-'Arif, *Tarikh Ghazza* (Jerusalem: Dar Al-Aytam Al-Islamiyya, 1943); Said 'Ashur, *Ghazza Hashim* (Amman: Dar Al-Diya', 1988).

9. See Nadine Meouchy and Peter Sluglett, eds., *The British and French Mandates in Comparative Perspectives* (Leiden: Brill, 2004), and Michael D. Callahan, *Mandates and Empire: The League of Nations and Africa, 1914–1931* (Brighton: Sussx Academic Press, 1999).

10. League of Nations Covenant, Article 22. Cited in Neta Crawford, *Argument and Change in World Politics: Ethics, Decolonization, and Humanitarian Intervention* (Cambridge: Cambridge University Press, 2002), 261.

11. As one commentator described this arrangement, "The mandatories . . . have not

sovereign powers, but are responsible to the League for the execution of the terms of the mandate" (H. W. V. Temperley, cited in Quincy Wright, *Mandates Under the League of Nations* [Chicago: University of Chicago Press, 1930], 23).

12. Campbell L. Upthegrove, *Empire by Mandate: A History of the Relations of Great Britain with the Permanent Mandates Commissions of the League of Nations* (New York: Brookman Associates, 1954), 17.

13. On this question see Quincy Wright, "Sovereignty of the Mandates" *American Journal of International Law* 17, 4 (1923): 691–703.

14. Antony Anghie, "Colonialism and the Birth of International Institutions: Sovereignty, Economy, and the Mandate System of the League of Nations," *NYU Journal of International Law and Politics* 34 (2001–2): 513–633, 569.

15. On the complexities of sovereignty and rule that have been part of all colonial endeavors, see Ann Stoler, "Degrees of Imperial Sovereignty," *Public Culture* 18, 1 (2006): 125–46.

16. Anghie, "Colonialism and the Birth of International Institutions," 545.

17. See Susan Pedersen, "Settler Colonialism at the Bar of the League of Nations," in *Settler Colonialism in the Twentieth Century*, ed. Caroline Elkins and Susan Pedersen, 113–34 (New York: Routledge, 2005).

18. Upthegrove, *Empire by Mandate*, 17.

19. There were three classes of mandates, distinguished on the basis of their perceived developmental level. On the development and management of the mandate system, see J. Stoyansky, *The Mandate for Palestine: A Contribution to the Theory and Practice of International Mandates* (London: Longmans, Green, 1928); Freda White, *Mandates* (London: Jonathan Cape, 1926); Wright, *Mandates Under the League of Nations*; Pitman Potter, "Origin of the System of Mandates under the League of Nations," *American Political Science Review* 16, 4 (1922): 563–83.

20. On modern European interests in and entrance into Palestine, see Alexander Scholch, *Palestine in Transformation 1856–1882: Studies in Social, Economic and Political Development*, trans. William C. Young and Michael C. Gerrity (Washington, D.C.: Institute for Palestine Studies, 1993).

21. As Herbert Samuel, the first high commissioner for Palestine, described British responsibility, "It is the clear duty of the mandatory power to promote the well-being of the Arab population in the same way as a British administration would regard it as its duty to promote the welfare of the local population in any part of the Empire. Measures to foster Arab well-being should be primarily those we should adopt in Palestine if there were no Zionist question and no Balfour Declaration" (cited in Norman and Helen Bentwich, *Mandate Memories: 1918–1948* [London, Hogarth Press, 1965], 71).

22. The Peel Commission Report used the phrase "dual obligation" specifically in reference to land management issues; it aptly describes the Mandate as a whole as well (*Palestine Royal Commission Report*. Cmd. 5479, July 1937, 221).

23. The period of the Mandate was marked by intensifying conflict between Zionist

settlers and Palestinian Arabs, conflict that periodically expressed itself in outright rebellion. On the history of the Mandate, see A. W. Kayyali, *Palestine: A Modern History* (London, Croom Helm, 1970); Bernard Wasserstein, *The British in Palestine: The Mandatory Government and the Arab-Jewish Conflict, 1917–1929* (London: Royal Historical Society, 1978); J. C. Hurewitz, *The Struggle for Palestine* (New York: Schocken Books, 1976).

24. *Palestine Royal Commission Report*. Cmd. 5479, July 1937, 362. Both the 1929 riots, which were sparked by rumors that Jews were planning to take over the *Haram al-Sharif* in Jerusalem, and the 1936 revolt provoked a serious reconsideration of British policy in Palestine.

25. The onset of World War II had put conflict in Palestine on the back burner, but it was not long after the war that the British gave up on their (clearly failed) effort to govern Palestine. In February 1947 they announced to the United Nations their intention to depart from Palestine. In November of that year the UN voted, over Arab objection, to support the partition of Palestine into two states, one Jewish and one Arab. War over the future of Palestine began well before the British departure from the country on 14 May 1948. Upon the British departure, the regular armies of the neighboring Arab countries entered the fight.

26. For an overview of political and economic aspects of this period, see Husayn Abu Naml, *Qita' Ghazza, 1948–1967: Tatawwarat Iqtisadiyya wa-Siyasiyya wa-Ijtimaiyya wa-Askariyya* (Beirut: PLO Research Center, 1979).

27. The defeat of Egypt's poorly organized forces had tremendous impact on both Gaza and Egypt. The defeat, and the scandal about defective weapons that followed, were significant factors in the Free Officers "revolution" in 1952 that brought an end to the monarchy in Egypt. See Anouar Abdel-Malek, *Egypt: Military Society, the Army Regime, the Left, and Social Change Under Nasser* (New York: Random House, 1968); Joel Gordon, *Nasser's Blessed Movement: Egypt's Free Officers and the July Revolution* (New York: Oxford University Press, 1992); Ilan Pappe, *The Making of the Arab-Israeli Conflict, 1947–51* (London: I. B. Tauris, 1992). On the war itself, see Fawaz Gerges "Egypt and the 1948 War: Internal Conflict and Regional Ambition," in *The War for Palestine: Rewriting the History of 1948*, ed. Eugene Rogan and Avi Shlaim, 151–77 (Cambridge: Cambridge University Press, 2001).

28. Haroun Hashim Rashid, *Qissat Madinat Ghazza* (al-Munazzama al-Arabiyya l-it-Tarbiyya wal-Thaqafa wal-'Ulum, nd), 65.

29. Neil Caplan, "A Tale of Two Cities: The Rhodes and Lausanne Conferences, 1949" *Journal of Palestine Studies* 21, 3 (Spring 1992): 5–34.

30. FO 371 file 96973.

31. *Al-Ahram*, 21 June 1950 and 9 June 1951. The British embassy in Cairo also described such requests, in one case reporting on Egyptian press coverage of a delegation from Gaza with that end in mind (FO 371, file 80398, from Embassy to Foreign Office, 17 March 1950), and in another describing a conversation with Gaza City's mayor, who indicated a first preference for annexation to Jordan with incorporation into Egypt

his second choice (FO 371, file 82256, from Embassy to Foreign Office, 6 August 1950).

32. PRO FO 371/96973, telegram from Foreign Office to British Embassies in Middle East, 9 April 1952.

33. PRO FO 371/104776, letter from G. H. Baker, Foreign Office, to S. Goddard, Board of Trade, Statistics Division, 13 August 1953.

34. The All-Palestine Government was established in the immediate aftermath of 1948 but never had any real power or functionality. Its declaration of independence was defiant but doomed: "The inhabitants of Palestine, by virtue of their natural right to self-determination and in accordance with the resolutions of the Arab League, have decided to declare Palestine in its entirety . . . as an independent state under a government known as the All-Palestine Government which is based on democratic principles" (Avi Shlaim, "The Rise and Fall of the All-Palestine Government in Gaza," *Journal of Palestine Studies* 20(1): 37–53, 41–42). Lacking any infrastructure or financial base, the All-Palestine Government was unable to operate effectively and could not maintain independence. As Avi Shlaim notes, "It claimed jurisdiction over the whole of Palestine, yet it had no administration, no civil service, no money, no real army of its own" (ibid., 43).

35. That the West Bank was incorporated as Jordanian territory, with Palestinians given citizenship, created a quite different governing dynamic (Joseph Massad, *Colonial Effects: The Making of a National Identity in Jordan* [New York: Columbia University Press, 2001]).

36. See Ilana Feldman, "Government Without Expertise?: Competence, Capacity, and Civil Service Practice in Gaza (1917–1967)," *International Journal of Middle East Studies* 37, 4 (November 2005): 485–507, and "Everyday Government in Extraordinary Times: Persistence and Authority in Gaza's Civil Service, 1917–1967," *Comparative Studies in Society and History* 47, 4 (2005): 863–91.

37. DW, *Qawa'im El-Mushir*, Group 41, File 90105, 17 December 1960, letter from Governor General to Director of the Defense Minister's Office.

38. On the National Union and subsequent Arab Socialist Union in Egypt, see Abdel Malek, *Egypt: Military Society;* John Waterbury, *The Egypt of Nasser and Sadat: The Political Economy of Two Regimes* (Princeton: Princeton University Press, 1983), 312–32; and Kirk Beattie, *Egypt During the Nasser Years: Ideology, Politics, Civil Society* (Boulder: Westview Press, 1994), esp. chapter 6.

39. *Al-Ahram*, 11 September 1964. See Yezid Sayigh, "Escalation or Containment? Egypt and the Palestine Liberation Army, 1964–67," *International Journal of Middle East Studies* 30, 1 (1998): 97–116.

40. Laurie Brand, "Nasir's Egypt and the Reemergence of the Palestinian National Movement," *Journal of Palestine Studies* 17, 2 (1998): 29–45, 41. After the establishment of conscription, Administration records indicate a number of instances of soldiers going absent without leave, though how prevalent this phenomenon was is not clear (see ISA, RG 115, box 1983, file 15).

41. One exception to this mandate was inside Israel: the Israeli government asked UNRWA not to operate in its territory.

42. For discussion of some of the debates that led to the distinctive status of Palestinian refugees, see Lex Takkenberg, *The Status of Palestinian Refugees in International Law* (Oxford: Clarendon Press, 1998).

43. In his history of UNRWA, Edward Buehrig cites a U.S. representative to the UN on the matter. Speaking in 1969, Joseph Johnson commented that the "special attention which the United Nations has, over a twenty-one year period, devoted to the Arab refugee problem is understandable . . . in light of the United Nations direct concern with the over-all problem that gave rise to the refugee situation" (*The UN and the Palestinian Refugees: A Study in Nonterritorial Administration* [Bloomington: Indiana University Press, 1971], 181).

44. See Buerhig, *The UN and the Palestinian Refugees*, and Benjamin N. Schiff, *Refugees Unto the Third Generation: UN Aid to Palestinians* (Syracuse: Syracuse University Press, 1995).

45. I follow Foucault here, who described his project in *The History of Sexuality* as "to move less toward a 'theory' of power than toward an 'analytics' of power: that is, toward a definition of the specific domain formed by relations of power, and toward a determination of the instruments that will make possible its analysis" (*The History of Sexuality*, Volume 1: *An Introduction* [New York: Vintage Books, 1980], 82).

46. Frantz Fanon, *The Wretched of the Earth* (New York: Grove Press, 1963).

47. For helpful discussions of these issues, see Nicholas Dirks, *Castes of Mind: Colonialism and the Making of Modern India* (Princeton: Princeton University Press, 2001); Dagmar Engels and Shula Marks, *Contesting Colonial Hegemony: State and Society in Africa and India* (London: I. B. Tauris, 1994); Peter Pels and Oscar Salemink, *Colonial Subjects: Essays on the Practical History of Anthropology* (Ann Arbor: University of Michigan Press, 1999).

48. John L. Comaroff, "Reflections on the Colonial State, in South Arica and Elsewhere: Factions, Fragments, Facts and Fictions" *Social Identities* 4, 3 (1998): 321–61, 340.

49. Ann Stoler, "Tense and Tender Ties: The Politics of Comparison in North American History and (Post)Colonial Studies," *Journal of American History* 88, 3 (2001): 829–65; David Scott, *Refashioning Futures: Criticism After Postcoloniality* (Princeton: Princeton University Press, 1999); Ann Stoler and Frederick Cooper, eds., *Tensions of Empire: Colonial Cultures in a Bourgeois World* (Berkeley: University of California Press, 1997).

50. Comaroff, "Reflections on the Colonial State," 329.

51. Whether one should study government or the state has been the subject of considerable debate in anthropology and beyond. Even as my focus is on government—explored primarily through state institutions and personnel—I hope to move beyond a taking sides approach. The literature on this debate is vast. For some helpful examples, see Philip Abrams, "Notes on the Difficulty of Studying the State," *Journal of Historical Sociology* 1 (1988 [1977]): 58–89; Philip Corrigan and Derek Sayer, *The*

Great Arch: English State Formation as Cultural Revolution (Oxford: Basil Blackwell, 1985); Timothy Mitchell, "The Limits of the State: Beyond Statist Approaches and Their Critics," *American Political Science Review* 85, 1 (March 1991): 77–96; Michel-Rolph Trouillot, *Global Transformations: Anthropology and the Modern World* (New York: Palgrave, 2003); Nikolas Rose, *Powers of Freedom: Reframing Political Thought* (Cambridge: Cambridge University Press, 1999). For a specific discussion of Arab states, see Nazih Ayubi, *Overstating the Arab State: Politics and Society in the Middle East* (London: I. B. Tauris, 1995).

52. Such exceptionalism is relied on far too often to explain Palestinian history—or, more precisely, to make it seem unnecessary to explain it. Mahmood Mamdani has noted a similar problem in South African studies, suggesting in that case that the assumption that the "exceptional" racism of the apartheid state explains South African history tends to preclude asking questions about the form and function of that state as well as its relation to other forms of governance (*Citizen and Subject: Contemporary Africa and the Legacy of Late Colonialism* [Princeton: Princeton University Press, 1996]). The same could be said for Zionism in the Palestinian instance. Scholars need to develop ways of accounting for the admittedly unique features of Palestinian history without presuming that this uniqueness is an answer in itself.

53. Michel Foucault, "Governmentality," in *The Foucault Effect*, ed. Graham Burchell, Colin Gordon, and Peter Miller, 87–104 (Chicago: University of Chicago Press, 1991). For a critique of what he sees as too generalized deployments of governmentality, see Frederick Cooper, *Colonialism in Question: Theory, Knowledge, History* (Berkeley: University of California Press, 2005).

54. See "The Birth of Biopolitics," in Michel Foucault, *Ethics: Subjectivity and Truth*, ed. Paul Rabinow, 73–79 (New York, New Press, 1997), for a discussion of the specificities of liberal governmentality. For particular investigations into workings of governmentality, see Andrew Barry, Thomas Osborne, and Nikolas Rose, eds., *Foucault and Political Reason: Liberalism, Neo-Liberalism and Rationalities of Government* (Chicago: University of Chicago Press, 1996).

55. For examples of anthropological explorations of government and the state, see Nicholas Dirks, *Castes of Mind*; James Scott, *Seeing Like a State: How Certain Schemes to Improve the Human Condition Have Failed* (New Haven: Yale University Press, 1998); Fernando Coronil, *The Magical State: Nature, Money, and Modernity in Venezuela* (Chicago: University of Chicago Press, 1997); Michael Taussig, *The Magic of the State* (New York: Routledge, 1997); Akhil Gupta, "Blurred Boundaries: The Discourse of Corruption, the Culture of Politics, and the Imagined State," *American Ethnologist* 22, 2 (1995): 375–402. Important Middle East specific investigations include Michael Meeker, *A Nation of Empire: The Ottoman Legacy of Turkish Modernity* (Berkeley: University of California Press, 2002); Yael Navaro-Yashin, *Faces of the State: Secularism and Public Life in Turkey* (Princeton: Princeton University Press, 2002); Martha Mundy, *Domestic Government: Kinship, Community and Polity in North Yemen* (London: I. B. Tauris, 1995); Brinkley Messick, *The Calligraphic State* (Berkeley: Univer-

sity of California Press, 1993); Timothy Mitchell, *Colonising Egypt* (Berkeley: University of California Press, 1988).

56. The phrase is obviously Foucault's, *Discipline and Punish: The Birth of the Prison*, trans. Alan Sheridan (New York: Vintage Books, 1979).

57. For discussion and examples of this work, see Pierre Bourdieu, *Outline of a Theory of Practice* (Cambridge: Cambridge University Press, 1977); Michel de Certeau, *The Practice of Everyday Life* (Berkeley: University of California Press, 1984); Michel de Certeau, Luce Giard, and Pierre Mayoal, *The Practice of Everyday Life*, Volume 2: *Living and Cooking*, trans. Timothy Tomasik (Minneapolis: University of Minnesota Press, 1998); Alf Ludtke, ed., *The History of Everyday Life: Reconstructing Historical Experiences and Ways of Life* (Princeton: Princeton University Press, 1995); Sherry Ortner, "Theory in Anthropology Since the Sixties," *CSSH* 26, 10 (1984): 126–66.

58. For a similar approach, see Ivan Evans, *Bureaucracy and Race: Native Administration in South Africa* (Berkeley: University of California Press, 1997).

59. Michel Foucault, "Questions of Method," in *The Foucault Effect*, 73–86, 75. Foucault was reflecting on the practice of imprisonment here, but the point is apt for bureaucracy as well.

60. Richard Sennett, *Authority* (New York: W. W. Norton, 1980), 20. Following this suggestion, and remembering Foucault's descriptions of power, one can think of authority as a node—perhaps a particularly dense one—in a network of force relations. The formation of this node, which can be momentary or long-lasting, requires repetition.

61. See E. Valentine Daniel, *Charred Lullabies: Chapters in an Anthropography of Violence* (Princeton: Princeton University Press, 1996); Partha Chatterjee, *The Nation and Its Fragments* (Princeton: Princeton University Press, 1993); Benedict Anderson, *Imagined Communities* (New York: Verso, 1991).

62. Michael Herzfeld, *The Social Production of Indifference: Exploring the Symbolic Roots of Western Bureaucracy* (Chicago: University of Chicago Press, 1992), 61.

63. For anthropological discussions of bureaucracy, see Akhil Gupta, "Blurred Boundaries"; Don Handelman, "Introduction: A Recognition of Bureaucracy," in *Bureaucracy and World View: Studies in the Logic of Official Interpretation*, ed. Don Handelman and Elliott Leyton, 1–14 (St. John's: Institute of Social and Economic Research, 1978); Josiah McC. Heyman, "Putting Power in the Anthropology of Bureaucracy," *Current Anthropology* 36, 2 (1995): 261–87.

64. Derrida argues that a performative (as a subjectifiying form of speech) could not work if it was not "identifiable as *conforming* to an iterable model, if it were not then identifiable in some way as a 'citation'" ("Signature, Event, Context," in *Limited Inc.* [Evanston, Ill.: Northwestern University Press, 1988], 18). Butler echoes Derrida and suggests that a performative succeeds "not because an intention successfully governs the action of speech, but only because that action echoes prior actions and, accumulates the force of authority through the repetition of citation of a prior and authoritative set of practices" (*Excitable Speech: A Politics of the Performative* [New York: Routledge, 1997], 51).

65. Butler, *Excitable Speech*, 51. This phrase is in italics in the original.

66. De Certeau, *The Practice of Everyday Life*, 189.

67. For examples from the voluminous literature on bureaucracy, including such critiques, see David Beetham, *Bureaucracy* (Minneapolis: University of Minnesota Press, 1987); Gerald Britan and Ronald Cohen, *Hierarchy and Society: Anthropological Perspectives on Bureaucracy*, (Philadelphia: Institute for the Study of Human Issues, 1980); David W. Haines, "Conformity in the Face of Ambiguity: A Bureaucratic Dilemma," *Semiotica* 78, 3/4 (1990): 249–69; Henry Jacoby, *The Bureaucratization of the World*, trans. Eveline L. Kanes (Berkeley: University of California Press, 1973); Elihu Katz and Brenda Danet, "Introduction: Bureaucracy as a Problem for Sociology and Society," in *Bureaucracy and the Public: A Reader in Official-Client Relations*, ed. E. a. B. D. Katz (New York: Basic Books, 1973); B. Guy Peters, *The Politics of Bureaucracy*, (New York: Longman, 1989).

68. Heyman argues that bureaucratic inculcation—the development of a worldview—combines with external power dynamics to consolidate inequalities ("Putting Power in the Anthropology of Bureaucracy").

69. Max Weber, *Economy and Society: An Outline of Interpretive Sociology*, volume 2, ed. Guenther Roth and Claus Wittich (Berkeley: University of California Press, 1968), 988.

70. Max Weber, *From Max Weber: Essays in Sociology*, ed. Hans Gerth and C. Wright Mills (New York: Oxford University Press, 1946), 228.

71. Studies of bureaucracy in stable settings like the United States and Western Europe, for example, suggest numerous points of connection. See Metin Heper, "The State and Public Bureaucracies: A Comparative and Historical Perspective," *Comparative Studies in Society and History* 27, 1 (1985):86–110; Michael Lipsky, *Street-Level Bureaucracy: Dilemmas of the Individual in Public Services* (New York: Russell Sage Foundation, 1980); Katz and Danet, eds., *Bureaucracy and the Public*; Peter Blau and Marshall Meyer, *Bureaucracy in Modern Society* (New York: Random House, 1971).

72. Max Weber, "Politics as a Vocation," in *From Max Weber*, ed. Gerht and Mills, 78.

73. For discussions of authority and legitimacy that use the terms almost interchangeably, see Scott Herscovitz, "Legitimacy, Democracy, and Razian Authority," *Legal Theory* 9 (2003): 201–20; Italo Pardo, ed., *Morals of Legitimacy: Between Agency and System* (New York: Berghahn Books, 2000); Joseph Raz, ed., *Authority* (Oxford: Basil Blackwell, 1990); Myron Aronoff, ed., *The Frailty of Authority* (New Brunswick: Transaction Books, 1986); William Connolly, ed., *Legitimacy and the State* (Oxford: Basil Blackwell, 1984).

74. Saskia Sassen traces historical transformations of authority and its relation to states in Europe (*Territory, Authority, Rights: From Medieval to Global Assemblages* [Princeton: Princeton University Press, 2006]).

75. Lisa Wedeen, *Ambiguities of Domination: Politics, Rhetoric, and Symbols in Contemporary Syria* (Chicago: University of Chicago Press, 1999).

76. This difference also highlights the ways in which Gaza's state was not exactly magical

in the sense that Fernando Coronil describes Venezuela, where a deified state that "sought to conquer rather than persuade" was implicated in a government of magical power which "by manufacturing dazzling development projects that engender collective fantasies of progress, . . . casts its spell over audience and performers alike" (*The Magical State*, 116).

77. Studies of colonialism have highlighted the always tenuous nature of its control, and in some ways Gaza represents an extreme point on a scale of surety and capacity. See Frederick Cooper, "Colonizing Time: Work Rhythms and Labor Conflict in Colonial Mombasa," in *Colonialism and Culture*, ed. Nicholas Dirks, 209–46 (Ann Arbor: University of Michigan Press, 1992); Sara Suleri, *The Rhetoric of English India* (Chicago: University of Chicago Press, 1992); Ann Stoler, "'In Cold Blood': Hierarchies of Credibility and the Politics of Colonial Narratives," *Representations* 37 (Winter 1992): 151–87. That nation-states often have similar problems of control and capacity has also been explored. See, for example, Danilyn Rutherford, *Raiding the Land of the Foreigners: The Limits of the Nation on an Indonesian Frontier* (Princeton: Princeton University Press, 2003).

78. De Certeau, *The Practice of Everyday Life*.

79. *Discipline and Punish*, 139.

80. Of course, limitations (especially fiscal ones) on the capacity of government are not unique to peculiar circumstances like those in Gaza. If anything about government is ubiquitous—part of colonial rule, liberal government, totalitarian despotism—it is the problem of limited resources. In each of these instances, though, the problem emerges from a different site, with different inflections and different effects.

81. Israel State Archives (ISA), RG 3, box 737, file 29/5, Town Planning Commission Minutes, June 19, 1947.

82. Dar al-Watha'iq [DW], *Qawa'im al-Mushir*, Group 41, file 90505, letter from Director of Palestine Affairs Administration to Governor General, March 7, 1960.

83. According to the Peel Commission Report, "Municipal organization of a sort existed in Turkish times, though in practice the Ottoman Governors exercised unlimited power of interference in municipal affairs." Mandate municipal organization, in this view, represented an immediate advance by attempting to "regularize the position of the municipalities and to impose fiscal reform" (*Palestine Royal Commission Report*, Cmd. 5479 [1937], 347).

84. Omar al-Barghouthi argued that mandate rule represented a serious setback for municipal autonomy: "The position of the municipality under the Turkish Government was one of dignity and independence. Government interference was very slight, consisting mainly of the appointment of the mayor from among the elected members. When the British came, however, this local self-government was seriously jeopardized." ("Local Self-Government—Past and Present," in *Palestine: A Decade of Development*, ed. Harry Vitales and Khalil Totah, 34–38 [Philadelphia: American Academy of Political and Social Science, 1932], 36). Along with this complaint, Barghouthi did note that the British had improved municipal services a great deal:

"Although it robbed the population of its rights [British administration] has tended to improve sanitary conditions, modernize the streets, and minimize corruption. . . . Thus, local freedom has been sacrificed to efficiency, and one wonders if the two could not be combined" (ibid., 37).

85. See 'Ali Jarbawi, "*al-Baladiyyat al-Filastiniyya (Min al-Nasha' Hata al-'Am 1967)*," *Shu'un Filastiniyya*, 221–22 (1991): 49–72.

86. See *Palestine Gazette* 1934 for the laws governing municipal councils, and ISA RG 2, box 206, file G/57/34 for examples of mayoral appointments.

87. Interview, Gaza City, 8 March 1998.

88. CO 733, file 3879, "Civil Service," letter regarding the organization of the Palestine Government, 14 January 1922.

89. "Report on Education in the Southern District, Feb. 1941–October 1945" A. L. Tibawi, submitted to the director of education, Government of Palestine, 1 May 1946.

90. For a discussion of Gaza's economy during this period, see Roy, *The Gaza Strip*.

91. The issue of tax farming is a good example of the circuits of policy formation. While tax farming had been the principal means of revenue collection under the Ottomans, British authorities preferred more direct forms of taxation. As they tried to amend the laws regulating municipalities to exclude tax farming, however, Mandate officials were forced to recognize that municipalities had neither the personnel nor the financial resources to take this task on themselves (ISA, RG 2, box 210, file G/99/35). Despite officials' strong preference to the contrary, Mandate practice had to bend to local requirements. The grudging recommendation of the Southern District commissioner states, "I enclose a list of the dues which the various municipalities in the Southern District desire to farm out. I am still hoping to cut down this list, as I think that we should aim at the gradual elimination of the farming system, but provisionally I must recommend them" (File G/99/35, letter from Southern District Commissioner to Chief Secretary, 2 July 1938).

92. For a more extensive discussion of these border crossings, see Ilana Feldman, "Home as a Refrain: Remembering and Living Displacement in Gaza," *History and Memory* 18, 2 (2006): 10–47.

93. See Benny Morris, *Israel's Border Wars, 1949–1956: Arab Infiltration, Israeli Retaliation, and the Countdown to the Suez War* (Oxford: Clarendon Press, 1993); Husayn Abu Niml, "Harb al-*Fida'iyyin* fi Qita' Ghazza," *Shu'un Filastiniyya* 62 (January 1979): 177–99; Ann Mosely Lesch, "Gaza: History and Politics," in *Israel, Egypt, and the Palestinians: From Camp David to Intifada*, ed. Ann Mosely Lesch and Mark Tessler, 223–37 (Bloomington: Indiana University Press, 1989).

94. Interview, Gaza City, 23 March 1999.

95. Though Ann Mosely Lesch notes that benefits did not accrue to everyone: "This trade benefitted a few wealthy Gaza merchants and fostered corruption both locally and within the Egyptian Administration" ("Gaza: History and Politics," 227).

96. ISA, RG 115, box 2024, file 14, Administration of general supervision of refugees, government aid, and social affairs, Annual Report, 1953.

97. ISA, RG 115, box 2007, file 15, speech given by head of Executive Committee of Arab UNRWA Employee in Jabalya Camp, 15 December 1964.

98. For some examples from the vast literature on the transformation of space and place in processes of rule, see Doreen Massey, *Space, Place, and Gender* (Minneapolis: University of Minnesota Press, 1994); Paul Rabinow, *French Modern: Norms and Forms of the Social Environment* (Chicago: University of Chicago Press, 1989); Mitchell, *Colonising Egypt*; Gwendolyn Wright, "Tradition in the Service of Modernity: Architecture and Urbanism in French Colonial Policy, 1900–1930," *Journal of Modern History* 59 (1994): 291–316; James Holston, *The Modernist City: An Anthropological Critique of Brasília* (Chicago: University of Chicago Press, 1989); Mike Davis, *City of Quartz: Excavating the Future in Los Angeles* (New York: Vintage, 1990). Many of these works describe interventions that were conceived on a much larger scale than the more constricted practices of government in Gaza.

99. Even as the importance of shaping the character of places and localities—to make them more amenable to government, to enable them to better meet the needs of the population—has been an articulated part of government practice, at the same time place or territory is often held to mark simply the boundaries of rule. Modern government proceeds in a place, over a place, but as if it is not essentially about place. In *The Magical State*, Coronil discusses the problems of how "nature is taken for granted" in both governmental practice and social analysis (Chicago: University of Chicago Press, 1997). Uday Mehta explores the difficulty of territory for liberalism, contrasting a Lockean approach with Burke's attitude (*Liberalism and Empire: A Study of Nineteenth-Century British Liberal Thought* [Chicago: University of Chicago Press, 1999]).

100. While there is some continuity of sources across the periods of the Mandate and the Administration, there are also important discontinuities. Broadly, sources from the Mandate provide more insight into policy development and debates and less on local practice, while those from the Administration provide a nearly reversed image. In the sources for this later period one finds an enormous amount of detail about the micropractices of government and much less analytic reflection on their purpose. While this difference in availability does not reflect an essential divergence in the modes of government employed by each regime (it reflects much more the vagaries of archival retention), it necessarily affects how I write my account.

101. ISA, RG 26, box 4973, file 15.

102. When Israel occupied Gaza in 1956 and then again in 1967, Egyptian Administration records were seized and transferred to the state archives (see chapter 2). Israel's first occupation of Gaza, part of the attack launched on Egypt by Israel, Great Britain, and France, lasted four months. Israeli forces departed under intense pressure from the United States, and in their wake UN troops came in to patrol the borders. The second Israeli occupation of Gaza began in June 1967, at the same time that Israel occupied the West Bank, the Sinai, and the Golan Heights.

103. Walking around Gaza City, one sees, in addition to the makeup of the population,

the boundaries of the territory, and the presence of refugee camps, buildings that have been in successive turns prisons, schools, and administrative offices. The laws which govern the place are an amalgam of amendments enacted by British, Egyptian, Israeli, and Palestinian bodies on an existing Ottoman framework.

104. I am aware of the risk that, in not giving the same attention to the personnel dynamic of British and Egyptian civil servants, "the Mandate" and "the Administration" may at times appear overly unitary and unified as categories. To undercut this appearance, while at the same time maintaining the focus that is important for my inquiry, I try throughout to gesture to this field of complication among "foreign" personnel.

2. Ruling Files

1. On Ottoman bureaucratic histories, see Stanford Shaw, *The Financial and Administrative Organization and Development of Ottoman Egypt, 1517–1798* (Princeton: Princeton University Press, 1962); Carter Findley, *Bureaucratic Reform in the Ottoman Empire: The Sublime Porte, 1789–1922* (Princeton: Princeton University Press, 1980); id., *Ottoman Civil Officialdom: A Social History* (Princeton: Princeton University Press, 1989); id., "The Ottoman Administrative Legacy and the Modern Middle East," in *Imperial Legacy: The Ottoman Imprint on the Balkans and the Middle East*, ed. L. Carl Brown, 158–74 (New York: Columbia University Press, 1996); Michael Meeker, *A Nation of Empire: The Ottoman Legacy of Turkish Modernity* (Berkeley: University of California Press, 2002).

2. For discussions of filing and government paper in other contexts, see Veena Das, "The Signature of the State: The Paradox of Illegibility," in *Anthropology in the Margins of the State*, ed. Veena Das and Deborah Poole, 225–52 (Santa Fe: SAR Press, 2004); Matthew Hull, "The File: Agency, Authority, and Autography in an Islamabad Bureaucracy," *Language and Communication* 23, 3, (2003): 287–314; Jane Caplan and John Torpey, eds., *Documenting Individual Identity: The Development of State Practices in the Modern World* (Princeton: Princeton University Press, 2001).

3. Disciplinary writing was marked by "the accumulation of documents, their seriation, the organization of comparative fields making it possible to classify, to form categories, to determine averages, to fix norms" (Foucault, *Discipline and Punish*, 190).

4. For example, Findley describes the new system of managing personnel records, under regulations issued in 1879 and: "The instructions also specified the form of the questionnaire that was to be the basic document in each file. This questionnaire was a large sheet of paper divided into boxes. The column on the right contained the printed questions which the respondent was to answer in the wider boxes running down the middle of the sheet. To the left was another column of boxes intended for 'observations' by the individual's superiors. . . . [After listing of family background and qualifications] there was to be a chronological account of the respondent's official service. This was to include dated entries for changes in salary or other forms of compensation as well as for changes of position" (*Bureaucratic Reform in the Ottoman Empire*, 272).

5. Ibid.

6. For an account of the importance of paper and its forms in producing "textual domination," see Brinkley Messick, *The Calligraphic State*.

7. *Discipline and Punish*, 190.

8. Archives have become a subject of considerable interest to anthropologists in recent years, as the possibilities inherent in pursuing "ethnography 'of' and 'in'" the archive have been increasingly elaborated (Ann Stoler, "Colonial Archives and the Arts of Governance," *Archival Science* 2, 1–2 [2002]: 87–109). See also Penelope Papailias, *Genres of Recollection: Archival Poetics and Modern Greece* (New York: Palgrave Macmillan, 2005). Historians too have turned new attention to the form and function of archives as institutions and processes, not simply as repositories of information. These attentions have been well described by Ann Stoler and others, and I will not repeat the history of the "archival turn" here. See, for example, Roberto Echevarría, *Myth and Archive: A Theory of Latin American Narrative* (Cambridge: Cambridge University Press, 1990); Nicholas Dirks, "Colonial Histories and Native Informants: Biography of an Archive," in *Orientalism and the Postcolonial Predicament: Perspectives on South Asia*, ed. Carol Brekenridge and Peter van der Veer, 279–313 (Philadelphia: University of Pennsylvania Press, 1993); Richard Thomas, *Imperial Archive: Knowledge and Fantasy of Empire* (London: Verso, 1993).

9. As Derrida says of the archive, "As much and more than a thing of the past, before such a thing, the archive should *call into question* the coming of the future" (*Archive Fever: A Freudian Impression*, trans. Eric Prenowitz [Chicago: University of Chicago Press, 1995], 33–34).

10. By discussing personnel files, police files, and administrative files within a single frame, I do not mean to suggest that they are all the same. I do, however, want to show how these kinds of files participate in filing practice.

11. Interview, Gaza City, 26 March 1998.

12. Ann Stoler uses the term "extractive history" to oppose what she argues is the more useful ethnographic history.

13. For example, the particular hierarchical relations evident in filing are frequently refigured in archives. Typically, these relations are in some ways flattened, all documents being of equal potential value for a researcher. In other ways, they are remade, such that a prolific filer might acquire a higher place in an archival hierarchy than s/he occupied in an administrative one.

14. Critical historians have highlighted the political character of archival narratives and the ways in which the forms of these archives operate to dictate particular kinds of narratives (see De Certeau *The Writing of History*; Hayden White, *The Content of the Form* [Baltimore: Johns Hopkins University Press, 1987]; Dirks, "Colonial Histories and Native Informants"; and Stoler, "'In Cold Blood'").

15. Brinkley Messick describes the importance of the Qur'an as the "authoritative original" for Islamic texts. He notes that "the paradigmatic, Urtext qualities of the Quran concern both content and textual form" (*The Calligraphic State*, 16).

16. The violent character of the shifts in Gaza's rulers has meant that the documents of its history have followed highly troubled paths. While no system of archiving documents, however comprehensive in its regulations, is ever perfectly actualized, the Gazan case has been especially difficult.

17. In addition to documents I gathered, my archive is constituted by those in whose production I was involved. I refer to my interviews with former civil servants and civilian Gazans, or, more precisely, to the transcripts of those interviews. By recording and then translating and transcribing (with the help of a research assistant) my interviews, I have transformed them into another type of document. Despite this transformation, the originally oral character of the interviews is not entirely lost in this process, as their rhythm and language remain distinct from a written form. Unlike most of the documents of my research, these interviews are conducted after the fact. Certainly the files I am using are at different levels of remove from a situation, ranging from in-the-moment, on-the-ground reporting to conclusions reached after study and reflection, but virtually all of them were formed in the period on which they report.

18. According to the ISA catalogue, "The records of these former administrations were not received in an orderly and organised fashion since neither the Turks nor the British wished to pass on to their successors the machinery of government. Most of the records salvaged at the end of the British Mandate were found in abandoned buildings and then transferred to temporary depots till a successor department eventually asked for the records. Therefore much of the archival material was lost by negligence or destroyed purposely" (P. A. Alsberg, *Guide to the Archives in Israel*, volume 1: *The Israel State Archives* [Jerusalem: Israel Archives Association, 1991], 13).

19. I deduce this from the files I was able to examine. I was not allowed to see files related to security matters.

20. There is a certain danger that in calling attention to content and style as being distinguished they will appear as distinct. I hope I succeed in highlighting the mutual imbrication as well as the differentiation of these two aspects of writing files.

21. ISA, RG 2, box 460, file U/333/43, Chief Secretary's Office, Office Order No. 1, 6 September 1946.

22. Such lapses were noted at the top of many of the notices.

23. ISA, RG 2, box 460, file U/333/43, Chief Secretary's Office: Office Notice No. 35, 15 December 1947.

24. Messick describes the authorizing gestures in copying in both scribal and mechanical reproduction. In the former, "as a 'copy' it is virtually the same thing as the original, not because it 'looks like' the original in the photo-identity sense accomplished by mechanical reproduction (cf. Benjamin 1968), but because it has passed through an authoritative process of human reproduction and collation" (*The Calligraphic State*, 240).

25. Chief Secretary's Office: Office Notice No. 35, 15 December 1947.

26. See, for example, ISA, RG 2, box 473, file U/2586/47 on the form of personnel files;

ISA RG 2, file 8/217, on early orders governing drafting and sending of official telegrams and correspondence; and ISA, RG 22, box 3395, file 53/44, on land registries.

27. Regulations governing filing specified that full-size, rather than half-size, sheets had to be used for minutes, indicating an interest that such minutes be neither lost nor appear like other than important parts of the file. At the same time, the regulations indicated that reference in minutes to other papers should indicate clearly whether that paper was a folio or a minute, highlighting the structured difference between the two types of writing in files (ISA, RG 2, box 460, file U/333/43, Office Orders No. 3 and 10).

28. CO 733, file 77168, Comment in minutes, 11 December 1930.

29. The importance of informal correspondence was noted in the Secretariat regulations. While the reason offered in the regulations for such informality was that "by this means useful exchange of ideas can be made without formally committing Heads of Departments or Government" (ISA, RG 2, box 460, file U/333/43, Office Order No. 35), the opportunity provided for officials to blow off steam seems equally important.

30. Competition among officers was often expressed through posturing about who had a clearer understanding of the Palestinian population or the impact of a specific policy on that population. This kind of posturing was evident in debates over issues as diverse as funding the rebuilding of Gaza (CO 733, file 12837), the drafting of a press law (CO 733, file 77168), and the reorganization of the police force (CO 733, file 57397).

31. Hayden White, *The Content of the Form* (Baltimore: Johns Hopkins University Press, 1987).

32. See Michel Foucault, "The Discourse on Language," appendix to *Archeology of Knowledge*, trans. A. M. Sheridan Smith (New York: Pantheon Books, 1972), for a related discussion about the necessity that statements fall "within the true" to even be subject to judgments about veracity.

33. Juan Cole describes the importance of print technologies in producing such transformations. When scribes were the primary means of reproducing texts, authors often relied on rhyming and repetition in order to protect their texts from corruption. As Cole notes, though, "the need for rhymes, parallelism, and synonyms sent authors to the dictionaries frequently, and caused them to resort to obscure terms inaccessible to ordinary folk" (*Colonialism and Revolution in the Middle East: Social and Cultural Origins of Egypt's 'Urabi Movement* [Princeton: Princeton University Press, 1993], 117). The growth of print in the Middle East toward the end of the nineteenth century had a dramatic effect on this writing style.

34. The journal was interested in the conditions of civil service in Egypt and does not address Gaza. However, insofar as I am interested in the ethos of rule under Egypt, this prescriptive discourse can tell us something about the milieu within which civil servants in Gaza likely approached their task.

35. "The Literature of Memos," *Majallat al-Muwazzafin* 1 (March 1956): 76–77.

36. Juan Cole, "Printing and Urban Islam in the Mediterranean World, 1890–1920," in *Modernity and Culture from the Mediterranean to the Indian Ocean, 1890–1920*, ed. Leila Fawaz and C. A. Bayly, 344–64 (New York: Columbia University Press, 2002), 350.

37. The use of civil service writing as a means of evaluating employees was certainly not new, though the grounds for evaluation had changed. Cole describes how an Ottoman civil servant was promoted "because the Sultan thought well of the rhetorical excellence he displayed in an article on preventing fires in Istanbul" (*Colonialism and Revolution*, 116).

38. The civil service in Gaza, like that in the United States, was organized by grades, which determined salary (separate from the specific job). Promotions were usually made according to seniority and less frequently for performance.

39. As is to be expected, the letters usually close with a plea to the addressee to turn his attention to this case and to fulfill his obligation (and desire) to see that right prevails.

40. In order to protect individuals' and their families' privacy, I have changed the names of the civil servants whose personnel files I examined as well as those I interviewed. Since last names in Gaza locate people quite specifically as members of certain families, I have not used last names at all, even as pseudonyms.

41. Pensions and Social Security Administration (PSSA), Gaza City, Personnel File #244.

42. PSSA, Personnel File #242/434.

43. The personnel files of the Egyptian Administration include numerous examples of civil servants being punished for delays in reporting changes in their family circumstances, indicating the seriousness with which this requirement was enforced (see, for example, PSSA, Personnel Files #665, 156/1959, and 1917).

44. The exact conditions which determined allowance eligibility changed over the course of the Administration. Because of this, there are instances of children reappearing in the files. For example, in 1963 the Executive Council ruled that unmarried female children over the age of seventeen should receive allowances. After this decision, many civil servants requested allowance increases and once again listed the names of their female children on their personal status forms. In 1965, sons who had come of age and who were still students were allowed to be counted for allowance purposes, and so they reappeared in files.

45. There is no way these files could have ever actually included all available information about behavior and attitudes in the Gaza Strip. As a practical matter that would be a little like building a life-size map. Furthermore, people must have been successful, at least on occasion, at keeping some of their thoughts and actions secret.

46. Well-known figures and important moments must have also been the subject of a great deal of police reporting. Not having been granted access to sensitive materials in the Israeli archives, I have not seen any such files. That they surely exist does not detract from my argument about how this particular kind of everyday surveillance operates. I explore this aspect of policing in greater detail in "Observing the Every-

day: Policing and the Conditions of Possibility in Gaza (1948–67)," *Interventions: International Journal of Postcolonial Studies* 9, 3 (2007): 415–34.

47. ISA, RG 115, box 2024, file 3, report from officer to *mabahith* inspector on "public opinion and general conditions in Khan Yunis," 1 April 1963.

48. This incidental accumulation, which was so effective in enhancing the authority of these police files, also highlights some of the limitations of compilation in filing. By gathering apparently everything (without discrimination about veracity) and composing a potential narrative within these files (without too much evident concern about actuality), these files also contained a built-in potential for failure. Because, of course, the police did maintain an active interest in hunting out the truth, and investigations might show rumors to be false and information inaccurate. These moments of failure, which were inevitable, did not necessarily destabilize the scaffolding of filing. Rather, and this is the dual aspect of accumulation, the same compilation effect which could lead to a false story in the files ensured that there would always be enough material in those files to rewrite that story better.

49. Foucault describes this lowering of the threshold of knowledge as central to the "epistemological 'thaw' of the sciences of the individual" (*Discipline and Punish*, 191).

50. For example, in a 1922 discussion about the organization of districts in Palestine, mention was made of a suggested appointment of an officer to Gaza. In touting this man's abilities, Gaza was offhandedly mentioned and defined: "The somewhat backward district over which it is proposed to place him will, I confidently believe, make considerable progress under his guidance" (CO 733, file 3879 "Civil Service," letter of January 14, 1992).

51. In addition to the files of the "Municipalities and Local Government" group of the Chief Secretariat, the primary kinds of files where particular files were dedicated to Gaza were town planning files (of the attorney general's office) and land registry files (of the Land Settlement Department).

52. ISA, RG 2, box 209, file G/44/35, Gaza Municipal bylaws, 1935. Signed by the mayor of Gaza and "confirmed. By His Excellency's Command" by the chief secretary.

53. ISA, RG 2, box 216, file G/8/41, letter from Gaza District Commissioner to Chief Secretary, 22 January 1941.

54. ISA, RG 2, box 206, file G/39/34 Municipal Elections—Gaza, petition to High Commissioner from Khalil Bseisso, Abdel Azim El Husseini, Husni Khayal, Adil Shawwa, Mousa Sourani, Osman Tabbah, Shaheen Ghalayini, Said Ramadan, Khader Tarazi, and Abdel Nour Ifranji, 9 January 1930.

55. Weber, *Economy and Society*, 992.

56. Ibid, 992.

57. "Except to the Attorney General in person" (ISA, RG 2, box 460, file U/333/43 Office Order No. 1, 5 September 1946). All citations that follow regarding secrecy regulations are from this file.

58. "Officers of the secret registry and officers of or above the rank of Administrative Assistant."

59. The copy of the order which I have is hand-marked as going to the office of the Khan Yunis administrative commissioner. Presumably the order was distributed at least to all of the regional administrative offices.

60. ISA, RG 115, box 2023, file 19, Circular #M/49 issued by the Director of Administrative Affairs of the Employee Affairs Administration, 1 March 1956.

61. Unlike British regulations, Egyptian filing practice did not appear to determine access to files based upon nationality. That such regulation was not felt to be needed is not surprising, given the different political circumstances between the two periods. During the Mandate, restricting certain files to British officers would serve only to protect them from entering into conflicts between Jews and Arabs and enable at least certain parts of administration to remain above the fray. Facing no such local national conflict, Egyptian administrators could sufficiently protect files from local politics by differentiation through rank and position.

62. Chief Secretary's Office: Order No. 35, 15 December 1947. Recall that this order was a restatement of the previously issued code, so despite its late date it is not an end of the Mandate order.

63. ISA, RG 2, box 460, file U/333/43, Chief Secretary's Office: Order #44, 11 November 1947.

64. Ibid.

65. Ibid., Office Order #3, n.d.

66. ISA, RG 115, box 2114, file 17, Decision #6 of the Executive Council for 1960, 6 November 1960.

67. Ibid., memo from head of Personal Investigation Bureau on "Permanent Orders for Movement of Files," 17 March 1965.

68. Ibid., Decision #6 of the Executive Council for 1960.

69. Ibid.

70. Such a problem was indicated in the complaint by the director of the Gaza Land Registry about the insufficiency of available archival space in the office ("Accommodation of Land Registry Gaza in Tegart Building," letter from Director of Land Registry to Chief Secretary, 29 June 1942).

71. There is, though, a certain inaccuracy in defining archiving as the chronological end of filing. Filing as a practice is not basically linear. Precisely since filing operates as a system through accumulation the various moments of filing that are sometimes synchronic and, even when occurring diachronically, do not follow a single trajectory.

72. The one specific requirement was that "particular care should be taken not to destroy files and documents relating to Government claims to land" (ISA, RG 2, box 460, file U/333/43, "Destruction of Old Files," 25 March 1947). All quotations in this paragraph are from this order.

73. ISA, RG 2, box 473, file U/2586/47, from Civil Service Commissioner, Staff Notice #26, 9 April 1848.

74. Ibid.

75. File U/2856/47, letter from Civil Service Commissioner to Dr. C. Stavropoulos of the United Nations Palestine Commission, 8 April 1948.

76. Cited in A. J. Sherman, *Mandate Days: British Lives in Palestine, 1918–1948* (New York: Thames and Hudson, 1997), 236.

77. ISA, RG 115, box 2114, file 17, Schedule of Bureau Documents, Issued by Head of Personal Investigation Bureau, n.d. 1966.

3. On Being a Civil Servant

1. Morroe Berger describes the classic images of European and Egyptian civil service: "The 'typical' British civil servant, with bowler and tightly-rolled umbrella, is reserved, aloof, and very correct. The 'typical' French *fonctionnaire* sits among his papers, inaccessible, and never permits the public business to prevent him, every day at the same time, from reaching into the bottom drawer of his desk for his lunch wrapped in brown paper. The 'typical' Egyptian clerical *muwazzaf*, for the author, is a man sitting at a desk in his overcoat, his *tarbush* (or fez) hanging on a nail on the wall behind him, his newspaper spread out, one hand holding his demitasse of Turkish coffee and the other reaching for his buzzer to call in a messenger" (Berger, *Bureaucracy and Society in Modern Egypt: A Study of the Higher Civil Service* [Princeton: Princeton University Press, 1979], 12).

2. Akhil Gupta's study of provincial government in India shows how sometimes even clerical employees are found in places other than offices ("Blurred Boundaries").

3. Interview, Gaza City, 23 February 1999.

4. 'Arif al-'Arif, *Tarikh Ghazza*, 310. Al-'Arif provides the following breakdown of Gazan civil service: First Division, 31–19 British and 12 Arab; Second Division, 243-13 British and 230 Arab; police officers, 2,193-130 British and 2,063 Arab; messengers/janitors, 308—all Arab. The settled population of the Gaza subdistrict was estimated to be 136,650 in 1944 (*A Survey of Palestine, prepared in December 1945 and January 1946 for the information of the Anglo-American Committee of Inquiry* (reprint. Washington D.C.: Institute for Palestine Studies, 1991, 1:152). Gaza City itself had a population of around 36,000 (Mosely Lesch, "Gaza: History and Politics," 225).

5. C. S. Peirce defines habit as "a rule, norm, or general pattern of what is appropriate under the circumstances . . . that is acquired dispositions to act in a certain way rather than in another" (quoted in Vincent Potter, *Charles S. Peirce on Norms and Ideals* [Worcester: University of Massachusetts Press, 1967], 126–27). That habit is a tendency, not a certainty, is crucial to Peirce's conception. If it were a certainty "habit would become wooden and ineradicable" (Peirce, *Collected Papers of Charles Sanders Peirce* [Cambridge, Mass.: Harvard University Press, 1935], 6:148).

6. Weber, *From Max Weber*, 229.

7. As Peirce argues, the capacity for habit change is a crucial part of the vitality of such habit.

8. Ibid., 228.

9. As Peirce says, "Doubt is an uneasy and dissatisfied state from which we struggle to

free ourselves and pass into the state of belief" and "the irritation of doubt is the only immediate motive for the struggle to attain belief" (Peirce, *Collected Papers*, 5:372, 5:375). While the notion of doubt refers immediately to an uncertainty in habits of thought, it can also permit us to understand uncertainty of action. As Douglas Anderson puts it, doubt, "in leaving us without guidance for acting, puts us in an unsettled state" (*Strands of System* [West Lafayette, Ind.: Purdue University Press, 1995], 94).

10. Kelly Parker, *The Continuity of Peirce's Thought* (Nashville: Vanderbilt University Press, 1998), 182. Parker also writes, "The ultimate purpose of ideas is thus to effect habit-change."

11. Anderson explains Peircean belief as "not merely verbal assent to a proposition but . . . a general conditional habit for conducting our lives given the circumstances of the physical and social environment" (*Strands of System*, 94). Murray Murphy notes that Peirce's ideas about belief were derived from those of Alexander Bain. He cites Bain to the effect that belief is "essentially related to Action, that is, volition. . . . Preparedness to act upon what we affirm is admitted upon all hands to be the sole, the genuine, the unmistakable criterion of belief. . . . The readiness to act is thus what makes belief something more than fancy" (*The Development of Peirce's Philosophy* [Cambridge, Mass.: Harvard University Press, 1961], 160).

12. Much has been written about the problem of memory in the collecting and analyzing of oral histories. People's memories are always shaped by subsequent experiences, and it is impossible to reach back across the years and capture a perfect image of what people felt then. At the same time, one should not replace an image of oral histories as uncluttered truth about the past (uncluttered because personal, or subaltern, or outside the state) with a counterimage of these memories as simply comments about the present spoken in the past tense or ideological constructions intended to fulfill some political purpose. The practice of narrating the past is much more complicated than either of these notions would suggest. On the complexity of memory and importance of "memory work," see Ann Stoler and Karen Strassler, "Castings for the Colonial: Memory Work in 'New Order' Java," *Comparative Studies in Society and History* 42, 1 (2000): 4–48. See also Paul Thompson, "Believe It or Not: Rethinking the Historical Interpretation of Memory," in *Memory and History: Essays on Recalling and Interpreting Experience*, ed. Jaclyn Jeffrey and Glenace Edwall, 1–16 (New York: University Press of America, 1994); Peter Burke, "History as Social Memory," in *Memory: History, Culture, and the Mind*, ed. Thomas Butler, 97–115 (Oxford: Basil Blackwell, 1989); and Maurice Halbwachs, *On Collective Memory*, ed. and trans. Lewis Coser (Chicago: University of Chicago Press, 1992). On oral history, see Elizabeth Tonkin, *Narrating Our Past: The Social Construction of Oral History* (Cambridge: Cambridge University Press, 1994); Luisa Passerini, *Fascism in Popular Memory: The Cultural Experience of the Turin Working Class* (Cambridge: Cambridge University Press, 1988); Paul Thompson, *The Voice of the Past* (New York: Oxford University Press, 1982).

13. This view of habit *is* a bit like Bourdieu's description of *habitus* as structuring structures that provide for possibilities of action. However, unlike Bourdieu, what I want to highlight in thinking about reflective habits is thought as a part of practice. While Bourdieu sees cognition as being part of practice, he sees *habitus*, "the durably installed generative principles of regulated improvisations"(*Outline of a Theory of Practice* [Cambridge: Cambridge University Press, 1977], 78), as operating largely "unconsciously." I do not mean to suggest as an alternative that people's actions are entirely self-conscious. Rather, I want to call attention to the ways in which thought processes, beliefs, ideas are also part of "systems of durable, transposable *dispositions*" (72) and the ways in which they are fully practice. Potter argues that Peirce's conception of habit is "flexible and allow[ing] for changes, modifications, growth and development" (*Norms and Ideals*, 129), and is therefore more differentiated than Bourdieu's notion of *habitus*. Conflict, contradiction, and distinction can be part of habitual thought and action.

14. For those people who were working in other jobs or were officers in one of the retired civil service associations, I had plenty of opportunities to observe their interactions with colleagues and members of the public and could confirm that habits recalled in interviews were not simply created for that context.

15. On the complexity of historical memory, see Ted Swedenburg, *Memories of Revolt: The 1936–1939 Rebellion and the Palestinian National Past* (Minneapolis: University of Minnesota Press, 1995); Shahid Amin, *Event, Metaphor, Memory: Chari Chaura, 1922–1992* (Berkeley: University of California Press, 1995); and Daniel, *Charred Lullabies*.

16. Even if people's memories of how they acted as civil servants (that they were polite, precise, etc.) may not always be accurate, they *are* evaluative statements about how civil servants *should* act. Perhaps someone did not actually act as he now recalls, but he has internalized those modes of behavior as being part of both his personal subjectivity and the general practice of civil service. Perhaps someone told me certain things because she thought it would make her look good to be seen as sympathetic, efficient, or selfless—in that case it indicates the importance attributed to those behaviors.

17. On the "silences" of history, see Michel-Rolph Trouillot, *Silencing the Past: Power and the Production of History* (Boston: Beacon Press, 1995); Ranajit Guha, "Discipline and Mobilize," in *Subaltern Studies VII: Writing on South Asian History and Society*, ed. Partha Chatterjee and Gyanendra Pandey (Oxford: Oxford University Press, 1992); Gayatri Spivak, "Subaltern Studies: Deconstructing Historiography," in *In Other Worlds: Essays in Cultural Politics*, 197–221 (New York: Routledge, 1988).

18. While I often felt that as people spoke to me they must be censoring their narratives because I was a foreigner, other people told me that they thought people were more willing to tell me things because of my outsider (and professional) status. My research assistants, who helped me transcribe the tapes, often told me that people would never tell them or other locals the things they told me.

19. Many of the women I spoke to who were civil servants during the Mandate told me their fathers were advocates for women's rights who considered permitting their daughters to work to be a form of activism.

20. Interview, Gaza City, 11 April 1999.

21. Interview, Gaza City, 19 April 1999.

22. Interview, Gaza City, 14 April 1999.

23. Interview, Gaza City, 12 November 1999.

24. Interview, Gaza City, 20 March 1999.

25. Interview, Gaza City, 28 February 1999.

26. As another retired civil servant put it, reiterating Salim's position, "The good *muwazzaf* commands the respect of his superiors and subordinates, as well as of the people. People loved the decent muwazzaf. Why wouldn't people love me as long as I am good with them?" (Interview, Gaza City, 8 June 1999).

27. Many people told me stories of how, even in their retirement, they derived benefits from their civil service respectability. For instance, Ibrahim Mahmoud told me a story about receiving special treatment during a visit to the hospital, which illuminates the currency generated by habits of respectability. While waiting in line to have his wife seen, he was spotted by a former student who was now a doctor. His student arranged for him to be taken out of the line, and he treated her right away. As Ibrahim said, "This behavior is more worthwhile than any money in my viewpoint. The physician appreciated me and . . . I consider this act as one of the advantages or fruits of my work in teaching" (Interview, Gaza City, 20 March 1999).

28. Interview, Gaza City, 30 April 1999.

29. At times, though, being respectable meant biting your tongue, not challenging your superiors. According to Muhammad Ghazi, "The word 'Hadir' [Yes, sir] is very important. It is not wrong when he says that you are transferred to another place. The employee has to accept this, and in any case will learn in the new position."

30. See Findley, *Bureaucratic Reform in the Ottoman Empire* and *Ottoman Civil Officialdom.*

31. Another way in which the service relationship was supposed to be different from the patron-client relationship often described as central to social organization in the Ottoman Middle East is that it was generalized: it is about categories, not individuals, and any person can receive their service from any civil servant. Authority also required not only the encounter or relationship itself, but the system which governed service provision. On the question of patronage, see Ernest Gellner and John Waterbury, eds., *Patrons and Clients in Mediterranean Society* (Hanover: Duckworth, 1977); S. N. Eisenstadt and Luis Roniger, *Patrons, Clients, and Friends: Interpersonal Relations and the Structure of Trust in Society* (Cambridge: Cambridge University Press, 1984); Luis Roniger and Ayse Gunes-Ayata, eds., *Democracy, Clientelism, and Civil Society* (Boulder: Lynne Rienner, 1994). For a case study, see Edward Reeves, *The Hidden Government: Ritual, Clientelism, and Legitimation in Northern Egypt* (Salt Lake City: University of Utah Press, 1990).

32. Interview, Gaza City, 7 June 1999.

33. The differences Hanan noted were not in fact preexisting distinctions between what would become the groups native and refugee. Rather, they mark a difference between the small urban elite of which she was a part and the broader population, both native and refugee.

34. Rachelle Taqqu, "Arab Labor in Mandatory Palestine, 1920–1948" (diss., Columbia, 1977), 261. This description of Palestinian civil servants taking up British manners is reminiscent of Homi Bhabha's argument about colonial "mimic men"—colonized persons who were encouraged to become "white, but not quite"—useful to colonial rulers but not equal to them ("Of Mimicry and Man: The Ambivalence of Colonial Discourse," in *The Location of Culture*, 85–92 [New York: Routledge, 1994]).

35. Taqqu, "Arab Labor in Mandatory Palestine," 262.

36. Interview, Gaza City, 4 May 1999.

37. Interview, Gaza City, 14 February 1999.

38. Ibid. Under the British Mandate, when education remained relatively rare, teachers were likely to be already privileged persons. During the Egyptian Administration they might just as well have been children of illiterate peasants who benefited from the Egyptian policy of universal education.

39. Throughout most of the Israeli occupation, people could make a great deal more money working as a laborer inside Israel than they could working for government. It was to these workers, now barred from going to Israel, that Abu Jamal referred.

40. Bseiso's choice to go to the attorney general, rather than to the SMC, with his complaint may have been a strategic effort to involve an outside party in a local conflict.

41. ISA, RG 2, file K/16/47, translation of Mustafa Bseiso's complaint, 19 July 1947.

42. The government response to this petition, while maintaining that the complaint overall had little merit, admonished the chief clerk to "maintain official office hours" (letter from Amin Abdul Hadi, for SMC, to Chief Secretary, 15 October 1947).

43. It is, of course, much easier to criticize another department, another employee, than to reflect critically on one's own practice and success. In this light, some of the details of Abu Jamal's critique should be taken with a grain of salt. Nonetheless, the general issue he raises of different kinds of capacities being evident in different government departments is a very important one.

44. Interview, Gaza City, 4 May 1999.

45. The municipality, he said, "offered better services than any other governmental department at the time of the Egyptians because it offered services such as cleaning, sewage, water, and electricity. Accordingly, the citizen was connected to the municipality . . . because it offered dozens of services for the citizen which were essential for his daily life and which solved his problems."

46. Gazans today often complain that under the Palestinian Authority one cannot get a job, a scholarship, or assistance without some kind of *wasta*. Great bitterness is expressed about this by refugees in the camps, who feel they suffered and struggled

during the years of occupation and *intifada* and that the fruits of their struggles are going to the well-placed returnees who have followed in the wake of the PLO.

47. Interview, Gaza City, 7 June 1999.

48. For examples of this attention, see ISA, RG 115, box 2024, files 14, 20, 27.

49. ISA, RG 115, box 2024, file 3, *mabahith* report, 20 January 1962.

50. Interview, Gaza City, 8 March 1998.

51. For brevity's sake, I describe only one example from each period, but this should not be taken to mean that civil servants were more appreciated during the Administration or more condemned under the Mandate. During the Mandate, the newspaper *Mir'at al-Sharq*, for example, praised both Arab and Jewish Palestinian civil servants even as it complained about their lack of opportunities for advancement. All the best positions went to the British, the paper argued, even though these officials did not do much work beyond putting "their honorable names on the papers which the national civil servants exhausted themselves in preparing" (30 December 1926). And during the Administration the press made complaints about the civil service. In 1949, *Sawt al-'Uruba* reported complaints that civil servants were taking bribes (14 October 1949).

52. *Al-Difa'* was founded in 1934 and was politically affiliated with the *Istiqlal* party, a pan-Arabist party (Qustandi Shomali, "al-Sahafa al-Filastiniyya fi 'Ahd al-Intidab: Jaridat Mir'at Al-Sharq (1919–1939)." *Shu'un Filastiniyya* no. 221–22 (August/September 1991): 72.

53. *Al-Difa'*, 2 May 1935.

54. *Sawt al-'Uruba*, 22 January 1950.

55. ISA, RG 22, box 3589, file 5/78, petition to Director of Land Registry, 2 February 1945.

56. Ibid.

57. The complaint stated, "If you would only meet members of the public in Gaza or converse with persons interested in transactions in the Land Registry or ask the Fellahin about the reputation of the Land Registry in Gaza you would discover that every person complains with bitterness of the behaviour of these two officers."

58. Examples of such complaints can be found in the following files: ISA, RG 115, box 1983, files 1, 14; box 2007, file 2; and box 2024, file 10.

59. ISA, RG 115, box 1983, file 1, letter from students to Director of Interior and Public Security, 24 March 1958.

60. I thank Val Daniel for suggesting this phrase.

61. William Connolly, "The Dilemma of Legitimacy," in *Legitimacy and the State*, 222–49, 225.

62. That the occupation was short and that people were aware from the outset that it might be certainly contributed to political beliefs trumping the duty of service in that case. In 1967, when it was clear that the occupation might be very long, many more civil servants did return to work.

63. Interview, Gaza City, 8 March 1998.

64. I am talking here about low-level civil servants, not high level, nationally known government officials. Such people, while still technically forbidden to engage in politics, were also recognized leaders and, given that British officials needed someone to talk to, a certain amount of activity was not only tolerated but almost necessary.

65. Interview, Gaza City, 19 April 1999.

66. Interview, Gaza City, 11 April 1999.

67. James Scott, *Domination and the Arts of Resistance: Hidden Transcripts* (New Haven: Yale University Press, 1990).

68. Alexei Yurchak critiques Lisa Wedeen and others for producing such binary distinctions (*Everything Was Forever, Until It Was No More: The Last Soviet Generation* [Princeton: Princeton University Press, 2006]).

69. On the activities of the underground Muslim Brotherhood in the first years of the Administration, see Ibrahim Skeik, *Ghazza 'Abr al-Tarikh: Qita' Ghazza Taht al-Idara al-Misriyya, 1948–1956* (1982).

70. Rema Hammami, "Between Heaven and Earth: Transformations in Religiosity and Labor Among Southern Palestinian Peasant and Refugee Women, 1920–1993" (diss., Temple University, 1994), 125.

71. See Ziad Abu 'Amr, *Usul al-Harakal al-Siyasiyya fi Qita' Ghazza, 1948–1967* ('Akka: Dar al-Aswar, 1987).

72. Beattie, *Egypt During the Nasser Years*, 131.

73. James Jankowski, *Nasser's Egypt, Arab Nationalism, and the United Arab Republic* (Boulder: Lynne Rienner, 2002), 152.

74. Interview, Gaza City, 16 February 1999.

75. I already mentioned one report about communist teachers smoking during Ramadan. Another report indicated that non-communist teachers were being discriminated against in UNRWA schools because the head of the education department was a sympathizer (ISA, RG 115, box 1983, file 1, report from *Mabahith*inspector to Director of Interior and Public Security, 9 February 1958).

76. Box 1983, File; box 2007, file 2; box 2096, file 22.

77. Interview, Gaza City, 20 March 1999.

78. Among the many such descriptions I heard are "The period of Abdul Nasser was the golden age for the Palestinian people" (interview, Gaza City, November 12, 1999); "The period between 1948 and 1967 was a golden period in the history of Gaza—to the extent that thousands of students graduated from university" (interview, Gaza City, March 8, 1998); and "Things [have] changed nowadays—the *Sulta* [PNA] came but the golden age was during the Egyptian period" (interview, Gaza City, 19 April 1999).

79. DW, Qawa'im al-Mushir, Group 41, file 90505, UNRWA Staff Circular No. A/1, 1 September 1959.

80. Ibid., letter from State Minister for War Matters to Deputy Foreign Minister, 24 November 1959.

81. In January 1961, for example, a committee of Gazan UNRWA employees petitioned

the agency, asking that employees who wanted to run for National Union office be allowed to do so (letter from committee of Arab UNRWA employees to UNRWA Gaza representative, 4 January 1961). Further meetings between the Administration and UNRWA failed to resolve the issue.

82. One conversation I had with a retired UNRWA teacher exemplified this attitude. When talking about UNRWA practice in general, Hamdi Hassan had nothing good to say, but when it came to his personal work experience, he was quite proud of what he had accomplished (interview, Gaza City, 10 March 1998).

83. Mary McGuire, in a 1996 dissertation, argues that civil service organizing in the United States and Germany had significant, long-term effects on the structural arrangement of the state, leading to the emergence of the state as "sovereign employer" as a means of containing such organizing ("Disciplining the State: Organized Civil Servants, State Formation and Citizenship in the United States and Germany, 1880–1925" [diss., University of Michigan, 1996]).

84. Ibid., 24.

85. ISA, RG 2, U/38/37 Vol. 1, memorandum on interview between members of proposed association and Chief Secretary, 10 February 1927.

86. Ibid., letter from B. Lewis for Provisional Executive Committee of Association to Chief Secretary, March 1927.

87. The terms *Senior* and *Junior* were later replaced by *First* and *Second Division*.

88. U/38/37, Annual Report of the President of the 1st Division Civil Service Association for 1944.

89. In the aftermath of the strike, the high commissioner described his dismay at the action, while at the same time affirming government's general sympathy toward civil servants. Outlining new policy recommendations, he said, the strike "was the result in the main of a lack of confidence on the part of the Second Division Civil Service in the Administration, for I can assure you that the recommendations I am making to the Secretary of State would have been the same had the strike not taken place. I wish to state that I am convinced that the foundation stone of any efficient public service is that there should be confidence in carrying out their duties towards the public. It has always been and will continue to be my earnest endeavour to establish these conditions amongst those with whom I serve, fully appreciating that it entails the protection of their rights and the adjustment of reasonable grievances" (statement by High Commissioner, issued by Chief Secretary, 26 April 1946). On the strike, see Zachary Lockman, *Comrades and Enemies: Arab and Jewish Workers in Palestine, 1906–1948* (Berkeley: University of California Press, 1996), 332–35, and David De Vries, "British Rule and Arab-Jewish Coalescence of Interest: The 1946 Civil Servants' Strike in Palestine," *International Journal of Middle East Studies* 36, 4 (2004): 613–38.

90. ISA, RG 2, U/38/37, vol. 2, note by Shaw, n.d.

91. McGuire, "Disciplining the State," 25.

92. Memorandum from Chief Secretary, 20 June 1944.

93. ISA, RG 2, U/38/37 vol. 3, Palestine Civil Service (1st Division) Association: Circu-

lar to all Members, Annual Report of the President of the Central Council for the Year ended 31st December, 1945.

94. ISA, RG 115, box 2007, file 15, letter from Chair of Executive Committee to Director of UNRWA, 24 February 1965.

95. Abu Sami, interview, Gaza City, 26 March 1998. Not surprisingly, it was not actually possible to keep politics—or even the appearance of politics—entirely outside of the workings of the association. A series of mabahith reports about a meeting held in January 1960 for the purpose of electing new officers for the association highlights the tendentious internal politics of the organization, politics which were intimately connected with the broader political conditions of the Gaza Strip (ISA, RG 115, box 2007, file 17).

4. The Civil Service Career

The full citation for this chapter's first epigraph is ISA, RG 2, box 441, file U/16/3318, *Report by a Committee Concerning the Establishment of a Permanent and Pensionable Cadre for the General Clerical Service*, 31 July 1926.

1. Thomas Blom Hansen explores such repertoires in the context of India, though he describes distinct sites of authority (informal authority, community, legality), while here I am interested in different deployments of authority within the civil service ("Sovereigns Beyond the State: On Legality and Authority in Urban India," in *Sovereign Bodies: Citizens, Migrants, and States in the Postcolonial World*, ed. Thomas Blom Hansen and Finn Stepputat, 169–91 [Princeton: Princeton University Press, 2005]).

2. Here I mean disinterested in its positive sense of being impartial, not personally motivated, etc., rather than disinterest as indifference in the sense described by Michael Herzfeld, *The Social Production of Indifference*.

3. On the relationship between generalists and specialists (experts) in civil service, see R. B. Upadhyaya and K. C. Sharma, *Management of Conflict between Generalist and Specialist Administrators in India* (Jaipur: Shashi Publications, 1987); Jaleel Ahmed, *The Expert and the Administrator* (Pittsburgh: Pittsburgh University Press, 1959); Gail Savage, *The Social Construction of Expertise: The English Civil Service and Its Influence, 1919–1939* (Pittsburgh: University of Pittsburgh Press, 1996); and, of course, Max Weber, *Economy and Society*.

4. Roy MacLeod, "Introduction," in *Government and Expertise: Specialists, Administrators and Professionals, 1860–1919*, ed. Roy Macleod (Cambridge: Cambridge University Press, 1988), 1.

5. It has been generally agreed that "the expert in the civil service is here to stay. . . . I do not believe there is anybody who seriously thinks that a modern government can do without the expert" (Ahmed, *The Expert and the Administrator*, 8).

6. There were, to be sure, experts in Gaza's government, including doctors, religious officials, judges, and, to a certain extent, teachers, but they did not form the bulk of the civil service.

7. On the consolidation and contours of the colonial civil service, see Charles Jeffries, *The Colonial Empire and Its Civil Service* (Cambridge: Cambridge University Press, 1938).

8. Robert Heussler, *Yesterday's Rulers: The Making of the British Colonial Service* (Syracuse: Syracuse University Press, 1963), xx. A pamphlet published in 1950 as an advertisement for the Colonial Service emphasized creativity, initiative, and enterprise, not particular skills, as the qualities needed to succeed as a colonial officer. In fact, the pamphlet warned potential applicants that their preservice training would not suffice to make them "competent and reliable." Whatever training one arrived with, "in order to become a craftsman at your job, you must learn it from the bottom. . . . you must face the fact that it will be some time before you can consider yourself competent and experienced" (Kenneth Bradley, *The Colonial Service as a Career* [London: His Majesty's Stationery Office, 1950], 23).

9. Timothy Mitchell, *Rule of Experts: Egypt, Techno-Politics, Modernity* (Berkeley: University of California Press, 2002), 36. I explore the question of expertise in Gaza's government at greater length in "Government Without Expertise?"

10. Thomas Osborne "Bureaucracy as a Vocation: Governmentality and Administration in Nineteenth-Century Britain," *Journal of Historical Sociology* 7 (1994): 289–313.

11. For consideration of the unethical outcomes of bureaucratic practice, see Kathleen Ferguson, *The Feminist Case Against Bureaucracy* (London: Sage, 1984); Zygmunt Bauman, *Modernity and the Holocaust* (Cambridge: Polity Press, 1989); and Heyman, "Putting Power in the Anthropology of Bureaucracy." Bucking a general trend of critiquing bureaucracy for its ethical absences, Paul du Guy (*In Praise of Bureaucracy: Weber, Organization, Ethics* [London: Sage Publications, 2000]) offers a defense of bureaucracy on precisely these grounds. My interest here is not so much in defending bureaucracy from its critics, but in understanding the ways in which ethical concerns shape its practices.

12. See Michel Foucault, *The Care of the Self: The History of Sexuality*, volume 3, trans. Robert Hurley (New York: Vintage Books, 1986), and id., *Ethics: Subjectivity and Truth*.

13. See, for example, Gayatri Spivak, "Can the Subaltern Speak?" in *Marxism and the Interpretation of Culture*, ed. Cary Nelson and Larry Grossberg, 271–313 (Urbana: University of Illinois Press, 1988), and Harald Fischer-Tiné and Michael Mann, eds., *Colonialism as Civilizing Mission: Cultural Ideology in British India* (London: Anthem Press, 2004).

14. Foucault identifies "the care of the self" as central to an ancient Greek ethos—"a way of being and of behavior"—that identified this care as central to the practice of freedom ("The Ethics of the Concern for the Self as a Practice of Freedom," in *Ethics: Subjectivity and Truth*, 281–301). In the case of Gaza's civil service, I am interested in the how "care of the self" was seen as part of one's service obligations.

15. Saba Mahmood, *Politics of Piety: The Islamic Revival and the Feminist Subject* (Princeton: Princeton University Press, 2005), 29.

16. Osborne, "Bureaucracy as a Vocation," 290.

17. Letter from D. N. Strathie, Income Tax Advisor, to Chief Secretary, 3 July 1941, cited in Taqqu, "Arab Labor in Mandatory Palestine," 256.

18. Carter Findley notes that the formation of a new civil bureaucracy in the Ottoman Empire demanded a restructuring of hiring practice. The older models of recruitment into government—patronage and apprenticeship primarily—were no longer sufficient to meet the demands of an increasingly rationalized administrative structure. Partly in order to meet this demand, widespread educational reform was undertaken. While the effects of the changing educational system were felt outside of the pool of potential civil servants, these schools were characterized by an "unabashed vocationalism" (*Ottoman Civil Officialdom*, 136). Consequently, Findley argues, "the advent of the secular civil schools did encourage the idea—found throughout the Middle East ever since—that they provided simply a way into official service" (ibid., 136).

19. CO 733/3, file 31764, letter from High Commissioner to Secretary of State, 15 June 1921.

20. CO 733/5, file 44554, letter from Secretary of State to High Commissioner, 22 September 1921.

21. ISA, RG 2, box 8, file 220, Organization of Palestine Government, letter to High Commissioner, 15 May 1924.

22. Ibid.

23. ISA, RG 2, box 465, file U/766/3/45, letter from Acting District Commissioner to Chief Sec., 30 October 1946.

24. Without previous civil service employment, it was nearly impossible to get a job, and, given the severe financial difficulties facing the Administration, even continuity of service was not always enough to guarantee a job. See, for example, DW, Qawa'im al-Mushir, group 8, which includes complaints of three persons who had worked for the Egyptian army during the war and were asking for salaries and further work (17 September, 27 September, and 2 October 1949) and the response from Administration that the army was a separate administration and that work for it bestowed no obligation on the Administration (6 November 1949); and UNRWA, *Annual Report of the Director: Covering the Period 1 July 1952 to 30 June 1953*. General Assembly, Official Records: Eighth Session—Supplement No. 12 (A/2470), 12: "There is a large surplus among the refugees of ex-government clerks and senior employees for whom no work can be found, farmers without land, former landowners without qualifications, and labourers without trade or special skills of any kind."

25. The complaint described the intricacies of their case, as they had moved from Beersheba to Gaza with the Egyptian army when it redeployed: "Those who came directly to Gaza from Beersheba found work in Gaza. We, however, were refused, being told that the budget did not allow for the transfer of those coming from the Jordanian areas of Hebron and Bethlehem. This prohibition was not supposed to include Beersheba employees" (DW, Qawa'im al-Mushir, group 8, complaint by Beersheba employees to War Minister, 21 June 1949).

26. Ibid., letter from Deputy Governor General to Governor General, 1 August 1949.

27. There is no further archival mention of these particular employees and their plight, so it is not known if they eventually received Administration jobs. One general way the Administration attempted to reconcile the desperate need for work with its severe fiscal limitations was by reducing civil service salaries by one-quarter, thereby stretching the budget (Salim Rashid, interview, Gaza City, 11 March 1999).

28. Personnel file held at *Awqaf* Ministry, Gaza City. Letter from [Hussam Abdullah] to Khan Yunis Administrative Governor, 10 May 1958.

29. Letter from *Awqaf* director to Administrative Governor of Khan Yunis, 26 May 1958.

30. As late as 1959 an Administration report indicated that 87 percent of the population of Gaza was unemployed (DW, Qawa'im al-Mushir, Group 42, file 91105. "Report on Educational Situation in the Gaza Strip").

31. Interview, Gaza City, 24 March 1999.

32. Interview, Gaza City, 14 February 1999.

33. The precise effects on the job are hard to trace—not surprisingly, no one I spoke with characterized their own work as less than meaningful or demanding. The effects of these changes on the wider perception of civil service are more evident. As long as there were few other opportunities for employment, civil service status remained high. As the economy expanded and as more people sent remittances from work abroad, civil service salaries were less exceptional, and its status went down.

34. Palestine Civil Service Second Division Association, "Report on the terms and Conditions of Service of Second Division Officers (by the nominee of the association on the Commission of Enquiry Mr. S Gadalla)," 1946.

35. ISA, RG 2, box 466, file U/1738/45, letter from Director of Labor Department to Chief Secretary, 5 November 1945.

36. Ibid., letter from Education Director to Chief Secretary, 25 January 1946.

37. ISA, RG 2, box 460, file U/329/43, "Memorandum: Training of Messenger Boys," 1 September 1943.

38. See, for example, PSSA, personnel files #4327, 186/(24), 181/1274, and 124.

39. Interview, Gaza City, 24 April 1999.

40. Pierre Bourdieu, among others, calls attention to the crucial importance of spatial relations in habit formation (*Distinctions: A Social Critique of the Judgement of Taste*, trans. Richard Nice [Cambridge, Mass.: Harvard University Press, 1984]). For a review of some of the literature on this question, see Setha Low, "Embodies Space(s): Anthropological Theories of Body, Space, and Culture," *Space and Culture* 6, 1 (2003): 9–18.

41. ISA, RG 22, box 3395, file 53/44, report to Acting Director of Lands from Land Officer, 4 August 1934.

42. ISA, RG 22, box 3395, file LD 53/4/7A, "Accommodation of Land Registry Gaza in Tegart Building," letter from Director of Land Registry to Chief Secretary, 29 June 1942.

43. Berger, *Bureaucracy and Society in Modern Egypt*, 13.

44. Interview, Gaza City, 17 March 1999.

45. The circumstances in Gaza occasionally led people to forego raises. For example, after 1948 UNRWA provided rations to refugees whose monthly income was below a certain amount. One person told me he refused promotion so as not to lose these rations: My salary was fourteen pounds and if I was promoted I would have taken fifteen pounds, and then my rations would have been cut. Rations were much better than a promotion" (interview, Gaza City, 7 June 1999).

46. ISA, RG 2, box 441, file U/16/3318, *Report by a Committee Concerning the Establishment of a Permanent and Pensionable Cadre for the General Clerical Service*, 31 July 1926. The committee recommended a five-grade system with separate salary scales for men and women such that, for men, "steady promotion and incremental progress will lead to maximum salary in forty-two years." For women the proposed time period was thirty-six years. In both cases, the goal was that civil servants should reach retirement age at the same time they reached their maximum salary potential. On the question of separate salary scales for men and women, the reported noted, "We are aware that among the female clerical officers there is some feeling that salaries should be paid for the amount of work performed and that, when man and woman perform the same amount of work, there should be no difference in salary. . . . To equate salaries of men and women is to weight the scales against marriage in the eyes of women, because, taking the whole body economic such an arrangement places a woman entering marriage at a decided economic disadvantage as against her employed sister or as against herself employed prior to marriage. . . . We think, therefore, that Government must strongly oppose attempts to equate women's salaries with those of men."

47. "Report," 9.

48. The Administration largely adopted the existing British procedure, though the framework for this procedure was somewhat revised. While the specific cadres and grades differed, the general principle remained the same. Raises and promotions were supposed to occur according to seniority, with certain positions requiring particular qualifications and abilities.

49. Interview, Gaza City, 4 May 1998.

50. Interview, Gaza City, 13 March 1999.

51. Interview, Shati camp, 14 March 1999.

52. Interview, Gaza City, 23 March 1999.

53. ISA, RG2, box 459, U/126/43II, letter from General Manager of Palestine Railways to Civil Service Commissioner, 1 November 1947. In this particular case, the dismissal resulted from a history of problems and a charge of insubordination. In his complaint about the dismissal, Farag Abadir did not entirely deny that there had been problems but suggested that there was a cause for his behavior and that the response was inappropriate. He furthermore argued that the context in which he appeared to be a bad employee was fomented by individuals who had personal interests against him. Disregarding Farag's claims, the general manager stressed his incompetence and noted that "this man is one of many engaged during the war years, when decent

labour was at a premium. . . . As we are now faced with the necessity of reverting to peace time establishments, it is impossible to contemplate the continued employment of such individuals."

54. ISA, RG 2, box 459, file U/126/43II, letter from Khalil Ibrahim Hammanieh to Chief Secretary, 15 January 1946.

55. Ibid., letter from General Manager, Palestine Railways to Chief Secretary, 4 February 1946.

56. An amendment to Article 206 of the Penal Code dated 1 August 1911 stated that in cases of abduction and rape "if the act of marriage is celebrated with the girl so carried away, and she is 20 years old, the prosecution will be suspended by her desistance, or by that of her guardian if she is not 20 years old." While the criminal code was revised in 1927, that clause was not changed (cited in 21 November 1931, Supreme Court decision, in *Collection of Judgments of the Courts of Palestine, 1919–33: Including Judgments of the Privy Council, Court of Appeal, High Court, Special Tribunal, District Courts, Land Courts, Criminal Courts, etc.* [Tel Aviv: L. M. Rotenberg, 1937], 557–58).

57. I have seen one account of such a dismissal in a file devoted to the investigation of an employee of the Deir Belah village council (one 'Adel Mahmud) who was fired because of a deficit in the village supply of lighting fuel (ISA, RG 115, box 2014, unnumbered file). 'Adel was hired in May 1959 but did not last long in the position. In May 1960 he was sent the following letter: "It has been decided to end your employment as tax collector and treasurer for the Deir Belah village council, effective from the beginning of May 1960. This is because of what was discovered in the investigation into the matter of missing lighting fuel belonging to the council. Please return to us the accounts of expenditures and revenues as well as all correspondence, registers, and other papers that you have in your possession" (letter from Administrative Qa'immaqam, 9 May 1960).

58. PSSA, Personnel File #1493.

59. Fines of up to one day's salary could be imposed by a civil servant's immediate superior. Fines of more than a few days had to be approved by the governor-general.

60. Letter from Director of Health Administration to Director of Civil Affairs Administration, 5 July 1964.

61. PSSA, Personnel File #841, letter from Director of Municipal and Village Affairs to Director of Civil Affairs, 29 October 1964.

62. PSSA, Personnel File #175/636, letter from Director of Civil Affairs to Governor General, 25 February 1958.

63. Statement by [Da'ud Khaled], 31 March 1958.

64. In conversation after conversation people told me they or their fathers still received a pension from the British government. People admired this respect for employee "rights" and contrasted it to their experiences with other administrators. For example, one man told me, "Someone who was working in the graveyard for the English receives his pension check in the mail until today. His rights are well-kept. . . . I, for example, worked with the Egyptians and when I retired—and you saw me at the

retirees office—I was not able to get my due either from the Egyptians or from the Palestinians except after long suffering" (interview, Gaza City, 16 February 1999).

65. Letter from Postmaster General to Chief Secretary, 22 March 1929.

66. ISA, RG 2, U/359/31, Gratuities to Pensionable women officers on marriage.

67. Letter from Postmaster General to Chief Secretary, 22 March 1929.

68. This mention of embarrassment brings to mind Virginia Woolf's discussion of the "odor" attached to the words "Miss" and "Mrs": "The word 'Miss' however delicious its scent in the private house has a certain odor attached to it in Whitehall which is disagreeable to the noses on the other side of the partition. . . . As for the word 'Mrs,' . . . such is the smell of it, so rank does it stink in the nostrils of Whitehall, that Whitehall excludes it entirely" (*Three Guineas* [New York: Harcourt, 1938], 52).

69. Letter from Treasurer to Chief Secretary, 25 May 1936.

70. Near the end of the Mandate the practice of forcing married women to retire was revoked, in light of similar changes in the British civil service (ISA, RG 2, box 466, file U/2011/45).

71. The Supreme Muslim Council, which held the authority to fire *shari'a* court officers, had been established as part of an effort to respond to the anomaly of having a non-Muslim body (in this case the Mandate legal department) serve as authority over Muslim religious institutions, as happened when the British occupied Palestine and ended Muslim Turkish rule over the country.

72. ISA, RG 2, box 446, file U/417/36, letter from Amery to Chancellor, High Commissioner, 11 December 1928.

73. Ibid., letter from Secretary of Palestine Senior Civil Servants Association to Chief Secretary, 2 July 1929.

74. Haj Amin al-Husseini, head of the Supreme Muslim Council, expressed a similar perspective in his correspondence with the high commissioner. He stressed that the position and the conditions of service of shari'a judges superseded any particular government: "Centuries have passed and Governments have come and gone, yet the rights of judges have been safeguarded in priority to all other officials. The established laws support this old practice." He noted further that "officials of Shari'a courts are considered as members of the Public Service in the Government which has close relations with such Courts, since Government confirms the appointment of senior officials in Shari'a Courts who are subject to medical examination in accordance with the Government's regulations; Audit officers are entitled to inspect and audit the books etc. of the Shari'a Courts; Fees collected by Shari'a Courts are paid into the Treasury; Salaries of Shari'a officials form part of the Government's budget; and therefore any purchase or transfer of immovable properties is effected by Shari'a officials, Shari'a Courts apply to the Government for authority. Officials of Shari'a Courts are required to attend regularly and perform their duties daily with diligence" (letter from Haj Amin al-Husseini to High Commissioner, 9 June 1929).

75. In a response to the Civil Servants' Association, the chief secretary admonished that the association did not have appropriate jurisdiction over these employees: "They

may not be regarded as Civil Servants for the purposes of your Association and therefore the question of their claims to pensions is not one which your Association can properly discuss with Government" (4 August 1929).

76. One government officer, Ruhi Bey Abdul Hadi, suggested that government offer pensions on the condition that the Supreme Muslim Council cede authority for hiring and dismissal (memorandum from Ruhi Bey Abdul Hadi, 10 January 1933). Yet another (Musa Alami) argued, however, that the defining regulations of the council made it impossible for it to make such a concession, given that one of the purposes for which the council was created was to ensure that "the authority at least of the Qadis should emanate from a Moslem body" (memorandum from Musa Alami, 24 January 1933). This need for Muslim authority within a non-Muslim government created a circumstance whereby the shari'a court became "a Government department except for the point that the appointment and dismissal of the Qadis is with the S.M.C."

77. Decision of the Executive Council, 17 May 1933. After the enactment of the pension law, the Supreme Muslim Council and government continued to tussle over the question of authority and control over the officers of the shari'a court.

78. Personnel files held at the *Awqaf* Ministry in Gaza City attest to this practice.

79. Interview, Gaza City, 8 May 1999. Not surprisingly, those people who had purchased land or houses with their money were much satisfied with the arrangement.

80. Interview, Gaza City, 3 May 1999.

5. Service in Crisis

In relation to the quotation in this chapter's first epigraph, in *Lords of the Lebanese Marches: Violence and Narrative in an Arab Society* (Berkeley: University of California Press, 1996), Michael Gilsenan discusses the narrative importance an orange acquired in the context of this famine as experienced in the Akkar region of Lebanon—when a man gave away an olive grove for one orange (120–24).

1. The elusiveness of such boundaries is discussed by Mitchell, "The Limits of the State," and Gupta, "Blurred Boundaries" and "Governing Population: The Integrated Child Development Services Program in India," in *States of Imagination: Ethnographic Explorations of the Postcolonial State*, ed. Thomas Blom Hansen and Finn Stepputat, 65–96 (Durham, N.C.: Duke University Press, 2001).

2. Carol Gilligan, *In A Different Voice: Psychological Theory and Women's Development* (Cambridge, Mass.: Harvard University Press, 1982), 62. Of course, according to Gilligan's argument, it is women who see the world as a web of relation and men who imagine hierarchy.

3. Foucault, "The Ethics of the Concern for the Self as a Practice of Freedom," 287.

4. Ibid., 286.

5. Tom Segev, *One Palestine, Complete: Jews and Arabs Under the British Mandate*, trans. Haim Watzman (London: Little, Brown, 2000), 19.

6. Municipality of Gaza, "Gaza Municipality: Between the Future and the Present" (1996), 9.

7. See the Shaw Commission Report (*Report of the Commission on the Palestine Disturbances of August, 1929*, Cmd. 3530, March 1930); the Hope-Simpson Report (Sir John Hope-Simpson, *Report on Immigration, Land Settlement, and Development in Palestine*, (Cmd. 3686, 1930); the Peel Commission Report (*Palestine Royal Commission Report*, Cmd. 5479, July 1937); and *A Survey of Palestine, prepared in December 1945 and January 1946 for the information of the Anglo-American Committee of Inquiry* (reprint. Washington D.C.: Institute for Palestine Studies, 1991).

8. *Survey of Palestine*, 682.

9. *Report of the Committee on Development and Welfare Services* (1940).

10. UNRWA, *Special Report of the Director Concerning Other Claimants for Relief*, A/2978/Add.1.

11. For more on the problem of aid to native Gazans, see Ilana Feldman, "Difficult Distinctions: Refugee Law, Humanitarian Practice, and Political Identification in Gaza," *Cultural Anthropology* 22, 1 (2007): 129–69.

12. *Al-Ahram*, 18 August 1951.

13. American Friends Service Committee materials, for instance, describe a population in crisis but not without sociality.

14. Alison Brysk, and Gershon Shafir, *People Out of Place: Globalization, Human Rights, and the Citizenship Gap* (New York: Routledge, 2004).

15. Christopher R. Duncan, "Unwelcome Guests: Relations between Internally Displaced Persons and Their Hosts in North Sulawesi, Indonesia," *Journal of Refugee Studies* 18, 1 (2005): 25–46; Jeffrey M. Peck, "Refugees as Foreigners: The Problem of Becoming German and Finding Home," in *Mistrusting Refugees*, ed. E. Valentine Daniel and John Chr. Knudsen, 102–25 (Berkeley: University of California Press, 1995). For more on the particular tensions of the Gazan refugee condition, see Feldman "Difficult Distinctions."

16. ISA, RG 115, box 2024, file 14, Department of General Supervision of Refugees, Government Assistance, and Social Affairs, *Annual Report 1953*, 2.

17. UNRWA, *Annual Report for 1 July 1951 to 30 June 1952*, 5, 3.

18. UNRWA, *Annual Report for 1 July 1955 to 30 June 1956*, 6.

19. UNRWA, *Annual Report for 1 July 1957 to 30 June 1958*, 19. As late as 1964, the Annual Report lamented the large number of men who were "not only unemployed but were virtually unemployable" because of the limited work opportunities in Gaza (UNRWA, *Annual Report for 1 July 1963 to 30 June 1964*, 2).

20. Interview, Gaza City, March 11, 1999. Salim and others also suggested that UNRWA relief was part of a Western imperial plot to make Palestinians accept the loss of their homeland.

21. Interview, Gaza City, 14 February 1999.

22. Interview, Gaza City, 19 April 1999.

23. As Hanan's remarks suggest, tension between natives and refugees and concern about refugees' "character" have not entirely dissipated, even as the figure of the refugee has become central to the Palestinian national imaginary.

24. Description of Gaza by a Reverend Father Waggett, cited in Butt, *Life at the Cross-roads*, 118.

25. The entire Levant suffered from a severe famine during this period, so the experience in Gaza was by no means unique. See Linda S. Schilcher, "The Famine of 1915–1918 in Greater Syria," in *Problems of the Modern Middle East in Historical Perspective: Essays in Honor of Albert Hourani*, ed. John Spagnolo (Reading: Ithaca Press, 1992).

26. Interview, Rafah, 2 May 1999. See also Butt, *Life in the Crossroads*: "Because of the succession of battles in and around Gaza, for example, the local population had had little opportunity to work the land and harvest crops—or to attend to cattle. This all contributed to a food shortage both among the [Turkish] military and the civilian population" (113).

27. Interview, Khan Yunis, 15 June 1999.

28. *Jaridat Filastin*, 18 July 1918.

29. For a more extended discussion of what development meant in the context of the Mandate, see Feldman "Government without Expertise?"

30. ISA, RG 2, 504, W/40/46, Summary of Col. Porteus' Report of June 1936 on Gaza Drainage.

31. The Gaza region as a whole had among the highest percentage of cultivatable land in Palestine—30 percent (David Gurevitch, *Statistical Abstract of Palestine 1929* [Jerusalem: Keren Hayesod, 1930], 78). It was not the most productive land. Sara Roy notes that in 1935 "the Gaza District accounted for 70 percent of the total area under barley cultivation but 30 percent of crop yield" (*The Gaza Strip*, 47)—but the capacity to grow a wide variety of crops was important to the area's economy and to people's eating habits.

32. Svetlana Boym describes the problematic of nostalgia that historians face: "On the one hand, elusive nostalgic affects undermine the historians' dispassionate attempts to write their chronicles; on the other hand, these affects help them to understand people's relationship to the lived or imagined experience and the infatuation with things past, because most of us experience history as nostalgia" (*Common Places: Mythologies of Everyday Life in Russia* [Cambridge, Mass.: Harvard University Press, 1994], 285). For further discussion of nostalgia and memories of home in pre-1948 Palestine, see Feldman "Home as a Refrain."

33. American Friends Service Committee [AFSC] Archives, FS Sect Palestine #36, "Background Material on Mughazy," 16 February 1949.

34. Hope-Simpson, *Report on Immigration, Land Settlement, and Development in Palestine*, 143. The report declared that such conditions could be alleviated only by improvements in "the method of cultivation . . . so that the fellah will be able to gain a reasonable livelihood from a smaller area of land than that which has been essential hitherto." A few years later, the Peel Commission argued that while land loss was a significant problem, in many other respects conditions had improved. According to the report, "Despite the disproportion between their numbers and the amount of cultivable land they occupy, the *fellaheen* are on the whole better off than they were in

1920. . . . The whole range of public services . . . has steadily developed, to the benefit of the *fellaheen*" (*Palestine Royal Commission Report*, 128). For further discussion of economic conditions during the Mandate, see Ylana Miller, *Government and Society in Rural Palestine, 1920–1948* (Austin: University of Texas Press, 1985), and Sarah Graham-Brown, "The Political Economy of Jabal Nablus, 1920–48," in *Studies in the Economic and Social History of Palestine in the Nineteenth and Twentieth Centuries*, ed. Roger Owen, 88–176 (Carbondale: Southern Illinois University Press, 1982). Roy describes Gaza's place in this broader dynamic in *The Gaza Strip*.

35. As a Quaker providing relief in Gaza in 1949 noted about one refugee, "He owned a bit of fruit trees too and on his earnings they lived in relative comfort in the little village before fright scattered them and their neighbors" (American Friends Service Committee [AFSC] Archives, FS Sect Palestine #36, "Background Material on Mughazy," 16 February 1949).

36. A similar "simplicity" in eating habits was described in a 1930 report by the head of the Zionist Agricultural Experimental Station of Tel-Aviv, Dr. Wilkansky, who described the dietary state of the Palestinian *fellah* [peasant] as "poor and monotonous." He continued, "His staple food is 'pittah' . . . which he bakes every day. A few pittahs, with onions or radishes form his morning and midday meals. . . . Most of his requirements are provided by his own fields, and he buys but little outside. . . . The fellah uses very little meat" (cited in Hope-Simpson Report, 65).

37. Joseph Massad describes the transformations in Jordanian eating habits under colonial rule (*Colonial Effects*). The *Survey of Palestine* described the challenges that variations in eating habits among Palestine's population caused for World War II rationing: "The distribution of foodstuffs in Palestine is the more difficult on account of the lack of homogeneity of the population in regard to nutrition. There exists a wide variety of standards of living, ranging from that of the nomadic Bedouin in the desert areas to that of the cultivated Europeans in the larger towns" (*A Survey of Palestine*, 817).

38. Interview, Khan Yunis, 15 June 1999.

39. Interview, Gaza City, 9 May 1999.

40. ISA, RG 2, W/RD/74, Unemployment Relief.

41. Robert Vitalis and Steven Heydemann describe the role of the Middle East Supply Centre (MESC) in regulating agricultural production (among other things) during the war ("War, Keynesianism, and Colonialism," in *War, Institutions, and Social Change in the Middle East*, ed. Steven Heydemann, 100–45 [Berkeley: University of California Press, 2000], 105).

42. *Survey of Palestine*, 817.

43. Majdal was a town in the Gaza district that, after 1948, lay across the armistice line from the Gaza Strip. The town was renamed Ashkelon, and the remaining Arab inhabitants of Majdal were expelled by the Israeli army in 1950.

44. ISA, RG 2, box 217, file G/5/4/42.

45. Letter from District Commissioner to Chief Secretary, 2 September 1942.

46. The proposals were approved, so the district commissioner's argument appears to have been accepted within government.

47. Interview, Gaza City, 22 March 1999.

48. Interview, Gaza City, 14 February 1999.

49. Interview, Khan Yunis, 15 June 1999.

50. Interview, Gaza City, 13 May 1999.

51. When Quaker volunteers arrived in Gaza they noted that "besides their own great and everpressing misery, the refugees are creating problems, both current and future, for the permanent population." They described practices similar to those mentioned by Im 'Amir, among them that "lack of fuel has driven refugees to denuding the land of every burnable thing, especially trees and shrubs." They further noted that "this drove a nearby landowner to shut off camp water taps until refugees promised not to cut anymore from his trees" (AFSC, #63 FSC Sect Palestine, "Background Material on Rafah," 1 February 1949).

52. De Certeau, *The Practice of Everyday Life*, 37.

53. Interview, Gaza City, 12 November 1999.

54. The establishment of UNRWA was an implicit recognition that the problem would not be solved immediately and that there had to be more than an ad hoc means of providing assistance to the Palestinian refugees.

55. Interview, Shati camp, 16 March 1999.

56. Not only was Egypt uncertain about its relationship to Gaza, but its failure in 1948 to "save" Palestine meant that in the first years after 1948 apolitical humanitarianism may have been the only credible mode of claiming to assist the Gazan population. That Gazans would not be forever satisfied with simple humanitarianism from Egypt was evident in the response of the Gazan press to the train's arrival. *Al-Raqib*, a local paper, took the opportunity to thank the Egyptian government for its assistance and to remind it that Palestinians were also waiting for other trains—trains that would return them to their villages, trains that would bring weapons and men ready to fight for the liberation of Palestine (*al-Raqib*, 30 December 1952).

57. Interview, Shati camp, 16 March 1999.

58. AFSC #41 FS Sect Palestine, letter from Howard Wriggins to Colin Bell, 18 February 1949.

59. The UNRWA director's report commented, "The regular monthly issues of flour, butter, cheese and milk given by the Egyptian and United States (through CARE) Governments provide only a basic 1,050 calories per person per day (compared to the Agency's basic provision of 1,500 to refugees in summer)" (*Special Report*). The Egyptian Administration's own Refugee and Government Assistance Administration reported on its ration distribution program that "the Egyptian government recognized the reality and began to provide assistance to 60,000 of the original inhabitants of the Strip—whose total number is 86,000.... every person among the 60,000 receives flour in the amount of 5–6 kilos per month. There is no doubt that this ration, in relation to what people need, is not enough to live on, but it does help, and covers their needs for

flour" (ISA, RG 115, box 2024, file 14, *Administration of General Supervision of Refugees, Government Aid, and Social Affairs: Annual Report, 1953*, 31). Neither UNRWA nor Administration officials deemed their rations sufficient.

60. Native inhabitants of Gaza were just as hungry as the refugees. These people had lost their lands and livelihoods, and many were, in fact, "in an even worse economic position than the refugees" (UNRWA, *Annual Report 1952*, 5). A 1955 report by the UNRWA director on "other claimants for relief" emphasized native Gazans' need for assistance: "In the case of the Gaza Strip, nearly the whole population is therefore in need as result of the establishment of the demarcation line and of the impossibility of moving goods and persons across it legally" (*Special Report*).

61. *Refugee Affairs Report*, 31.

62. Ibid.

63. In this case, in order to assure stability of food provision, the bureau occasionally had to borrow flour from UNRWA. So even the apparently clear (and reiterated) distinction of jurisdiction was not always so clear, and UNRWA, in a roundabout way did provide food services to native Gazans.

64. AFSC, #53 FS Sect Palestine, letter from AFSC Gaza Unit to C. Pickett, AFSC Headquarters, 12 October 1949.

65. Interview, Gaza City, 11 March 1999.

66. Some people, at least in retrospect, did argue that this dynamic and the acceptance of UNRWA services were damaging to Palestinian political aspirations. One person recounted a story from the early days of UNRWA that was meant to underscore this point. He told me that a friend of his met an American working with UNRWA who tried to give him some political advice: "The American told my friend: 'about this food you eat from UNRWA—I want to tell you something but do not say that I told you. If you reject the provisions and do not eat and twenty people die of hunger, then they will let you back soon to your homes.' But we did not have that awareness. If we told people to do so they would have refused" (interview, Gaza City, 13 March 1999).

67. CO 733 group 4, file 33635, "Rebuilding of Gaza," September 27, 1920, letter from Herbert Samuel, High Commissioner, to Earl Curzon of Kedleston, Secretary of State for Foreign Affairs.

68. Ibid.

69. In response to a proposal that the government guarantee a bank loan for Gaza, one official commented, "I do not want to encourage the Palestine municipalities to think they can reasonably expect advances from banks on security of this kind. The amount is so small that the Bank probably would have done it if we pressed them, but there can be no question that the transaction would be a thoroughly unsound one" (CO 733, group 4, file 33635, "Rebuilding of Gaza," Minutes, July 1921).

70. ISA, RG 22, box 3464, file 7, 21 October 1930, Comment in Minutes on Secretariat File No. L/132/32.

71. CO 733, group 54, file 33039, "Rebuilding of Gaza," 18 June 1923, letter from Governor of Southern District to Chief Secretary.

72. One official (Keith-Roach, the assistant chief secretary for administration) expressed an extreme view that Gazans were so incapable as to render the entire scheme nearly irrelevant: "We need not excite ourselves about this scheme of building houses on sand. I doubt whether any sites will be sold and if sold whether the purchasers will ante up with the cash. . . . I think all now serving in Palestine will have passed on before the war damaged houses in Gaza have been repaired, judging by the local apathy of the people and the lack of money among would be purchasers" (CO 733, group 65, file 12837 "Rebuilding of the town of Gaza," comment in the minutes, Keith-Roach). Keith-Roach suggested that the value of the plan, if there was one, lay in its being a "big bluff," providing a ready answer if "the Arabs complain and say Jews would have and do get better treatment."

73. Among the causes for delay were "(a) stultification of the Town Plan by shiftings of sand, (b) stultification of the Town Plan by encroachments of alleged Government land, (c) part of the site proposed was claimed for the establishment of a Stud Farm by Director of Agriculture, (d) demands for easier terms by prospective purchasers" (ISA, RG 22, box 3464, file 7, 14 April 1930, letter from Commissioner of Southern District to Chief Secretary).

74. ISA, RG 22, Box 3464, File 7, 8 September 1932, letter from Acting Commissioner of Southern District to Chief Secretary.

75. ISA, Record Group 22, box 3464, file 7, 14 February 1941, "Memorandum on the Gaza Development Scheme."

76. Ibid.

77. There is no evidence in the archival record to suggest that monies from the sale of lands in "new Gaza" were actually deposited in a loan fund.

78. The idea of a government-supported housing plan did not entirely disappear, however. Records from the latter years of the Mandate indicate that Gaza's mayor was pushing for such a scheme and that the district commissioner rejected the idea on the grounds that "there is no real need for such a scheme. Houses are badly required but should be, and are being, erected by private enterprise" (ISA, RG 2, box 513, file WH/3/46, letter from District Commissioner to Chief Secretary, 4 May 1946).

79. ISA, RG 3, box 737, file 29/5 Minutes of Gaza District Town Planning Commission, 1940–47.

80. ISA, RG 3, box 737, file 29/5A, Letter from Town Planning Advisor to Solicitor General, 3 July 1945.

81. Commission Minutes, 18 October 1940. In an effort to cut down on construction outside the confines of the plan, the commission restricted the issuance of building permits and, on occasion, ordered the demolition of buildings that had been begun before obtaining a permit (Commission Minutes, 7 April 1941).

82. Commission Minutes, 18 October 1940. Involving itself in the aesthetics of home building as well, in 1942 the commission adopted a suggestion made by the town planning advisor that "he should produce about twelve different type plans of houses to suit all pockets." Each of these twelve designs would share certain fundamental

features, including: "1) Each house would have a loggia and terrace; 2) Plastering of the outside walls would be compulsory; 3) Each type would have overhanging eaves and tiled roofs, preferably "Roman" tiles, would be compulsory" (Commission Minutes, 30 June 1942). Most of the (now) old houses in the Rimal quarter of Gaza do conform to this general design.

83. Commission Minutes, 19 June 1947.

84. Ibid.

85. Interview, Gaza City, 8 May 1999.

86. Interview, Rafah, 12 June 1999.

87. Interview, Khan Yunis, 15 June 1999.

88. One refugee told me that Gazans treated them like brothers: "They shared their homes with us. He, whose house was small, told the women of the two families to sleep together. And did the men. They shared everything they had, and we are grateful for that. They offered us every service, every respect" (interview, Gaza City, 3 May 1999).

89. Interview, Gaza City, 16 February 1999. Another person recalled how the women of Gaza mobilized to help the refugees: "All women participated in receiving refugees and in helping them by putting them in schools, mosques, and empty places—until we had the Quakers organization" (interview, Gaza City, 11 April 1999).

90. Personnel files of mosque imams maintained by the Awqaf Administration (now Ministry) record their transfer to positions in other mosques for the period that refugees were housed there, indicating that mosques were turned over entirely to the project of housing refugees.

91. ISA, RG 115, box 2024, file 14, Annual Report of General Supervision of Refugees, Government Aid, and Social Affairs Administration, 1953.

92. Ibid.

93. These houses, in which many refugees still live, are made of concrete blocks and roofed with asbestos.

94. The 1955 UNRWA Annual Report noted, "The new camp construction programme in Gaza was completed before the onset of the winter of 1954–55, and now no refugees in camps in Gaza remain in tents. The Agency's Gaza officer has, however, some 2,800 applications for shelter from persons outside camps; in addition births, marriages, and other social changes create a demand for shelter that has so far not been met" (UNRWA, *Report of the Director Covering the Period 1 July 1954 to 30 June 1955*, 3).

95. UN A/1905 28 September 1951.

96. Ibid.

97. UNRWA, *Annual Report of the Director for the Period 1 July 1953 to 30 June 1954*, 2.

98. UNRWA Camp Regulations, Form C, n.d.

99. UNRWA Camp Regulations and Administrative Instructions Concerning Contraventions and Permits, 13 May 1961.

100. Many camps were created on the sites of World War II–era military camps. In addition to state lands, however, refugees also settled on land owned by native

Gazans. In 1953, the Administration authorized a tax exemption for landowners who did not have use of their land because refugees were living on it. UNRWA paid rent for private lands on which it established camps (ISA, RG 115, box 2024, file 11, correspondence on tax exemptions, 1953).

101. Some people had initially settled in towns, whether using savings to rent houses or staying with relatives or friends. Even as their funds began to dwindle and some people sought to move into camps, limited space could not accommodate everyone. UNRWA reports noted pressure to increase camp size as those refugees "who owned considerable property and other worldly goods under their former living conditions . . . have reached, or are reaching, the end of their resources and are now living under the ordinary conditions applying to refugees in the area" (UN A/1451/Rev.1, 6 October 1950).

102. During the course of the Administration, five lotteries were held to distribute land. The first two lotteries took place before the 1956 Israeli occupation, during which the Israelis seized the records of these sales. In these first two lotteries approximately twelve hundred one-dunam plots were made available at prices ranging from forty to sixty pounds per plot, though no details are available as to who purchased the land (*Waqa' i' al-Filastiniyya*, #47, Announcement about sales of government lands to civil servants, 10 May 1955; #58, Sales of government land to civil servants, second lottery, 9 January 1956). The Housing Ministry does, however, have registers from the last three lotteries. These registers list the names and government departments of the purchasers.

103. The deferred nation-state was Palestine, not Gaza alone. Gaza might have been "the last independent part of Palestine," as Egyptians liked to say, but it alone was not enough to be Palestine.

104. One former civil servant told me, "The employee was very much relieved as they [Egyptians] gave him a dunam of land for a symbolic price. The employee could sell half of this dunam and build a building for himself or could sell it and work in trading and so on. The employee at the time of the Egyptians was very lucky: he took a good salary and owned a piece of land" (interview, Gaza City, 4 May 1999).

6. Servicing Everyday Life

1. This according to Ibrahim Skeik, a practicing local historian (*Ghazza 'Abr al-Tarikh: Taht al-Intidab al-Britani* [1981], 106).

2. Hilmi Abu Sha'aban, *Tarikh Ghazza: Naqd wa Tahlil* (Jerusalem: Matba'at Bayt al-Maqdis, 1943), 9.

3. Ibid., 58.

4. Donna Haraway, "Situated Knowledges: The Science Question in Feminism and the Privilege of Partial Perspective," in Haraway, *Simians, Cyborgs, and Women: The Reinvention of Nature*, 183–202 (New York: Routledge, 1991).

5. It is precisely these kinds of practices that produce the relation with and sense of place that is then transformed into ideology (or idea) in nationalist thought.

6. Michel de Certeau and Luce Giard refer to these creative possibilities as pluralization: "Ordinary culture hides a fundamental diversity of situations, interests, and
contexts under the apparent repetition of objects that it uses. *Pluralization* is born
from ordinary usage, from this immense reserve that the number and multiple of
differences constitute" ("A Practical Science of the Singular," in *The Practice of Everyday Life*, Volume 2: *Living and Cooking*, ed. Luce Giard, trans. Timothy Tomasik,
251–56 (Minneapolis: University of Minnesota Press, 1998), 256.

7. ISA, Mandate Publications, box 4382, file 01/3/161, Report on Palestine Administration, July 1920–December 1921.

8. ISA, RG 2, box 219, file G/37/45, telegram from heads of al-Agha, Zu'rub, al-Najjar,
al-Astal, and Abdallah families to Chief Secretary, 6 January 1946.

9. Government's response to this complaint indicated that it had explored whether
municipal actions had contravened any of the regulations established by government
(whether it had stepped outside its domain, in other words). Finding that they had
not, it saw no reason to intervene (ibid., letter from Chief Secretary to Anton Atalla
[lawyer for the Khan Yunis families], 26 January 1946).

10. ISA, RG 115, box 2014, file 4, letter from *Qaimaqam* to Governor General, 9 March
1960.

11. In fact, the administrative governors of the different areas of the Gaza Strip were as
responsible as the councils for the maintenance of quiet and order. The details of this
responsibility were not identical to that of the councils, but there was a clear overlap.
According to the regulations, "Every administrative governor is responsible for security and order in the area . . . and for taking the necessary steps to secure peace and
security" (ISA, RG 115, box 2024, file 21, Jurisdiction of the Administrative Governors,
1956). In order to secure this order, administrative governors were given a wide range
of tasks. They were supposed to submit monthly reports to the governor-general;
track public opinion in the area; forward local complaints to the appropriate authorities; supervise police; oversee appointment of mukhtars; protect public buildings and
employees; and be in "constant contact" with local powers and cooperate with them
in activities on behalf of the common good. This last assignment at least partially
explains the interference about which Abu Sharkh complained, though it does not
tell us if the Deir Belah governor was acting inappropriately in the details of his
interventions.

12. Interview with former council member, Gaza City, 6 June 1999. See also minutes of
Legislative Council meetings, DW, Qawa'im al-Mushir, group 41, file 90205. Haidar
Abdul Shafi, a physician who founded the Gaza branch of the Palestinian Red
Crescent Society, was a major figure in Palestinian politics. He was one of the
Palestinian representatives in the 1991 Madrid Conference and in the negotiations
that followed (until the Oslo process took over). He was a member of the Legislative
Council and a cofounder of al-Mubadara, a new political movement founded during
the second *intifada* to provide an alternative to Fatah and Hamas. In no small part
due to what was perceived as his integrity—in a political landscape in which this is a

rare trait—he was consistently one of the most respected figures on the Palestinian political scene. Abdul Shafi died in September 2007.

13. See, for example, ISA, RG 115, box 2007, unnumbered file, debate about purchasing a cart to transport meat from Rafah slaughterhouse; ISA, RG 115, box 2014, file 2, debate about Deir Belah water project; ISA, RG 115, box 2014, file 4, debate about paving Rafah road.

14. Interview, Shati Camp, 15 March 1999.

15. Of course, there are still Palestinian villages which lack such services and provide their own electricity with private generators. And during the summer even large cities like Gaza and Hebron are without water much of the time.

16. Interview, Jabalya Camp, 13 May 1999.

17. This particular concentration of resources reminds us that even as government in Gaza was incapable of large-scale concentrations on the order described by Timothy Mitchell in *Rule of Experts* or invoked by Bourdieu in "Rethinking the State," the concept and practice of concentration were not foreign to its tactical government.

18. 'Arif al-'Arif, *Tarikh Ghazza*, 281.

19. In addition to municipal wells, both authors described the importance of private wells—of which al-'Arif said there were forty-eight in the city—in providing water for the population. Abu Sha'ban recounted how "most of the people drank from wells that were next to their homes, or brought water from nearby wells in jugs or jars" (Abu Sha'ban, 68).

20. Al-'Arif, *Tarikh Ghazza*, 283.

21. Abu Sha'ban, *Naqd wa-Tahlil*, 68.

22. Ibid., 68–69. Khan Yunis faced a similar issue about compelling people to pay fees since "there are private wells from which families obtain their water." Ultimately, as in Gaza, a law was enacted "for the payment of water fees by all residents of Khan Yunis whether water is supplied or not" (ISA, RG 2, box 208, G/165/34, letter from District Commissioner to Chief Secretary, 22 April 1935).

23. ISA, RG 22, box 3464, file 7, 8 September 1932, letter from Acting Commissioner of Southern District to Chief Secretary.

24. CO 733, file 97471, letter from High Commissioner to Secretary of State for Colonies, 10 December 1932.

25. Unfortunately, there are no records that describe the well-digging process, how the site was chosen, etc., details of which would no doubt shed considerable light on the practical relations between government and municipality.

26. Al-'Arif, *Tarikh Ghazza*, 382.

27. Abu Sha'ban, *Naqd wa-Tahlil*, 70. In 1939, another well was dug that supplied water to Rimal. This well, the Safa well, al-'Arif described as supplying "the sweetest water found in Gaza by far" (al-'Arif, *Tarikh Ghazza*, 283).

28. ISA, RG 2, box 504, file w/40/46, "Gaza Drainage—Summary of Col. Porteous' Report of June 1936." The report also noted, "There is no lack of under-ground water, wells in and around the Municipal area being numerous."

29. Both Arturo Escobar and Jim Ferguson note the ways in which development discourse and practice identify local incapacities, which it can then "treat and reform." Arturo Escobar, *Encountering Development: The Making and Unmaking of the Third World* (Princeton: Princeton University Press, 1995), and James Ferguson, *The Anti-Politics Machine: "Development," Depoliticization, and Bureaucratic Power in Lesotho* (Minneapolis: University of Minnesota Press, 1994).

30. Gaza City Council, Minutes of 27 May 1936 Meeting.

31. There were plenty of instances during the Mandate when the central government did take over municipal or village operations. Faluja is a case in point.

32. Minutes of 4 June 1936, meeting.

33. ISA, RG 2, box 216, file G/25/41, Petition to Chief Secretary, 1 April 1941.

34. The petitioners complained that their quarter was being unfairly singled out for meters (the other quarters of the city did not have them) and argued that the new system was unfair to the poor, who would now be charged at the same rate as the wealthy.

35. This woman explained to me that her father was a mukhtar, not an official one, but someone recognized by other villagers as being a notable. This nobility was evident, she suggested, in his water practices: "My father had a farm, there was a waterwheel in our farm called the village's basin. Everybody came to the basin. My father sat near the waterwheel and welcomed everybody" (interview, Shati Camp, 16 March 1999).

36. Roy explains that "existing municipal services could not possibly keep pace with the excess demand placed on them. . . . Gaza City, for example, with a prewar population of 35,000 and an annual income of £P 100,000, now had to provide services to a population of 170,000 on the same budget" (*Gaza Strip*, 78).

37. ISA, RG 115, box 2024, file 14, *Refugee Affairs Report*. Under this system, camp residents were able to get ten liters of water a day per person. The report noted that ordinary daily consumption for residents of Gaza City was thirty to forty liters a day.

38. Administrative Instructions concerning contravention and permits issued by Director of Social Affairs and Refugees on 13 May 1961.

39. Interview, Gaza City, 8 May 1999.

40. *New York Times*, "Israel Ousts Mayor and Council of Gaza," 23 October 1972.

41. Mosely Lesch, "Gaza: History and Politics." She further indicates that when Shawwa returned to his position in 1975 he claimed it was because Israeli agreed to "freeze" that order (232).

42. Interview, Gaza City, 4 May 1999.

43. Interview, Gaza City, 17 March 1999.

44. ISA, RG 2, box 2024, file 20, *Mabahith* report on political activity in Gaza area for period between 8 June and 20 June 1966.

45. When I interviewed Abu Jamal, he read me a long letter that he had written on behalf of the Retired Civil Servants Association to the director of the Pensions Administration, asking for higher pension payments for retirees.

46. Interview, Gaza City, 4 May 1999.

47. This equivalence of water servicing has not been sustained in Gaza. At the time I was doing my research, Gaza faced a severe water shortage. During the summer many homes had no water at all during the day. If, however, one could afford a generator and pump, it was possible to keep the water flowing. Additionally, the quality of the water that flowed from the faucets was not generally acceptable for drinking, though this quality varied from neighborhood to neighborhood.

48. De Certeau and Giard, "A Practical Science of the Singular," 256.

49. Government offices still follow this 8 A.M. to 2 P.M. schedule, though, unlike offices in the United States, they are open six days a week.

50. De Certeau and Giard, "A Practical Science of the Singular," 256.

51. Nuseirat, Bureij, and Maghazi are known known collectively as the midcamps because of their position in the middle of the Strip.

52. ISA, RG 115, box 2096, file 21.

53. Report from mabahith director to Director of Social Affairs and Refugees, 16 April 1967.

54. In all the statements, everyone, however strong their objection to the project, denied having any knowledge of 'Ali Harb's destroying pumps in the camp. This despite the conviction of the mabahith that he did so. In the absence of any other information on this case, the facts are difficult to judge. It is certainly possible that the local mabahith officers were simply mistaken or were pinning the blame on Harb (an UNRWA employee) as a means of distancing the Administration from any responsibility for the broken pumps. On the other hand, it is equally possible that the Nuseirat residents, while willing to object to Harb's plan, were not willing to denounce him, a local, as a saboteur.

55. Report from police officer to mabahith inspector, 4 April 1967.

56. A particular absence in the investigative record leaves me wondering. None of the statements, with their objections to the plan, were taken from women. What might these refugees, the ones who did the work of getting water from the pumps, have said about the proposal to pipe water directly into their homes? I do not think it is a foregone conclusion that women would have supported the project (I'm sure they would have seen a lot of other uses for their ten pounds), but it would be extremely interesting to be able to know what they said about it.

57. Statement from Block c resident, 20 April 1967.

58. Report from police officer to *mabahith* inspector, 16 April 1967.

59. Interview, Gaza City, 20 March 1999.

60. Interview, Jabalya camp, 13 May 1999.

61. Interview, Gaza City, 7 June 1999.

62. ISA, RG 2, box 484, file w/197/33, letter from Fahmi Husseini, Rushdi Shawa, Yousif Sayegh, Musa El-Borno, Musa Sourani, Haj Raghib Abu Sha'ban, 'Abdel Nour Franji, et al. to High Commissioner, 21 July 1933.

63. ISA, RG 12, box 4101, file 9/33/1/1, memo from Public Works Department, 16 October 1946.

64. Ibid., letters between District Commissioner and Public Works Department, 27 November and 5 December 1944.

65. ISA, RG 12, box 4100, file 9/33/1, "Extract from Arabic Press," 14 December 1935.

66. ISA, RG 2, box 485, file w/295/33, letter from Beersheba sheikhs to High Commissioner, 29 November 1936.

67. Letter to Chief Secretary from Arab Chamber of Commerce, 15 February 1937.

68. Letter from the High Commissioner to the Chief Justice, Law Courts, 25 March 1938.

69. For example, an article from 18 June 1935 chastised the Majdal municipal authorities for cleaning the streets only when government health inspectors came to town, which, as the article said, "does not show concern for the people."

70. Al-Difa', 2 January 1935.

71. Al-Difa', 28 May 1935. The problem of restricted access to roads has returned with a vengeance during the Israeli occupation, and now it is not simply the location of roads that makes them exclusive, but a set of regulations that bar Palestinians from using roads reserved for Israeli settlers.

72. Those who could not read or could not afford to purchase newspapers did often hear these papers read aloud. For those living in a small village, this required that at least someone in the village be able to read. As Abu Said recalled, "No one knew reading or writing—only one . . . he read the newspaper . . . [the people] came to listen to the news."

73. The political character of transportation services was evident during the 1936–39 revolt and after, when telephone lines and railroads became objects of attack in the rebellion. As the years went on, these events became more frequent causes of service interruption.

74. DW, Qawa'im al-Mushir, group 8, file 1–27/s g/14, "Administration of the Areas Controlled by Egyptian Forces in Palestine," memo on telephone/telegraph in Gaza-Rafah Area, 17 July 1949.

75. In October 1949, the interior minister, at the request of military intelligence, agreed to open the telephone lines between Gaza and Egypt (ibid., report on telephone conversation between Interior Minister and representative of Military Intelligence).

76. DW, Qawa'im al-Mushir, group 42, file 99905, al-Tahrir, "The Train of Troubles and the Transportation Problems," 10 October 1959.

77. Ibid., letter from Inspector General for Transportation to Governor General, 14 October 1959.

78. Ibid., letter from Gaza and Southern Villages Car Company to Director of Public Works and Transportation, 31 October 1959.

79. Interview, Shati Camp, 15 March 1999.

80. ISA, RG 115, box 2024, file 3, report from police officer to mabahith inspector, 10 July 1963.

81. ISA, RG 115, box 2024, file 3, report from police officer to mabahith inspector, 10 July 1966.

82. This was not an isolated incident, and the *mabahith* report noted further that there was a group of civil servants from the southern part of the Strip who were awaiting the resolution of this matter in order to present their own similar petition.

7. Formations of Civic Life

The full citation of this chapter's second epigraph is Bylaws of Arab UNRWA Employees Association, ISA, RG 115, box 2056, file 26, Bylaws of Arab UNRWA Employees Association, 3 March 1961.

1. For a discussion of security services in Gaza, see Ilana Feldman, "Interesting Times, Insecure States: The Work of Government and the Making of Gaza in the British Mandate and the Egyptian Administration, 1917–1967" (Ph.D. diss., University of Michigan, 2002).

2. Pierre Mayol, "Propriety," in *The Practice of Everyday Life*, 2:15–34, 17.

3. Ibid.

4. Colin Gordon, "Governmental Rationality: An Introduction," in *The Foucault Effect: Studies in Governmentality*, ed. Graham Burchell, Colin Gordon, and Peter Miller, 1–51 (Chicago: University of Chicago Press, 1991), 2.

5. While Jewish and Christian services were also part of this public service domain, given the almost entirely Muslim population of Gaza, my discussion is limited to Islamic services.

6. Robert Eisenman, *Islamic Law in Palestine and Israel: A History of the Survival of the Tanzimat and Shari'a in the British Mandate and the Jewish State* (Leiden: E.J. Brill, 1978), 12–19.

7. Associational life has been recognized as a crucial part of "the public sphere" (see Jurgen Habermas, *The Structural Transformation of the Public Sphere: An Inquiry into a Category of Bourgeois Society*, trans. Thomas Berger [Cambridge: MIT Press, 1989]. See also Geoff Eley, "Nations, Publics, and Political Cultures: Placing Habermas in the Nineteenth Century," in *Habermas and the Public Sphere*, ed. Craig Calhoun, 298 [Cambridge: MIT Press, 1992]).

8. Gaza's religious services were particular and inflected by its particularities but by no means unique. Considering the case of Saudi Arabia, Talal Asad argues that Islamic tradition offers a path for political-moral debate in the form of *nasiha* (moral advice): "[*Nasiha*] reflects the principle that a well-regulated polity depends on its members being virtuous individuals who are partly responsible for one another's moral condition—and therefore in part on continuous moral criticism" ("The Limits of Religious Criticism in the Middle East: Notes on Islamic Public Argument," in *Genealogies of Religion: Discipline and Reasons of Power in Christianity and Islam*, 233 [Baltimore: Johns Hopkins University Press, 1993]). Egyptian Islamists, who perceive themselves as being in opposition to the Egyptian government (a perception shared by the government) participate in a similar practice of moral advising, as do sanctioned *'ulama'* in Saudi Arabia. *Da'wa*, Charles Hirschkind writes, is "understood as an ethical form of speech and action aimed at improving the moral conduct of one's

fellow community members" ("Civic Virtue and Religious Reason: An Islamic Counterpublic," *Cultural Anthropology* 16, 1 [2001]: 7).

9. For a detailed examination of the establishment and operations of the Supreme
Muslim Council in Mandate Palestine, see Uri M. Kupferschmidt, *The Supreme
Muslim Council: Islam under the British Mandate for Palestine* (New York: E. J. Brill,
1987).

10. See, in addition to Kupferschmidt, Michel Dumper, "Forty Years Without Slumbering: Waqf Politics and Administration in the Gaza Strip, 1948–1967," *British Journal
of Middle East Studies* 20, 2 (1993): 174–90.

11. Cited in Kupferschmidt, *The Supreme Muslim Council*, 39.

12. *Report by His Majesty's Government in the United Kingdom of Great Britain and
Northern Ireland to the Council of the League of Nations on the Administration of
Palestine and Trans-Jordan for the Year 1936*, Colonial no. 129 (1937), 39–40.

13. There was considerable overlap in these categories, as SMC employees were often
considered community leaders and no doubt frequently joined these societies.

14. 'Uthman al-Tabba', *Ithaf al-A'izza fi Tarikh Ghazza*, ed. Abd al-Latif Abu Hashim
(Gaza: Maktabat al-Yaziji, 1999), fn. 1 (by Abu Hashim), 339.

15. Kupferschmidt, *Supreme Muslim Council*, 250

16. Al-Tabba', *Ithaf al-A'izza*, 339.

17. Michael Cook, *Commanding Right and Forbidding Wrong in Islamic Thought* (Cambridge: Cambridge University Press, 2000). The index provides a quick glimpse of
this variety.

18. Asad, "Religious Criticism in the Middle East," 216.

19. Saba Mahmood, *Politics of Piety*, 61–62.

20. Al-Tabba', *Ithaf al-A'izza*, 339.

21. Kupferschmidt indicates that active concern about missionary activity increased after
1929, partly connected, he suggests, to the fact that a missionary conference was held
in Jerusalem in 1928. He also notes that the number of converts was undoubtedly
small (*The Supreme Muslim Council*, 247–48).

22. This delineation of a Palestinian agenda should also make clear the complexity of
concerns during the Mandate. The conflict with Zionism was the most prominent
issue among Palestinians during this period, but it was by no means the only one.

23. Ibid., 250.

24. UT, Papers of *Jam'iyyat al-Amr bi-l -Ma'ruf wa-l -Nahy 'an al-Munkar*, Ghazza.

25. Papers of *Jam'iyyat al-Amr bi-l -Ma'ruf*, letter from Society to head of SMC, n.d.

26. Whether the society was formally granted authority over government preachers, I do
not know.

27. Weldon Matthews, *Confronting an Empire, Constructing a Nation: Arab Nationalists
and Popular Politics in Mandate Palestine* (London: I. B. Tauris, 2006), 138. Matthews
describes the Istiqlal party's use of all of these terms in its articulation of the nation.

28. The current popularity of Hamas (the Islamic Resistance Movement) as a nationalist
organization is a relatively recent phenomenon. See Jean-François Legrain, "The

Islamic Movement and the Intifada," in *Intifada: Palestine at the Crossroads*, ed. Jamal R. Nasser and Roger Heacock, 175–89 (New York: Praeger, 1990); Lisa Taraki, "The Islamic Resistance Movement in the Palestinian Uprising," in *Intifada: The Palestinian Uprising Against Israeli Occupation*, ed. Zachary Lockman and Joel Beinin, 171–77 (Boston: South End Press, 1989); and Shaul Mishal and Avraham Sela, *The Palestinian Hamas: Vision, Violence, and Coexistence* (Columbia: Columbia University Press, 2000).

29. Reporting on their efforts, one group of *mukhtars* wrote to the society president in January 1937 to say they had preached against abomination, had encouraged sincerity, and called for struggle "to defend the nation and protect their lands" (letter from 5 *mukhtars* to President of Society, 9 January 1937). Not all preachers had the same success. Hassan Hamad, who had been sent in April 1936 to preach in the main mosque of the Shaja'iyya quarter of Gaza City, reported that when he arrived at the mosque his entrance was blocked by some of the worshipers. Not knowing who they were and not wanting trouble in "God's house," Hassan left the scene. He was later given the names of the objectors by witnesses to the incident and, in his report to the society, he stated, "There were a large number of worshipers present and [the objectors'] actions constitute a lack of respect for mosques, non-implementation of the decisions of the Society, and a personal insult to me as the lecturer. I am completely convinced that these troublemakers are motivated by personal interests." Hassan closed by asking the society to inform government about what had happened and ask it to take steps to prevent such behavior from continuing (letter from Hassan Hamad to President of the Society, 5 April 1936).

30. Letter from Said Muhammad Allah to Society President, 26 February 1936.

31. In addition to preaching, the society also published calls to moral conduct. In a *bayan* (declaration) published in late 1935 or early 1936, the society chastised the people for their poor morals, saying "the majority of them are neglectful of prayer, don't give *zakat*, drink alcohol, partake of usury and gambling . . . they have crossed the line and angered God who will deny them entrance into heaven" (announcement from society, n.d.). The society published its announcement to encourage people to return to God and religion, assuring them that "there is no doubt of God's mercy if they believe."

32. Ibid., letter from Society to High Commissioner, n.d.; Monthly Report for Sha'ban 1355 from Gaza Society to Head of Central Society in Jerusalem, November 1936; Monthly Report for Muharram 1356 from Gaza Society to Head of Central Society, April 1937.

33. Letter to President of the Society, 25 May 1936.

34. This concern was evident in the society's papers. In 1934, a member of the society wrote to the head of the organization, telling him that "in Gaza there is an English hospital and inside it there is a missionary school, which is spreading poison to the children of this nation [*umma*]. It claims to be about education and cultivation of the mind, but it is a mission—from the Protestant Missionary Association. Large num-

bers of Muslim children have joined the school. . . . I have great hope that you will ask these people not to send their children to the school" (UT, *Papers of Jam'iyyat al-Amr bi-l Ma'ruf*, letter from member of Society to President, 11 March 1934).

35. Ibid., Society Monthly Report, April 1936.

36. Monthly Report, 17 June 1936—from Pres. of Assoc.—to the Head of Central Assoc.

37. See letter from preacher to Society, 16 December 1935; Society Monthly Report for Shawwal 1355 [December/January 1936/7]; letter from preacher to Society 20 Ramadan 1355 [4 December 1936]; and Monthly Report for Muharram 1356 [March/April 1937].

38. This was how Salim Rashid, a civil servant discussed in chapter 2, described the best civil service work.

39. Dumper, "Forty Years Without Slumbering," 178.

40. Ibid., 179. The basic problem was that the SMC was designed to be a national body overseeing a number of different "local" councils. Gaza being the only remnant of Palestine, there was only one council to oversee.

41. Ibid., 180.

42. DW, *Qawa'im al-Mushir*, Group 8, file number 1–27/s g/14, folder 1 "Administration of the Areas Controlled by Egyptian Forces in Palestine," letter from Governor General to Agent of Awqaf Ministry, October 1949.

43. Ibid., report about Palestine Administration, 26 October 1949.

44. Ibid. and letter from Governor General to Minister of Social Affairs, October 1949.

45. ISA RG 115, box 2014, unnumbered file, Deir Belah council minutes, 25 August 1953; ISA, RG 115, box 2023, file 23, letter to Director of Municipal Affairs, 2 August 1957.

46. Despite the evident utility of the dispersal of religious services throughout the departments of government, the transformation was not entirely smooth. For example, authority over the entire shari'a court system was transferred to the Appeals Court, but the appointment of a staff to manage these responsibilities lagged behind. In 1959, a member of Gaza's Legislative Council expressed his frustration that the court "has a large administrative responsibility without any administrative employees" (DW, *Qawa'im al-Mushir*, group 42, file 91215, Report on 5th Council Session). In another redistribution of responsibility, in 1958, oversight for teachers of the Fallah school, the premier *waqf* school in Gaza, was transferred to the Education Department (PSSA, file #183/2000, personnel file of Fallah schoolteacher). This transfer engendered problems of equivalency among the personnel, specifically, how to calculate the length of service for pension purposes of Fallah schoolteachers in relation to teachers in secular schools, which had been part of the Education Department since 1948.

47. Rema Hammami, "Between Heaven and Earth: Transformations in Religiosity and Labor Among Southern Palestinian Peasant and Refugee Women, 1920–1993" (diss., Temple University, 1994).

48. ISA, RG 115, box 2007, file 22, Bylaws of the Society of the Followers of Sunna in Khan Yunis, April 1953.

49. Ibid., from Head of Khan Yunis *Mabahith*, to Administrative Governor of Khan Yunis, 5 March 1959.

50. From Khan Yunis Administrative Governor to Director of *Mabahith*, 24 June 1959. Restriction did not mean a total ban on social religious groups though. Police files record, for instance, the case of a group of people who "claim to be Sufi" (ISA, RG 115, box 2096, file 13) being given permission to operate a *zawiya* (religious establishment) after the members, including many civil servants, were personally interviewed by the police director and after the group swore "that we will not allow any one who is suspected or wanted to the security services to enter our place" (ISA, RG 115, box 2096, file 13, letter to Chief Judge of Shari'a Appeals Court, 25 Sept. 1966; statement by *Zawiya*, 29 October 1966). In this case, the group acquired its permission by agreeing to take on the control functions of government itself. And since the permission was conditional, the Administration could shut down this (and any other) organization if it ever appeared threatening.

51. "Between Heaven and Earth," 136–37.

52. Ibid., 141–42.

53. *Putting Islam to Work: Education, Politics, and Religious Transformation in Egypt* (Berkeley: University of California Press, 1998), 78.

54. Hammami cites a passage from a 1965 textbook that underscores this point: "We treated among the subjects that the Islamic religion is the religion of happiness and respect, and that it is the religion for individual life, and for the family, and for the group, for the community and for all" ("Between Heaven and Earth," 142).

55. ISA, RG 115, box 2096, file 21, from Awqaf Commissioner to preachers and teachers in mosques, 21 May 1967.

56. Education is crucial for governments of all kinds. Colonial states, as Homi Bhabha has argued, sought to produce a class of educated "natives" who would mimic English ways and be "almost the same, but not quite" ("Of Mimicry and Man: The Ambivalence of Colonial Discourse," in *The Location of Culture* [New York: Routledge, 1994], 86). Education has also been undeniably important for the development of bureaucratic government (Ian Hunter, *Rethinking the School: Subjectivity, Bureaucracy, Criticism* [St Leonards, Australia: Allen and Unwin, 1994]). In the Middle East, "secular" schools were created as mechanisms for producing government personnel (see Findley, *Bureaucratic Reform in the Ottoman Empire*).

57. James Holtson and Arjun Appadurai, "Introduction: Cities and Citizenship," in *Cities and Citizenship*, ed. James Holston, 6 (Durham, N.C.: Duke University Press, 1999).

58. Miller, *Government and Society in Rural Palestine*, 92.

59. As Miller notes, the terms of the Mandate itself "protected the right of each community to educate its own children" (ibid., 90). The only way it would have been possible to create a single school system would have been to have already created the broad Palestinian society that joint schooling could have promoted.

60. Precise statistics about the number of schools in the Gaza district (later subdistrict)

during the Mandate are difficult to come by. As a general guide, the Annual Reports of the Department of Education provide some information. The 1925–26 report, for example, indicated that in the Gaza subdistrict there were thirty government schools, with a total of 1,788 students (1,436 boys and 352 girls) (Government of Palestine, Department of Education, *Annual Report for the Scholastic Year 1925–1926* [Jerusalem, 1927]). A 1946 report by A. L. Tibawi on the conclusion of his tenure as education inspector for the Southern district (made up at that point of the Lydda and Gaza subdistricts) attests that, whatever the number of schools in Gaza, it was not enough to meet the demand: "The admission of pupils to the three types of schools combined [government, foreign missionary, and private Arab] left every year an appreciable number of pupils without places in school" (*Report on Education in the Southern District, February 1941–October 1946, by A. L. Tibawi, Submitted to the Director of Education, Government of Palestine*). Secondary schooling in Gaza was limited, as of 1941, to one school in Gaza City, which offered two years of postelementary education. By 1945, Majdal was able to offer one year of such schooling. For the most part, Gaza students who wanted to pursue their education beyond elementary schooling had to hope to obtain one of the few seats available in a Jerusalem high school. As for girls' education, Tibawi placed the number of village schools for girls at fourteen, ten of which had been built just in the five years previous. In terms of overall numbers, he indicated that in 1945 there were 5,161 girls in school in the entire Southern District (out of a total of 24,584), compared to 3,563 in 1941 (out of a total of 16,574).

61. Interview, Gaza City, 8 March 1998.

62. Interview, Gaza City, 14 February 1999.

63. Interview, Gaza City, 19 April 1999.

64. The restrictions on political participation continued to rankle after the Mandate. In 1951 the Gazan newspaper *al-Raqib* published a complaint about an UNRWA regulation that its teachers get permission before publishing anything in the papers. This policy resembled the British restrictions on participation, restrictions which were, the paper argued, "part of an effort to distance civil servants from their society and to make of these civil servants human machines, with no right to act except with permission of their boss" (*Al-Raqib*, 27 November 1951).

65. See Palestine Government, Education Department, *Curriculum for Government Elementary Boys' Schools in Cities and Villages* (1921) and Department of Education, *Elementary School Curriculum* (1927).

66. Humphrey Bowman, *Middle-East Window* (London: Longmans, Green, 1942), 279.

67. Tibawi, *Arab Education in Mandatory Palestine: A Study of Three Decades of British Administration* (London: Luzac, 1956), 86–87.

68. Ibid., 88. British officials also came to recognize some of the inadequacies of the curriculum in Arab schools. The 1940 "Report of the Committee on Development and Welfare Services" noted the importance of producing textbooks with "local knowledge." The report indicated that an English publisher had agreed to take on

this project, and it further commented, "Until these books become available for pupils the teaching of history and geography in the whole Arab system must remain largely ineffective."

69. Interview, Gaza City, 19 April 1999.

70. Interview, Gaza City, 8 March 1998.

71. Government of Palestine, "Education Ordinance, no. 1 of 1933," *Ordinances: Annual Volume for 1933*.

72. *Palestine Royal Commission Report*, Cmd. 5479 (July 1937), 97.

73. A teacher could not so easily escape repercussions from political activity. Skeik noted that punishment for misbehavior or conflict at work was often transfer to a post far from home (*Ghazza 'Abr al-Tarikh: Dhikrayat wa-Intaba'at 'an Ghazza Qabl Nusf Qarn* (n.d.), 80).

74. Tibawi, *Report on Education in the Southern District*.

75. Hammami argues that "by the end of the 1950s, Nasserist Arabism was the hegemonic political ideology in Gaza." and she cites education as one of the most important factors in "creating consent for the Egyptian regime, if not always for the local authority that represented it" ("Between Heaven and Earth," 139).

76. Interview, Gaza City, 12 November 1999.

77. Interview, Gaza City, 3 May 1999.

78. Interview, Gaza City, 13 March 1999.

79. Interview, Gaza City, 15 April 1999. Indeed, the AFSC did support a schooling program as part of their relief work.

80. This phenomenon was also noted by Quakers, AFSC, #60 FS Sect Palestine, Report on Education Activities for December 1949. In addition to employing Palestinians, the Egyptians brought teachers from Egypt to meet the demand for education, which initially exceeded the local capacity to provide educators. Eventually, Gazans who had benefited from the expanded educational opportunities took over teaching and became an important source of teachers for other parts of the Arab world.

81. One native Gazan described to me how the interest in education among refugees had enabled them to get ahead, even of native Gazans: "Then the refugees exceeded us in education, and civilization. They took high positions outside [the country], but when they came back during the PNA period, they all came millionaires. In my house I have water and electricity, but he is living in a shack, so he says to himself, 'Why do not I go to Saudi Arabia and bring money?' Of course he studied and worked. They loved to be educated more than we were. The refugee says that he lost his home and education, so he had to study. The native says that his father has an orchard so why should he study. The refugee says, 'I want to have a better social status. I want to leave the shack. I want a good house. I want to have a car. I want to marry a beautiful woman.' That is why they are more educated than we are" (interview, Gaza City, 23 March 1999).

82. For more on the distinctions and tensions between refugees and natives, see Feldman, "Difficult Distinctions."

83. *Al-Raqib*, 17 May 1952.

84. DW, *Qawa'im al-Mushir*, Group 42, file 91105, "Report of the technical committee's visit to some of the elementary schools in Gaza from January 4–8, 1959." The committee noted that a few government classes used local books (which may well have been Mandate leftovers) and that all UNRWA schools used Egyptian books.

85. DW, *Qawa'im al-Mushir*, Group 41, file 90505, letter from Director of Palestine Affairs Administration to Governor General, 7 March 1960.

86. Ibid.

87. DW, *Qawa'im al-Mushir*, Group 42, file 91105, "Report on Education in Gaza," 1959.

88. Given the difficulties in creating an economic infrastructure inside the Strip, it was also nearly impossible to develop educational services that were truly equipped to meet these immediate needs. The recommendations of the report indicate this difficulty. The best suggestion it could come up with was neither to change education in the Strip, nor to improve the economy there (both worthwhile but seemingly impossible goals), but rather to increase work opportunities for Gazans abroad and then impose a tax on those salaries.

89. For the most part UNRWA, seeing work as part of the basket of services provided by the agency, employed refugees only. Ibrahim had a college degree when he began working in 1952 (a rarity at the time), and he told me that those qualifications overrode the hiring restrictions (interview, Gaza City, 20 March 1999).

90. Ibrahim commented that the committee also worked to establish a parents' council to give parents advice about how to raise their children in ways that would complement the work of the schools.

91. Ibrahim's description of his work closely resembles Gregory Starrett's discussion of education in Egypt at this time: "Education was not merely for the amelioration of illiteracy, but the 'enculturation of the children of the nation's masses,' 'leading them to an appropriate national life'" (*Putting Islam to Work*, 78). Gaza's schoolbooks came from Egypt, so this convergence is not surprising.

92. ISA, RG 115, box 1983, file 1, memo from Education Director to school principals, 7 January 1958; file 2, Report from police officer to police inspector on meeting held between Governor General and school principals, 2 October 1959.

93. ISA, RG 115, box 2007, file 2.

94. Statement by Bureij School teacher, 12 October 1959; letter from Deir Belah Governor to Mabahith Director, 17 October 1959.

95. Report to police inspector, 4 January 1960; Police Inspector memo, 9 January 1960.

96. Mu'in Basisu, *Descent into the Water: Palestinian Notes from Arab Exile* (Wilmette, Ill.: Medina Press, 1980), 32–40.

97. On party activity in Gaza during this time, see Ziad Abu 'Amr, *Usul al-Harakat al-Siyasiyya fi Qita' Ghazza*.

98. While Basisu was a communist, Ibrahim said that he and many other teachers were falsely accused of party affiliation. His only crime, he insisted, was to demand support for the Palestinian struggle. Basisu notes how closely connected teacher and

communist were in the Administration's imagination. Describing interrogation, he says that when a teacher identified himself as such the response was, "Teacher? That means Communist, you son of a bitch" (*Descent into the Water*, 68).

99. UN Archives, S-0530-0151, file C-32, letter from UN General Counsel to Under Secretary and Legal Counsel, 22 April 1965.

100. Sayigh, "Escalation or Containment?"

101. UN Archives, S-0530-0151, file C-32, Palestine Gazette (*al-Waqai' al-Filastiniyya*), Law Number 4 of 1965 Concerning Military and National Service, 10 March 1965 (UN Translation).

8. Conclusion

1. Nikolas Rose, "Governing 'Advanced' Liberal Democracies," in *Foucault and Political Reason*, 37–64, 46. See also Michel Foucault, "The Birth of Biopolitics."

2. See Ann Stoler and Fred Cooper, eds., *Tensions of Empire*; Gyan Prakash, *Another Reason: Science and the Imagination of Modern India* (Princeton: Princeton University Press, 1999); Mehta, *Liberalism and Empire*.

3. This point has long since been taught us by feminist historians. For a classic example, see Joan Kelly-Gadol, "Did Women Have a Renaissance?" in *Becoming Visible: Women in European History*, ed. Renate Bridenthal and Claudia Koonz, 148–52 (Boston, 1977).

4. See Homi Bhabha, "In a Spirit of Calm Violence," in *After Colonialism*, ed. Gyan Prakash, 326–43 (Princeton: Princeton University Press, 1995); Suleri, *The Rhetoric of English India*; Ann Stoler, "Sexual Affronts and Racial Frontiers: European Identities and the Cultural Politics of Exclusion in Colonial Southeast Asia," *Comparative Studies in Society and History* 34 (1992): 514–51; Cooper, "Colonizing Time."

5. Coronil, *The Magical State*, 116.

6. Das, "The Signature of the State."

7. See, for example, Eric Davis, *Memories of State: Politics, History, and Collective Identity in Modern Iraq* (Berkeley: University of California Press, 2005); Meeker, *A Nation of Empire*; Martin van Beek, "Public Secrets, Conscious Amnesia, and the Celebration of Autonomy for Ladakh," in *States of Imagination: Ethnographic Explorations of the Postcolonial State* (Durham, N.C.: Duke University Press, 2001).

8. For a damning account of U.S. governing practices in Iraq, see Rajiv Chandrasekaran, *Imperial Life in the Emerald City: Inside Iraq's Green Zone* (New York: Knopf, 2006).

9. Weber, *Economy and Society*, 989.

10. For discussions of Gaza under Israeli occupation, see, in addition to Roy, *The Gaza Strip*; Butt, *Life at the Crossroads*; Paul Cossali and Clive Robson, *Stateless in Gaza* (London: Zed Books, 1986); Richard Locke and Antony Stewart, *Bantustan Gaza* (London: Zed Books, 1985).

11. Nimrod Raphaeli, "Gaza Under Four Administrations," *Public Administration in Israel and Abroad* 9 (1968): 40–51, 47.

12. Quote from Israeli Army magazine, December 1968; cited in Raphaeli, *Gaza Under Four Administrations*, 48.

13. Interview, Gaza City, 13 March 1999.

14. "Arabs Get Ultimatum to Turn in Arms," *New York Times*, 20 June 1967.

15. "Dayan Visits Gaza and Wins Arab Aid," *New York Times*, 22 June 1967.

16. Mosely Lesch, "Gaza: History and Politics," 229.

17. Ibid., 229–30; and Roy, *The Gaza Strip*, 104–6.

18. The mayor and council had been dismissed once before, in January 1971. See Mosely Lesch, "Gaza: History and Politics," 231. The councils outside Gaza City seem to have been permitted to continue, but details about their operations are lacking. See Muhammad al-Khass, "Municipal Legal Structure in Gaza," in *A Palestinian Agenda for the West Bank and Gaza*, ed. Emile A. Nakhleh, 102–6 (Washington, D.C.: American Enterprise Institute, 1980).

19. Roy, *The Gaza Strip*, 105.

20. As the *New York Times* reported at the time, "The Israelis, without major publicity and without making their ultimate intentions completely clear, are evicting families from the three most crowded camps here, offering them other quarters—mostly in El Arish, south of the Gaza Strip—and bulldozing their homes" ("Gaza a Monument to Wretchedness Caused in Mideast," 20 August 1971).

21. Recognition of the politics of moving refugees did not always stop people from appreciating these new houses. After his move one refugee told a reporter, "This house is bigger, better and cleaner than the old one. . . . We have electricity, running water and room to breathe here." But another insisted, "I had no choice. . . . They came and said I had to go. . . . It's a miserable place with only three small rooms" (*New York Times*, "Israel's Refugee-Resettling Project Is Transforming Gaza Strip," 2 April 1973).

22. For discussion of Israeli work with space, see Rafi Segal and Eyal Weizman, eds., *A Civilian Occupation: The Politics of Israeli Architecture* (London: Verso, 2003).

23. Tom Segev, *1967: Israel, the War, and the Year that Transformed the Middle East*, trans. Jessica Cohen (New York: Metropolitan Books, 2007), 455.

24. Pursuant to the Oslo Accords the West Bank and Gaza were divided into three categories: Area A (approximately 65 percent of Gaza and 3 percent of the West Bank), where Palestinians had both security and civil control; Area B (about 23 percent of the West Bank), where Palestinians had civil control and the Israelis retained military control; and Area C, where Israel had full control.

25. In the years since, an electricity plant was built in Gaza and then was destroyed by Israeli forces in the summer of 2006.

26. Serge Schmemann, "Palestinians Say Israeli Aim Was to Destroy Framework, from Archives to Hard Drives," *New York Times*, 16 April 2002. These would have been West Bank records.

27. According to a *New York Times* report from fall 2005, Eyad Sarraj, founder and head of the Gaza Community Mental Health Program, diagnosed a near total breakdown:

"'Who rules Gaza?' He asked. 'It's certainly not the central Palestinian Authority.' There is no law or security here, he said, adding, 'The reality is that the Gaza Strip is controlled from outside by Israel and from inside by groups intertwined with security forces and tribes'" (Steve Erlanger, "In Unruly Gaza, Clans Compete in Power Void," *New York Times*, 17 October 2005).

28. For discussions of how to conceptualize "modernity," in its different guises, see Talal Asad,"Conscripts of Western Civilization," in *Civilization in Crisis: Anthropological Perspectives*, ed. Christine Gailey, 333–51 (Gainesville: University of Florida Press, 1992); Timothy Mitchell, ed., *Questions of Modernity*, (Minneapolis: University of Minnesota Press, 2000); Dipesh Chakrabarty, *Habitations of Modernity: Essays in the Wake of Subaltern Studies* (Chicago: University of Chicago Press, 2002); and Bruce Knauft, ed., *Critically Modern: Alternatives, Alterities, Anthropologies* (Bloomington: Indiana University Press, 2002).

29. James Ferguson, *Global Shadows: Africa in the Neoliberal World Order* (Durham, N.C.: Duke University Press, 2006); Aihwa Ong, *Neoliberalism as Exception: Mutations in Citizenship and Sovereignty* (Durham, N.C.: Duke University Press, 2006); Rose, *Powers of Freedom*.

30. Akhil Gupta and James Ferguson, "Spatializing States: Toward an Ethnography of Neoliberal Governmentality," *American Ethnologist* 29, 4 (2002): 981–1002; Jamie Peck and Adam Tickell, "Neoliberalizing Space," *Antipode* 34, 3 (2002): 380–404; Benjamin Chesluk, "'Visible Signs of a City Out of Control': Community Policing in New York City," *Cultural Anthropology* 19, 2 (2004): 250–75.

31. Trouillot, *Global Transformations*, 95. Trouillot does not argue that bureaucracy is an inappropriate object of anthropological inquiry. His point is that anthropology is especially well suited to investigate other sorts of state effects. My contention is that anthropological techniques can in fact illuminate features of bureaucratic practice to which other approaches might not pay attention.

32. George Marcus, "Ethnography in/of the World System: The Emergence of Multi-Sited Ethnography," in *Ethnography through Thick and Thin*, 79–104 (Princeton: Princeton University Press, 1998).

33. See Ong, *Neoliberalism as Exception*; Victoria Bernal, "Eritrea Goes Global: Reflections on Nationalism in a Transnational Era," *Cultural Anthropology* 19, 1 (2004): 3–25.

34. Sassen, *Territory, Authority, Rights*.

35. Foucault, "Questions of Method," 75.

BIBLIOGRAPHY

Archives and Libraries

American Friends Service Committee Archives [AFSC], Philadelphia
Dar al-Kutub, Egyptian National Library, Cairo
Dar al-Watha'iq (DW), Egyptian National Archives, Cairo
Israel State Archives (ISA), Jerusalem
Jewish National Library, Jerusalem
Library of Congress, Washington, D.C.
The National Archives [formerly Public Record Office], London
New York Public Library, New York, N.Y.
'Omari Mosque Library, Gaza City
United Nations Archives, New York, N.Y.

Government Offices and Private Papers

Awqaf Administration (AA), Palestinian National Authority, Gaza City
Gaza City Municipal Council, Gaza City
Housing Ministry, Palestinian National Authority, Gaza City
Pensions and Social Security Administration (PSSA), Palestinian National Authority, Gaza City
Papers of 'Uthman al-Tabba' (UT)

Government Publications

Gaza City Municipality. *Gaza Municipality: Between the Future and the Present,* 1996.
Palestine Government. *Annual Report to the Council of the League of Nations on the Administration of Palestine and Trans-Jordan,* 1924–39.
Palestine Government Education Department. *Curriculum for Government Elementary Boys' Schools in Cities and Villages,* 1921.
——. *Elementary School Curriculum,* 1927.

——. *Annual Reports*, 1925–39.

Palestine Police Force. *Annual Administrative Reports*, 1934–38.

Palestine Royal Commission Report. Cmd. 5479, July 1937.

Report of the Commission on the Palestine Disturbances of August, 1929. Cmd. 3530. London, March 1930.

Sir John Hope-Simpson, *Report on Immigration, Land Settlement, and Development in Palestine.* Cmd. 3686, 1930.

A Survey of Palestine, Prepared in December 1945 and January 1946 for the Information of the Anglo-American Committee of Inquiry. Reprinted Washington D.C.: Institute for Palestine Studies, 1991.

United Arab Republic. *Gaza: Springboard for the liberation of Palestine.* Cairo: Information Department, n.d.

United Nations Publications

Progress Report of the United Nations Mediator on Palestine. Supplement No. 11 (A/648), 1948.

Progress Report of the United Nations Acting Mediator on Palestine. UN, ed. Supplement No. 11A (A/689, A/689/Corr. 1 and A/689/Add. 1), 1948.

Refugees and Stateless Persons and Problems of Assistance to Refugees: Report of the United Nations High Commissioner for Refugees. UN Official Records: Sixth Session—Supplement No. 19 (A/2011), 1952.

United Nations Relief and Works Agency for Palestinian Refugees in the Near East [UNRWA]. *Annual Reports*, 1951–67.

——. *Special Report of the Director Concerning Other Claimants for Relief.* A/2978/Add. 1, 1955.

——. *UNRWA: A Brief History, 1950–1982.* Vienna: UNRWA, 1982.

Periodicals

Al-Ahram
Al-Difa'
Filastin
Jaridat Filastin
Majallat al-Muwazzafin
Mir'at al-Sharq
Palestine Gazette
Al-Raqib
Sawt al-'Uruba
Al-Waqai' al-Filastiniyya

Books and Articles

Abdel-Malek, Anouar. *Egypt: Military Society, the Army Regime, the Left, and Social Change Under Nasser.* New York: Random House, 1968.

Abrams, Philip. "Notes on the Difficulty of Studying the State." *Journal of Historical Sociology* 1 (1988 [1977]): 58–89.

Abu 'Amr, Ziad. *Usul al-Harakat al-Siyasiyyah fi Qita' Ghazza, 1948–1967*. Akka: Dar al-Aswar, 1987.

Abu-Ghazaleh, Adnan. *Arab Cultural Nationalism in Palestine*. Beirut: Institute for Palestine Studies, 1973.

Abu Naml, Husayn. "*Harb al-Fida'iyyin fi Qita' Ghazza.*" *Shu'un Filastiniyya* 62 (January 1979): 177–99.

——. *Qita' Ghazza, 1948–1967: Tatawwurat Iqtisadiyya wa-Siyasiyya wa-Ijtima'iyya wa-Askariyya*. Beirut: PLO Research Center, 1979.

Abu Sha'ban, Hilmi. *Tarikh Ghazza: Naqd wa Tahlil*. Jerusalem: Matba'at Bayt al-Maqdis, 1943.

Ahmed, Jaleel. *The Expert and the Administrator*. Pittsburgh: University of Pittsburgh Press, 1959.

Alsberg, P. A. *Guide to the Archives in Israel*. Volume 1: *The Israel State Archives*. Jerusalem: Israel Archives Association, 1991.

Amin, Shahid. *Event, Metaphor, Memory: Chari Chaura, 1922–1992*. Berkeley: University of California Press, 1995.

Anderson, Benedict. *Imagined Communities*. New York: Verso, 1991.

Anderson, Douglas R. *Strands of System: The Philosophy of Charles Peirce*. West Lafayette, Ind.: Purdue University Press, 1995.

Anghie, Antony. "Colonialism and the Birth of International Institutions: Sovereignty, Economy, and the Mandate System of the League of Nations." *NYU Journal of International Law and Politics* 34 (2001–2): 513–633.

al-'Arif, 'Arif. *Tarikh Ghazza*. Jerusalem: Dar al-Aytam al-Islamiyya, 1943.

Aronoff, Myron, ed. *The Frailty of Authority*. New Brunswick, N.J.: Transaction Books, 1986.

Asad, Talal. "The Limits of Religious Criticism in the Middle East: Notes on Islamic Public Argument." In *Genealogies of Religion: Discipline and Reasons of Power in Christianity and Islam*, 200–238. Baltimore: Johns Hopkins University Press, 1993.

'Ashur, Said. *Ghazza Hashim*. Amman: Dar al-Diya', 1988.

Ayubi, Nazih. *Overstating the Arab State: Politics and Society in the Middle East*. London: I. B. Tauris, 1995.

al-Barghouthi, Omar Bey Salih. "Local Self-Government—Past and Present." In *Palestine: A Decade of Development*, edited by Harry Vitales and Khalil Totah, 34–38. Philadelphia: American Academy of Political and Social Science, 1932.

Barry, Andrew, Thomas Osborne, and Nikolas Rose. "Introduction." In *Foucault and Political Reason: Liberalism, Neo-liberalism and Rationalities of Government*, edited by Andrew Barry, Thomas Osborne, and Nikolas Rose, 1–17. Chicago: University of Chicago Press, 1996.

Basisu, Mu'in. *Descent into the Water: Palestinian Notes from Arab Exile*. Wilmette, Ill.: Medina Press, 1980.

Bauman, Zygmunt. *Modernity and the Holocaust*. Cambridge: Polity Press, 1989.

Beattie, Kirk. *Egypt During the Nasser Years: Ideology, Politics, Civil Society*. Boulder: Westview Press, 1994.

Beetham, David. *Bureaucracy*. Minneapolis: University of Minnesota Press, 1987.

Bentwich, Norman, and Helen Bentwich. *Mandate Memories: 1918–1948*. London: Hogarth Press, 1965.

Berger, Morroe. *Bureaucracy and Society in Modern Egypt: A Study of the Higher Civil Service*. Princeton: Princeton University Press, 1979.

Bernal, Victoria. "Eritrea Goes Global: Reflections on Nationalism in a Transnational Era." *Cultural Anthropology* 19, 1 (2004): 3–25.

Bhabha, Homi. "Of Mimicry and Man: The Ambivalence of Colonial Discourse." In *The Location of Culture*, 85–92. New York: Routledge, 1994.

——. "In a Spirit of Calm Violence." In *After Colonialism*, edited by Gyan Prakash, 326–43. Princeton: Princeton University Press, 1995.

Blau, Peter, and Marshall Meyer. *Bureaucracy in Modern Society*. New York: Random House, 1971.

Bourdieu, Pierre. "Rethinking the State: Genesis and Structure of the Bureaucratic Field." In *State/Culture: State-Formation after the Cultural Turn*, edited by George Steinmatz, 53–75. Ithaca: Cornell University Press, 1999.

——. *Distinctions: A Social Critique of the Judgement of Taste*, trans. Richard Nice. Cambridge, Mass: Harvard University Press, 1984.

——. *Outline of a Theory of Practice*. Cambridge: Cambridge University Press, 1977.

Bowman, Humphrey. *Middle-East Window*. London: Longmans, Green and Co., 1942.

Boym, Svetlana. *Common Places: Mythologies of Everyday Life in Russia*. Cambridge, Mass.: Harvard University Press, 1994.

Bradley, Kenneth. *The Colonial Service as a Career*. London: His Majesty's Stationary Office, 1950.

Brand, Laurie. "Nasir's Egypt and the Reemergence of the Palestinian National Movement." *Journal of Palestine Studies*, 17, 2 (1998):29–45.

Britan, Gerald, and Ronald Cohen. *Hierarchy and Society: Anthropological Perspectives on Bureaucracy*. Philadelphia: Institute for the Study of Human Issues, 1980.

Brysk, Alison, and Gershon Shafir. *People Out of Place: Globalization, Human Rights, and the Citizenship Gap*. New York: Routledge, 2004.

Buerhig, Edward. *The UN and the Palestinian Refugees: A Study in Nonterritorial Administration*. Bloomington: Indiana University Press, 1971.

Burke, Peter. "History as Social Memory." In *Memory: History, Culture, and the Mind*, edited by Thomas Butler, 97–115. Oxford: Basil Blackwell, 1989.

Butler, Judith. *Excitable Speech: A Politics of the Performative*. New York: Routledge, 1997.

Butt, Gerald. *Life at the Crossroads: A History of Gaza*. Nicosia, Cyprus: Rimal Publications, 1995.

Caplan, Jane, and John Torpey, eds. *Documenting Individual Identity: The Development of State Practices in the Modern World*. Princeton: Princeton University Press, 2001.

Caplan, Neil. "A Tale of Two Cities: The Rhodes and Lausanne Conferences, 1949." *Journal of Palestine Studies* 21, 3 (spring 1992): 5–34.

Chandrasekaran, Rajiv. *Imperial Life in the Emerald City: Inside Iraq's Green Zone*. New York: Knopf, 2006.

Chatterjee, Partha. *The Nation and Its Fragments*. Princeton: Princeton University Press, 1993.

Chesluk, Benjamin. "'Visible Signs of a City Out of Control': Community Policing in New York City." *Cultural Anthropology* 19, 2 (2004): 250–75.

Cole, Juan. "Printing and Urban Islam in the Mediterranean World, 1890–1920." In *Modernity and Culture from the Mediterranean to the Indian Ocean, 1890–1920*, edited by Leila Fawaz and C. A. Bayly, 344–64. New York: Columbia University Press, 2002.

——. *Colonialism and Revolution in the Middle East: Social and Cultural Origins of Egypt's 'Urabi Movement*. Princeton: Princeton University Press, 1993.

Comaroff, John L. "Reflections on the Colonial State, in South Africa and Elsewhere: Factions, Fragments, Facts and Fictions." *Social Identities* 4, 3 (1998): 321–61.

Connolly, William. "The Dilemma of Legitimacy." In *Legitimacy and the State*, ed. William Connolly, 222–49.

Connolly, William, ed. *Legitimacy and the State*. Oxford: Basil Blackwell, 1984.

Cook, Michael. *Commanding Right and Forbidding Wrong in Islamic Thought*. Cambridge: Cambridge University Press, 2000.

Cooper, Frederick. *Colonialism in Question: Theory, Knowledge, History*. Berkeley: University of California Press, 2005.

——. "Colonizing Time: Work Rhythms and Labor Conflict in Colonial Mombasa." In *Colonialism and Culture*, ed. Nicholas Dirks, 209–46. Ann Arbor: University of Michigan Press, 1992.

Coronil, Fernando. *The Magical State: Nature, Money, and Modernity in Venezuela*. Chicago: University of Chicago Press, 1997.

Corrigan, Philip, and Derek Sayer. *The Great Arch: English State Formation as Cultural Revolution*. Oxford: Basil Blackwell, 1985.

Cossali, Paul, and Clive Robson. *Stateless in Gaza*. London: Zed Books, 1986.

Crawford, Neta. *Argument and Change in World Politics: Ethics, Decolonization, and Humanitarian Intervention*. Cambridge: Cambridge University Press, 2002.

Daniel, E. Valentine. *Charred Lullabies: Chapters in an Anthropography of Violence*. Princeton: Princeton University Press, 1996.

Das, Veena. "The Signature of the State: The Paradox of Illegibility." In *Anthropology in the Margins of the State*, edited by Veena Das and Deborah Poole, 225–52. Santa Fe: SAR Press, 2004.

Davis, Eric. *Memories of State: Politics, History, and Collective Identity in Modern Iraq*. Berkeley: University of California Press, 2005.

Davis, Mike. *City of Quartz: Excavating the Future in Los Angeles*. New York: Vintage, 1990.

de Certeau, Michel. *The Writing of History*. Translated by Tom Conley. New York: Columbia University Press, 1988.

———. *The Practice of Everyday Life*. Berkeley: University of California Press, 1984.

de Certeau, Michel, Luce Giard, and Pierre Mayoal. *The Practice of Everyday Life*. Volume 2: *Living and Cooking*. Translated by Timothy Tomasik. Minneapolis: University of Minnesota Press, 1998.

de Certeau Michel, and Luce Giard. "A Practical Science of the Singular." In *The Practice of Everyday Life*, 2:251–56.

Derrida, Jacques. *Archive Fever: A Freudian Impression*. Translated by Eric Prenowitz. Chicago: University of Chicago Press, 1995.

———. "Signature, Event, Context." In *Limited Inc*. Evanston, Ill.: Northwestern University Press, 1988.

De Vries, David. "British Rule and Arab-Jewish Coalescence of Interest: The 1946 Civil Servants' Strike in Palestine." *International Journal of Middle East Studies* 36, 4 (2004): 613–38.

Dirks, Nicholas. *Castes of Mind: Colonialism and the Making of Modern India*. Princeton: Princeton University Press, 2001.

———. "Colonial Histories and Native Informants: Biography of an Archive." In *Orientalism and the Post-Colonial Predicament*, edited by Carol Breckenridge and Peter van der Veer, 279–313. Philadelphia: University of Pennsylvania Press, 1993.

du Guy, Paul. *In Praise of Bureaucracy: Weber, Organization, Ethics*. London: Sage Publications, 2000.

Dumper, Michael. "Forty Years Without Slumbering: Waqf Politics and Administration in the Gaza Strip, 1948–1967." *British Journal of Middle East Studies* 20, 2 (1993): 174–90.

Duncan, Christopher R. "Unwelcome Guests: Relations between Internally Displaced Persons and Their Hosts in North Sulawesi, Indonesia." *Journal of Refugee Studies* 18, 1 (2005): 25–46.

Echevarría, Roberto. *Myth and Archive: A Theory of Latin American Narrative*. Cambridge: Cambridge University Press, 1990.

Eisenman, Robert. *Islamic Law in Palestine and Israel: A History of the Survival of the Tanzimat and Shari'a in the British Mandate and the Jewish State*. Leiden: E. J. Brill, 1978.

Eisenstadt, S. N., and Luis Roniger. *Patrons, Clients, and Friends: Interpersonal Relations and the Structure of Trust in Society*. Cambridge: Cambridge University Press, 1984.

Eley, Geoff. "Nations, Publics, and Political Cultures: Placing Habermas in the Nineteenth Century." In *Habermas and the Public Sphere*, edited by Craig Calhoun, 289–339. Cambridge, Mass.: MIT Press, 1992.

Engels, Dagmar, and Shula Marks. *Contesting Colonial Hegemony: State and Society in Africa and India*. London: I. B. Tauris, 1994.

Escobar, Arturo. *Encountering Development: The Making and Unmaking of the Third World*. Princeton: Princeton University Press, 1995.

Evans, Ivan. *Bureaucracy and Race: Native Administration in South Africa*. Berkeley: University of California Press, 1997.

Fanon, Frantz. *The Wretched of the Earth*. New York: Grove Press, 1963.

Feldman, Ilana. "Difficult Distinctions: Refugee Law, Humanitarian Practice, and Political Identification in Gaza." *Cultural Anthropology* 22, 1 (2007): 129–69.

——. "Observing the Everyday: Policing and the Conditions of Possibility in Gaza (1948–67)." *Interventions: International Journal of Postcolonial Studies* 9, 3 (2007): 415–34.

——. "Home as a Refrain: Remembering and Living Displacement in Gaza." *History and Memory* 18, 2 (2006): 10–47.

——. "Everyday Government in Extraordinary Times: Persistence and Authority in Gaza's Civil Service (1917–1967)." *Comparative Studies in Society and History* 47, 4 (2005): 863–91.

——. "Government Without Expertise?: Competence, Capacity, and Civil Service Practice in Gaza (1917–1967)." *International Journal of Middle East Studies* 37, 4 (November 2005): 485–507.

——. "Interesting Times, Insecure States: The Work of Government and the Making of Gaza in the British Mandate and the Egyptian Administration, 1917–1967." Ph.D. diss., University of Michigan, 2002.

Ferguson, James. *Global Shadows: Africa in the Neoliberal World Order*. Durham, N.C.: Duke University Press, 2006.

——. *The Anti-Politics Machine: "Development," Depoliticization, and Bureaucratic Power in Lesotho*. New York: Cambridge University Press, 1990.

Ferguson, Kathleen. *The Feminist Case Against Bureaucracy*. London: Sage, 1984.

Findley, Carter. "The Ottoman Administrative Legacy and the Modern Middle East." In *Imperial Legacy: The Ottoman Imprint on the Balkans and the Middle East*, edited by L. Carl Brown, 158–74. New York: Columbia University Press, 1996.

——. *Ottoman Civil Officialdom: A Social History*. Princeton: Princeton University Press, 1989.

——. *Bureaucratic Reform in the Ottoman Empire: The Sublime Porte, 1789–1922*. Princeton: Princeton University Press, 1980.

Fischer-Tiné, Harald, and Michael Mann, eds. *Colonialism as Civilizing Mission: Cultural Ideology in British India*. London: Anthem Press, 2004.

Foucault, Michel. "The Birth of Biopolitics." In *Ethics: Subjectivity and Truth*, edited by Paul Rabinow, 73–80. New York: Free Press, 1997.

——. "The Ethics of the Concern for the Self as a Practice of Freedom." In *Ethics: Subjectivity and Truth*, edited by Paul Rabinow, 281–301.

——. *Ethics: Subjectivity and Truth*. Edited by Paul Rabinow. New York: New Press, 1994.

——. "Governmentality." In *The Foucault Effect: Studies in Governmentality*, edited by Graham Burchell, Colin Gordon, and Peter Miller, 87–104. Chicago: University of Chicago Press, 1991.

——. "Questions of Method." In *The Foucault Effect*, edited by Graham Burchell, Colin Gordon, and Peter Miller, 73–86.

———. *The Care of the Self: The History of Sexuality*. Volume 3, translated by Robert Hurley. New York: Vintage Books, 1986.

———. *The History of Sexuality*. Volume 1: *An Introduction*. New York: Vintage Books, 1980.

———. *Discipline and Punish: The Birth of the Prison*. Translated by Alan Sheridan. New York: Vintage Books, 1979.

———. "The Discourse on Language." Appendix to *Archeology of Knowledge*. Translated by A. M. Sheridan Smith. New York: Pantheon Books, 1972.

Gellner, Ernest, and John Waterbury, eds. *Patrons and Clients in Mediterranean Society*. Hanover: Duckworth, 1977.

Gerges, Fawaz. "Egypt and the 1948 War: Internal Conflict and Regional Ambition." In *The War for Palestine: Rewriting the History of 1948*, edited by Eugene Rogan and Avi Shlaim, 151–77. Cambridge: Cambridge University Press, 2001.

Gilligan, Carol. *In a Different Voice: Psychological Theory and Women's Development*. Cambridge, Mass.: Harvard University Press, 1982.

Gilsenan, Michael. *Lords of the Lebanese Marches: Violence and Narrative in an Arab Society*. Berkeley: University of California Press, 1996.

Gordon, Colin. "Governmental Rationality: An Introduction." In *The Foucault Effect: Studies in Governmentality*, ed. Graham Burchell, Colin Gordon, and Peter Miller, 1–51. Chicago: University of Chicago Press, 1991.

Gordon, Joel. *Nasser's Blessed Movement: Egypt's Free Officers and the July Revolution*. New York: Oxford University Press, 1992.

Graham-Brown, Sarah. "The Political Economy of Jabal Nablus, 1920–48." In *Studies in the Economic and Social History of Palestine in the Nineteenth and Twentieth Centuries*, edited by Roger Owen, 88–176. Carbondale: Southern Illinois University Press, 1982.

Guha, Ranajit. "Discipline and Mobilize." In *Subaltern Studies VII: Writing on South Asian History and Society*, edited by Partha Chatterjee and Gyanendra Pandey. Oxford: Oxford University Press, 1992.

Gupta, Akhil. "Governing Population: The Integrated Child Development Services Program in India." In *States of Imagination: Ethnographic Explorations of the Postcolonial State*, edited by Thomas Blom Hansen and Finn Stepputat, 65–96. Durham, N.C.: Duke University Press, 2001.

———. "Blurred Boundaries: The Discourse of Corruption, the Culture of Politics, and the Imagined State." *American Ethnologist* 22 2 (1995): 375–402.

Gupta, Akhil, and James Ferguson. "Spatializing States: Toward an Ethnography of Neoliberal Governmentality." *American Ethnologist* 29, 4 (2002): 981–1002.

Habermas, Jürgen. *The Structural Transformation of the Public Sphere: An Inquiry into a Category of Bourgeois Society*. Translated by Thomas Berger. Cambridge, Mass.: MIT Press, 1989.

Haines, David W. "Conformity in the Face of Ambiguity: A Bureaucratic Dilemma." *Semiotica* 78, 3/4 (1990): 249–69.

Halbwachs, Maurice. *On Collective Memory*, edited by and translated by Lewis Coser. Chicago: University of Chicago Press, 1992.

Hammami, Rema. "Between Heaven and Earth: Transformations in Religiosity and Labor among Southern Palestinian Peasant and Refugee Women, 1920–1993." Ph.D. diss., Temple University, 1994.

Handelman, Don. "Introduction: A Recognition of Bureaucracy." In *Bureaucracy and World View: Studies in the Logic of Official Interpretation*, edited by Don Handelman and Elliott Leyton, 1–14. St. John's: Institute of Social and Economic Research, 1978.

Hansen, Thomas Blom. "Sovereigns beyond the State: On Legality and Authority in Urban India." In *Sovereign Bodies: Citizens, Migrants, and States in the Postcolonial World*, edited by Thomas Blom Hansen and Finn Stepputat, 169–91. Princeton: Princeton University Press, 2005.

Haraway, Donna. "Situated Knowledges: The Science Question in Feminism and the Privilege of Partial Perspective." In Haraway, *Simians, Cyborgs, and Women: The Reinvention of Nature*, 183–202. New York: Routledge, 1991.

Heper, Metin. "The State and Public Bureaucracies: A Comparative and Historical Perspective." *Comparative Studies in Society and History* 27, 1 (1985): 86–110.

Herscovitz, Scott. "Legitimacy, Democracy, and Razian Authority." *Legal Theory* 9 (2003): 201–20.

Herzfeld, Michael. *The Social Production of Indifference: Exploring the Symbolic Roots of Western Bureaucracy*. Chicago: University of Chicago Press, 1992.

Heussler, Robert. *Yesterday's Rulers: The Making of the British Colonial Service*. Syracuse: Syracuse University Press, 1963.

Heyman, Josiah McC. "Putting Power in the Anthropology of Bureaucracy." *Current Anthropology* 36, 2 (1995): 261–87.

Hirschkind, Charles. "Civic Virtue and Religious Reason: An Islamic Counterpublic." *Cultural Anthropology* 16, 1 (2001): 3–34.

Holston, James. *The Modernist City: An Anthropological Critique of Brasilia*. Chicago: University of Chicago Press, 1989.

Holston, James, and Arjun Appadurai. "Introduction: Cities and Citizenship." In *Cities and Citizenship*, edited by James Holston, 1–20. Durham, N.C.: Duke University Press, 1999.

Hull, Matthew. "The File: Agency, Authority, and Autography in an Islamabad Bureaucracy." *Language and Communication* 23,3 (2003): 287–314.

Hunter, Ian. *Rethinking the School: Subjectivity, Bureaucracy, Criticism*. St. Leonards, Australia: Allen and Unwin, 1994.

Hurewitz, J. C. *The Struggle for Palestine*. New York: Schocken Books, 1976.

Jacoby, Henry. *The Bureaucratization of the World*. Translated by Eveline L. Kanes. Berkeley: University of California Press, 1973.

Jankowski, James. *Nasser's Egypt, Arab Nationalism, and the United Arab Republic*. Boulder: Lynne Rienner, 2002.

Jarbawi, 'Ali. "*Al-Baladiyyat al-Filastiniyya (Min al-Nasha' Hata al-'Am 1967)*." *Shu'un Filastiniyya* 221–22 (1991): 49–72.

Jeffries, Sir Charles. *The Colonial Empire and Its Civil Service*. Cambridge: Cambridge University Press, 1938.

Johnson, Nels. *Islam and the Politics of Meaning in Palestinian Nationalism*. London: Kegan Paul International, 1982.

Katz, Elihu, and Brenda Danet. "Introduction: Bureaucracy as a Problem for Sociology and Society." In *Bureaucracy and the Public: A Reader in Official-Client Relations*, edited by Elihu Katz and Brenda Danet, 3–30. New York: Basic Books, 1973.

Katz, Elihu, and Brenda Danet, eds. *Bureaucracy and the Public: A Reader in Official-Client Relations*. New York: Basic Books, 1973.

Kayyali, A. W. *Palestine: A Modern History*. London: Croom Helm, 1970.

Kelly-Gadol, Joan. "Did Women Have a Renaissance?" In *Becoming Visible: Women in European History*, edited by Renate Bridenthal and Claudia Koonz, 148–52. Boston: Houghton Mifflin, 1977.

Khalidi, Rashid. *Palestinian Identity: The Construction of Modern National Consciousness*. New York: Columbia University Press, 1997.

al-Khass, Muhammad. "Municipal Legal Structure in Gaza." In *A Palestinian Agenda for the West Bank and Gaza*, edited by Emile A. Nakhleh, 102–06. Washington, D.C.: American Enterprise Institute, 1980.

Knauft, Bruce, ed. *Critically Modern: Alternatives, Alterities, Anthropologies*. Bloomington: Indiana University Press, 2002.

Kupferschmidt, Uri M. *The Supreme Muslim Council: Islam under the British Mandate for Palestine*. New York: E. J. Brill, 1987.

Legrain, Jean-François. "The Islamic Movement and the Intifada." In *Intifada: Palestine at the Crossroads*, edited by Jamal R. Nasser and Roger Heacock, 175–89. New York: Praeger, 1990.

Lesch, Ann Mosely. "Gaza: History and Politics." In *Israel, Egypt, and the Palestinians: From Camp David to Intifada*, edited by Ann Mosely Lesch and Mark Tessler, 223–37. Bloomington: Indiana University Press, 1989.

Lipsky, Michael. *Street-Level Bureaucracy: Dilemmas of the Individual in Public Services*. New York: Russell Sage Foundation, 1980.

Locke, Richard, and Antony Stewart. *Bantustan Gaza*. London: Zed Books, 1985.

Lockman, Zachary. *Comrades and Enemies: Arab and Jewish Workers in Palestine, 1906–1948*. Berkeley: University of California Press, 1996.

Lockman, Zachary, and Joel Beinin, eds. *Intifada: The Palestinian Uprising Against Israeli Occupation*. Boston: South End Press, 1989.

Low, Setha. "Embodied Space(s): Anthropological Theories of Body, Space, and Culture." *Space and Culture* 6, 1 (2003): 9–18.

Ludtke, Alf, ed. *The History of Everyday Life: Reconstructing Historical Experiences and Ways of Life*. Princeton: Princeton University Press, 1995.

MacLeod, Roy. "Introduction." In *Government and Expertise: Specialists, Administrators and Professionals, 1860–1919*, edited by Roy Macleod, 1–24. Cambridge: Cambridge University Press, 1988.

Mahmood, Saba. *Politics of Piety: The Islamic Revival and the Feminist Subject*. Princeton: Princeton University Press, 2005.

Mamdani, Mahmood. *Citizen and Subject: Contemporary Africa and the Legacy of Late Colonialism*. Princeton: Princeton University Press, 1996.

Marcus, George. "Ethnography in/of the World System: The Emergence of Multi-Sited Ethnography." In Marcus, *Ethnography through Thick and Thin*, 79–104. Princeton: Princeton University Press, 1998.

Massad, Joseph. *Colonial Effects: The Making of a National Identity in Jordan*. New York: Columbia University Press, 2001.

Massey, Doreen. *Space, Place, and Gender*. Minneapolis: University of Minnesota Press, 1994.

Matthews, Weldon. *Confronting an Empire, Constructing a Nation: Arab Nationalists and Popular Politics in Mandate Palestine*. London: I. B. Tauris, 2006.

Mayol, Pierre. "Propriety." In *The Practice of Everyday Life*. Volume 2: *Living and Cooking*. Edited by Luce Giard, 15–34. Minneapolis: University of Minnesota Press, 1998.

McGuire, Mary. "Disciplining the State: Organized Civil Servants, State Formation and Citizenship in the United States and Germany, 1880–1925." Ph.D. diss., University of Michigan, 1996.

Meeker, Michael. *A Nation of Empire: The Ottoman Legacy of Turkish Modernity*. Berkeley: University of California Press, 2002.

Mehta, Uday. *Liberalism and Empire: A Study of Nineteenth-Century British Liberal Thought*. Chicago: University of Chicago Press, 1999.

Meouchy, Nadine, and Peter Sluglett, eds. *The British and French Mandates in Comparative Perspectives*. Leiden: Brill, 2004.

Messick, Brinkley. *The Calligraphic State*. Berkeley: University of California Press, 1993.

Meyer, Martin A. *History of the City of Gaza from Earliest Times to the Present Day*. New York: Columbia University Press, 1907.

Miller, Ylana. *Government and Society in Rural Palestine, 1920–1948*. Austin: University of Texas Press, 1985.

Mishal, Shaul, and Avraham Sela. *The Palestinian Hamas: Vision, Violence, and Coexistence*. Columbia: Columbia University Press, 2000.

Mitchell, Timothy. *Rule of Experts: Egypt, Techno-Politics, Modernity*. Berkeley: University of California Press, 2002.

——. "The Limits of the State: Beyond Statist Approaches and Their Critics." *American Political Science Review* 85, 1 (March 1991): 77–96.

——. *Colonising Egypt*. Berkeley: University of California Press, 1988.

Morris, Benny. *Israel's Border Wars, 1949–1956: Arab Infiltration, Israeli Retaliation, and the Countdown to the Suez War*. Oxford: Clarendon Press, 1993.

al-Mubayyid, Salim. *Ghazza wa-Qita'uha: Dirasa fi Khulud al-Makan wa-Hadarat al-Sukkan min al-'Asr al-Hajari Hatta al-Harb al-'Alamiyya al-Ula*. Cairo: al-Haya al-Misriyya al-'Amma lil-Kitab, 1987.

Mundy, Martha. *Domestic Government: Kinship, Community and Polity in North Yemen*. London: I. B. Tauris, 1995.

Murphy, Murray. *The Development of Peirce's Philosophy*. Cambridge, Mass.: Harvard University Press, 1961.

Muslih, Muhammad. *The Origins of Palestinian Nationalism.* New York: Columbia University Press, 1990.

Nasser, Jamal, and Roger Heacock, eds. *Intifada: Palestine at the Crossroads.* New York: Praeger, 1990.

Navaro-Yashin, Yael. *Faces of the State: Secularism and Public Life in Turkey.* Princeton: Princeton University Press, 2002.

Ong, Aihwa. *Neoliberalism as Exception: Mutations in Citizenship and Sovereignty.* Durham, N.C.: Duke University Press, 2006.

Ortner, Sherry. "Theory in Anthropology since the Sixties." *Comparative Studies in Society and History* 26 10 (1984): 126–66.

Osborne, Thomas. "Bureaucracy as a Vocation: Governmentality and Administration in Nineteenth-Century Britain." *Journal of Historical Sociology* 7 (1994): 289–313.

Papailias, Penelope. *Genres of Recollection: Archival Poetics and Modern Greece.* New York: Palgrave Macmillan, 2005.

Pappe, Ilan. *The Making of the Arab-Israeli Conflict, 1947–51.* London: I. B. Tauris, 1992.

Pardo, Italo, ed. *Morals of Legitimacy: Between Agency and System.* New York: Berghahn Books, 2000.

Parker, Kelly. *The Continuity of Peirce's Thought.* Nashville: Vanderbilt University Press, 1998.

Passerini, Luisa. *Fascism in Popular Memory: The Cultural Experience of the Turin Working Class.* Cambridge: Cambridge University Press, 1988.

Peck, Jamie, and Adam Tickell. "Neoliberalizing Space." *Antipode* 34, 3 (2002): 380–404.

Peck, Jeffrey M. "Refugees as Foreigners: The Problem of Becoming German and Finding Home." In *Mistrusting Refugees*, edited by E. Valentine Daniel and John Chr. Knudsen, 102–25. Berkeley: University of California Press, 1995.

Pedersen, Susan. "Settler Colonialism at the Bar of the League of Nations." In *Settler Colonialism in the Twentieth Century*, edited by Caroline Elkins and Susan Pedersen, 113–34. New York: Routledge, 2005.

Peirce, Charles Sanders. *Collected Papers of Charles Sanders Peirce.* Cambridge, Mass.: Harvard University Press, 1935.

Pels, Peter, and Oscar Salemink. *Colonial Subjects: Essays on the Practical History of Anthropology.* Ann Arbor: University of Michigan Press, 1999.

Peters, B. Guy. *The Politics of Bureaucracy.* New York: Longman, 1989.

Potter, Pitman. "Origin of the System of Mandates under the League of Nations." *American Political Science Review* 16, no 4 (1922): 563–83.

Potter, Vincent. *Charles S. Peirce on Norms and Ideals.* Amherst: University of Massachusetts Press, 1967.

Prakash, Gyan. *Another Reason: Science and the Imagination of Modern India.* Princeton: Princeton University Press, 1999.

Quandt, William, Fuad Jabber, and Ann Mosely Lesch. *The Politics of Palestinian Nationalism.* Berkeley: University of California Press, 1973.

Rabinow, Paul. *French Modern: Norms and Forms of the Social Environment.* Chicago: University of Chicago Press, 1989.

Raphaeli, Nimrod. "Gaza Under Four Administrations." *Public Administration in Israel and Abroad* 9 (1968): 40–51.

Rashid, Harun Hashim. *Qissat Madinat Ghazza*. Al-Munazzama al-'Arabiyya lil-Tarbiyya w-al Thaqafa w-al-'Ulum, nd.

Raz, Joseph, ed. *Authority*. Oxford: Basil Blackwell, 1990.

Reeves, Edward. *The Hidden Government: Ritual, Clientelism, and Legitimation in Northern Egypt*. Salt Lake City: University of Utah Press, 1990.

Roniger, Luis, and Ayse Gunes-Ayata, eds. *Democracy, Clientelism, and Civil Society*. Boulder: Lynne Rienner, 1994.

Rose, Nikolas. *Powers of Freedom: Reframing Political Thought*. Cambridge: Cambridge University Press, 1999.

——. "Governing 'Advanced' Liberal Democracies." In *Foucault and Political Reason: Liberalism, Neo-liberalism and Rationalities of Government*, edited by Andrew Barry, Thomas Osborne, and Nikolas Rose, 37–64. Chicago: University of Chicago Press, 1996.

Roy, Sara. "Why Peace Failed: An Oslo Autopsy." *Current History*, 101, 651 (2002): 8–16.

——. *The Gaza Strip: The Political Economy of De-development*. Washington, D.C.: Institute for Palestine Studies, 1995.

Rutherford, Danilyn. *Raiding the Land of the Foreigners: The Limits of the Nation on an Indonesian Frontier*. Princeton: Princeton University Press, 2003.

Sassen, Saskia. *Territory, Authority, Rights: From Medieval to Global Assemblages*. Princeton: Princeton University Press, 2006.

Savage, Gail. *The Social Construction of Expertise: The English Civil Service and Its Influence, 1919–1939*. Pittsburgh: University of Pittsburgh Press, 1996.

Sayigh, Yezid. "Escalation or Containment? Egypt and the Palestine Liberation Army, 1964–67." *International Journal of Middle East Studies* 30, 1 (1998): 97–116.

Schiff, Benjamin N. *Refugees unto the Third Generation: UN Aid to Palestinians*. Syracuse: Syracuse University Press, 1995.

Schilcher, Linda S. "The Famine of 1915–1918 in Greater Syria." In *Problems of the Modern Middle East in Historical Perspective: Essays in Honor of Albert Hourani*, edited by John Spansolo. Reading: Ithaca Press, 1992.

Scholch, Alexander. *Palestine in Transformation 1856–1882: Studies in Social, Economic and Political Development*. Translated by William C. Young and Michael C. Gerrity. Washington, D.C.: Institute for Palestine Studies, 1993.

Scott, David. *Refashioning Futures: Criticism After Postcoloniality*. Princeton: Princeton University Press, 1999.

Scott, James. *Seeing Like a State: How Certain Schemes to Improve the Human Condition Have Failed*. New Haven: Yale University Press, 1998.

——. *Domination and the Arts of Resistance: Hidden Transcripts*. New Haven: Yale University Press, 1990.

Segal, Rafi, and Eyal Weizman, eds. *A Civilian Occupation: The Politics of Israeli Architecture*. London: Verso, 2003.

Segev, Tom. *1967: Israel, the War, and the Year That Transformed the Middle East*. Translated by Jessica Cohen. New York: Metropolitan Books, 2007.

——. *One Palestine, Complete: Jews and Arabs Under the British Mandate*. Translated by Haim Watzman. Boston: Little, Brown, 2000.

Sennett, Richard. *Authority*. New York: W. W. Norton, 1980.

Shaw, Stanford. *The Financial and Administrative Organization and Development of Ottoman Egypt, 1517–1798*. Princeton: Princeton University Press, 1962.

Sherman, A. J. *Mandate Days: British Lives in Palestine, 1918–1948*. New York: Thames and Hudson, 1997.

Shlaim, Avi. "The Rise and Fall of the All-Palestine Government in Gaza." *Journal of Palestine Studies* 20 no. 1 (Fall 1990): 37–53.

Shomali, Qustandi. "al-Sahafa al-Filastiniyya fi 'Ahd al-Intidab: Jaridat Mir'at al-Sharq (1919–1939)." *Shu'un Filastiniyya* no. 221–22 (September 1991).

Skeik, Ibrahim. *Ghazza 'Abr al-Tarikh: Taht al-Intidab al-Britani*. 1981.

——. *Ghazza 'Abr al-Tarikh: Qita' Ghazza Taht al-Idara al-Masriyya, 1948–1956*. 1982.

——. *Ghazza 'Abr Al-Tarikh: Dhikrayat wa-Intaba'at 'An Ghazzah Qabl Nusf Qarn*. n.d.

Spivak, Gayatri. "Can the Subaltern Speak?" In *Marxism and the Interpretation of Literature*, edited by Cary Nelson and Larry Grossberg, 271–313. Urbana: University of Illinois Press, 1988.

——. "Subaltern Studies: Deconstructing Historiography." In Spivak, *In Other Worlds: Essays in Cultural Politics*, 197–221. New York: Routledge, 1988.

Starrett, Gregory. *Putting Islam to Work: Education, Politics, and Religious Transformation in Egypt*. Berkeley: University of California Press, 1998.

Stoler, Ann. "Degrees of Imperial Sovereignty." *Public Culture* 18, 1 (2006): 125–46.

——. "Colonial Archives and the Arts of Governance." *Archival Science* 2, 1–2 (2002): 87–109.

——. "Tense and Tender Ties: The Politics of Comparison in North American History and (Post)Colonial Studies." *Journal of American History* 88, 3 (2001): 829–65.

——. "'In Cold Blood': Hierarchies of Credibility and the Politics of Colonial Narratives." *Representations* 37 (1992): 151–87.

——. "Sexual Affronts and Racial Frontiers: European Identities and the Cultural Politics of Exclusion in Colonial Southeast Asia." *Comparative Studies in Society and History* 34, 3 (July 1992): 514-51.

Stoler, Ann, and Fred Cooper, ed. *Tensions of Empire*. Berkeley: University of California Press, 1996.

Stoler, Ann, and Karen Strassler. "Castings for the Colonial: Memory Work in 'New Order' Java." *Comparative Studies in Society and History* 42, 1 (2000): 4–48.

Stoyansky, J. *The Mandate for Palestine: A Contribution to the Theory and Practice of International Mandates*. London: Longmans, Green, 1928.

Suleri, Sara. *The Rhetoric of English India*. Chicago: University of Chicago Press, 1992.

Swedenburg, Ted. *Memories of Revolt: The 1936–1939 Rebellion and the Palestinian Past*. Minneapolis: University of Minnesota Press, 1995.

al-Tabba', 'Uthman, *Ithaf al-A'izza fi Tarikh Ghazza*, ed. 'Abd al-Latif Hashim. Gaza: Maktabat al-Yaziji, 1999.

Takkenberg, Lex. *The Status of Palestinian Refugees in International Law.* Oxford: Clarendon Press, 1998.

Taqqu, Rachelle. "Arab Labor in Mandatory Palestine, 1920–1948." Ph.D. diss., Columbia University, 1977.

Taraki, Lisa. "The Islamic Resistance Movement in the Palestinian Uprising." In *Intifada: The Palestinian Uprising Against Israeli Occupation*, edited by Zachary Lockman and Joel Beinin, 171–77. Boston: South End Press, 1989.

Taussig, Michael. *The Magic of the State.* New York: Routledge, 1997.

Thomas, Richard. *Imperial Archive: Knowledge and Fantasy of Empire.* London: Verso, 1993.

Thompson, Paul. "Believe It or Not: Rethinking the Historical Interpretation of Memory." In *Memory and History: Essays on Recalling and Interpreting Experience*, edited by Jaclyn Jeffrey and Glenace Edwall, 1–16. New York: University Press of America, 1994.

——. *The Voice of the Past.* New York: Oxford University Press, 1982.

Tibawi, A. L. *Arab Education in Mandatory Palestine: A Study of Three Decades of British Administration.* London: Luzac, 1956.

Tonkin, Elizabeth. *Narrating Our Past: The Social Construction of Oral History.* Cambridge: Cambridge University Press, 1994.

Trouillot, Michel-Rolph. *Global Transformations: Anthropology and the Modern World.* New York: Palgrave, 2003.

——. *Silencing the Past: Power and the Production of History.* Boston: Beacon Press, 1995.

Upadhyaya, R. B., and K. C. Sharma. *Management of Conflict between Generalist and Specialist Administrators in India.* Jaipur: Shashi Publications, 1987.

Upthegrove, Campbell L. *Empire by Mandate: A History of the Relations of Great Britain with the Permanent Mandates Commissions of the League of Nations.* New York: Brookman Associates, 1954.

van Beek, Martin. "Public Secrets, Conscious Amnesia, and the Celebration of Autonomy for Ladakh." In *States of Imagination: Ethnographic Explorations of the Postcolonial State*, edited by Thomas Blom Hansen and Finn Stepputat, 365–90. Durham, N.C.: Duke University Press, 2001.

Vitalis, Robert, and Steven Heydemann. "War, Keynesianism, and Colonialism." In *War, Institutions, and Social Change in the Middle East*, edited by Steven Heydemann, 100–45. Berkeley: University of California Press, 2000.

Wasserstein, Bernard. *The British in Palestine: The Mandatory Government and the Arab-Jewish Conflict, 1917–1929.* London: Royal Historical Society, 1978.

Waterbury, John. *The Egypt of Nasser and Sadat: The Political Economy of Two Regimes.* Princeton: Princeton University Press, 1983.

Weber, Max. *Economy and Society: An Outline of Interpretive Sociology.* Edited by Guenther Roth and Claus Wittich. Berkeley: University of California Press, 1978.

——. *From Max Weber: Essays in Sociology.* Edited by Hans Gerth and C. Wright Mills. New York: Oxford University Press, 1946.

Wedeen, Lisa. *Ambiguities of Domination: Politics, Rhetoric, and Symbols in Contemporary Syria.* Chicago: University of Chicago Press, 1999.

White, Freda. *Mandates.* London: Jonathan Cape, 1926.

White, Hayden. *The Content of the Form.* Baltimore: Johns Hopkins University Press, 1987.

Wright, Gwendolyn. "Tradition in the Service of Modernity: Architecture and Urbanism in French Colonial Policy, 1900–1930." *Journal of Modern History* 59 (1994): 291–316.

Wright, Quincy. *Mandates Under the League of Nations.* Chicago: University of Chicago Press, 1930.

——. "Sovereignty of the Mandates." *American Journal International Law* 17, 4 (1923): 691–703.

Yurchak Alexei. *Everything Was Forever, Until It Was No More: The Last Soviet Generation.* Princeton: Princeton University Press, 2006.

INDEX

Page references in italics indicate illustrations.

authority (*cont.*)

pertoires of, 92, 98, 264n1. *See also* civil
service competence and career trajectory

ayyam al-balad (village days; pre-1948 period), 33–34

Bain, Alexander, 257n11
Barclay's Bank, 164
al-Barghouthi, Omar, 246–47n84
Basisu, Mu'in, 217, 292–93n98
Ba'th party, 85, 216, 225
Beersheba, 179–80
Berger, Morroe, 256n1
Bhabha, Homi, 260n34, 289n56
Bourdieu, Pierre, 258n13, 281n17
Boym, Svetlana, 273n32
British Mandate (1917–48): acceptance of,
237n1; administrative difficulties and
limitations of, 19, 246n80; authority of,
15; British vs. Ottoman municipal organization under, 21, 246–47nn83–84;
centralized government under, 48–49,
157–58, 165–66, 282n31; Chief Secretariat's regulations on filing under, 38–
41, 52–55, 57, 252n27, 252n29; crises
during, 126–27; as crisis time for Palestinian peasants, 21, 131–33, 274n36;
documentary materials from, 25–26,
248n100; dual obligations of British
under, 6–7, 19, 239nn21–22; end of, 7,
38, 59, 127, 210, 240n25; Gaza as district under, 5–6; information flow under, 55; jurisdictional struggles under,
157–58; legitimacy of, 17–18; map of,
xiv; military rule during, 237n1; Palestine as a colony under, 6–7; pensions
and, 116, 269–70n64; persistence via
bureaucracy, 14; on promotions for
civil servants, 110, 268n46; relationship
of, with place, 24; riots and revolt during, 126, 133, 284n73; taxation under,

247n91; temporal insecurity of, 19;
town and housing planning during,
142–47, 153–54, 277nn72–73, 277n78,
277n81, 277–78n82; Zionist settler–
Palestinian Arab conflict under, 7, 126,
239–40nn23–24. *See also* crisis services; files; Gaza district; Palestine; Supreme Muslim Council
bureaucracy: authority and, 14–17, 90–92,
119–20, 219–21, 225, 234, 244n60; citation and, 16; as everyday life, 233; importance of, 225; inculcation of, 16,
245n68; present-day vs. Mandate / Administration, 26–27; as regime of practices, 12–14, 233–34; across regimes, 1–
2; rule vs. reason in, 16–17; Weber on,
1–2, 15–17, 52, 66, 220, 225, 226. *See
also* civil servants; civil service competence and career trajectory; files
Bureij Middle School for Refugees, 216
Bureij refugee camp (Gaza), 283n51
buses, 183–84
Butler, Judith, 16, 244n64

Cairo, 222
care of self, 96–97, 125, 265n14
cars, 178
Christian services, 285n5
Churchill, Winston, 98–99
citation, 16, 244n64
citizenship and nationality, 204–5, 207–8,
210
civic life, as shaped by community services. *See* community services
civil servants (*muwazzafin*), 63–79; associations of and organizing by, 87–90,
263n87, 263n89, 264n95; authority of,
challenges to, 13; on bad habits of colleagues, 76–79, 260nn42–43, 260
n.45; benefits of vs. tensions in service,
65, 73–76; British manners taken up
by, 74–75, 260n34; class and social sta-

community services (*cont.*)

nity and, 191; educational services, 190–91, 204–17, 212–13, 289–90nn59–60, 290–91n68, 291nn80–81, 292n88; moral improvement and, 193, 195, 198, 285–86n8, 287n31; overview of, 189–92; propriety and, 190–92; religious associations and, 194–200, 286n13, 287n29, 287n31, 287–88n34; religious services, 190–203, 285–86n8, 285n5, 288n46; surveillance of education and, 216; surveillance of religious activities and, 202, 289n50. *See also* Supreme Muslim Council

Connolly, William, 82

Cook, Michael, 195

Coronil, Fernando, 245–46n76, 248n99

crisis services, 123–54; contours of crisis and, 126–30; definitions of needs and, 132; development projects and, 126–27, 131, 273–74n34; ethic of care and, 125, 131, 133–38, 142, 153; as exceptional, 221; flour distribution, 140–41, 276n63; food services after 1948, 134–42, 139, 141, 275n56, 275–76n59, 276n60, 276n63, 276n66; food services by Quakers, 134, 137–38; food services during British Mandate, 123, 131–35, 153–54; housing service as social service, 147–54, 150, 278nn93–94, 278–79n100, 279n101; *mukhtars'* role in, 140; municipal control of, 134–35, 144–47, 275n46; for native Gazans vs. refugees, 127–28; overview of, 123–26; relief efforts and, 126–27; security concerns surrounding, 124, 126, 142, 153; stealing and, 136–37, 275n51; town and housing planning during British Mandate, 142–47, 153–54, 277nn72–73, 277n78, 277–78n81, 278n82; UNRWA on, 275–76n59, 276n60; water services, 145

da'wa, 285–86n8

de Certeau, Michel: on citation, 16; on ordinary practices, 174; on pluralization, 280n6; on tactics, 18–19

deferral and distraction. *See* distraction and deferral

Deir Belah Council, 201

Deir Belah (Gaza), 158–59, 159, 177, 280n11

Department of Refugee Supervision, Government Assistance, and Social Affairs, 170

Derrida, Jacques, 16, 244n64, 250n9

development discourse, 164, 282n29

diet, eating habits, 132–33, 274nn36–37. *See also* crisis services

al-Difa', 79, 181–82, 261n52, 284n69

disciplinary writing, 32–33, 249n3

distraction and deferral: through crisis services, 125, 135, 148, 152–53; effectiveness and limits of, 172, 179, 210, 217, 222; through everyday services, 182; importance of, to Mandate government, 7; meaning of, 20; propriety and, 191; tactical mobilization of, 28

District Town Planning Commission, 146–47, 277–78n81, 278n82

Dumper, Michael, 200

education: agricultural training school, 214; for civil service, 92, 98, 103–5, 266n18; curricula, 207–8, 210–11, 213–14, 290–91n68; in Egypt, 202–3, 289n54, 292n91; for girls, 290n60; importance of, to governments, 289n56; Jewish vs. Arab schools, 205, 289n59; number of schools, 289–90n60; parents' role in, 292n90; of refugees, 19–20, 23, 211–12, 211–12, 216, 291nn80–81; secular civil schools, 266n18; services, 190–91, 204–17, 212–13, 289–90n59, 290n60, 290–91n68, 291nn80–

expertise, 94, 264nn5–6. *See also* civil service competence and career trajectory

Fallah school (Gaza), 288n46
famine, 132, 273n25
Farouq, King, 85
Fatah, 231–32
Ferguson, Jim, 233, 282n29
fida'iyyin (guerilla) units, 23
Filastin, 179
files, 31–61; access to and control of, 36–37, 52–57, 255n61; accumulation of authority and, 35, 48–52; Administration filing practices, 31, 36, 41–42, 53–54, 59–60, 255n59, 255n61; Administration writing practices and, 37, 41–42; administrative conversation in, 39–41, 252nn29–30; archives and, 33–37, 57, 250n13, 255nn70–71; audience for, 37; authority of, 32–33, 35, 38, 42, 47, 251n24; autonomy of filing, 60–61; Chief Secretariat's regulations on, 38–41, 52–55, 57, 252n27, 252n29; circulation of, 52, 54–57; civil servants' writings about themselves in, 42–44, 253nn38–39; compilation of, and categories of people and place, 48–52; content and style of writing of, 37, 39, 251n20; copies of, 38, 54–55, 251n24; criminal records, 56–57; definition of, 34; disruption and loss and, 33; elite's use of, 50; on Gaza locality, 48–51, 49, 51, 254nn50–51; generality of conventions and technology of, 31–32; hierarchy of producers of, 34, 250n13; horizontal vs. vertical relations in, 34; indexing of, 57–58; interviews, 251n17; Israeli seizure of, 34–35, 230–31; land claim and registry, 106, 254n51, 255n72; limits of content of, 45–47; Mandate filing practices, 31, 36, 38–41, 40, 52–53, 59, 251n18, 251n22, 255n61; Mandate

writing practices and, 37; memos, 41–42; minutes, 39–41, 40, 252n27, 252n30; as mundane and quotidian, 35; Ottoman filing practices, 31–32, 249n4; overview of, 31–33; of Palestine government correspondence, 39–40; personnel records, 45, 58–59, 109, 249n4, 253nn43–44; police reports and surveillance, 45–47, 46, 253nn45–46, 254n48; privacy concerns and, 56–57, 107; production of, 37–52; regularity and uniformity of, 16, 32–33, 38–39, 42, 220; secret, 52–54, 254–55n58, 255n59; storage and destruction of, 57–60, 255n70, 255n72; town planning, 254n51; types of, 33, 35, 250n10; Weber on, 31
Findley, Carter, 32, 249n4, 266n18
First Division Association, 88–89
food services. *See under* crisis services
Foucault, Michel: on analytics of power, 242n45; on care of self, 125, 265n14; on disciplinary writing, 32–33, 249n3; on ethical self-cultivation, 96–97; on governmentality, 12; on imprisonment, 244n59; on lowering of threshold of knowledge, 254n49
Free Officers revolution (1952), 85, 240n27

Gaza: Alexander's conquest of, 238n8; bank loan proposal for, 276n69; cultivable land in, 131, 273–74n34, 273n31; curfew in, 4; as district under Mandate, 5–6; documentary materials and, 25–26, 36, 248n100, 248n102, 251n16; economic decline of, 4–5; Egypt's reconnection with, 183–85, 284n75; government practice and shaping of, 20–26, 28, 248–49n103; history of disruption in, 5–10, 238n8; improvement projects in, 4; *intifada* (second) and, 5; Israeli closure of, 4–5, 230; Israeli oc-

Ilana Feldman is assistant professor of anthropology and international affairs at George Washington University.

Library of Congress Cataloging-in-Publication Data
Feldman, Ilana
Governing Gaza : bureaucracy, authority, and the work of rule, 1917–1967 /
Ilana Feldman.
p. cm.
Includes bibliographical references and index.
ISBN-13: 978-0-8223-4222-9 (cloth : alk. paper)
ISBN-13: 978-0-8223-4240-3 (pbk. : alk. paper)
1. Gaza Strip—Politics and government—20th century.
2. Representative government and representation—Gaza Strip. I. Title.
DS110.G3F45   2008
953'.1—dc22   2007046082